YAHOO!®

THE ULTIMATE 2002 REFERENCE TO THE WEB

YAHOO!®

THE ULTIMATE 2002 REFERENCE TO THE WEB

Your Indispensable Companion to the Internet

Edited by HP Newquist

An Original Publication of ibooks, Inc.

Pocket Books, a division of Simon and Schuster, Inc.
1230 Avenue of the Americas, New York, NY 10020

An ibooks, Inc.

Distributed by Simon & Schuster, Inc.
1230 Avenue of the Americas

ibooks Inc.,
24 West 25th Street
New York, NY 10010.

The ibooks World Wide Web Site Address is:
http://www.ibooksinc.com/

You can visit the ibooks Web site for free first chapters of all the ibooks titles:
http://www.ibooksinc.com/

ISBN 0-7434-4477-9
First ibooks printing April 2002
10 9 8 7 6 5 4 3 2 1

Cover design by Tom Draper
Interior design by Tom Draper and Andy Omel

Printed in the U.S.A.

CONTENTS

PREFACE

We've all experienced the frustration of getting lost in the vastness of the web. Your search begins with something as simple as, say, last night's baseball score, yet you soon find yourself stuck in a morass of Shaker furniture sites and links to Civil War chat rooms, courtesy of a broad interpretation of your interest in the Yankees. Fortunately there's Yahoo!, the most trusted portal on the web. Its simple yet logical approach is the model for all others.

Yahoo! The Ultimate 2002 Reference to the Web is an analog companion to the digital version. This guide cuts to the chase by categorizing the most enduring, most useful and informative sites on the web in a wide array of topics, from Business to Entertainment to Health. This easy-to-use book will be valuable to novice and experienced surfers alike.

Yahoo! The Ultimate 2002 Reference highlights a thousand great sites, and along the way offers useful tips on how to get the most information and services from the web. Whether you're looking for travel information, health advice, free stuff, job leads, auction sites, or consumer reports, this guide points you in the right direction, saving you hundreds of hours of research.

INTRODUCTION

As of this writing, it is estimated that there are more than several hundred million websites residing on servers all over the world. That's a monstrous number of sites, and it translates into somewhere between 5 billion and 550 billion actual pages. That's billion, with a "b." And the number is growing by thousands every day. The web has gotten so large that no one human can ever hope to visit every website in his or her lifetime.

My guess is that you want to use the Internet to find information, news, articles, wisdom, knowledge, and the occasional recipe or sports statistic. However, finding what you want among those millions of sites is not an easy task. Yahoo! can help narrow your hunt. But even 20 or 30 sites are a lot to browse through when you're in a hurry. And that's the reason for this book—the definitive reference for Internet users.

We've identified and profiled those sites that best serve the needs of people looking for information on a vast range of subjects. That's it, plain and simple. To achieve that, we've built on the Yahoo! principle of making the web easy to access, easy to use, and fun to wander around in. Yahoo! is the premier portal, or launch pad, for people logging on to the Internet. It's *the* place to go when you want to find content with just a click or two of your mouse.

Looking for the best sites on the web while you're actually on the web is not for the faint of heart. It's a lot like learning how to drive a car by getting thrown behind the wheel of a speeding vehicle. You need a sense of the entire car—the ignition, gas tank, mirrors—before you can go roaring down the highway. Consider this book your driver's ed class for the information superhighway, providing you with the map to the sites you will need for your particular off-road explorations. Once you are comfortable behind the wheel, you can explore the side streets at your leisure.

This book is divided into numerous categories comprising many hundreds of sites. Whether you're into astronomy and aromatherapy or horticulture and horror, you'll find what you are looking for. In many cases, these categories will include a site that we consider to be the ultimate in its class—they are what I call "category killers." Using these sites as the benchmark has enabled us to eliminate lots of sites that may have decent levels of info, but not quite enough to make the cut. Our goal for *Yahoo! The Ultimate 2002 Reference to the Web* was to include only those sites that serve either as the ideal destination or as a great point of departure for additional searches.

Other criteria also came into play for designating a killer site. This is a book about great websites and great resources, not just the web addresses of the best-known brand names. Even with a great name, you still need a great site. It's amazing that so many of sites in this book are run by individuals on their own time, and that they can compete with other sites in the category—even those maintained by corporations, institutions, or universities. In short, a category killer site has to dominate its field nearly to the exclusion of other sites covering similar ground. Take the movie category, for example. Yahoo!'s Movie Index lists more than 15,000 related sites, including actors, movie titles, and trivia. Some of these sites are amazing, while others are mind-numbingly awful. Do you really need 15,000 movie sites to find the answers to the majority of your questions? No. You need one site—a great one. And we've selected it and reviewed it here for you.

Unfortunately, however, not all areas of interest have category -killer sites, which is why there are multiple listings for various categories. In some cases, you will need more than one site simply because of the breadth of the topic or the absence of one tremendously strong site. History, for instance, is extremely fragmented on the web, as is science fiction. Thus we have multiple entries for these (and other) categories because it takes several sites to provide you with one superb resource. Diversity also proved tricky to handle: How, for instance, can national politics be covered in one site in the face of numerous political parties, loads of factions, and enough opinions to crush an elephant and a donkey? To be comprehensive, we obviously had to include multiple listings.

As with any desk reference, this book is a single source providing information on a range of subjects in an easily accessible format. The next step for the adventurous information seeker is to plug into the best search engines and learn the fine art of data mining and search refinement. And the best engines, of course, are listed here.

That the web needs a guide such as this is indicative of how big, how pervasive, and how important it has become. To keep it in perspective, think of the web as a resource and research library. You can go and sit in a library all day long every day that it's open and browse through books, magazines, and newspapers until your heart's content. It doesn't cost you a dime, and they don't kick you out until they close the doors for the night. The web improves on the experience because it never closes, you can crank your stereo, you can eat and drink while looking at the selections, and no one shushes you. The web is like having a library crammed into a 7-Eleven. It's open when you want it to be, and you can even buy stuff there.

We've done our best to choose sites that have proven staying power, but nowhere is the adage "the only constant is change" more true than on the Internet. We purposely avoided news-oriented sites that hadn't been updated recently; we also stayed away from sites where the relevant information on a particular topic appears twenty levels below the main page, like when the chemistry links you need are listed below the plot summaries of the webmaster's all-time favorite episodes of *Seinfeld*.

Web sites are constantly evolving, and many of them change frequently. In some cases, the design of websites is updated on a regular basis, changing the way a particular site looks and how you navigate through it. We expect that a small percentage of sites will look different from the way we've described them by the time you get to them. Fortunately, design changes rarely affect content, so—no matter how they look—these sites will give you what you need.

Those sites selected for inclusion have a number of features that suggest longevity: first, how long they've been around; second, how a site compared to others in the category; third, who or what organization maintains the site. Finally, we depended on our instincts and included sites that are just too good to ignore.

Thus, out of the millions of sites on the web, those profiled here are simply better than the rest. No matter what the future of the web may be, the sites contained in this book should continue to survive and—with your encouragement—thrive.

HP Newquist

INTRODUCTION TO DATA MINING & SEARCH ENGINES

Finding.

It takes a lot of effort to find stuff. Your car keys, your wallet, your place in line. Some things are harder to find than others: the entrance to the subway in a strange city, the nearest public bathroom, a great restaurant. Other things are almost impossible to find: a good deal, intelligent life on Mars, decent sitcoms, and a great margarita.

The result is that we spend a great deal of time searching—in hopes of finding. But we're not talking about large, philosophical searches here, for the perfect mate, liberty, happiness, a first edition of Truman Capote's *In Cold Blood*; rather, we're talking about those finds that add genuine pleasure to our days—a record that you've been looking for for years, a toy that's always out of stock, a phone number that you thought you'd never find again, tickets to a sold-out concert, the answer to a nagging question. These are the kinds of searching, and finding, that we deal with every day.

So let's talk about searching and how it relates to finding. And then we'll talk about the Internet. To start, picture a little boy who has been given $10 and let loose in a modern, well-stocked candy store all by himself. There he stands, faced with an overwhelming array of choices; it seems to be a dream come true. But he looks to be on the verge of tears. It's too much; he's not sure exactly what he wants; all he knows is that he wants candy. Enter the shopkeeper. He guides the boy by asking questions. Let's narrow it down a bit, shall we? he asks. Do you want chocolates? Jellybeans? Hard candy? Gum? The boy wants hard candy. Okay, do you want peppermint, sourballs, jawbreakers? The little boy answers sourballs. Right. Do you want citrus flavored, berry flavored, grape? Citrus. Great, almost there. Lemon, lime, orange, grapefruit? Lime it is. The little boy has found what he wants by having his choices selectively pared down.

In this scenario, the boy is the user, the store is the Internet, and the shopkeeper is the search engine. The official technoterm for this process is *data mining*. It implies that by asking the right questions you will unearth the information that you want. Search engines are software applications that digitally prowl online content based on commands they're given. They're called engines because they "drive" the process of searching. But not every search engine "drives through" every site, which is why many web users employ different engines at different times. Why use more than one? Part of it has to do with the process of searching itself.

Every search engine employs what are called, variously, agents, spiders, crawlers, or bots (short for robots). During periods of low traffic on the Internet, a search engine host sends its bots out to the registered servers on the Internet. These bots retrieve the content of the pages and sites on that server and bring it back to be stored and catalogued in a database. It is this database that is searched when you look for something on the Net. That is why search engines seem to work almost instantaneously, because they are searching a single database and not scanning the global Internet. However, if a site isn't registered with a particular search engine, odds are that the bots won't find it, especially if it's a personal page or not part of a larger site. Therefore, a detailed search may require the use of more than one search engine.

There are a few other things to keep in mind about search

engines. Different search engines work in different ways. Yahoo!, for instance, is actually an index, or directory. After Yahoo! collects data from millions of websites using an Inktomi search engine, nonelectronic life forms known as people evaluate the sites, make notes about them, and determine whether they should be included in the Yahoo! directory. This is why Yahoo! is such an excellent launch point for your searches; its sites have been prescreened to ensure that you won't get articles on the zeppelins used during World War II when you're looking for the album *Led Zeppelin II*.

Yahoo! is also the place to start if you're looking for information in an area where you're a novice. Let's say you want to do a little research on small aircraft and you're new to the subject. Probably you wouldn't begin by looking at the Mooney Aircraft or ultralight website, because presumably you don't know about them. Rather, you start by looking in Yahoo! under Recreation & Sports, which takes you to Aviation (along with sports, travel, outdoors, etc.). Within Aviation you can find dozens of topics related to airplanes that are hand-picked by the Yahoo! staff. If you want more sites—or more specifically defined sites—you can type the words "small aircraft" in the Yahoo! search box and every one of its listings with that exact combination of words (including sites under Business & Economy, and Regional, in addition to Recreation) will appear. The value of searching this way is that you're guaranteed to get only those sites dealing with small aircraft.

Other search engines scan some portion of a page's text and store that information, categorizing the site using selected keywords that they extract from the text. Most search engines rely heavily on lines of software code known as *metatags* or *metanames*. The vast majority of websites have metatags but you can't see them. Essentially, they're identifiers that allow the search engines to categorize the site in areas that the owner feels the site most belongs. A site on the Boston Bruins, for example, might include tags such as "hockey," "Boston," "sports," and "NHL" so that the site will appear whenever you search for any or all of those terms.

Bait and Switch on the Web

People can put words like "baseball" and "banking" on their site even if the content has absolutely nothing to do with either baseball or banking—it could be a get-rich-at-home site for all you know. You can't see the words "baseball" and "banking," but bots can. They'll log the tags in the search engine database and every time you look for baseball or banking, you'll get a pointer to that site on making millions of dollars with just a few hours a week. Why do sites do this? Because a lot of people are looking for information on baseball and banking, and the site owner hopes that by some stretch of the imagination you'll actually be lured into visiting his or her site since you're in the neighborhood. They figure if you see it listed with other sites you're interested in, you'll drop by. Just so you know, this is considered an incredibly impolitic practice, and the use of "bait and switch" tags is pretty much limited to sites you wouldn't visit by choice.

If you've become knowledgeable in a particular area, you will want to use search engines simply because they guide you more directly to those sites that contain data you know you want or need. This raises the issue that different search engines use different search methods and rely on different identifiers, so you have to make sure that you use the proper methods for searching in each one. There are a variety of these methods, most of which are based on a form of mathematics known as Boolean logic. Search engines using this logic employ what are called *operators*, comprising words (AND, OR, NOT, NEAR) and/or symbols (+, -, =) to filter for the search terms. Since the use of Boolean logic is so pervasive in search engines, we've provided the following chart to assist you in using this method for your search purposes. To demonstrate its use, we'll go back to our earlier example the lighter-than-air-craft "graf zeppelin" versus the heavier-than-metal rock band known as Led Zeppelin.

The primary value of Boolean logic is that it lets you create specific relationships in your search by joining words and phrases using either quotation marks or brackets.

Word	Symbol	Alt. Symbol	Result
AND	&	+	When you use AND, the search engine retrieves only those documents that contain all of the specified words or phrases. So, *graf* AND *zeppelin* finds documents that contain both words, reducing the likelihood of finding info on Led Zeppelin.
OR	|		Using OR finds documents that contain at least one of the specified words or phrases. Thus, *graf* OR *zeppelin* finds documents that contain either the word *graf* or the word *zeppelin*. In some cases the document will have both words, but that is by chance, not design.
NOT	!	-	NOT helps trim down those searches where you know there is going to be some overlap. *Zeppelin* AND NOT *led* finds documents with the word *zeppelin* but they cannot contain the word *led*. Therefore, no documents that contain the words *led* and *zeppelin* will be retrieved.

Word	Symbol	Alt. Symbol	Result
NEAR	~		When you employ NEAR, the search engine finds documents that contain the specified words within a certain distance of each other—usually 10 to 20 words apart. For example, you may be looking for the Baron von Zeppelin. Of course his whole name is Baron Ferdinand von Zeppelin, but if you type in simply Baron von Zeppelin, you'll miss references that use his whole name. So, you want any instance of *zeppelin* that has reference to *Baron* nearby, whether it's one word away or half a dozen. By employing *baron* near *zeppelin*, you cover all bases.
Grouping	()	" "	Parentheses or quotation marks act as signifiers for complex Boolean phrases (meaning more than one word), such as "led zeppelin" or "graf zeppelin." Using them makes sure that specific terms are found in the order, and specific grouping, in which you'd like them retrieved.

Sites use variations of the above, so make sure you know which sites use which methods, or you'll get nowhere fast. Fortunately, many search engines use pull-down menus to help you make these relationships, or, like Yahoo!, they allow you to specify the mode of search up front (by clicking buttons that specify the operators AND or OR).

In addition to the use of Boolean logic, many search engines also offer the ability to search using words that are part of a website's title or part of its URL (as opposed to its content). Others will even allow you to search within specific dates, or offer utilities for partial matches (Yahoo! calls this "wildcard matching").

Furthermore, other types of searches are becoming popular, most notably natural language, which allows you to ask for information in a normal, conversational way. Engines employing natural language identify your intent from the way you've ordered your words, giveing weight (or importance) to each one word to determine what you are asking for. It's a little less accurate than Boolean searches, but a little less complicated as well.

All of the methods described here are excellent ways to do advanced searching on the web. We've kept our descriptions simple here because this is only an introduction and not a master class in computer programming. If you're so inclined, you can find much more information on the web itself, especially in the reference sites listed and reviewed in this work.

A Nickel History Tour of the Internet and Search Engines

In the late 1950s, access to the few computers in the United States was incredibly limited. Demand was high, and only several military labs, research centers, and academic institutions were granted access. The power of those early mainframe computers was, by today's standards, laughably weak (less than that of a palm-size electronic organizer), and any simple calculation ate up an incredible amount of time and memory. The institutions with on-site computers, such as MIT and Stanford, wielded a lot of power of a different sort.

To prevent computer monopolies from forming, the federal government's Department of Defense (DOD) set up a network called the ARPANET (Advanced Research Projects Agency Network) that linked universities and research labs to computers wherever they were available. At the same time, these labs were also researching the possibilities of artificial intelligence (the DOD was a major funder of ARPANET and AI), something that would have great relevance to the creation of the Internet as we know it.

Consequently, during the ARPANET years, an amazing anomaly existed: College students and professors had access to data that big corporations couldn't touch (at least in theory). As such, the ARPANET grew as a repository of huge amounts of academic research. But with the end of the cold war, the government removed most of the restrictions from ARPANET use, which became known in nonmilitary parlance as the Internet. Private citizens could now pay to get access to this big network of computers if they desired.

At that time, all content was text-based; there were no graphics, no cartoons. Dull, dull, dull. And there was no effective means for finding data. Sure, there were plenty of pointers to file transfer protocol (FTP) sites, the early all-text sites. These pointers were created by a small group of dedicated individuals who generated specialized indices for sites in particular areas of interest. But by and large, anyone scanning the Internet (post-ARPANET) had to know who or which institution was housing the data they needed, which they learned either by word of mouth or by reading notices posted online. Then they had to find the online location of that institution.

Enter Tim Berners-Lee, a researcher working at CERN (Conseil Européen pour la Recherche Nucléaire), the European Laboratory for Practicle Physics, based in Geneva, Switzerland. As early as 1980, Berners-Lee had proposed a standard for viewing information in a multimedia format over the nascent Internet. Such a format would allow users of the Net to generate pictures, photographs, audio, and video on their personal computers. His concept came to be known as the HyperText Transfer Protocol, or http, the prefix we're now all familiar with. Thus, the World Wide Web was born in 1990. The web, a multimedia network that uses the Internet's pathways and computers, offered users a way to view and post various data types online, from animation to interactive hypertext links. Since then, the web has been the driving force of the Internet. The web is not separate from the Internet, just as Usenet groups and ftp sites are not separate; they all "lie on top" of the Internet's existing structure. Think of them as different rooms in the same house. The subsequent advent of HyperText Markup Language (commonly known as HTML) and a standardization of part of the Internet kicked the doors open for the general public. The remaining obstacle was to enable easy access to all that information being loaded into Internet computers.

The dilemma caused the resurgence of the artificial intelligence researchers, whose heyday in the 1980s saw the development of creating commercial technologies for large corporations and the government. By the early 1990s, many of the technologies they had developed were being incorporated into standard programs, notably for querying databases and in grammar and spelling checkers in word processing programs. AI research has moved on to an area known as recognition, the capability of computers to "recognize" patterns, human speech, context, and even concepts. An extension of this, "recognition" also refers to the capability of computers to identify the content of files and documents stored in memory. Bingo. This, as they say in geek speak, was the "killer app" for the web.

Using AI techniques, various companies created programs that could monitor the various computers operating on the Internet and catalog their contents, a process similar to performing a file search on a personal computer; but these applications did it automatically and kept a record of it. As the Internet grew more and more quickly, the importance of these applications grew along with it. However, no one was keeping a master list of which files (now called homepages) were contained on all these computers, and no one was really sure how many computers there were. Today's search engines were the solutions, and they are now known by their "brand" names: Yahoo!, Lycos, Hotbot, AltaVista, and others.

Y! tips

- Pages with heavy graphic content can sometimes take a long time to load and may give the impression that either nothing is happening or the page is empty. Checking the loading line (in Netscape it appears in the lower left-hand corner within the border) lets you know whether you should keep waiting or move on.

- Don't assume that a web address ends in "dot.com." The information in a URL (Uniform Resource Locator) is ordered in importance from right to left, with the last three letters on the right being called the top-level domain name. The most common of these are .com (for commercial), .org (organization), .net (network), .edu (educational institution), and .gov (government agency).

- A URL is divided into three parts: the top-level domain name is the part after the dot (as in .com), the second-level domain name is the middle part of the URL (such as "yahoo"), while the third-level domain name is the segment that comes right after the slashes (such as "www").

- Deleting all the information after the top-level domain (most often .com) and hitting return will usually take you to the main page of any given site, or at least to the host of the site. This is useful when a page doesn't contain a "back" button or a link to its homepage.

- Site locations change over time. If you find that a site you've bookmarked is gone or seems to have moved with no forwarding address, go back to a search engine and look for it there by typing in the name of the page. It's like starting over, but it's better than losing a site forever.

ARTS & HUMANITIES

[acting]

The Acting Workshop Online

● http://www.redbirdstudio.com/AWOL/acting2.html

There are acting schools all over the world, but only one significant acting site on the web. AWOL is a no-frills site that directs visitors to a cornucopia of links for professional and aspiring actors, writers, and those interested in various aspects of the business. The site has 14 category links covering everything including unions, professional groups and organizations, actresses and actors, casting, Shakespeare, film festivals, publications, and community theater. Select a specific category and a new list of choices quickly appears. From there you choose direct links to websites.

Free acting and technique tips and information on nonunion work opportunities, auditions, agents, and services are available for perusal or study. If you're looking for books, the list of book recommendations automatically takes you to Amazon.com. And if you scroll to the bottom of the page you'll find current weather conditions, temperatures, and local times for Los Ang eles, Chicago, and New York—a reminder, perhaps, that if you can't stand the heat, don't go into the kitchen.

Two things stand out in this site:1) the breadth of information and 2) the absence of advertisers. What this site lacks in Hollywood-style sex appeal is made up for in content. Break a leg.

[american arts]

American Masters

● http://www.pbs.org/wnet/americanmasters/

If you think there is no connection between Louis Armstrong and John Cage or between Lucille Ball and Sarah Vaughan, then a visit to the Six Degrees Game at American Masters —a website devoted to the cultural identity of American arts—will change your mind. Film, television, literature, music, and performing arts are all featured in this cross-genre site developed by the Public Broadcasting Service in 1984. The database of film stars, dancers, singers, painters, and sculptors is thorough. There are even educational resources with lesson plans for all grade levels. And don't miss the PBS program summaries and schedules. PBS's mission is clearly and eloquently stated: "Without art we would, as a society, lack a soul and a voice." American Masters is a valuable continuation of this endeavor.

[architecture]

In large cities, buildings comprise our natural environment and architecture is their guide. New York, for example, has among its many specimens the Art-Deco-inspired Chrysler Building and the skyscraping beacon of the Empire State Building, as well as the modern lines of the Met Life Building.

Architecture is a subject that lends itself particularly well to the web. Many architectural firms have stunning websites (Skidmore Owings & Merrill at som.com is a fine example) and there are hundreds of pages devoted to renowned architects, such as Frank Lloyd Wright and Stanford Wright, and notable structures, such as the Empire State Building and the Taj Mahal. The sites listed here provide the best look at architecture from three perspectives: skyscrapers, great buildings of the world, and architects and their projects.

ArchINFORM

● http://www.archinform.de/

When you look at a new skyscraper or a monstrous new addition to some international airport, how often do you think about the people who actually dreamed it up? Generally, only certain names stick in our memory because they are associated with big commissions (I.M. Pei's glass pyramid for the Louvre, Frank Gehry's organic alien structure for the Bilbao Guggenheim, Norman Foster's see-through Hong Kong & Shanghai Bank in Hong Kong). This site goes beyond the top names to list more than 10,000 projects by more than 600 architects, categorized and linked by a variety of criteria, from country to kind of building (hotel, office, etc.) to project and architect. Clicking on Cesar Pelli, for instance, shows text listings of many of his buildings, as well as those of his firm, in addition to pictures of some of his most famous works, including the Petronas Towers.

This the most comprehensive site regarding architects as a

YAHOO! ALSO LISTS: [acting]

- **http://www.abwag.com/**
ABWAG to learn acting: details the feel, think, do technique.
- **http://free.prohosting.com/~jez/**
Actors Resource for Basic Technique: fundamentals of the craft.
- **http://www.actorsource.com/**
The Actor Source Web page,
- **http://www.geocities.com/Broadway/Stage/4196/AA03.html**
Footlight Notes: explores the lives and careers of performers from the 1850s to the 1920s.
- **http://www.theatrgroup.com/Method/**
Method Acting Procedures

major category; in addition, it represents the business of architecture with a sleek design while looking at a large cross-section of modern-day architects and their projects. Note: This is a German site, so make sure you click on English on the homepage.

The Great Buildings Collection

● http://www.greatbuildings.com/

Many of the world's premier cities are identified by the great buildings that form the jagged teeth of their skylines: Bombay by the Taj Mahal, New York by the Empire State Building, Hong Kong by the Bank of China, Washington, D.C. by the Capitol. These buildings and many more are celebrated at the Great Buildings Collection. A gateway to architecture from around the world and across history (at least, that's what the site says, and we completely agree), this site presents hundreds of

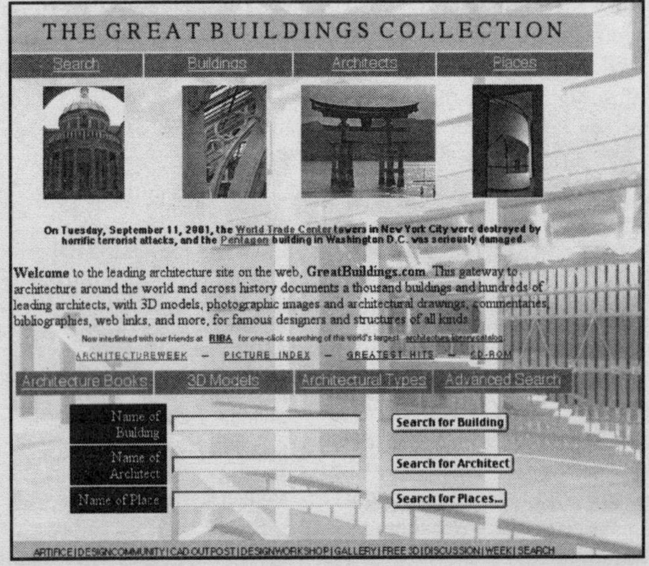

buildings and leading architects with a combination of 3D models, photographic images, and architectural drawings. Not content to stop there, the site has commentaries, bibliographies, and Web links to famous designers and structures of all kinds.

The search engine on the main page consists of three search boxes: Name of Building, Name of Architect, and Name of Place. Other aspects of the site, include: 3D Models and Architectural Types. There are also links to architectural support resources, such as galleries, 3D and CAD programs, and discussion groups.

Once you get to one of the 750 buildings featured on the site, the photographs alone are worth the effort. Each building profile also has historical data, ranging from dates of construction to materials used and style of architecture, as well as a link to the architect's other buildings on the site (for example, I.M. Pei has 10 buildings featured here). Finally, there is a free downloadable program, Design Workshop, that allows you to view the 3D models on the site; you can even construct some simple models of your own. If you ever wanted to try your hand at designing the next Westminster Abbey or Palace of Versailles, this might just be the place to begin your apprenticeship.

Skyscrapers.com

● http://www.skyscrapers.com/

Dallas and Kuala Lumpur have almost the same number of high-rise buildings—273 and 299 respectively. Chicago, on the other hand, has 1,281 and still pales in comparison to New York—which clocks in at 2,808. And these are just simple statistics. Skyscrapers.com includes information from the technical to the trivial about more than 29,000 high-rise buildings as well as hundreds of churches and other structures, such as observation towers and masts, in cities all over the world. Information on each city also includes population counts and a gallery of photos. There are message boards for visitors to post messages about their favorite buildings and a spotlight on a different building every day. As if all this weren't enough, daily weather forecasts for each city, sponsored by the Weather Channel, are posted.

[art]

Art is a mirror. Art is a hammer. Art is a hammer smashing that mirror. Whatever art is, there sure is a lot of it. The beauty of the Net is that much of the world's art is here, and you can view it in all its splendor. From the serenity of Seurat to the grimness of Giger, there is a website, or collection of websites, covering every major artist you can think of.

And if you want to expand your knowledge, stop by the world's best art museums (listed under our MUSEUMS section) or take a class in art history from one of the sites listed below. Or type the name of your favorite artist into the Yahoo! search engine and watch art from every corner of the planet fill up your screen. It's a lot cheaper than trying to buy an original van Gogh, and you can change the picture any time of day or night without needing a Swiss bank account or an armed guard.

ADAM Art Search

● http://adam.ac.uk/sindex.html

Compiled by England's top librarians, ADAM—the Art, Design, Architecture & Media Information Gateway—is a fabulous site to have in your kit of art history research tools. The service helps you find useful, quality-assured information on the Internet in the following areas: Fine Art (painting, prints and drawings, sculpture, and other contemporary media), Design (industrial, product, fashion, graphic, packaging, and interior design), Architecture (town planning and landscape design—but not building construction), Applied Arts (textiles, ceramics, glass, metals, jewelry, and furniture), Media (film, television, broadcasting, photography, and animation), and Museum Studies and Conservation.

ADAM has an online catalog of Internet resources, which include websites and electronic mailing lists, set up to mimic the way libraries organize bibliographic resources. Using this system, you can create and personalize a virtual library of digital art, design, architecture, and media resources. Start with the search engine to find interesting articles on artists or styles; if you require more depth, try a Power Search to which you can add more parameters. For instance, if you plug in "Picasso NOT Cubism," you'll find sites relating to the artist's early and later work, but not the Cubist works from the teens. For anyone with a real interest in art, features like this make ADAM more flexible and more accessible than a paper library.

Artcyclopedia

● http://www.artcyclopedia.com/

Artcyclopedia.com is a handy and comprehensive guide to museum-quality art on the Internet. Created by John Malyon of Calgary, Canada, the site features a database of more than 7,500 artists where visitors can search by artist, work, or museum. Painters, sculptors, and photographers of all cultures and eras are included. Through the AllPosters.com-sponsored area, visitors can order posters of various artworks. The site lists its top 30 most popular art works, art museums worldwide, and art news headlines and stories. There's a monthly art feature (with archives of past articles) and links to other art websites, making Artcyclopedia.com a great place to view art without leaving home.

Art History Research Centre

● http://www.art-history.concordia.ca/AHRC/

"The Internet as a Research Medium for Art Historians" is the title of an essay on this site, and it exemplifies what the Art History Research Centre is all about. The site's bold intro claims that "The AHRC is the first and foremost tool for art historical research on the Internet. It shares key resources and methods of online research so that art historians can find the resources relevant to their work."

Fully embracing the Digital Age, this site shows you how to use newsgroups, get on e-mail lists, use a search engine, search through articles and the holdings of university art history departments, and find your way through a variety of arcane art servers on just about any subject that comes to mind. There's even a section devoted to the proper method of citing material taken from electronic sources. In a nutshell, the Art History Research Centre not only shows you where the information is, but teaches you how to be a digital-era art historian and get the most out the World Wide Web.

Art History Resources on the Web

● http://witcombe.sbc.edu/ARTHLinks.html

A massive clearinghouse of art history links, this site will provide students, researchers, and art lovers with hundreds of places to visit on the web. Completely text-driven, Art History Resources breaks down each style of Western art into major subdivisions, which can be further broken down into more specific morsels of inquiry. For example, the Renaissance section is separated into 15th-Century Art in Northern Europe and Spain, 15th-Century Italian Art: Early Renaissance, 16th-Century Italian Art: High Renaissance and Mannerism, and 16th-Century Art in Northern Europe and Spain. If you pick, say, 15th-Century Art in Northern Europe and Spain, that will take you to a long list of more detailed pages, covering everything from the Ghent Alterpiece to a variety of sites on the Neuremberg Chronicle, as well as dozens (if not hundreds) more. Some sites have corresponding images of the artwork.

Art History Resources equally details every phase of art history, including the Baroque, Impressionism, Postmodernism, and even Prehistoric art. There's also a reference section devoted to the world's major art museums and galleries, all categorized by country.

ArtLex

● http://www.artlex.com/

Intimidated when people ask you about your opinion on the "Pre-Raphaelite Brotherhood?" Don't know the difference between baroque and rococo, or Dali and Dada? Fear no more. ArtLex (as in "art lexicon") is an amazing resource for artists, students, and educators, ArtLex is a giant dictionary of art-related terms. There are over 3,000 entries that cover styles, techniques, materials, tools, and much more. You can search by art movement, culture, and materials, or browse through alphabetical listings. For example, the PF-to-PIM page will give you in-depth definitions for philately (the study of postage stamps), photoCD (a digital storage system), photogravure (a photomechanical print-making process), and dozens more. Many of the entries include photo links to JPEG images of the work in question, as well as links to additional sites related to the topic. And a Shortcuts menu leads you to numerous articles on a variety of subjects, from abstract expressionism to watercolor.

ArtMuseum.Net

● http://www.artmuseum.net/

If you don't have the plane fare to travel across the United States and Europe to see major art exhibitions on van Gogh and American art in the twentieth century, you can save yourself a trip to the airport by visiting ArtMuseum.net. This site is a feast for the eyes, pure and simple, with incredible graphics and excellent digital reproductions of artworks. This Intel-sponsored site seeks to enhance the museum-going experience by providing online tours of exhibitions at major art museums, including the recent "van Gogh's van Goghs" from the van Gogh Museum in Amsterdam and the "American Century" from the Whitney Museum in New York. And because it's from Intel, the site is ambitious technology-wise. These exhibition guides are not just composed of press re-

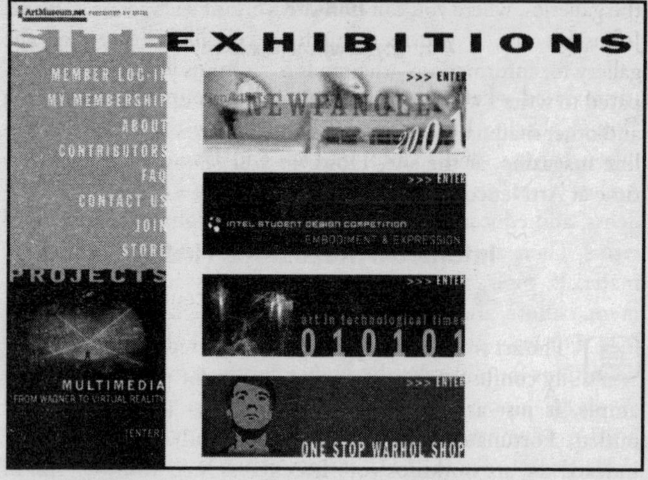

leases and a few JPEG images. ArtMuseum.net makes full use of plug-ins like Shockwave, Flash, and RealPlayer to convey the full picture—so to speak. Once you sign up as a member, you can take various gallery tours, look at video and audio clips, get info on upcoming exhibitions, and participate in discussions. It's the next best thing to being there.

ArtNet.com

● http://www.artnet.com/

Whether you're a serious collector or just looking for one special piece, ArtNet.com has almost everything you need to find, appraise, buy, and sell art online. In effect, ArtNet.com has harnessed the power of the Web to create an international art market, complete with price information, exhibitions, and inventory from hundreds of galleries and artists. You can participate in online auctions, which have featured works by such notables as Andy Warhol, Frank Stella, and Jim Dine. If you don't want to go the auction route, you can cruise the galleries, where you can find the work of such icons as Jasper Johns for sale. If you see something you like, just e-mail the gallery for information—though if it's a Johns you want, be prepared to write a check with lots of zeros. You can also find books and other materials about specific artists, or read through the online magazine, at the site. However you choose to spend your time at ArtNet.com, you're sure to get an eyeful.

InternetArtResources (IAR)

● http://www.artresources.com/

The art world is complex, and art-related content can easily confuse search engines. A search for paintings, for example, is just as likely to turn up hardware stores and craft outlets. Fortunately, ArtResources has already categorized and indexed the art world for you. It contains links to thousands of online art resources: to be exact, 4,998 galleries, 1,213 museums, and 3,193 artists, plus art reviews, books, articles, and catalogs. All are searchable alphabetically or by using the ArtResources search engine.

Arts Wire

● http://www.artswire.org/

Having trouble establishing an online presence for your art or art group? Try Arts Wire. If you're an artist or a member of an arts group, this site is a good place to learn new skills, network, and get your group the aid it needs to survive, enlighten, and strengthen your local community. The group's mission is to provide the arts community with a communications network whose core is composed of the strong voices of artists and community-based cultural groups. This communal approach to supporting the arts pervades the site. You'll find news on national funding efforts for the arts; new facilities for museums, music, and dance companies; job opportunities; and art conference dates. Using the SpiderSchool section, you can also tour various museums around the country, such as the Cooper-Hewitt in New York City or the DeCordova Museum & Sculpture Park outside of Boston. You can also find tips for buying and selling art online, for conducting art-related searches, and for launching fund-raising efforts.

The PartheNet

● http://home.mtholyoke.edu/~klconner/parthenet.html

Parthenon + Network = PartheNet. PartheNet is a resource page that guides students to many general websites on a variety of art history subjects. Click on, say, Winslow Homer in the "Nineteenth and Twentieth Century in America" section, and you're greeted with a wide array of links to delve into. For Homer, you get a capsule biography, a bibliography by noted scholars, and leads to find more on the famed artist. One nice touch is that there are sites that help you put Homer in the context of his time (turn-of-the-century music, literature, and other arts).

In addition to the genre sites is a list of museum sites, as well as photo archives and links to other art-history resource pages.

[history]

American Memory

● http://memory.loc.gov/

America's collective memory was captured before TV and radio were invented in photographs, on printed paper, and in paintings. These images are usually featured in schoolbooks or in documentaries—immigrants crowding into Ellis Island, George Washington crossing the Delaware, suffragettes marching for the vote. Now they are online in an extensive visual collection called American Memory.

This component of the Library of Congress site was created in conjunction with the National Digital Library Program,

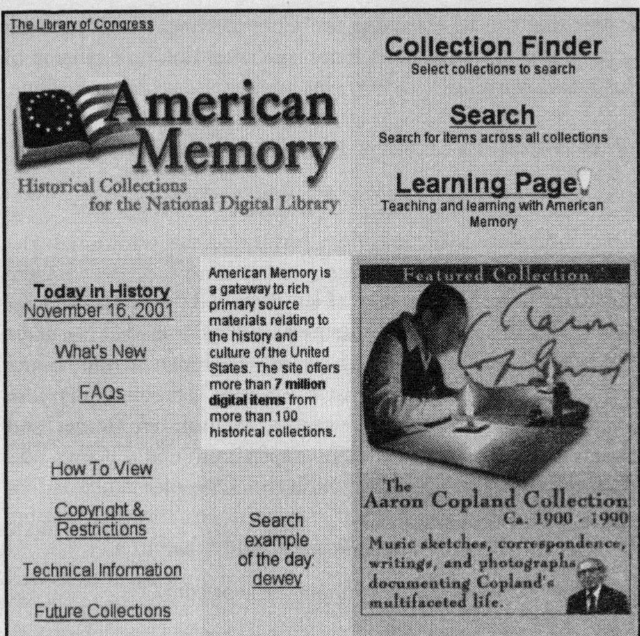

which is digitizing select books, photos, drawings, manuscripts, maps, music, movies, and more. The rationale behind the creation of the American Memory online collection was the popular demand for reproductions of the images owned by the Library. From the Library's millions of pieces, this site will feature those most in demand.

Currently, there are more than 60 collections at American Memory, including Panoramic Maps, Portraits of the Presidents and First Ladies, Touring Turn-of-the-Century America, Early Films of San Francisco, American Sheet Music, Architecture and Interior Design, Jackie Robinson and Other Baseball Highlights, and Civil War Photographs. Visitors can search by keyword or browse the collections, all of which are annotated and contain images that can be expanded for better viewing. Those wanting to stroll down America's memory lane need look no farther than this marvelous site.

WWW-Virtual Library: History Central Catalogue

● http;//www.ukans.edu/history/VL

Need information on maritime history or the traditional costumes of Estonia? If you're looking for history content on the Net, start here. This section of the Virtual Library (see our review under LIBRARIES) contains dozens of links that can serve as a jumping-off point for history-related research. Maintained at the University of Kansas, this V-Lib page is broken down into geographical areas (India, Australia, Bolivia, etc.), eras and epochs (Ancient Egypt, Modern Europe, etc.), and genres (the Holocaust, Women's History, Indigenous Peoples, etc.).

The History Net

● http;//www.thehistorynet.com/

"As I watched the advance of the Communist forces in March and April of 1975, I feared Vietnam would be partitioned again, as it had been in 1954, and that they were going to draw a line across the country just north of Saigon. I figured we would be able to stay behind that line and fight and survive for maybe a year. My feeling at the time was that if we tried this, then a lot of people would die, but the Americans, at some point in time, would come back and support us because they would see that we were doing the heroic thing in standing against the enemy armies. But I was wrong. . ." So writes a Jesuit priest in Vietnam during the American evacuation. This and other personal stories are recounted in the History Net's Eyewitness Accounts section, where you can read recollections by witnesses to epic moments in history. But this is just one section of a most accessible and enjoyable site for history buffs of every era. Sections include World War II, the Civil War, World History,

American History, and Aviation & Technology, as well as interviews with interesting figures (when we visited, there was a fascinating discussion with World War II Luftwaffe ace Günther Rall). Other features include a calendar of exhibits and events and an article-search database. The History Net is full of gripping, powerful stories and seemingly endless fascinating facts. As is often said, if we don't learn from history, we are doomed to repeat it; a site like this can ensure that we do learn.

The History Place

● http://www.historyplace.com/

An audio clip of Gerald Ford pardoning Richard Nixon. Neil Armstrong speaking from the surface of the moon. Photographs from seven campaigns of genocide in the twentieth

century. You can find all these at the History Place, where the motto is "The Past into the Future." This is a vast history site that covers everything from the American Revolution to Napoleon to the Irish potato famine and much more. Dedicated to students, educators, and all those who love history, the History Place grants easy access to its numerous documents and photos. Though the overall feeling is scholarly—but not academically dry—in other hands this site could be a disaster. The History Place handles this content masterfully.

As you look around, you can find (to cite just a few) background material on the Dred Scott decision, which helped trigger the Civil War; photos of John F. Kennedy's early political career; and the complete text of British prime minister Neville Chamberlain's address to Parliament just after Germany invaded Poland in 1939. Behind all these facts, there's a helpful section for students with tips on "How to write a better history paper." This is one of the best-organized and most user-friendly history sites on the Internet.

Horus' Web Links to History Resources

● http://www.ucr.edu/h-gig/

How do you like your history? By country? By time period? By historic site? Or just alphabetically? This site from the University of California in Riverside, called Horus, will deliver it to you in any of these forms. It contains an interesting collection of history links that are a bit out of the ordinary; they include museums, historical societies, genealogy resources, antiques catalogs, real estate ads for historic properties, and more. Devised to expand teaching methods, the Horus site links to many traditional historical topics as well, from world history and the military to women and Asian-and African-Americans.

If, say, you wanted to do research on the tiny Arabic country of Bahrain, Horus gives you four sites to explore, and each section gives you different angles of inquiry, such as Culture, Geography, Tour Guide, History, Government, Business, and

Transport. As you peel away the layers to get more specific about your subject matter, Horus steers you to sites that should help fulfill your research needs. If you have a term paper coming or just want to dig up some facts for your own learning pleasure, this links-only site has much to offer burgeoning history buffs.

Hyperhistory Online

● http://www.hyperhistory.com/online_n2/History_n2/a.html

Did you know that Picasso, Einstein, and Stalin were contemporaries? Or that the American Revolution was fought during the peak of the world slave trade? Most of us learn history as a chronology of events in our own culture, disconnected from the events that happened at the same time in other parts of the world. Hyperhistory Online can fill those gaps in our historical knowledge. Containing 1,400 files on 3,000 years of history, Hyperhistory makes use of colorful charts to point out pivotal events happening concurrently throughout history, which is a lot more meaningful than lists of names and dates.

National Archives

● http://www.nara.gov/

The National Archives and Records Administration (NARA) is an independent federal agency that helps preserve U.S. history by overseeing the management of all federal records. Its mission is to ensure ready access to the essential evidence that documents the rights of American citizens, the actions of federal officials, and the overall national experience. And thanks to the Internet, access to this information is easier than ever.

This website has many categories to choose from: an Exhibit Hall, containing such documents as the *Apollo 11* Flight Plan; a Digital Classroom, which encourages teachers and students to use archival documents and shows how to use them; and an Archives & Preservation area offering help to professionals concerning management and preservation of archives.

These are actual historical documents—records, really—and you can view them from your home, thanks to the Internet. They, and hundreds of other important American texts, are included in this wonderful site, all of which will make you glad you live in this democracy. Grab your flag and let it fly.

Today in History

● http://lcweb2.loc.gov/ammem/today/today.html

Pick a date, any date: say September 6th. In 1860 it's the birth date of social reformer Jane Hull, who began a number of crucial welfare programs for Chicago's poor. In 1901, it's the date President William McKinley was assassinated by the anarchist Leon Czolgosz. This wonderful site from the Library of Congress lets visitors time-travel to the colorful historic events on any day they choose. Each item at Today in History is described in an interesting essay and is connected to useful links and cross-references. For example, you can learn more about McKinley's presidency and his last day and see a vintage reenactment of his assassin's execution, filmed not long after the president's death and now downloadable on your computer as an MPEG file or QuickTime movie.

This is another site that proves how vital the Internet is as a teaching tool for history—it has an immediacy and vibrancy that books often can't duplicate. Definitely bookmark the Today in History site and stop back often. As you'll find out, there's something new every day . . . in history.

whowhatwhen

● http://www.sbrowning.com/whowhatwhen/

The whowhatwhen database is a unique site that generates graphic timelines of periods in history or of the events in the life of an individual. You can ask a question—say, what war was fought during Edgar Allan Poe's lifetime—and get the answer in a bar graph/text form, or you can type a day, year or name to learn the names of people who lived and died on that date. You can even chart a time line of contemporary people and events in one of 14 different categories. A nice finishing touch is that you can click on an icon next to a person's name to go directly to a Google search for other sites related to that person. Developed by Steve Browning (an engineer at Lockheed), this is a fantastic example of what one person with a good idea can bring to life via the web.

[humanities]

Social Science Information Gateway (SOSIG)

● http://sosig.esrc.bris.ac.uk/

Humanities is an extremely broad category of study. Where else can you explore the impact of evolution (anthropology), then discuss what it costs to dig up the evidence of evolution (economics)? SOSIG has the breadth of humanities covered from top to bottom. Designed as a Yahoo!-like index, the site has a number of "parent" headings: SOSIG tackles Economics, Education, Environmental Sciences, Ethnology/Ethnography/ Anthropology, Geography, European Studies, Government,

YAHOO! ALSO LISTS: [humanities]

- **http://edsitement.neh.fed.us**
  EDSITEment: a guide to humanities websites, with online teaching materials, lesson plans, etc.
- **http://www.sil.org/humanities/resources.html**
  Humanities Resources on the Internet
- **http://users.ox.ac.uk/~humbul/**
  Humbul Humanities Hub
- **http://vos.ucsb.edu/**
  Voice of the Shuttle: Humanities Research metapage of humanities resources designed for the research user.

Law, Philosophy, Politics, Psychology, Social Science General, Social Welfare, Sociology, Statistics, and Women's Studies. The University Social Science Departments have additional separate categories.

The links under the subheadings lead to articles, papers, reports, books, FAQs, journals, organizations and societies, research projects and centers, and related categories. These pages contain lengthy summaries of each resource before taking you to the actual site. SOSIG claims to have thousands of links on topics from applied psychology to statistical theory. FYI, the SOSIG site is maintained by funds from the European Union and the Economic & Social Research Council.

[languages]

travlang

● http://www.dictionaries.travlang.com/

Knowing how to say hello and thank you in Spanish just won't cut it if you've gotten food poisoning in Norway or are being detained in Yugoslavia. Really serious travel calls for some really serious translation capabilities, and you'll find them here at Travlang (assuming, of course, that you can access the Internet wherever you are). Travlang is a substantial collection of translation dictionaries, with an emphasis on European dialects. Each section on the page—and it is all on one page—is segmented by language. Within each of these is a list of possible translation paths, both from and to (e.g., English to Czech or Czech to English), in German, Dutch, English, French, Portuguese, Italian, Danish, Finnish, Norwegian, Frisian, Afrikaans, Magyar, Czech, Latin, and several others. A Quick Jump feature takes you to pulldown menus for a specific from-to translation.

The site contains a hidden gem: a link to Travlang's Foreign

YAHOO! ALSO LISTS: [language]

- **http://www.allwords.com/**
  allwords.com: English dictionary with multilingual search capability.
- **http://www.geocities.com/SoHo/Studios/9783/phond1.html**
  Dictionary of English Phonesthemes: Phonesthemes, or sound-symbols, play an important role in word formation and psycholinguistics.
- **http://www.ctv.es/USERS/alberfon/dicsear1.htm**
  Dictsearch: all-in-one search of monolingual and bilingual dictionaries.
- **http://www2.echo.lu/edic/**
  Eurodicautom: looks up words in a number of European languages. Offers subject filters and display options.
- **http://www.cs.cmu.edu/~dougb/ident.html**
  Language Identifier: Enter some text and this program will try to guess which language (of 12 Romance and Germanic languages) it is written in.
- **http://www.speech.cs.cmu.edu/egads/mingo/**
  Mingo Egads: texts, grammar, dictionary, and learning resources for this Iroquoian language.
- **http://tis.consilium.eu.int**
  Terminological Information System (TIS): online version of the database used by terminologists and translators working in the General Secretariat of the Council of the European Union.
- **http://www.wordbot.com/**
  Wordbot: When you load a page through Wordbot, you can click on any word to look up its meaning in a dictionary, including English translation from a number of languages.

Languages for Travelers, where you can select your native tongue, then click on a flag icon of the language you want to learn, from Austrian to Zulu. This jumps you to a page with a list of conversation categories, such as basic words, numbers, shopping/dining, travel, directions, and places. Click on a category, press the Submit button, and you're taken to long lists of relevant words and phrases. Not only that, but you can listen to a recording of each word using RealAudio. Additional components include data on the countries where these languages are spoken. Travlang is an invaluable site for international travelers, as well as for anyone who wants to brush up on a foreign language or take the first steps into learning a new one.

[literature]

The Complete Works of William Shakespeare

● http://chemicool.com/shakespeare/

This is Shakespeare the way it should be studied. Full of hyperlinks, support material, and even a discussion group, this certainly beats listening to some professor emeritus drone on about the wonders of the bard while you try to read six-point type in a thirty-pound book.

Hosted by those preternaturally bright people at MIT, this site includes the complete works of Shakespeare (yes, even the sonnets), along with a word and phrase search for the works, a chronological and alphabetical listing of plays, Bartlett's Familiar

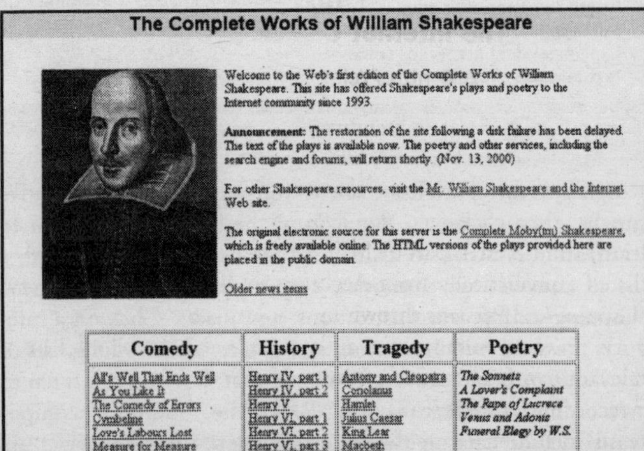
The Complete Works of William Shakespeare
Welcome to the Web's first edition of the Complete Works of William Shakespeare. This site has offered Shakespeare's plays and poetry to the Internet community since 1993.
Announcement: The restoration of the site following a disk failure has been delayed. The text of the plays is available now. The poetry and other services, including the search engine and forums, will return shortly. (Nov. 13, 2000)
For other Shakespeare resources, visit the Mr. William Shakespeare and the Internet Web site.
The original electronic source for this server is the Complete Moby(tm) Shakespeare, which is freely available online. The HTML versions of the plays provided here are placed in the public domain.
Older news items
Comedy
History
Tragedy
Poetry
All's Well That Ends Well
As You Like It
The Comedy of Errors
Cymbeline
Love's Labours Lost
Measure for Measure
The Merry Wives of Windsor
The Merchant of Venice
Henry IV, part 1
Henry IV, part 2
Henry V
Henry VI, part 1
Henry VI, part 2
Henry VI, part 3
Henry VIII
King John
Antony and Cleopatra
Coriolanus
Hamlet
Julius Caesar
King Lear
Macbeth
Othello
Romeo and Juliet
The Sonnets
A Lover's Complaint
The Rape of Lucrece
Venus and Adonis
Funeral Elegy by W.S.

Shakespearean Quotations, Shakespeare resources on the Internet, a Shakespeare discussion area, and a glossary.

The Perseus Project

● http://www.perseus.tufts.edu/

Passionate about the classics? No, not cars or golden-oldie tunes but *real* classics like Latin and Greek literature. Perseus is a great place on the Internet to find information about celebrated works, including Shakespeare and other authors of the English Renaissance. The Perseus Digital Library, a nonprofit site, is federally funded with the support of Tufts University and private donations. Hosted by the Department of the Classics at Tufts University, the goal of the site is stated simply: "to bring a wide range of source materials to as large an audience as possible." And do they ever. The site includes Latin texts in English and, a section on early modern English literature, complete with historical sources and secondary reference works. The site provides free access to its collections to foster appreciation of the humanities.

Text
The Internet Classics Archive

● http://classics.mit.edu/

If classic literature is all Greek to you—and that's the way you like it—then check out the Internet Classics Archive, a website that connects you to more than 400 works of mainly Greco-Roman literature, all in English translation. Sponsored in part by MIT, the archive includes 59 authors, listed alphabetically from Aechines to Xenophon—with a few Chinese and Persians thrown in for perspective.

Click on your favorite author, perhaps Virgil, and a list of available works is presented for your perusal. Choose his masterwork *The Aeneid* and you'll find the book's text divided into 12 easily digestible sections. The text is peppered with links to related sites on the web, which in some cases allow you to actually

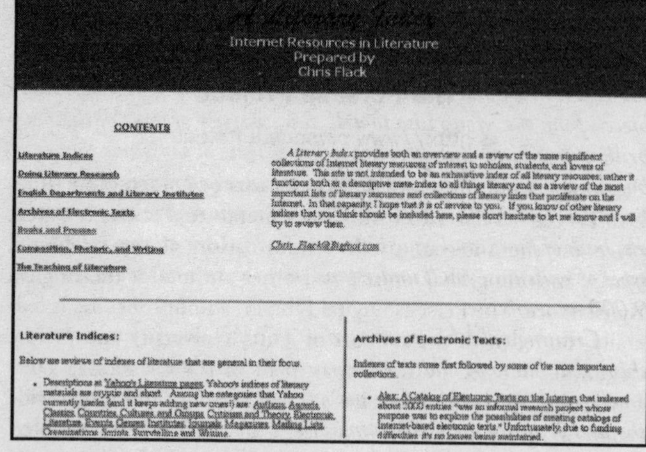

read some of these works in the original Greek. The works are appended with reader comments, and if you attach your e-mail address to a specific work, you'll receive notification each time a new comment is submitted. For those who'd rather collect and read these texts the old-fashioned—shall we say "classic"—way, there are links to Amazon.com and Barnesandnoble.com.

Finally, the site features a current trivia question. Recently, the question posted was "What was the vote in the condemnation of Socrates?" which suggests that the pursuit of factual minutiae is timeless.

[museums]

Most of the world's great museums are located in the world's great cities. The problem is that most of the people in the world don't live there. If you don't live in Europe, or don't travel there, for instance, you might never make it to the Louvre, the Orsay, or the London Science Museum. And if you never get to New York, you might not have a chance to explore the wonders of the American Museum of Natural History or the Museum of Modern Art.

The web changes all that. From the comfort of your armchair, you can look at some of the world's great collections and individual pieces, from the Mona Lisa to a T. Rex, courtesy of some of these brilliant websites. But there are so many types of museums that it boggles the mind. If you can think of it, there is a museum for it, from barbed wire to basketball. And, once you realize that memorials, halls of fame, and civic historical exhibits are all considered types of museums, you'll understand why the web has more than 9,000 museum sites.

Creating valuable websites to handle this diversity is something that has to be addressed by the museums themselves. In a reference guide such as this, it is not our intention to point readers to the sites of all the great museums, or to uncover the truly interesting yet obscure ones. Rather, we have looked to the best institutions in the world and determined which have made the most effective use of the web. Those websites must be entertaining or at least enjoyable, and they must have substantial depth of information that could be considered valuable by someone doing basic research.

The American Museum of Natural History (AMNH)

● http://www.amnh.org/

The American Museum of Natural History in New York City is the kind of place where you can wander around for days and never get bored, and the website is no different. This huge site contains the best of the best from the permanent exhibits of the AMNH, including its famous Tyrannosaurus Rex, its Hall of Biodiversity, and its Gem Collection.

There is a monstrous amount of information here, and in true natural-history-museum style, you find much of it by wandering down an unexpected hallway or turning into a small side gallery. Most visitors will want to explore what made the museum famous, namely its fossil collections. Expedition: Fossils and its attendant prehistoric time line comprise a beautifully laid-out tour through the world of fossils, fossil exploration, and stages of vertebrate evolution. The photos and diagrams used here are the same ones featured on the museum's online computer consoles.

The AMNH really excels at transferring its current exhibitions to online format, with full multimedia presentations ranging from Shackleton's exploration of the Antarctic to the epidemics that ravage the world to tracking humpback whales in Madagascar. The site also keeps some of its superb past exhibitions online as well, such as the Leonardo Codex Leicester and the Nature of Diamonds.

Finally, a large and superb Just for Kids section on the site offers ideas, printouts, and projects that relate to the museum's offerings (notably its dioramas) and current exhibitions. Floor plans can be printed out in .pdf format as well.

Franklin Institute Online

● http://sln.fi.edu/

Did you know that Ben Franklin invented a glass armonica, a musical instrument that creates sounds by rubbing water on differently shaped glasses? Philadelphia's Franklin Institute is packed with such interesting facts, in several virtual exhibits. One worth a visit is on the heart, which has QuickTime videos of heart surgery and of functioning hearts. Though this site doesn't have enough online exhibits to rank it among the top tier of museum sites, it does have one nice feature for visitors: After you've taken the virtual tour, you can print out a discount coupon for use when you visit the real museum.

London Science Museum (LSM)

● http://www.sciencemuseum.org.uk

  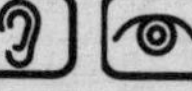

LSM's approach to teaching science online is an excellent example of what can be done when the Internet is used to its fullest potential. When we visited the site, we found an impressively diverse set of topics, including Fusion, Materials, Electrons, the *Apollo* missions, History of Industrialization, Cloning and Dolly the Sheep, the Relationship between the Brain and the Eye, and half a dozen others.

Each virtual exhibit is a website unto itself. For instance, the Discovery section of the Electron exhibit starts with a page on the discovery of the electron in 1897. From there, it discusses the theories and experiments leading up to J. J. Thomson's revelation. Next a QuickTime movie shows a reconstruction of Thomson's original experiment, followed by a Shockwave animation that allows viewers to try their hand at conducting the same experiment interactively. Farther into the Discovery section is an archive recording of Thomson discussing his work, along with a biographical text. There are seven more segments to this exhibit, including electron events, electrons in atoms, seeing with electrons, electrons in our lives, and relevant links.

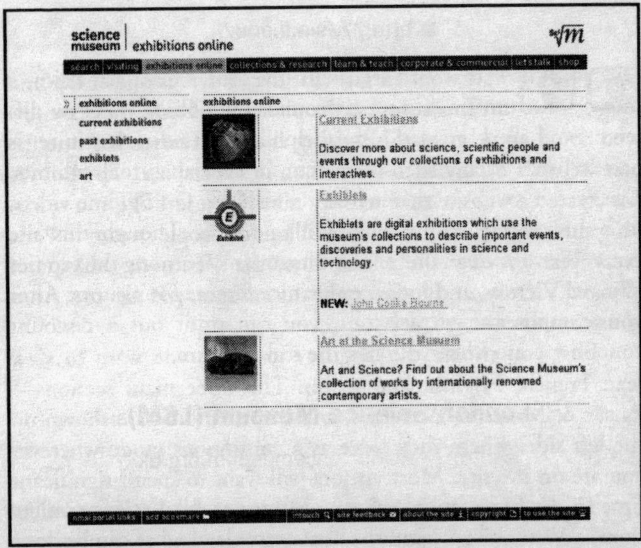

Thanks to the imaginative design and use of multimedia throughout the site, LSM's online museum makes good use of hands-on, or interactive, segments of exhibits, featuring a variety of experiments and tests that the visitor can participate in. Throughout all the virtual exhibits, the museum employs a wide array of Internet technologies (such as QuickTime VR and Shockwave), which help realize the sensation of being deep within the museum itself. This also makes learning about science a pleasurable experience.

In addition to the virtual presentations, an entire research "wing" on the LSM website, contains extensive lists of research projects, resources, and library materials. Of course, you'll also find the standard information about the museum itself, and a set of links to its regular collections. In short, the LSM has done a singularly brilliant job of making this website one of its very finest exhibits.

The Louvre

● http://www.louvre.fr

Few would argue that the Louvre is one of the best art museums on the planet. And now there are few who could argue as of this writing that the Louvre has one the best websites of any such institution in cyberspace. The Louvre has created a website that actually makes you feel like you're visiting this spectacular museum. Millions of people stream to Paris every year to view the Mona Lisa, the Venus de Milo, and Winged Victory, and today, right this minute, you can too, from your computer.

First you choose the language in which you want to view text: French, English, and so on. The three main sections—Palace & Museum, Activities, and Information—are shown on the left side, where they serve as a continuous guide wherever you are on the site. Most visitors will want to spend significant time in the first section, where a history of the Louvre, Collections, a Virtual Tour, and the museum magazine are found.

Y! tip

The top domain name (the .com part of a URL) is frequently different for sites in countries outside the United States. Instead of .com, .org, or .net, France has .fr, Australia has .au, Germany has .de, etc.

The eight primary collections of the museum are here, including Egyptian Antiquities, Paintings, Objets d'Art, and Prints and Drawings. Click on the picture above any of these headings and you are taken to a description of the collections, links to major works, and location within the museum. The Major Works section of the Painting Collection, for example, contains an additional 13 links to works ranging from French fourteenth century to paintings from Great Britain. (Okay, we knew you were going to ask, so here it is: The Mona Lisa is in the Italian sixteenth century collection.)

Within each major collection are a varying number of artifacts (averaging about eight pieces). Clicking on any one takes you to a larger image of it, as well as a description and info on its creator. Finally, clicking on the piece at this stage returns a full-screen image of it. The entire process is very museumlike: going to a particular room, viewing a piece, reading its info, then examining it. You can also take a virtual tour of the museum, which is astounding in its own right, but note that to do so requires a QuickTime plug-in for your machine.

This is a perfect way to get a quick education in art without flying to France (although that is still the preferred way to view the wealth of art at the Louvre). This site is one that could be incorporated into school curriculums in the near future, as it makes the process of learning about art and history truly interactive.

Musée d'Orsay

● http://www.musee-orsay.fr

The Musée d'Orsay is one of the world's most beautiful and navigable museums, set in an old railway station in the heart of Paris across the Seine from the Louvre. Its website is similarly striking and efficient, with displays of stunning pieces from Renoir's *Dance at Le Moulin de la Galette* to Cézanne's *Apples and Oranges*.

The Orsay homepage allows the viewer to select from three languages (English, French, and Italian). The site opens to nine different areas, most of which deal with museum business, shops, its internal use of multimedia, and so on. Among these is a fine historical look at the building itself and its origins as a train station. The Collections and Programs sections are the true attractions of this site. Collections details more than two dozen of the museum's most famous and influential works from artists such as van Gogh, Manet, and Seurat, among others. Clicking on the picture of the piece takes you to a detailed description and history and a brief discussion of the artist. Clicking on the picture enlarges it to full-screen size.

It is in the current exhibitions section (listed under Programmes) where the Orsay is outstanding. In fact, the attention paid to the temporary exhibitions is more extensive than that paid to its permanent collections. Recently, it included a retrospective of Marcel Proust and an exhibition of the collection of Theo van Gogh, Vincent's brother. A full description of these current exhibitions, along with photos of the artwork and a biography of the artists are all included. Previews of upcoming exhibitions are especially worthwhile; this is a tactic that should result in return visits to the site (or the actual museum).

The Museum of Modern Art

● http://www.moma.org/

The great thing about this site is its design, which, complete with commentary, is very contemporary and sleek, leaning toward the minimalist. But, hey, what is modern art if it isn't about design? Several pieces from the collection are on display here, including van Gogh's *The Starry Night* and Rousseau's *The Dream*, but we recommend you go to this site to see what modern technology can do with a modern medium like modern art.

The National Gallery of Art

● http://www.nga.gov/

"Data on all of the more than 100,000 objects in the National Gallery of Art's collections can be found using the search capabilities." That line, from the National Gallery of Art, almost captures your need to know about how great this site is. We could add lots of superlatives, but our jaws dropped when we reviewed this site, so not many words were forthcoming. Like the IMDB site for movies, this should be a model for any site where huge amounts of data need to be cross-referenced and cat-

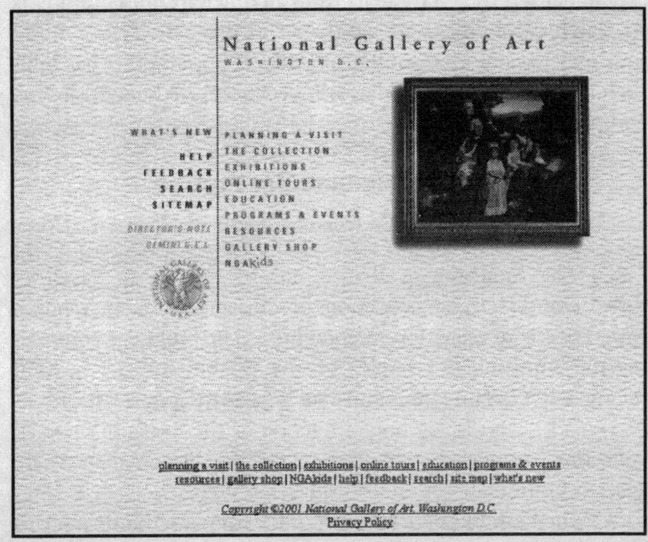

egorized according to the needs of the individual user.

There are amazing works of art here, from Gilbert Stuart's portraits of the presidents and Salvador Dali's *The Sacrament of the Last Supper* to John Singleton Copley's famous pre-*Jaws* terror, *Watson and the Shark*. The site is magnificent in its simplicity. Searches can be done by artist's name, title of the work, or subject matter. Or you can scroll through an indexed list of artists, after typing the appropriate data into a specific box. From there, you can access images of more than 4,000 objects in the National Gallery's collection and nearly 9,500 related details. Once you find an artist or work, there is a brief description, a list of other works in the collection by the artist, and—if there is an image—a full-screen viewing option.

Several virtual exhibitions actually walk you through a particular tour (using either browser plugins or a slide show). You can also tour the museum by medium (paintings, sculpture, etc.) and school. And like all good international sites, this one is accessible in five different languages.

What sets the NGA apart from all other art museum sites is its search capabilities and the size of its database. Other museums may have more stunning collections, but no other has built such a definitive resource that will benefit researchers, art lovers, and passersby alike.

The Smithsonian Institution

● http://www.si.edu/

The Smithsonian Institution (SI) claims to have the world's largest collection of museum artifacts, ranging from rockets to television memorabilia. The buildings comprising the Smithsonian complex on the Washington, D.C., Mall (along with satellite museums such as the Cooper-Hewitt in New York) can display only a fraction of the museum's overall collection. So what better place to exhibit the rest than where space is unlimited—on the World Wide Web.

Virtual exhibits here range from the history of filmmaking to

Edison after 40 to the development of the wine industry in the United States. This isn't a collection of recycled or older displays; you'll find a virtual *Star Wars* tour and an exhibition on the history of electric guitars. But you have to get to know the site to find your way around (after all, the actual museum is spread out over several cities).

All in all, this is a tremendous resource in almost every area of study you can imagine. As with the real thing, you can spend way too much time here—and enjoy every minute of it.

Virtual Library museums page (VLmp)

● http://www.icom.org/vlmp/

This site, sponsored by the International Council of Museums, is a part of the Virtual Library project (see specifics under LIBRARIES), is primarily a text-only list of museums and galleries that have websites. This page provides links categorized by country, type of museum, links to museum resources and contacts around the world, and a search engine for doing keyword searches through the site database. Beyond this, there is a history of the site, dates of additions to the database, and general housekeeping information.

This site serves as an excellent reference point for visiting museums you never knew existed, or for finding museums with similar focus, such as aviation museums or those that have Picasso collections. The search for Picasso turns up such diverse resources as the Museo Picasso Virtual and Washington D.C.'s Kreeger Museum.

[philosophy]

Philosophy Links

● http://www.philosophers.co.uk/links.htm

Philosophers wrestle with the "big" problems while the rest of us worry about the stock market and how to get our VCR timers to stop blinking. Questions such as "Is God dead?" and "Can computers think?" aren't easy to answer, which is why serious minds have spent so much time pondering them. If you like to ponder such questions, too, you can link to many of these people and read their thoughts at Philosophy Links.

Unlike the site listed previously, the emphasis here is not on texts but rather on a larger cross-section of philosophers and schools of thought. The site also has a wider range of links, with more attention paid to diversity of thought. For instance, covered here are atomism and the Turing Test (a mechanism for investigating whether machines can think like humans), as are notable nonclassic philosophers such as Noam Chomsky and Alfred Whitehead. The links are arranged categorically by philosophical organizations, individual philosophers, ancient philosophy, pre-twentieth-century philosophy, modern philosophy, and contemporary philosophy and journals. BTW, this site is a component of the Philosopher's Magazine Online.

Philosophy Texts Online

● http://eserver.org/philosophy

Everyone should have a philosophy, whether it be something simple, such as "I think therefore I am" or "The unexamined life is not worth living," or something more profound, such as a belief in every tenet of existentialism. If you don't have a philosophy of your own and want one, you can find it at Philosophy Texts Online. This single page links to works by nearly every philosopher worthy of intellectual discussion: Aristotle, Plato,

Socrates, Descartes, Hegel, Hume, Kant, Lao-tzu, Marx, Engels, Mill, Nietzsche, and more. There are also links to particular schools of thought—such as relativism—as well as schools of the college and university variety.

The site is laid out alphabetically, and the actual texts are located on servers all over the globe, primarily at academic institutions. If you only pretended to read this stuff in school—or have forgotten what it was it was trying to convey—here is the place to get back in touch.

YAHOO! ALSO LISTS: [philosophy]

- **http://www-personal.monash.edu.au/~dey/phil/**
  Philosophy in Cyberspace: annotated guide to philosophy resources, including schools of thought, concepts and terms, formal education, and organizations and associations.
- **http://eng.hss.cmu.edu/philosophy/**
  CMU English Server: Philosophy: collection of canonical philosophic texts and links to related resources.
- **http://www.epistemelinks.com/**
  Episteme Links: connections to a variety of philosophy resources including events, texts, images, journals, university departments, and more.
- **http://www.lucifer.com/~sasha/thinkers.html**
  Great Thinkers and Visionaries on the Net: list of pages of great thinkers and visionaries on the Net as well as other references to visionary websites.
- **http://www.earlham.edu/~peters/philinks.htm**
  Guide to Philosophy on the Internet
- **http://www.libraries.rutgers.edu/rulib/artshum/phil/phil1.html**
  Guide to Philosophy Resources: Rutgers University
- **http://noesis.evansville.edu/**
  NOESIS: topical index of philosophical research online.
- **http://www.phil.ruu.nl/philosophy-sites.html**
  Philosophy on the Web: directories, bibliographies, e-journals, FAQs, Gophers, and working papers.
- **http://www.bu.edu/sth/Library/contents.html**
  Religion and Philosophy Resources on the Internet: features comments on each item to provide guidance in Internet explorations.

Stanford Encyclopedia of Philosophy

● http://plato.stanford.edu/

Want to learn more about actualism? Who is Friedrich Wilheml Joseph von Schelling? There is a place on the web to find the answers to these burning questions and to discover other tidbits of interest to philosophers. The Stanford Encyclopedia of Philosophy was established in 1995 as a dynamic reference work on the Internet. The site is a publication of the Metaphysics Research Lab at Stanford University and is funded by the National Science Foundation, the National Endowment for the Humanities, the American Philosophical Association, the Canadian Philosophical Association, and the Philosophy Documentation Center. It includes a search engine, archives, editorial information, and tables of contents for navigational ease. The website is constantly updated with information about philosophical theories and concepts; the entries are maintained by experts in the field of philosophy.

[poetry]

Poetry on the web makes freedom of expression a double-edged sword: On the one side, anyone can publish a website with his or her favorite musings—or the words of a favorite poet—for all the world to read. The other side is that way too many people choose to do this, which makes putting together a definitive reference guide next to impossible.

It turns out that the majority of websites with any relationship whatsoever to poetry are individual sites for posting personal poetry or communal sites for posting poetry of a single mind. We found only one that addresses poetry on a larger scale, and that one is listed below. We also found a lot of websites that were about poetry, but they tended to be hosted by vanity publishers—companies that usually charge writers for publishing their work or make money by selling published poems back to the poets in bound compilations.

YAHOO! ALSO LISTS: [poetry]

- **http://www.netten.net/~bmassey/**
  Literature and Poetry Page: compendium of sites containing literature and poetry references; some commentary is included.
- **http://www.geocities.com/Paris/1416/**
  Poetry on the web
- **http://www.pmpoetry.com/**
  Poetry Resource: featuring an index of poets.
- **http://www.geocities.com/Athens/Delphi/2889/**
  Poetry Webring
- **http://www.poem.org/index.html**
  www.poem.org

We're not going to pass judgment on these companies, so if you want to check them out, you'll find them at www.poets.com and www.poetry.com. Not surprisingly, they're related to each other.

The Academy of American Poets

● http://www.poets.org/

This site is a rare surprise: an unexpected and engaging look at an art form many people dismiss out of hand. Designed with compelling graphics (no Hallmark sappiness here), the site is a veritable repository of information about American poets and poetry. A straightforward table of contents lists ongoing awards, programs, and events. Find the Poet is a biography search feature, and an impressive FAQ helps poets looking to get published and warns against the dangers of vanity publishing.

By far, Poets.org's most impressive section is its series of online exhibitions, which are quite comprehensive in their review of certain eras or genres of poetry. Within each exhibit, poets who are mentioned or cited are linked to their biographies elsewhere on the site. These bios include photos, links to the poet's work, and in some cases to audio recordings of their work. This site makes poetry and poets so interesting that we wish we hadn't slept through Poetry 101 in college.

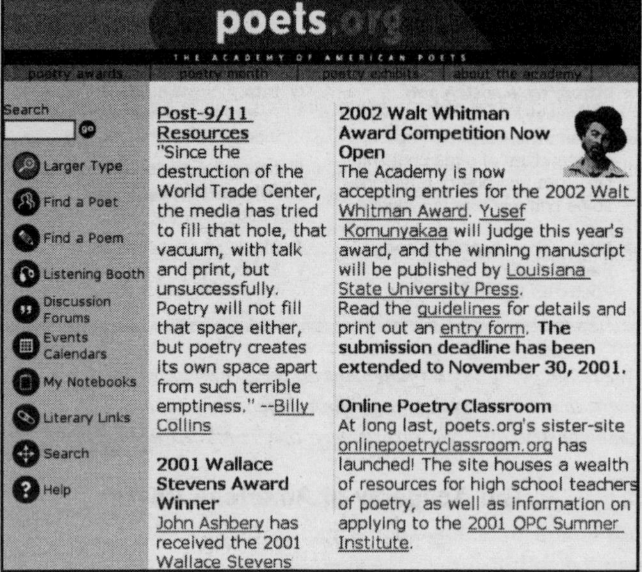

[sculpture]

International Sculpture Center

● http://www.sculpture.org/

As all art forms, sculpture has many styles, from Michelangelo's life-size marble wonders to the solid geometrical forms of Alexander Calder's stabiles. All are well represented at the Web residence of the International Sculpture Center, a not-for-profit organization founded in 1960. Members include sculptors, collectors, architects, developers, journalists, curators, historians, critics, educators, foundries, galleries, and museums—in short, anyone with an interest in the art of sculpture.

The site's best asset is its numerous links, giving you zillions of leads to find sculpture, take courses, join local groups, talk to other sculpture lovers, and in general learn more about this art form (there's even a *Sculpture* magazine you can subscribe to). You can find beautiful images of sculpture in the Portfolio section, from small tabletop pieces to giant outdoor installations. In the Commission section, you can have a piece designed just for you. You never know: A 20-foot-high abstract metal sculpture might look great in the front yard.

[writing]

Screenplays
Drew's Script-O-Rama

● http://www.script-o-rama.com/

Reading scripts is a great way to learn the art of telling a good story bound for film. Getting those scripts, however, used to mean that you had to know somebody who knew somebody in Hollywood. But thanks to the Internet, you don't have to go to Hollywood; just visit this websites. Pick a category (film scripts, TV stuff, movie haiku, anime), then scroll through the list of titles. Movies are listed alphabetically from *Amadeus* (which be-

Y! tip

Unless you have this book in front of you at all times (which is what we recommend), URLs can be hard to remember. By either bookmarking a site or adding it to your list of favorites, you can always find the site at the click of a button on your computer. To ensure access to the URLs no matter where you are, My Yahoo! has a feature that enables you to store all your bookmarks online.

gins with Salieri screaming, "Mozart! Mozart! Mozart. Forgive me! Forgive your assassin! Mozart!") to *Young Frankenstein* (containing the immortal "great knockers" and "werewolf" jokes). You'll also find four different drafts of *Star Wars*, *The Graduate*, *Dr. Strangelove*, and other classics. While you're there, surf to pages containing contests, chat rooms, and awards.

Society For Technical Communication

● http://stc.org/

All those computer manuals, product brochures, and technical instructions on how to run your software. Who writes this stuff? Unsung wordsmiths, who have to translate computerese and programmer jargon into language that the rest of the world can understand, that's who. Those interested or involved in this behind-the-scenes form of writing should take notes at the STC site. Tech writers can find resources, employment listings, conference and seminar dates, and educational information on all aspects of the craft, from translation services to usability resources. Really brave writers can also get programming and coding tips for website development.

BUSINESS & ECONOMY

[business]

Corporate Information

● http://www.corporateinformation.com/

Corporate Information is a bit of an understatement for this site. Corporate Everything is more like it. When you type in the name of a company here, you get links to a wide spectrum of online data and reports that analyze, probe, review, and profile that company. We looked up Disney, and found more than three dozen sources of data, including EDGAR, Quicken, PR Newswire, Bloomberg UK, Red Herring, Vault Report, Yahoo! Finance News, Lehman Brothers Equity Research, Stocksheet Profile, and plenty of others. Within these you get all the basics: most-recent-year sales, number of employees, market capitalization, total shares outstanding, stock chart, stock price history, officers' names, and a list of competing companies in the same industry. You can do this for companies in the most economically aggressive countries (notably the G7), and you can also see which companies in those countries are currently making news headlines. You aren't likely to get more data on your corporate pick anywhere else—unless you've got some inside sources, and there are people in the government who might frown on that.

GTE Superpages

● http://yp.superpages.com/

Online, not even your fingers have to do the walking. You can direct monstrous searchable directories like the GTE Superpages to do it for you. This site will find businesses anywhere in the country with asimple click of a mouse. In addition to phone, fax, and toll-free numbers, this directory has addresses, maps and directions, and URLs where appropriate. You can search for businesses by combinations of addresses and names, and by categories and phone numbers.

FYI, many portals, like Yahoo!, have their own directory services (http://www.yp.yahoo.com), some of which incorporate popular online directories. Another good way to find corporate websites is at Companies Online (http://www.companiesonline.com), which lets you search a gigantic database to find the URLs of more than 100,000 public and private companies.

Quicken.com

● http://www.quicken.com/small_business/

Do you have a small business? Thinking about starting one? Don't do a thing without first stopping by the small business site presented by Quicken.com. Entrepreneurs can get information about stocks, top business news, and Quicken products and promos, and learn more about the financial world in the Quicken learning center. You can customize the web page and subscribe to a newsletter. The site is divided into three areas: Start a Business, Run a Business, and Grow a Business. You can learn how to get a business license, manage employees more effectively, get more customers, and manage your finances. There's a search engine sponsored by Excite, a glossary of terms, and links to other business websites on the Net. The site is free, but many of the features presented require Quicken software. Whether you are running a business or just thinking about it, this site is sure to at least give you a head start.

Business and Companies: Resources
Accel: Resources for Entrepreneurs

● http://www.accel.com/entrepreneurs/index.html

Accel is a venture capital firm that doesn't mind sharing its wisdom and advice for free. At its site, the company posts articles that its partners have presented over the years, including "Advice for the First-Time Entrepreneur" and "How to Win a Venture Capitalist." A venture capital survey from PriceWaterhouseCoopers is included, and there are links to various entrepreneurial organizations and must-read venture mags such as *Red Herring* and *Inc.*

Business@Home

● http://www.gohome.com/

With $1,000 or less, plus some ingenuity and hard work, you can start a great company. Using that premise—and case studies to support it—Business@Home offers information to people who are ready to start a business in their home, garage, den, or spare bedroom. The site's motto is "making a life while making a living," and to that end it provides detailed data, articles, and

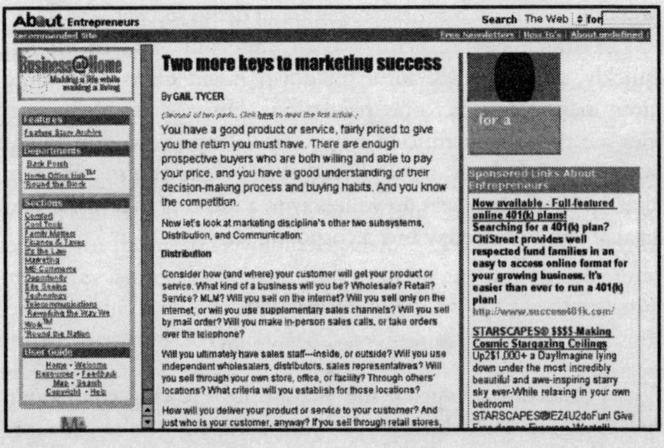

columns on everything from comfort and family matters to finance, taxes, marketing, and telecommunications. There are tips on building your website (get free code from the Netscape site for creating a newsletter signup system), being a good boss to yourself, getting credit reports, and following up and following through. The site points out that the most dangerous obstacles to success for at-home businesses may not be the competitors, but the refrigerator, the bed, and the TV, not to mention the wet bar. A good observation—from a great site.

Business Resource Center

● http://www.morebusiness.com/

Planning on launching the next multinational corporation in your spare bedroom? Need some *practical* business advice? The Business Resource Center has a huge number of articles on starting and running your own business. You'll also find some helpful templates, such as sample agreements that you can use as a foundation for creating your own; a complete business plan for a hypothetical company; or a sample proposal format for responding to RFPs (request for proposals). And if you're not in the business of reinventing the wheel, make use of the Tools area, where you can download business shareware or demo software for free.

A search engine helps you to find your areas of interest quickly, and a Quick Find pulldown menu offers everything from marketing tips to tax regulations. Hint: Many of the articles are rather academic in nature, and lengthy, so you might want to print them out and read them while you're sitting in that coach airplane seat on your way to a meeting that just might enable you to someday buy a corporate jet.

Inc. Magazine

● http://www.inc.com/

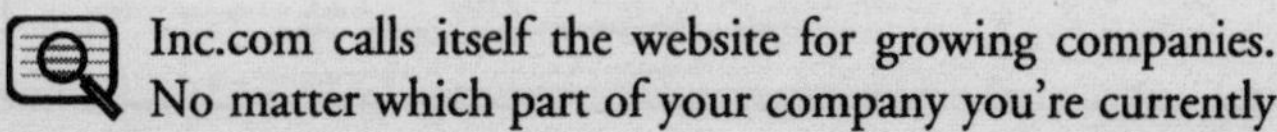

Inc.com calls itself the website for growing companies. No matter which part of your company you're currently trying to improve, you'll find plenty here to assist you. The site contains more than just reprints of articles from *Inc.* magazine; it features plenty of business tools to assist you with some of the more pressing matters of managing a company—regardless of its size. For instance, if you have budgetary questions, visit the Guide to Finance. Or if you are completely in the dark as to what kind of network you should build for your company, get help from the Guide to Biz Tech. Additional information can be found on the Bulletin Boards; check out Starting a Company, Networking by Industry, and the Virtual Consultant, to name a few. Virtual Consultant, for example, offers 301 Great Business Ideas. And be sure to make use of the spreadsheets and forms templates; they'll save you time and money.

Industry Search

● http://www.industrysearch.com/

Despite all the media coverage of the technology-based business boom, most businesses still make "things." This site guides you to those companies, which produce everything from cameras and cable to chemicals and copper fittings. Industry Search comprises several search engines, including the USA Industrial Directory, which lists more than 1 million manufacturers and suppliers; New Products, which has updates on product introductions; Library of Articles, which archives manufacturing articles and company press releases; Calendar of Events, across industries; and Industrial Links, to trade and industry organizations.

SBA–Starting Your Business

● http://www.sba.gov/starting

This comprehensive, no-nonsense site from the federal government's Small Business Administration (SBA) will help you find answers to almost every question you'll have as you set out to make your dream of professional independence come true. Its Startup Kit guides you through all the steps of creating a company and explains rules and regulations you have to consider in the process. And be sure to take the SBA's Business Plan Road Map to Success—a Tutorial and Self-Paced Activity to help you write your business plan.

Another excellent resource at the site is the shareware area, where you'll find helpful utilities and programs to download, including business letters, credit card validation programs, and a program for creating print ads.

Venture Capital
Venture Capital Resource Library

● http://www.vfinance.com/

If you need big bucks to start up your company, you've got to go to the VCs, the venture capitalists, the people with the millions and billions to invest in the next Apple, Amazon.com, or Yahoo!. This site has links to a huge number of venture capital firms, plus news from and about various VC firms. There are also downloadable business plans and contact info on investment banks, financial advisers, lenders, and "angel" investors, with descriptions of each. Professional services links will connect you to accountants, attorneys, public relations experts and others; and research links will hook you up to sites like EDGAR, the SEC, and the Tax Code. News on the financial industry and an update on IPOs top off the site.

[classifieds]

Free Classified Ad Links

● http://www.freeclassifiedlinks.com/

Looking for used golf clubs? How about a secondhand guitar amplifier? Maybe a ham radio? Or a tricycle? Instead of heading to the local newspaper classifieds, go to the Internet's thousands of classified "sections." You'll find a lot more to wade through than a few pages in the paper. And you can access more than 800 of them by stopping in at the Free Classified Ad Links page. The site divides its links into free, pay, charity links (where you can become an "Internet Philanthropist"), and business resources. The sites are listed in alphabetical order and range from Aardy Aardvark's Amazing Ads to the Virtual Dumpster. With choices like this, you'll never go back to the Sunday paper.

[e-commerce]

E-commerce and E-markets (research, articles)

● http://www.brint.com/Elecomm.htm

This gigantic page links to documents, articles, e-commerce sites, resources, online guides, and everything else that relates to the marketplace. Running straight down the page, there seems to be a series of links to authoritative sites including academic institutions, the government, the *Wall Street Journal, Information Week, BusinessWeek, Inc.*, and numerous others. Each link is accompanied by a short description of the accompanying article.

The site is maintained by the BizTech Network, whose master site can be accessed by deleting everything after the .com in the URL. If you're not fully informed about all aspects of e-commerce after spending quality time on this site, you aren't paying attention.

Ecommerceone

● http://www.ecommerce1.com/

This site is an excellent resource for information on digital cash, cybercash, cyberbanking, online business, and e-business. Ecommerceone is a set of links to sources of e-commerce information. It has a news section (with links to *ComputerWorld, Information Week, TechWeb*, and other online and print publications), e-commerce servers, software and hardware providers, digital cash vendors, security companies, smart card developers, and consulting and financial services.

Electronic Commerce Guide

● http://ecommerce.internet.com/

Electronic Commerce Guide is a magazine-style site that covers all that is e-commerce: auctions, e-payment systems, credit cards, software solutions and trends, and on and on. The bulk of the site's content is in the form of opinions and trends articles, plus product reviews and e-commerce news. A library has check-outable articles from other business publications and web-based news sources such as *The Economist* and *TechWeb*. The Solutions area addresses issues such as site improvement and product management.

One of the site's outstanding elements is its E-commerce Webopedia, which provides excellent descriptions of the terms and jargon bandied about in the e-commerce world. Not only that, it provides links to sites related to those terms, such as digital cash and Internet banking. A free weekly newsletter is available via a quick signup process.

FYI, Electronic Commerce Guide is an Internet.com site, which maintains a series of like-themed websites that provide information to Internet industry and technology professionals.

[economics]

The Beige Book

● http://www.federalreserve.gov/formc/beigebook/2001/

You know when you hear news reports that lead off with "The Fed announced its index of leading indicators today. New home starts were down . . ."? This document that contains those newsworthy economic tidbits. It is the text of the

Federal Reserve Board's Summary of Commentary on Current Economic Conditions by Federal Reserve District. Better known by its popular name, the Beige Book, this report is published eight times per year. Each of the 12 Federal Reserve Banks gathers anecdotal information on current economic conditions through reports from bank directors and interviews with key business contacts, economists, market experts, and other sources.

YAHOO! ALSO LISTS: [economics]

- **http://econwpa.wustl.edu/EconFAQ/EconFAQ.html**
  Resources for Economists on the Internet: comprehensive annotated directory of related resources.
- **http://www.oxy.edu/~gsecondi/dev.html**
  Development Economics and Economic Development: list of links to sites that provide information on development economics.
- **http://www.progress.org/econolink/**
  Econolink: links to the best websites that have anything to do with economics.
- **http://www.oswego.edu/~kane/econometrics/**
  Econometric Resources on the Internet
- **http://www.peachnet.edu/galileo/internet/business/econdata.html**
  Economic Data: annotated links to sources of economic data for the U.S. and foreign countries.
- **http://www.nuff.ox.ac.uk/Economics/Growth/**
  Economic Growth Resources: comprehensive set of resources for growth researchers, including data sets, key references, literature surveys, and links.
- **http://www.economicsearch.com/**
  Economicsearch.com: research links, course tutorials, job center, and a discussion board for economists and students of economics.
- **http://php.indiana.edu/~rmtucker/frmlempr.html**
  Formal and Empirical Political Theory Research Resources: a wide variety of resources for those interested in social science methodology. Individual pages include material on game theory, econometrics, dynamic models, and artificial intelligence.
- **http://hsb.baylor.edu/html/gardner/RESORC.HTM**
  Gardner's World Economics: structured links to about 650 world economic sites, organized by region and country.
- **http://altaplana.com/gate.html**
  International Economics Gateway Page

This is all compiled, summarized, and analyzed here.

A calendar motif on the home page allows the viewer to pick which report is to be read, and offers a list of each district (Boston, New York, Philadelphia, Cleveland, Richmond, Atlanta, Chicago, St. Louis, Minneapolis, Kansas City, Dallas, and San Francisco), along with all its relevant info. In addition to the current year's reports, there are four years worth of reports archived here. This is an excellent site for investors, students of economics, and anyone who gets off on leading indicators.

[employment]

Internships
Everett Public Sector

● http://www.everettinternships.org/

The Everett Public Service Internship Program funds more than 200 summer internships at progressive public service organizations. According to the site, interns get to do lots of heady things primarily in places like Washington, D.C. and New York; for example, prepare congressional testimony and legislative research, organize grassroots activity, write policy papers, and implement communication strategies (hey, isn't this what politicians are paid to do?).

The site's search engine puts you in touch with public opportunities after you select a city and a field of interest. The results not only include a list of the internships available, but give detailed summaries about the organizations and the positions. Before you know it, you'll be helping some senator draft a new amendment to the Constitution, or perhaps be doing it all by yourself.

Tripod Internship Database Search

● http://www.tripod.com/explore/jobs_career/intern_visa/

Tripod defines internships as a rewarding "monitored work or service experience." The main component of this site is its search engine. Type in a city or state (if you have a preference), and select a job category from more than 100 options. These run the gamut from accounting to zoos, with record labels, theme parks, and film companies in between. Then pick a desired weekly compensation, ranging from None to $500. Trust us, you'll get a lot more hits by selecting None.

At this point, you have to join the site, which involves providing a little more personal data. Just do it, because this is no wild-goose chase. The jobs are there, and some are actually quite appealing. Big-name companies are represented in various locations in all categories here.

FYI, the job database is sponsored by the Princeton Review.

Monster Board Job Database

● http://www.monster.com/

One of the, ahem, monster sites in the employment category is Monster.com. Everything you need to get started in your search for the perfect job is on this site. It even acts as a virtual office while you're putting out those feelers, by enabling you to search jobs, store your resume, research companies (by state or alphabetically), explore Monster Zones (areas of career interest), and join chat rooms. Even better is the Quick Search box where you enter the name of the job you're looking for, say CEO of a major international corporation, and you're on your way. The site also features the Monster Talent Market, which is essentially an auction whereby you can sell yourself to the highest bidder. In the old days, this had a different name—today they call it free agency.

There are a host of additional resources (news, career assessments, etc.) and a wide variety of message boards (e.g., Ask the Career Guru, Making the Transition From Military to Civilian Work).

There's even a section for employers who are looking for candidates. Werewolves, vampires, and other monsters need not apply.

Resumes

Resume Magic

● http://www.liglobal.com/b_c/career/res.shtml

Guide to Resume Writing

● http://www.jobweb.org/catapult/guenov/res.html#explore

Most employment sites on the web, including those described here, have tips on writing quality resumes. Here are two additional sites you might want to check out before you prepare your resume, as they offer different perspectives.

Resume Magic is a long article on crafting your curriculum vitae, with examples. Career Center's Guide to Resume Writing uses a sample resume format to introduce various ways to construct a resume. The two sites should give you enough info to put together an effective resume, regardless of your background.

Seasonal Employment

CoolWorks (recreational, US)

● http://www.coolworks.com/

"Live & Work Where Others Only Visit." That's the slogan of CoolWorks, an employment site that lists jobs across the United States, primarily in recreational, outdoor environments. Places that meet this criteria—and that comprise CoolWorks' categories—include National Parks, Resorts, Jobs on Water, Guest Ranches, Ski Resorts, Camp Jobs, Amusement Parks, and State Parks.

You can also search by state: On the map graphic, click on the area of the country where you want to work to go to directories that lead to the organizations offering jobs—some 70,000 in all. A lot of the jobs offered sound more like a cross between spring break and *Baywatch* than work: winter jobs at a ranch in sunny Arizona, working at the Knot's Berry Farm amusement park or at Jackson Hole.

Summer Jobs (worldwide)

● http://www.summerjobs.com/

Want to be a summer camp counselor in the Czech Republic? Or a food and beverage server at a beach resort in Thailand? No problem. From the exotic to the esoteric, Summerjobs.com has plenty of jobs in great places around the world to choose from to make summertime bucks.

Start your search by scanning the list of all the countries that have job listings. Pick a country and enter the job of your choice. The results comprise a full-page description of the job, who or what is offering it, and some superficial discussion of salary. And, of course, you'll find contact information, including, when applicable, a website and an e-mail link. Beats flipping burgers at the local mall.

Temps
Net-Temps

● http://www.net-temps.com/

Like all good employment sites, Net-Temps allows you to post your resume, access interviewing and jobs resources, and peruse a big database of jobs. What's unique about this site is that it's devoted to part-time work. Nevertheless, the categories are as broad as those for full-time jobs—engineering, finance, sales and marketing, information technology, and so on.

You can jump directly to a specific job category or you can search the whole database, by state or by metropolitan area. Then you select the kind of job you're looking for. The results can be substantial. If you see one you like, click on the link to the contact's e-mail address and send your resume or message indicating interest via the Net. There is also a list of recruiting firms in the area you select if you decide you want to pay someone to search for you. Just keep in mind that part-time means no benefits.

Yahoo! Careers

● http://careers.yahoo.com/

$ While you may never know what you want to be when you grow up, Yahoo! Careers can help you make a living while you figure it out.

Virtual job hunters will find navigation easy using a group of icons called Career Resources, which features job searches, resume posting, research, and advice. The Career Track Section is set up like Yahoo!'s main page, with categories including College Central, International, Getting Ahead, Entrepreneurialism, High Tech, and Human Resources. Those in the market for a new job should head straight to the job search area, where you can enter the parameters of the type of job that interests you. Choose a business area from a pull-down menu (such as administrative, creative, legal, etc.), specify a particular, add a specific level, type in keywords (such as health care), pick a location in the country, and watch the opportunity knock.

Yahoo! Careers hosts a daily column from the *Wall Street Journal's* career site, along with weekly features such as "Ask the Headhunter" and "Working Wounded." Another interesting feature is the extensive relocation resources that include salary and city comparisons.

[fashion and clothing]

Fashion Net

● http://www.fashion.net/

Wish you could sit front and center at a fashion industry runway show? Need to know what was featured in the hottest collections for this season? Then pull up your chair and start eyeing the proceedings at Fashion Net. This site is a portal to the entire fashion industry, from its designers and manufacturers to its associations and schools. Sporting excellent video and slick graphics, as well as one of the coolest site maps around, Fashion Net's headings move like they're on a catwalk.

The site is divided into three primary segments: sites, content, and career. Subgroups of these sections include Fashion Sites and Online Magazines, Fashion News and Designer Bias, and Job Listings and a how- to section describing how to land a job as a fashion designer or even a fashion photographer. There's also a section titled "This Week's News," which offers current weekly information around the globe in the fashion world.

[finance]

Yahoo! Finance

- http://finance.yahoo.com/
- http://bonds.yahoo.com/
- http://biz.yahoo.com/funds/
- http://biz.yahoo.com/r/
- http://taxes.yahoo.com/
- http://vision.yahoo.com/

No other single industry has been affected by the web to the degree that the financial services industry has. Before the web, only stockbrokers, insurance agents, mortgage bankers, and a select few others had direct access to the kind of financial data that the rest of us had to pay dearly for. With the web, we all have access. Free stock quotes, online and after-hours trading, comparison shopping for loans, insurance tools,and estimating calculators are all available now to anyone with access to the Internet. Nice how the balance of power has shifted, isn't it?

The Internet has changed the intrinsic nature of finance and financial transactions just since 1994. It is believed that the wild mood swings experienced by the stockmarket in the late 1990s was started by day traders—people using their own computers and the web to make their own trades without the intervention, or time delay, of stock brokers or large trading firms. One wonders where all these brokers will be 10 years from now when the Web is piped into every single home, car, and place of business in the United States.

Yahoo! lists nearly 200 categories of finance, from investments and insurance to corporate and personal finance. If you're looking for a place to put your money, or looking for a place to make more money, you're bound to find some assistance on the web, and the sites listed here are the best of the best. Beware, though: As in the real world, there are plenty of financial services sites that are designed to separate you from your hard-earned currency with little concern for providing you with anything of value. These range from stock sites to insurance brokers, so make sure you're dealing with a reputable firm—or at least one that can be checked out and vetted. Most of the major sites are owned and backed by established firms, so you're safe there.

Yahoo! offers the best gateway to the world of finance (http://finance.yahoo.com), allowing you to track your portfolio online, get free stock quotes, chart the performance of your stocks (with charts and graphs—the kinds of things that financial planners used to charge you money for), and even get stock alerts and investment advice. You can do this by setting up your own My Yahoo! page or creating an online portfolio manager. Once you've done that, you can keep tabs on your money from any computer in the world. Sure makes more sense than leaving it all under your mattress.

Bonds
Investing in Bonds

● http://www.bondmarkets.com/research.shtml

To understand the bond market, you have to do some bond research. This component of the Bond Market Association site has statistical tables (for cross-market, municipal, mortgage-backed, treasury, and asset-backed bonds), reports on each type of bond, a municipal swap index, and articles and historical information (for tracking the growth of bonds). It also has an outstanding news section with highlights, summaries, and analyses.

Bonds Online

● http://www.bondsonline.com/

Bonds Online differs from the preceding site in that it provides quotes, ratings, call features, and data on specific bonds. You can search its database of more than 12,000 bonds—from several hundred trading desks—to find those that best suit your needs. The site gives Treasury prices and yields in real time, with frequently updated offerings on all other bonds, including municipal, corporate, CMO, and zero-coupon. There are also links to a substantial number of research resources, including the SEC, Moody's, and Standard & Poor's.

Financenter

- http://www.financenter.com/

With 110 calculators, this site can help you figure out anything. This website offers Solution Centers for your auto, credit card, home, retirement, and several other areas crucial in figuring money management. You can calculate how much you should spend a month in a certain time period to pay off bills. It also offers Planners and Analyzers to evaluate your financial situations.

Kiplinger's

- http://www.kiplinger.com/calc/calchome.html

Kiplinger's has 10 calculators designed to help you with the ins and outs of investing: Stocks, Mutual Funds, Retirement, Investments, Saving & Borrowing, Your Home, Insurance, Taxes, Kids & Money, and Spending. You can choose any one of them to help you make a variety of financial decisions, explore your economic options, test possible investment scenarios, and figure out how to keep more of your cash. The calculators take you from the mundane ("How will taxes and inflation affect my savings?") to the motivational ("What will it take to become a millionaire?"). What you choose to do with this information is your business, but if you never make the big bucks, don't blame Kiplinger's calculators.

Estate Planning/Retirement Investor Guide

- http://www.investorguide.com/retirement.html

The Investor Guide is a large site that covers a multitude of topics; specifically, its Retirement section (located at the URL here) is a basic primer on retirement financial planning, walking readers through the topics of 401(k)s, IRAs, Social Security, After Retirement, Estate Planning, Calculators, Discussion Groups, Learning, and Organizations. Each topic text is embedded with useful links; the IRAs paragraph, for one, provides links to four IRA services, including those from the Vanguard and Strong mutual fund families. The Calculators paragraph includes connections to a number of retirement, annuity, and longevity calculators. Organizations linked with the Investor Guide Retirement page include the Profit Sharing Council of America and the Retirement Income Association.

The page also provides links to other Investor Guide discussions on such related topics as Retirement Software, Taxes, and Roth IRAs. And an Answers—Retirement section lists many more links that address specific retirement-related questions on wills, filing for Social Security benefits, and the like. In summary, this page functions as a no-frills, minimalist starting point for investors who are beginning to contemplate those future lazy days in the sun.

Mutual Funds
Brill's Mutual Fund Interactive

● http://www.fundsinteractive.com/

Another "all-service" mutual fund site, Brill's Mutual Fund Interactive seeks to be your one-stop source for investing in mutual funds. A Funds 101 section runs such articles as "Converting IRAs to Roth IRAs," and "Ready, Set, Invest!" Search engines are available to locate investing info, discussion groups, and current fund price quotes. On the lighter side are visitor polls that ask pressing questions such as "Whom would you rather have over for dinner: Peter Lynch, John Bogle, Warren Buffett, or Steven Spielberg?" (When we visited, billionaire Warren Buffett was edging out Peter Lynch for the lead.) But seriously, folks, Mutual Fund Interactive is a good, workmanlike site to refer to for your mutual fund needs.

Mutual Fund's Investor Service

● http://www.mfea.com/

Run by the Mutual Fund Education Alliance, this site is an excellent way for investors to bone up on the world of mutual funds. You can track fund prices, read articles, get relevant news stories, and assemble and track your own portfolio. There's a full-blown Retirement Center where you can learn about such plans as the IRA, Roth IRA, and 401(k)s. An article sampler includes "Key Things Every Investor Should Know," "Do No-Loads Always Beat Load Funds?" and the investment philosophy of former Magellan Fund manager and investment guru Peter Lynch. Or you can buy books at the Bookstore, learn about tax implications in the Education Center, or begin saving for your children's college tuition in the Planning Center. Whether you're an experienced investor or a financial newbie, this site contains plenty of useful information for your investment plans.

CNN Money

● http://money.cnn.com/

CNN Money is the website complement to CNN and *Money* magazine, providing research and resources for the business and finance professional. The homepage is simple and straightforward, with News, Markets & Stocks, Services, and Site Index tabs providing immediate direction for first-time visitors. A fill-in-the-box search engine also allows you to search either the Money.cnn site or the entire Internet, and the site index gives a succinct two-page topic listing grouped by tabs.

In addition to the litany of market indexes, news, and information services that are part and parcel of all good finance websites, CNN Money allows surfers to watch the Financial Network in real time using Media Player. The Personal Finance section is directly linked to Quicken.com, which furnishes such investing and planning tools as a refinance calculator, a stock screener, and a retirement planner. CNN Money also serves as a gateway to various services and e-commerce sites (under the Services link) that cover an array of commercial interests including a broker center; a "power shopper" that links users to Internet vendors for almost every conceivable good or service; and a travel center that allows users to register at Biztravel.com for help in making reservations and getting information on weather, events, and highlights of various destinations.

Marketwatch.com

● http://www.cbsmarketwatch.com/

It may be that every conceivable type of financial-market information is available at CBS Market Watch (popularly known as Marketwatch.com). The Front Page offers hundreds of connections to market data, feature stories, and sections on Mutual Funds and Newswatch. Up-to-the-minute data is available from all major exchanges, as is the latest news from wire services and foreign

markets. Market addicts may want to tune in to this site 24 hours a day. Commentary is provided by dozens of noted financial experts and includes video and audio clips, so that, for example, you can hear a report on how Silicon Valley firms are attempting to lure Australian technical experts to the United States.

The mix of hard-core technical data and personal finance information (such as finding good car loans or credit card and mortgage rates) makes the site valuable to experts and novices alike, while the CBSMW MarketPlace offers numerous ways to spend your earnings. A free membership to the site grants access to thousands of research reports, while a number of search engines allow users to search in a variety of ways: by topic-specific information, with market information (by typing in ticker symbols), and via market symbols. Finally, a plethora of links will take you elsewhere for additional research—though you'd be hard-pressed not to find what you need right here.

The Money Page

● http://www.moneypage.com/

Looking for financial advice and information on the Internet for the first time is not always an easy task. As the number of entries in this section indicate, there is a wealth of data and an excellent selection of websites to choose from. For those individuals making their first tentative clicks in the realm of web finance, the Money Page, "The Net's Consumer Guide to Investment, Banking and Finance," may be the easiest place to start.

Essentially a link service, the Money Page lists connections under such topic headings as Investor's Guide, Electronic Money, Real Estate, News, and MoneyTalk. Sans site map and search engine (there are links to other search engines such as AltaVista and Yahoo.finance), each listing is subdivided by topic and provides quick-jumping to the subject of choice. For example, in the Investor's Guide, clicking on the Online Trading subheading you to a list of more than 60 services—and that's not counting the more than 30 links under the Brokerage Firms subheading. The Money Page also has topic headings such as ATMs, Credit Unions, and Travel, plus Other "Stuff" links to the U.S. Postal Service, the World Clock, and the Bureau of Labor Statistics, among other goodies.

Functioning as a basic financial-connection address book—or book of bookmarks—the Money Page provides a valuable service to the novice online consumer and investor.

The Motley Fool

● http://www.fool.com/

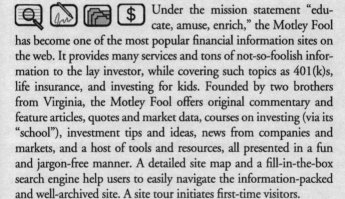

Under the mission statement "educate, amuse, enrich," the Motley Fool has become one of the most popular financial information sites on the web. It provides many services and tons of not-so-foolish information to the lay investor, while covering such topics as 401(k)s, life insurance, and investing for kids. Founded by two brothers from Virginia, the Motley Fool offers original commentary and feature articles, quotes and market data, courses on investing (via its "school"), investment tips and ideas, news from companies and markets, and a host of tools and resources, all presented in a fun and jargon-free manner. A detailed site map and a fill-in-the-box search engine help users to easily navigate the information-packed and well-archived site. A site tour initiates first-time visitors.

Via free registration, members get access to high-traffic message boards and members-only features; can track individual portfolios; receive discounts on books, software, and Motley Fool apparel (available at the FoolMart); and can create their own MyFool pages. After you've learned enough to begin investing, the Motley Fool will help you find a broker so you can safely join in the foolishness.

International
Worldly Investor

● http://www.worldlyinvestor.com/

The Internet enables investors to conduct research beyond their national borders and forces markets to open their doors to after-hours trading. The result is a 24-hour global market place that can change drastically while you're dreaming (literally) of the previous day's big deals. Claiming that it is "interpreting the world for individual investors," Worldly Investor offers news, analyses, commentary, global indices, quotes, and rankings for the international player. Its Investor's Atlas can be used to gauge the geographical impact on global markets. Other sections contain investment news by region (Americas, Asia, Europe, emerging markets), investing fundamentals, and a glossary (defining terms such as "amortization" and "zero-coupon bonds"). If you need to know how Japan's Nikkei close affected the Hong Kong Hang Seng and the London Ftse, drink your coffee while logged on to this site every morning.

IPOs (Initial Public Offerings)
IPO.com

● http://www.ipo.com/

IPOs have changed the face of the stock market. Everyone wants to be in a company that has an initial public offering, or, barring that, they want to get in on the ground floor of somebody else's IPO. IPO.com presents detailed information on upcoming IPOs, and reports on the success of current and recent IPO. (Note: The picture is not always rosy a few months down the road.) The listings here include pricing data, recent filings, company summaries, and news articles. You can also consult a calendar for upcoming offerings and search for offerings from specific underwriters. Finally, you can find out which companies have withdrawn their IPOs—a sign that the IPO market isn't a guaranteed path to riches.

Yahoo! Finance—Initial Public Offerings

● http://biz.yahoo.com/ipo/

This Yahoo! site offers a detailed one-page summary of the past week's IPO filings, pricing, and withdrawals, with links to its own profiles, charts, and news. It also provides a rating of best and worst performers over the past year; IPO lists by company, industry, and underwriter; and links to IPO message boards and newsletters. This is part of Yahoo!'s larger Finance component, which can be incorporated with its My Yahoo! feature to give you updated information whenever you check *your* Yahoo!.

Reports
EDGAR

● http://www.edgar-online.com/

One of the smartest things the SEC ever did was create EDGAR, the corporate electronic filing system. All public companies have to post their information there, so if you want to know anything about any company—its finances or executives—you can find it here. Visitors have unlimited access to historical company filings, as well as to EDGAR Online People, which searches Proxy Filings (DEF14A) by individual name; Full Search, which accesses specific filings using any combination of 10 criteria; EDGAR Online Glimpse, an extract of the Management Discussion and Analysis of the company's operating results; and the Financial Data Schedule (FDS), a feature that downloads a company's balance sheet and vital financial statistics directly into a Microsoft Excel spreadsheet for easy analysis.

All you have to do is fill out a visitor registration form and this website provides most of the data that individual investors need to conduct through research on their own. The site is easy to get around, as searches are done by name or ticker symbol.

Stock Markets
NASDAQ and Amex

● http://www.nasdaq-amex.com/

NYSE

● http://www.nyse.com/

With media attention focused on the ups and downs of the Dow, it's easy to forget that the stock markets are actual places. These sites serve as a reminder of what goes on at the bricks-and-mortar New York Stock Exchange, the American Stock Exchange, and National Association of Securities Dealers (the latter two are joined on the web and in real life).

Both sites track the day's events and list their respective major market gainers and losers. FAQs explain how the exchanges work and delve into their histories. You'll also find listed companies, schedules and calendars, market reports, and delayed stock quotes. And those who want to feel the excitement of being there when the big deals go down can watch the NASDAQ-Amex goings-on live via webcast (with RealPlayer) and view the NYSE trading floor panoramas (using IBM's HotMedia). At this rate, the stock exchanges will soon be as much fun as a theme park . . . or is it the other way around?

Taxes
The IRS

● http://www.irs.gov/

We've reviewed the IRS site in our GOVERNMENT section, but it's worth noting here too, for one simple reason: The more you know about your taxes, the more ways you can find to get out of paying them.

Essential Links to Taxes

● http://www.el.com/elinks/taxes/

Finding tax data on the web can be—to put it mildly—taxing. Skip the heartache (there will be enough of that on April 15) and go straight to El.com. This is a site with "essential links" to a lot of subjects on the web, but its tax list is truly essential. It contains summaries of more than 100 resources, which go way beyond the content of the IRS and H&R Block sites (although they're represented here, too). EL digs up sites for state taxes, tax forms, international taxes, tax law, the tax code, tax tips, tax software, tax-related associations and publications, tax news, tax professionals, tax calculators, tax discussion groups, and even tax history. This site has done so much of your tax homework for you that you'll feel like you're almost done by the time you sit down with your 1040. Of course, the key word here is "almost."

[insurance]

Insure.com—Consumer Insurance Guide

● http://www.insure.com/

Insure.com is an exceptional consumer site that gives you the help you need to effectively research and choose appropriate insurance coverage for your car, business, health, life, home, and annuities. The Consumer Insurance Guide helps you protect yourself whether your laptop computer crashes or a birch tree crashes into your bedroom. You can also review Standard & Poors' ratings of all insurers, find out which companies have received the most complaints, and learn which have lawsuits pending against them.

A great segment called the Basics has educational information on shopping for insurance, lists the top 100 auto insurers and top 100 home insurers, supplies Standard & Poors' rating tools provides instructions on how to file a complaint or a claim, defines your consumer rights, lists the most frequently stolen cars, and more. This is good reading for anyone who is responsible for handling insurance issues for themselves or their families.

Of course, there are links to news, plus articles in specific areas such as Your Car, Your Health, Your Home, and so on. An exhaustive list of category links helps users educate themselves on all aspects of insurance, get company ratings, and find local resources. After spending time on this site you will be prepared to shop competitively for the insurance package that best suits your needs.

InsWeb

● http://www.insweb.com/

InsWeb will act as your personal, virtual insurance agent. The site has essential tools and a broad knowledge base that will assist users in getting a handle on the potential cost of all kinds of insurance. In a section titled Insurance 101, a number of estimator, analyzer, and calculator tools are supplied for figuring the cost of auto, life, home, renter's, and health insurance. These tools can be applied to a wide range of insurance concerns. For example, the Homeowner's Quick Estimate in short order will give you a rough idea of what annual homeowner's insurance will cost based on the age of your house, the number of rooms it has, and its type and location. Other helpful features in the Insurance 101 section include Ask the Expert, Glossary, and Articles.

[mortgages]

So you think you're ready to buy a home. Know the benefits of buying versus renting? Know the national average interest rates? How about the long-term ramifications of choosing rate over points? If not, maybe you should spend some time at the sites listed here, each of which has tools for helping you figure out exactly how to proceed.

Buying a home is a complex and complicated process, and these sites can make it a whole lot easier.

Home Path

● http://www.homepath.com/

The United States is a diverse, multicultural place, and Fannie Mae—the "mother of the mortgage industry"—has paved an online path to home ownership for just about every citizen. This site walks house-hunting hopefuls through the buying process and features some incredibly useful tools, such as calculators that present a variety of what-if scenarios to help you figure out how much house you can afford. Once you know your price range, there are three ways to proceed: HomePurchasePath (ready to buy), HomeStarterPath (ready to begin the process), or HomeRefinancePath (thinking about refinancing). Fannie Mae also offers online resources such as guides to lenders, home-buyer education, and lists of financial advisers in your area.

Quicken

● http://www.quicken.com/mortgage/

Quicken's Home & Mortgage Center comes with an incredible toolkit that you can use to prepare you for the nitty-gritty financial work of figuring out your mortgage. Tools include calculators for credit assessment, home affordability, and determining the benefits of rate and points; online services for comparing loans, drafting a prequalification letter, and getting a preapproval letter. Interest-rate junkies can get the high, low, and average lending rate by banks in their state for the most common loan packages. Quicken will also help you access neighborhood info and credit reports, and pair up with a mortgage broker if you choose. Quicken's other financial sites can also be accessed from this page.

[real estate]

Builders
Builder Online

● http://www.builderonline.com/

Are you a construction worker, contractor, homebuilder, or developer? If building is in your blood, this site will become an extremely valuable resource. Unlike home-fix-it-type sites, Builder Online caters to professionals who need timely info on new products, mortgage rates, the latest real estate laws, and more. Visitors get online access to *Builder* magazine, which contains story snippets such as "20 Hi-Tech Building Tips," and stay abreast of various building and buying trends. Builders can also go to the Q&A to post a question or dig up information about the hot construction topic of the year—hardwiring new homes for the twenty-first century.

Buying
Realtor.com

● http://www.realtor.com/

Realtor.com simplifies the often complex and occasionally acrimonious world of home buying and selling. Rather than calling up Realtors and waiting for them to get back to you, Realtor.com lets you speed up the process by putting you in control of house hunts. You can search by area, price range, Realtor, and more. If you're a buyer, you can answer the questions on the handy worksheet about the kind of house you're looking for, then delve into the site's massive database to find houses that match your specifications. You can even look at photos of many of the homes for sale—an important time saver. There are also complete sections on home selling, making an offer, closing the deal, and more.

Realtors will find a section devoted to them, which makes this the complete real estate rescue for all those involved in the house hunt. Before you make the life-altering decision to buy a house, consult Realtor.com to lay your foundation.

Commercial
Commercial Real Estate Network (CCIM)

● http://www.ccim.com/

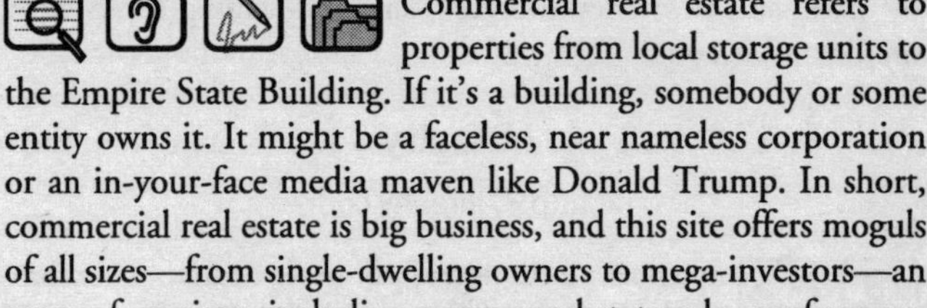

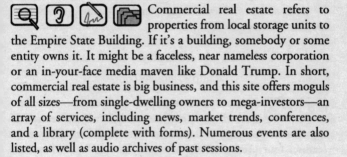

Commercial real estate refers to properties from local storage units to the Empire State Building. If it's a building, somebody or some entity owns it. It might be a faceless, near nameless corporation or an in-your-face media maven like Donald Trump. In short, commercial real estate is big business, and this site offers moguls of all sizes—from single-dwelling owners to mega-investors—an array of services, including news, market trends, conferences, and a library (complete with forms). Numerous events are also listed, as well as audio archives of past sessions.

Investments
Creative Real Estate Online

● http://www.creonline.com/

Ready to put some money into an apartment building, a skyscraper, a shopping mall, or a hotel? Real estate investors looking for tips, ideas, and peer support should pay a visit to Creative Real Estate Online, a website dedicated to real estate investing, creative financing, nothing-down and no-money-down real estate techniques. The bulk of Creonline.com is dedicated to information and original articles in several categories: How-to Articles, Money-Making Ideas, Legal Corner, and Cash Flow Forum. Among the 40-plus articles found under Money-Making Ideas are titles such as "Cashing in on Roadside Motels," "Benefits of Local Real Estate Clubs," and "How to Handle Telephone Calls."

Creonline.com presents several membership opportunities, including subscription to a free e-mail newsletter, the Insider's Club (discounts on products, advance notice of new tools and articles, and a dedicated chat area), and the Players Club, an area for investment professionals "conducive to sophisticated discussions and deal-making opportunities." The Online Catalog has investment books and courses for sale, and the site also posts classified ads. There are testimonials from investors in Success Stories and links to local real estate investment clubs, cataloged by state, and to money sources—lenders—willing to advertise on Creonline.com.

InRealty

● http://inrealty.com/

Novices need not apply at InRealty, an action-packed source of "Internet information for institutional and commercial real estate investments." This detailed site features four primary sections: Realty Stocks, Realty Research, Realty Books, and Realty Mortgages. The abundance of info represented makes it certain you'll find what you're looking for. For instance, if you need info on casino-stock IPOs, two clicks and you're at IPO Maven's site within the InRealty portal. If you need a listing of developer or construction associations, InRealty's got it. There's a useful Real Estate Job Line area, and a Commercial Realty Information Directory (CRID) groups topics and links within 40 real estate categories from accounting to taxes, with stops at banks, hotels, mobile home parks, and resorts in between.

By becoming an InRealty member for an annual fee, you get access to restricted areas that include additional information on more than 300 public realty companies, plus discounts on publications, special updates and reports, and access to affiliated sites; registration for a monthly newsletter is available at no charge.

Real Estate Investment Trusts
National Association of Real Estate Investment Trusts

● http://www.nareit.com/

The website for the National Association of Real Estate Investment Trusts is useful for both the industry professional and the person trying to figure out just what the heck a REIT is. The About REITs section is the place to read the history of these investments; it is designed to help small investors invest in commercial real estate. Discussions detail how to invest in REITs, and a useful glossary of terms ensures that it all makes sense. Professionals will be interested in the Government Relations section, which delves into regulation developments and issues, and the Research and Statistics section, which contains performance stats and market snapshots, as well as annual 1099 tax-reporting information. There's also a Real Time Market Index for monitoring investments and property performance, in addition to a host of special features available only to the more than 2,000 members of NAREIT, including a REIT Watch Online service and information on REIT offerings. Finally, there's an extensive list of links to REITs and other publicly traded real estate companies.

Tenants and Landlords
TenantNet

● http://tenant.net/

You know the purpose of this from its lead-off definition from *The Devil's Dictionary*: "LANDLORD, n. A pillar of society as necessary to its existence as a tick is to a hound." Clearly, this is a tenants' site, whose mission is to keep tenants from, ahem, getting screwed by their landlords. Though it focuses primarily on tenant information for New York (the capital of rent raising and rapaciousness), it addresses tenant concerns in many states through links to state laws, local newspaper articles and investigations, and advocacy groups. TenantNet instructs all visitors on the fine art of forming tenant groups, staging demonstrations, and protesting commercial invasion into their buildings or neighborhoods.

By the way, landlords concerned about militant tenants are advised to visit the Landlord's Resource Centre (http:// www.lrcinc.com), which has forms and advice available for them.

COMPUTERS & INTERNET

[advice]

Ask Slashdot

● http://slashdot.org/askslashdot

If you are having serious computer problems—and we're not talking about trouble installing a printer—go to Ask Slashdot. The site bills itself as "News for Nerds. Stuff That Matters." In addition to providing tons of hard-core techie news about computers and software (including the introduction of new Apple machines and the discovery of holes in Microsoft's security programs), the owners of the site answer seriously geekish questions. Here are sample topics: using SSH on non-U.S. sites for crypto development, Pentiums, sockets, and Coppermine; perplexing PPP problems; and optimizing Apache/MySql for a production environment. This is not your average watercooler discussion material. Questions posted on the site are answered by Slashdot's editors or by visitors to the site. If you can't get an answer to your computer question here, there may not be one.

University of Victoria Computer Help Desk

● http://helpdesk.uvic.ca/

If you're tired of waiting for a tech support person to pick up the phone, it may be faster to cross the border into Canada—virtually, that is. Though the UVic Computer Help Desk was designed for the computer users at the University of Victoria, this website is a real find for people in computer distress everywhere. It serves as an online hub for routing users to technical support and documentation both within the university and at sites maintained by specific vendors such as Microsoft, Apple, and HP. The primary features, in addition to general support data, are a Task Index (which shows you which application will help you accomplish which task) and an Application Index (which shows you how to do certain tasks within applications). There are also sections for specific operating systems, with information about their Internet capabilities, viruses, printing processes, and various applications.

[anti-hate]

HateWatch

● http://www.hatewatch.org/

Taking the First Amendment at its word, the Internet provides a forum for any and all agendas. That means that the bigoted, racist, fascist, misogynist—you name it—can also have their say online. With a little bit of time and a domain name, any neo-Nazi or white supremacist can put up his rants for the world to see.

HateWatch is an organization whose purpose is to combat bigotry on- and offline. It has many sections, but first and foremost it provides a daily news report (available via e-mail) on hate crimes and related trials, laws, and events around the world. Sadly, this section is pretty busy every day.

HateWatch lists sites that fight bias and those that promote it. It contains descriptions and links to dozens of civil rights and activist groups such as the Anti-Defamation League, the Simon Weisenthal Center, Outrage, the National Urban League, Equality Now, and others. You can search for hate by category (white supremacists, anti-gay, Holocaust denial, more), hate by country, symbols of hate, and more, then scan HateWatch's annotated listing of the hundreds of websites that fall into those categories.

[buying]

MacCentral

● http://maccentral.macworld.com/

Macintosh users are a loyal bunch, and MacCentral is a great place to indulge their passion. Mac news and reviews are included on the site. There's even a section devoted to finding the best deals on computer products and services. The *Macworld* Classifieds let you browse products or post a listing to sell a product. Free newsletters keep Mac enthusiasts who always want to be in the know informed about Mac issues and deals. Forums are indexed by sponsors, operating system, hardware and software, and many other threads. Visitors can register with the site, create a profile, and see who else is using the site, which makes MacCentral a true online community for Macintosh users.

Macintosh
Apple

● http://www.apple.com/

The Mac is back! And this site is the mecca for Macintosh users, plain and simple. In addition to providing up-to-date info on products, upgrades, and tools, the site includes reams of white papers and help sections to assist those looking to max their Macs. Special sections address the needs of educators, developers, and those in the design and publishing industries.

Linux

● http://www.linux.org/

Linux is the language cum operating system that its inventor and devotees hope will change the computing world. An offshoot of UNIX, Linux holds the promise of making the operating system at the heart of all computers freely available to all, while maintaining compatibility between programs. Developed by Linus Torvalds, the system's grassroots fervor could change computing in the twenty-first century. This site is the official home of the language that Linus wrote—although the most popular commercial Linux site belongs to Red Hat (www.redhat.com). Between the two, and accompanied by the penguin mascot every step of the way, you can find everything you need to know about the merits and implementation of Linux.

Windows
Microsoft

● http://www.microsoft.com/windows/default.asp

Hundreds of sites provide Windows information, but this is where the Religion of Redmond gets posted first. It's only natural to check up on the latest version of the Windows operating system at the mother ship. This is where all the info on all the Microsoft applications (Office, Word, Excel, etc.) can be found.

Yahoo! Computers

● http://shopping.yahoo.com/computers

$ Anyone who owns or is looking to buy a computer knows: There are a lot of brands out there and a lot of places to buy them with a lot of different price tags. Sorting through the maze of promotions and peripherals is like piecing together a map of the world—with your eyes closed. Yahoo!

comes to the rescue. Its computer shopping site is an efficient, easy way to buy computers. This attractive, user-friendly site guides you to the right computer, printer, accessory, or peripheral for you—all at very competitive prices.

To search for what you need, you choose from a long list that includes desktop computers, laptops, books, components, monitors, scanners, modems, and more. If you're brand-driven you can also pick the manufacturer you want: Apple, Dell, Hewlett-Packard, Iomega, Gateway, and every other major computer-gear vendor. We sussed out the goods on a purple iMac by following the links for iMac Grape. Soon we had a full list of specs on the system, as well as a discounted price from an Internet retailer that has partnered with Yahoo!. Once we entered our vital stats, the iMac was scheduled to be shipped to our door in a few days. The process couldn't have been faster or easier. It made us wonder how much longer people will continue to buy computers from bricks-and-mortar stores.

[clip art]

Clipart.com

● http://www.clipart.com/

Nowhere else on the web will you find everything from Jesus Christ to Images, Icons to International Traffic Signs. And nowhere do such graphics masterpieces exist outside the realm of clip art. Clip art was originally an "art form" provided in monstrously thick catalogs from which images could be clipped and pasted into newsletters, advertisements, and so on. With the advent of illustration software, scanners, and photo manipulation software, you might think that clip art would have died off. Instead, it has found new life on the web, where it thrives like mosquitoes in a Florida swamp. Perhaps the reason is that clip art is, by and large, offered for free there. On thousands of sites around the world, you can cut, copy, and paste clip art images into your digital documents, from e-mail to faxes.

Unfortunately, because a number of these sites are maintained by individuals who make the art available to the masses, many of these sites disappear quickly or move with their owners to new addresses. So the best way to start digging through clip art is via Clipart.com, which keeps an updated list of links to clip art sites (including commercial sites) with brief descriptions. Clipart.com also allows website owners to register their pages as part of the Clipart network. There are hundreds and hundreds of sites to choose from, so you're on your own determining the quality of each site.

One caveat: Don't look for free photo images on the web. Occasionally a site might pilfer and then offer the photography of another site or person for free (clip art seems to imply public domain status that doesn't apply to photography), but photographers have gotten a lot more savvy about protecting and charging for their work. If you want photos, you're probably going to have to buy them.

YAHOO! ALSO LISTS: [clip art]

- **http://www.webplaces.com/html/clipart.htm**
  Clip Art Review: guide to sites offering free graphic images.
- **http://www.clipart.com/**
  Clip Art Directory
- **http://www.clipartsite.com/**
  Clipartsite.com: a guide to the top free clip art, font, and animation sites.
- **http://www.free-clip-art.to**
  Free Clip Art: resources for finding images and designers.
- **http://webclipart.about.com/**
  Mining Co. Clip Art: provides resource backgrounds, textures, animation, graphics, icons, and more.
- **http://www.itec.sfsu.edu/multimedia/multimedia.html**
  Multimedia and Clip Art: a large collection of multimedia, clip art, and icon resources.

[companies]

Apple

- http://www.apple.com/

Dell

- http://www.dell.com/

Gateway

- http://www.gateway.com/

Hewlett-Packard

- http://www.hp.com/

Microsoft

- http://www.microsoft.com/

Sun Microsystems

- http://www.sun.com/

Talking about computer companies and their websites in a book about the Internet is a lot like talking about the deities in *Bullfinch's Mythology*: There are some good ones, some bad ones, some major ones, and some minor ones. In the race to "control" the Internet, all of these computer companies have something at stake. We're not going to be part of the ongoing battle over which company really has the best interests of websurfers at heart, nor are we going to make recommendations that might bias the reader toward the purchase of specific hardware or software; instead, we'll point you to the players and let you be the judge. Note that most of the savvy computer companies got their URLs early, so if you're looking for a company you don't see here, try typing its name with .com slapped on after it.

The hundreds of other computer companies you may come into contact with—Oracle, Computer Associates, 3Com, and so on can be found easily by typing their names in the Yahoo! search engine.

[e-mail]

Yahoo! Mail

● http://mail.yahoo.com/

Free e-mail for life? Yahoo!. Yahoo! does indeed offer free e-mail for life on its homepage, right near the top.

Many Internet portals offer free e-mail because it draws people into their sites on a regular basis. You give them a little bit of personal information, and they give you a free e-mail account. A fair trade, considering that an Internet mailbox can be a beautiful thing. Unlike many private mail systems, a Yahoo! mail account can be accessed from any browser at any time in any city on earth.

The requirements are few: Click on the Yahoo! Mail link, agree to the terms of use, give some personal information of the name-rank-and-serial-number kind, fill out (or not) a few optional lines, pick out a user name and password, and you're on your way. After that, you can retrieve your mail from the Yahoo! site regardless of whose computer you're using.

Of course, you need Internet access before you can check

Y! tip

Take the time to customize your browser. This is one of the simplest things you can do on your computer, and it takes about a minute. Set your homepage to a site you visit regularly (like My Yahoo!), so that whenever you log on to your browser, it takes you directly to that site.

your e-mail on the Internet, and more and more ISPs are offering free e-mail when you sign up with them. Still, a Yahoo! mail account can be a very valuable commodity; it is useful as a personal or secret account, especially if you're sharing one computer in a household or if your primary e-mail account belongs to your employer. It also serves as a nice backup and storage facility, where you can store your e-mail, with file attachments (up to three megabytes worth), for access from any computer on the Internet.

The only problem with any free e-mail service is, of course, spam. No matter how vigilant the mail providers are, spam of all sorts (primarily offering cheapo computer components, get-rich-at-home schemes, and pornography) is going to make its way to your e-mail. It's part of the deal, and spam or no spam, it's a sweet deal.

One thing we have to say—and we're only going to say it once—write down your user name and password. It takes some of the joy out of free e-mail when you have to sign up for a new account because you haven't the faintest idea which alias you used the last time around.

[fonts]

The Font Fairy

● http://www.printerideas.com/fontfairy/

Used to be that you were stuck with the one font provided by your typewriter: Courier. How times have changed. A standard computer today comes with dozens of fonts in every style one could wish for, from Arial to Zapf Dingbats. For those with a serious font fetish, this site links to hundreds of free font sites on the web. Developed by author Kay Hall, the front page explains her motivation and then leads into a simple list of links in a modified HTML format. There is a description of each font style and whether it is available for Macintosh or Windows. Links point to commercial sites that have sample fonts offered for free.

[internet and the world wide web]

Streaming Media World

● http://www.streamingmediaworld.com/

The promise of audio and video on the web means your TV and your computer will one day be the same thing. Today, though, there are competing standards, concepts, and formats for Net-based audio and video, so making it all work for you can be a little on the daunting side. Media World is a site for anyone who wants to add audio and video to his website, for anyone who wants to know how to make streaming audio and video work, or for anyone who just wants to understand the technology. The categories are News & Views, Making It (tutorials on creating streaming media), Power Tools (software to make streaming media), Cool Streams (examples of audio, video, animation, and multimedia culled from other sources—a demo from Porsche, a look at the Getty Museum), Just SMIL (info on the Synchronized Multimedia Integration Language), Info Sites (other web resources), and Streaming Talk (discussion). The main ingredients of the site are the links to nearly every conceivable player product and the various tutorials—both company-sponsored and independent—that explain how to implement these players.

[personal pages]

If you've been spending a lot of time websurfing, perhaps it's time to stake your own claim in cyberspace. Then, of course, you'll have to build on it—that is, create a homepage. Once you finish that, you'll want to build out—add extensions, do renovations; well, you get the idea. Clearly, developing a successful website takes commitment, resources, time, and maintenance. These sites offer the resources. The rest is up to you.

C/NET builder.com–Creating Web Pages

● http://builder.cnet.com/

It's no doubt stating the obvious that the best place for finding information on building a website is on the web itself. Sure, you can design a website by reading a book, but that's sort of like learning to drive by watching a movie—the active process of doing is a much better way to learn.

C/NET is well known as an Internet source for all sorts of

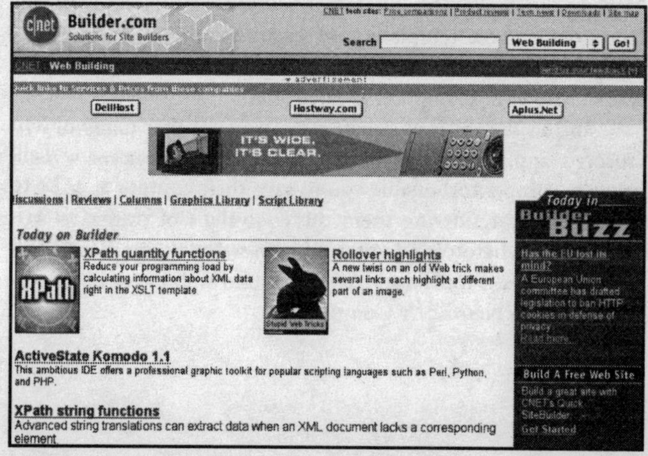

computer information—in vast quantities—and its guide to building websites is excellent. To amplify specific aspects of web design (under these category headings: Basics, Web Services, Tips & How-to's, lots more), it supplies downloadable tools, which help make the process both more efficient and more enjoyable.

The Building section includes data that goes beyond actual site construction; it has information on branding your site, finding the right ISP, and creating an e-commerce server. It also offers reviews of website design. It's a lot to digest, but well worth sorting through if you're serious about carving out your own piece of the Web.

Netscape

● http://home.netscape.com/browsers/createsites/index.html

Microsoft

● http://www.microsoft.com/frontpage/

Netscape takes the HTML out of site building. It has made personal site design easier than you can imagine. From this page on Netscape's site you can create pages in no time using Netscape Composer, whose templates and wizards walk you through the process in unbelievably simple steps. You can even integrate Java scripts into your Composer-created sites.

And in the spirit of equanimity, we note that many of Microsoft's application programs (Microsoft is Netscape's main browser competitor) enable you to save their content as HTML code, thereby rendering them the equivalent of primitive web pages. And Microsoft's Explorer browser has a complementary program called FrontPage that helps build web pages in a manner similar to Netscape's Composer.

Reallybig.com— The Complete Resource for Web Builders

● http://reallybig.com/default.shtml

Reallybig.com hits you like a ton of bricks, claiming that it is the complete resource for all web builders, and then following up with links to every type of web tool imaginable. In its own words, Reallybig.com has "more than 5,000 resources for web builders including free scripts, CGI, counters, fonts, HTML, Java, animation, backgrounds, icons, HTML editors, buttons, photographs, site promotion, and much more." And there's enough data here to back up that claim.

For anyone building a website, "shopping" at Reallybig.com is the equivalent of letting loose a child in a toy store: "I'll have one of those, and two of those, and that looks really cool; do I have room for that? Let's see how this one works. . ." Among the building tools are animated gifs, backgrounds, font managers, hit counters, icons, Java resources, and site promoters. These tools are located on other sites but indexed here.

[privacy/encryption]

Internet Privacy

Since the day that the first World Wide Web page appeared,people have been concerned about the downsides of being "wired," not only to each other, but to the government, businesses, and entities that we ultimately don't want to be connected with (you know what they are).

The fact is, we are linked to all of the above, whether We like it or not. Having accepted this as a condition of being members of a digitally networked society, we then have to figure out how to protect our privacy and limit abuses in information disclosure, while maintaining our right to say just about any damn thing we please, whenever we please without interference. This raises a lot of dis-

parate issues, some of them in apparent conflict. Think about it: we want access to anything and everything, but we want total privacy. We want to say anything that comes to mind—whether important or impolitic—but we don't want information about our personal lives to be trafficked like a public commodity.

The organizations listed in this category address various components of these issues. As information providers and activists, they form the front line both in defending and promoting the web. Regardless of how you use the web—or what you think about it—the potential for abuse and government interference is huge. Without invoking images of Big Brother and George Orwell, suffice it to say that diligence is required.

Center for Democracy and Technology (CDT) Encryption Issues Page

● http://www.cdt.org/crypto/index.shtml

The government may not like it, but secret codes are alive and well at the CDT site. Like the other organizations mentioned here, the CDT is concerned with individual rights and technology. This page, though, deals specifically with issues surrounding encryption—the stickiest sticking point between the government and privacy activists. Basically, encryption allows digital messages to be secretly encoded so that only participants in the exchange can read, hear, or understand the message. The problem? The government doesn't want any of it, and the activists want a lot more of it.

As with all the other privacy sites, news items dominate this site, but you should head to the image of a set of keys with article titles over them. This is where you can learn about encryption and the attendant issues. And use the zip code box to find out how your congressperson has voted on encryption legislation. Or link to discussions of current administration policy, to publications, and to related topics such as digital authorization, data privacy, and wiretapping.

Electronic Frontier Foundation (EFF)

● http://www.eff.org/

The EFF is perhaps the most visible and active of all the civil liberties and technology organizations. Founded in 1990, the group sponsors events, presents white papers, and generally campaigns on behalf of defending civil liberties with in the context of advanced technology and the Internet.

This site provides summaries of all the group's recent efforts (forums, presentations, protests, calls to action, etc.) and gives you an opportunity to become a member of the EFF. The archive section is especially expansive, with 15 categories of information such as Activism & Government, Intellectual Property & Fair Use, Censorship & Free Expression, and Net Culture & Online Community, each of which has dozens of directories, collections, FAQs, and documents all relating to the issue of protecting privacy in an increasingly wired world.

Electronic Privacy Information Center (EPIC)

● http://epic.org/

The EPIC site serves as a place to review news and issues regarding so-called cyber-liberties and to get hard facts on privacy tools. The site offers a list of resources and guides, including Bill-Track, which follows pending legislation, and an online guide to privacy resources, where you can get software tools to protect your phones, e-mail, computer files, and so on. There's also a listing of the latest news, especially government bills concerning privacy and encryption that are under consideration or have been approved. And a policy archives of epic proportions covers everything from airline passenger profiling to caller ID and wiretapping.

The Privacy Page

● http://www.privacy.org/

The Privacy Page contains links to privacy information all over the web. The main section of the page features links to recent news stories from a variety of sources, including MSNBC, *The Washington Post*, *The San Jose Mercury News*, CNN, and a host of others. Hot buttons link to privacy groups, which are listed by specialty (consumer, international, kids, resources, etc.). This page is sponsored in part by EPIC (see above).

[programming]

Resources
Dr. Dobb's Journal (DDJ)

● http://www.ddj.com/

Dr. Dobb's has long been known as a programmer's paradise in print, revealing undocumented instructions on microprocessors and exploring ternary search trees. The good Doctor is known for giving code lovers insight on the issues that comprise the heart of computer applications and operating systems. Now all this is available on the DDJ website, along with its online equivalent of buried treasure, the Programmer's Vault. The Vault has tips, tutorials, data, and downloads available in areas such as writing Java apps and designing software games. DDJ posts many of its articles and editorials, along with the source code featured in those articles—which is archived for nearly a decade.

Programming Language Research

● http://www.cs.cmu.edu/afs/cs.cmu.edu/user/mleone/web/language-research.html

Those looking to delve into the mysterious world of computer programming languages can find paths to knowledge in the links stored at this site. From calculi for mobile processes to run-time code generation and skeletal parallelism, there are hotlinks here for both the novice and the seasoned programming pro. Most of the links lead to other universities, research labs, and even some vendors, all of which are excellent resources for researching language theory, design, and implementation.

[reference]

Whatis

● http://www.whatis.com/

"In information technology and other specialized areas, technobabble is the use of technical or 'insider' terms that, to the uninitiated, have no meaning." For example, "kludge" is an awkward or clumsy solution to a programming or hardware designer implementation problem. Whatis explains acronyms such as URL and TCP/IP and takes the mystery out of "twip" and "futzing." And because terms are constantly submitted by visitors as well as the techies running the site, Whatis always knows what is new. In addition, you'll find sections on how to use the Internet and on how it works in general; you can learn to set up websites, and find descriptions of most HTML tags, graphic design, new technology, and cyberculture. Our Latest Discovery reviews websites, such as the amazing Atlas of Cyberspaces and to How to Learn Perl (and if you don't know what that is, visit the site).

Our recommendation: Always have a second browser window open for Whatis. That way you'll always know "what is" in case you're suddenly confronted with geek speak.

[searching the internet]

Google

- http://www.google.com/

Archives and Articles
Northern Light

- http://www.northernlight.com/

Hoovers Online

- http://www.hoovers.com/

Multimedia
Scour.Net

- http://www.scour.net/

Ditto

- http://www.ditto.com/

Yahoo! Image Surfer

- http://gallery.yahoo.com/

People
Infospace

- http://www.infospace.com/

KnowX

- http://www.knowx.com/

Search Engines and Directories
Alta Vista

- http://www.altavista.com/

Excite

- http://www.excite.com/

Infoseek

- http://www.infoseek.com/

Lycos

- http://www.lycos.com/

Yahoo!

- http://www.yahoo.com/

Metasearches

The Big Hub

- http://www.thebighub.com/

Mamma

- http://www.mamma.com/

ProFusion

- http://www.profusion.com/

CNET Search.com

- http://www.search.com/

There are a numerous ways to conduct searches on the web. The obvious place to start is Yahoo! No matter what category of information you want, Yahoo! has it wired. If you've selected so specific a topic that Yahoo! doesn't have a category for it, its Inktomi engine will perform a webwide search.

For more specific searches, where you're looking for very detailed information, go to Alta Vista, Excite, Lycos, or InfoSeek. Each of these search sites have advanced features and employ different forms of logic functions. Big note: You can find out which one accepts which form by asking for "help," on the homepage. Some take the Booleans AND, OR, NOT, NEAR, while others do searches with Boolean symbols. Look the site over to make sure you're using the right methods. And remember, hitting return does not always activate the engine; sometimes you actually have to click on the "go" button.

In addition to these engines, there are others for specific industries or areas of interest, many of which we've included in this book (scubasearch.com, musicsearch, bibliofind, etc.). These sites have already narrowed the results to pages dealing with the subject at hand. They are usually compiled and indexed by the editors of a particular site so that when you look up, say, "snorkel" you don't get sites for rock bands with the same name.

If using one search engine at a time doesn't do it for you, go to some of the metasearch sites, which utilize several engines at once. This is useful if you are, or become, a veritable power user of the Net. These search "portals" integrate a variety of search engines into one page, sending each of these engines off to seek your solution without your having to consult each one individually (sort of like sending a pack of dogs off hunting instead of just one). Some of the notable metasearchers are Mamma.com (http://www.mamma.com/), CNET Search.com (http://www.search.com/), The Big Hub (http://www.thebighub.com/), and Profusion (http://www.profusion.com/). Mamma.com bills itself as "the mother of all search engines" and, along with the Big Hub and ProFusion, lets you select from several engines and choose the types of search. SavvySearch goes a step further in the way of volume, giving you a choice of up to 100 search engines to employ in its searches. Ultimately, your use of these comes down to personal taste as they all present information in different ways from different sources.

If you are searching for data that might be embedded within a magazine or newspaper site, try Powerize.com. This engine takes you behind the scenes of some sites that don't normally get crawled through by bots or agents. These are often subscriber sites that don't allow access past the homepage without registration. To get deeper into the archives of some of these sites, or into archives of a more traditional sort, try Northern Light (http://www.northernlight.com/). This site has data on articles that have appeared in 6,000 different periodicals, from daily newspapers to business weeklies. It acts as a reprint service, so you do have to pay if you want a complete article, but the summary is enough to let you know whether you want to pay for the whole thing.

For looking up people, there are dozens of white pages on the Web, but we suggest a couple of precision sites, namely InfoSpace (http://www.infospace.com/) and KnowX (http://www.knowx.com/). InfoSpace is a popular white-pages-style search engine that lets you search for people via name, phone number, or e-mail address. KnowX is a little more interesting and will appeal to those who need to do some serious sleuthing. The site is the equivalent of hiring a private detective to find information about people—not just where they live. It does this by searching through sites that contain public records—which is perfectly legal though somewhat daunting. There is a charge for these documents, but it sure beats paying a private eye or doing the legwork yourself.

All of the above directories and metasearchers are text-based search engines, which look for information based on keywords and/or concepts. But what if you're looking for an image or a sound? For this type of search, go to Scour.Net (http://www.scour.net/) or Ditto (http://www.ditto.com/), which will perform searches based on your description of an image, video, or sound. The new Yahoo! Image Surfer (http://gallery.yahoo.com/) also offers you a way to scan through images.

You can't go wrong with any of these sites—they're all good, though it may help to use more than one for a search, to cover more ground quickly.

[security]

Vmyths.com

● http://www.vmyths.com/

Taking advantage of rampant computer-virus paranoia are pranksters who like to spread viruses that are nothing more than practical jokes. This site aims to separate the real from the malicious. It has an A-Z list of hoax viruses and lists some urban legends, hands out Computer Virus Hysteria Awards, and offers news items and recent reports of hoaxes as reported on other Internet sites. The site also analyzes the ramifications of such well-known viruses as Melissa and Michelangelo and describes other non-virus-related Internet problems—spam e-mails and chain letters—that, for example, offer trips to Disney World or gifts from Bill Gates (yeah, right).

The tone here is humorously strident and certainly worth reading. It will make you think twice about the real impact of viruses versus the media-generated impact, but that doesn't mean you shouldn't protect yourself. It's said that even Nostradamus carried an umbrella.

[software]

Reviews
Freeware and Shareware
Shareware.com

● http://www.shareware.com/

Free. It's one of our favorite words, especially as it relates to the computer industry, a business whose every product and peripheral has a pricey price tag. So when you hear that some computer product is free—or can be had for a nominal fee—you should pay attention. For the same reason, you should pay attention to Shareware.com, one of the excellent "subsites" of the massive C/NET technology news/products/reviews website. In this case, C/NET has archived a quarter of a million files that can be downloaded for free or purchased directly from the creator for a small fee. You can search for applications by your area of interest (say MP3 players or viewer programs) or the type of operating system you're using (Windows, Macintosh, Linux). Shareware.com also ranks the software by popularity, determined by number of "weeks on the chart" and downloads this week. You know that MP3 player we mentioned? It's playing right now. Know how much it cost us? Nada. Nothing. Zip. Life is good. Visit C/NET.

ZDNet

● http://www.zdnet.com/

[$] Ziff-Davis is the publisher of such popular personal computing magazines as *PC Week,* and *PC Computing,* to *Macworld,* and *FamilyPC.* This site brings the resources of all those magazines—and more—to the Web, with a leviathanlike homepage crammed with daily news, reviews, polls, industry highlights, and free downloads. And that's not counting its "channels," nearly three dozen indexed categories with links to the entire high-tech universe. These include auctions, benchmarks, careers, development libraries, events, investments, product guides, small businesses, and much more.

This site is aimed at users of all experience levels, so higher-end techies might also want to check out TechWeb (http://www.techweb.com/), maintained by Miller Freeman/CMP.

[sounds]

SoundAmerica

● http://www.soundamerica.com/

If you like to accessorize your answering machine message with film dialogue ("Feel lucky, punk?") or use audio cartoon snippets on your computer desktop ("What's up, doc?"), SoundAmerica is your kind of place. This is an excellent resource for downloadable audio files, boasting more than 26,000 of them.

Sounds are grouped by category. Cartoons are weighted with '90s animated shows, such as *South Park*, *Beavis and Butt-head*, and *Spawn*. Comedy offerings range from old-timers such as Jack Benny to shockers of the Sam Kinison ilk. Miscellaneous contains everything from Casey Kasem to the ubiquitous "Got milk?" soundbite. Movies are grouped alphabetically from *12 Monkeys* to *Young Frankenstein*. Sound Effects has, of course, numerous belches, as well as the requisite boings, bells, and bangs. Barney, the repulsive purple dinosaur, has his own folder under Spoofs, while the TV Shows category contains ever-popular *Seinfeld* clips. There's even a grab bag of sounds in Unsorted Stuff.

An important component of SoundAmerica is that it leads users through the necessary steps to obtain the free software to enable use of the site's audio files.

[technology]

Advanced

Advanced technology is that technology which doesn't yet rest comfortably in the hands of consumers. While this is a simple definition, attempting to define individual technologies is a much more daunting task. Artificial intelligence, artificial life, neural networks—these sound like components of a sci-fi movie. Yet they are actually viable technologies used in various ways on our PCs and even on the Net. Like most good technologies, the best ones work so well that you don't even know they're there.

The categories we've included below are primarily computer-driven technologies, and that by definition limits the field (we've stayed away from propulsion technology, for instance). Most of these sites serve as indices to the technology world around them, and none of them are category killers—advanced technology is just too fragmented. If you want some basic introduction to many of these technologies and their underlying concepts, especially those related to artificial intelligence and virtual reality, the best site for an overview is the Relayer Group's Technology Page (http://www.newquist.net/technology). It provides nontechnical introductions to many of the specific sites listed below.

Botspot

● http://www.botspot.com/

Bots (short for robots) are the software programs that crawl around the Net identifying and categorizing websites. In fact, bots are the lines of code that make surfing the Net possible. They are the spawn of the original artificial intelligence programs developed in the 1970s, and they have become a class of program unto themselves.

Botspot discusses all things related to bots: research projects, news, categories of bots, (from chatter bots to stock bots), feature articles, and introductions to bots as well as tips on using bots and employing them in website design. FYI, the site identifies 18 different kinds of bots; chances are you've already encountered several of them without knowing it.

Institute for Information Technology—AI Resources

● http://ai.iit.nrc.ca/ai_point.html

Artificial intelligence (AI) is the attempt to teach computers to behave like humans, particularly in the areas of thought, speech, hearing, seeing, and understanding. This site has links to over 110,000 documents containing information relevant to AI, from bibliographies, books, companies, and conferences to journals, software repositories, and projects. The searches can be done by category or via a search engine that scans all the links on the site. This site is maintained as part of the National Research Council of Canada.

Genetic Algorithms (GA)
The Genetic Algorithms Archive

● http://www.aic.nrl.navy.mil:80/galist/

Genetic algorithms (GA) are computer programs or models that attempt to identify the dominant and weak characteristics of an entity using a simulated evolutionary processes. It's sort of like watching time-lapse evolution. Computer-generated entities are assigned specific traits; their evolution is monitored to define and identify desirable outcomes. A good example would be a model of an IPO stock that could grow and evolve even in difficult economic times.

The GA Archives is a list of extremely well-annotated links maintained by the Naval Research Laboratory. Contained on a single page, the links lead to upcoming events, online programs, university projects, and GA societies.

Biotechnology
BioSpace

● http://www.biospace.com/

Biotechnology—the manipulation of biology through technology—draws a fine line between pure research and commercial endeavor. Work in biotechnology raises hope for cures of various diseases, for better crops, and much more. But not all work being conducted in biotech labs has practical application in the real world, leading to some wonder if the science is more hype than promise.

BioSpace opens this research world to the public in the form of news from both the commercial realm and labs. Its content varies from breaking news and career help to finding investors, companies, industry events, and resources. It also offers a marketplace, BioBuzz (treatments, biological warfare, etc.), and search engines. The news stories, gleaned from respected sources such as CNN, lean toward the corporate, although labs and universities are also represented. A good portion of the site is devoted to the stock market and how its ups and downs affect biotech stocks. There is a BioSpace Radio page that features streaming audio from various biotech and financial conferences.

Cloning
Conceiving a Clone

● http://library.thinkquest.org/24355/

Would you consider having yourself cloned if it required giving up only a few of your microscopic cells? Opening with a graphic of Dolly the cloned sheep—the benchmark clone to date—Conceiving a Clone addresses all the issues surrounding the practice of cloning. There are three primary areas: the Details (time lines, profiles, techniques, media center), Reactions (misconceptions, implications, the debate, regulations), and Interactions (discussions, create a clone, and questionnaire). Each section contains an encyclopedic amount of related information in the form of biographies, lists of significant events, and references to types of cloning (nuclear transfer, Honolulu Technique, etc.).

Conceiving a Clone addresses most of the issues that have arisen surrounding cloning, and the fact that it leaves the commercial world out of the discussion is a nice plus. It should be noted that this is a ThinkQuest site (see under SCIENCE), a group of webpages that are of such high quality, they should consider cloning themselves.

Neural Networks
Neural Announcements & General Information

● http://www-xdiv.lanl.gov/XCM/neural/neural_announcements.html

Neural nets are yet another offshoot of AI. They are software, and occasionally hardware, models of the brain, attempting to mimic human thought patterns and perform pattern recognition using interconnected "neurons." The concept is that if many neurons are working on a problem simultaneously and sharing information, they can arrive at a solution faster than traditional computers do. Neural nets have already been used successfully in detecting credit card fraud and in identifying patterns too complex for humans to recognize (notably in photographic surveillance). This Los Alamos site is the best available resource for reaching the neural net world, not only covering the lab's own efforts, but charting sites that range from the commercial to the community-based.

Speech Recognition
Commercial Speech Recognition

● http://www.tiac.net/users/rwilcox/speech.html

Speech recognition is a subset of artificial intelligence that strives to make computers understand human speech. Many telephone systems and customer service centers now use speech recognition to move customers quickly toward their desired information, and there are now several popular speech programs that integrate a microphone and a PC so that individuals can control their computers via voice commands.

This page is an index of links to the world of speech recognition. Each is categorized and summarized, then divided into sections including news, Usenet groups, corporate websites (recognition engines, resellers, integrators), applications and peripherals, computer telephony integration vendors, major research labs, text-to-speech and speech synthesis, and tons more. In short, everything you really need to hear about speech recognition.

Virtual Reality on the Net—VR

● http://www.hitl.washington.edu/projects/knowledge_base/onthenet.html

Virtual reality (VR) is a technology that lets users immerse themselves in "alternate" and computer-generated realities. The basic idea is that you strap on a helmet with 3D computer goggles and a data glove that lets you "touch" objects in the virtual world, and you're free of the bonds of the real world. Virtual realities have become popular as arcade and video games but are also being used for scientific research, architecture, design, and manufacturing.

This site, maintained by the University of Washington's renowned Human Interface Technology Laboratory—nicknamed the HIT Lab—serves as a link repository to VR sites across the Internet. It is made up of several directories, beginning with a Full Listing that provides a comprehensive list of the web's commercial sites, research labs, and VRML-related sites. The Whole Thing presents the organization's entire VR database, complete with the disclaimer "Warning!! Very Long!!" Other directories include Resources (software and sound), VRML (authoring tools, browsers, repositories, etc.), Applications (everything from architecture and augmented reality to manufacturing and medical), and Guides (papers, bibliographies, conferences).

[telecommuting]

Smart Valley Inc.'s Telecommuting Web Pages

● http://smart2.svi.org/PROJECTS/TCOMMUTE/webguide/

Given the chance, most people would probably give up their houses to work at home. Fortunately, more and more companies are offering their employees the option of telecommuting. (It is not entirely altruistic; it's a way to give employees more perks without shelling out more cash.) So with the growing number of people in the workforce who now telecommute—either part- or full-time—it's surprising that the Web doesn't have more information to offer in this area. Though there are a plethora of work-at-home sites, stay-at-home-dad sites, and the like, nothing fully addresses telecommuting from a practical perspective.

Smart Valley's site comes closest to describing the personal and professional ramifications of logging in from home. It is primarily a series of brief articles, both on- and offsite, for telecommuters and their managers. Articles and links are categorized by the Basics of Telecommuting, Implementation of Telecommuting, Changes in Work and Lifestyle, Experiences with Telecommuting, Technology, and Resources, plus links to search engines. Real-life experiences share page space with case studies and corporate wisdom. Ultimately, a lot more space—here and across the entire web—should be devoted to the issue of telecommuting. To its credit, Smart Valley has taken the first step.

[translations]

Alta Vista: Translations

● http://babelfish.altavista.com/

There are millions of sites not in your native language, making some corners of the web a veritable Tower of Babel. Unlike the builders of that ill-fated structure, you can continue to communicate with the world of the Web thanks to babelfish, a translation component of the Alta Vista search engine. Translations are performed using a form of artificial intelligence called machine translation, here supplied by a company called Systran. Translations are available from English to French, Italian, Spanish, German, and Portuguese, and from each of these back into English.

The layout is very similar to that of the famous search engine. You can choose one of two translation options: translating text you supply or translating the information in a particular site. In the first instance, you simply type in the words you want translated, select a language, then click on the Translation button. In the second instance, you type in the URL of the site you want translated, and it brings up the site itself, with the text translated entirely into the language you chose. This feature can also be accessed from the Alta Vista search engine itself.

Mind you, always get an accurate translation; in particular, sites don't translate well when they contain lots of slang or jargon. But that's a minor complaint. (One of the major complaints with machine translation systems is that they can't comprehend cultural references. For example, during the Cold War, the English phrase "The spirit is willing but the flesh is weak" translated into the Russian "The vodka is strong but the meat is spoiled."). One interesting diversion: View your own site in another language.

EDUCATION

A quick scan of the Net uncovers that quality courses, stellar research, and comprehensive curricula are available for free to anyone who wants to educate themselves.

The World Wide Web can supplement curriculum by offering alternative means of exploring subject matter, beyond the classroom and in an environment that is essentially self-paced and one-on-one. Don't want to pay for courses taught at MIT? Then explore them online—free. There is, of course, the issue of degrees and accredidation, but some of the websites listed in this section address these concerns, from A to Z.

Education on the web isn't limited to the college-age students. Everyone who wants to learn on their own and expand their personal horizons will find a wealth of information here. Individuals looking to complete their postgraduate degrees or to get ahead of their classmates will also find pages to serve their needs. Self-starters in particular will find the web to be a haven of data that they can use to enrich their existing knowledge of a subject or serve as the basis—indeed, the complete course—for beginning the learning process.

Will the web one day supplant colleges as the main source of higher education in the world? That remains to be seen. Education was once considered the means by which people would have the opportunity to become intellectual and philosophical equals. The cost of education has certainly put that thought to rest, but the web is wiping the slate clean and leveling the playing field.

[colleges & universities]

Peterson's

● http://www.petersons.com/

In real life, most college advisers aren't nearly as helpful as this site by Peterson's, one of the premier names in college information and resources. Peterson's is very likely the only web resource many students will ever need. It acts as an online guidance counselor in their quest to find the right college or colleges, complete applications, and seek financial aid. And it includes grad schools, private secondary schools, summer programs, boarding schools, distance learning centers, special schools, executive education, and on and on. The site is monstrous (more than 1,000 pages deep). The mind reels.

Each type of education has its own section, which means you can look up institutions and information, as well as featured articles ranging from how colleges evaluate applications to the pros and cons of transferring. But the main attraction of Peterson's is a single component called CollegeQuest. Once you've registered (for free) with CollegeQuest, you are sent a personal organizer page, which allows you to build your college wish list and keep track of key dates (deadlines for application submissions and the like). It also lets you compare different colleges side by side, by reviewing student-teacher ratios, how entrants scored on their SATs, housing options, athletic programs, number of

Y! tip

When looking for academic institutions, you can oftentimes go straight to the source by typing in the name of the school or its abbreviation with .edu attached in place of .com.

organizations that recruit on campus, and more. Peterson's even has a "virtual campus" section containing news, quick and detailed fact sheets, and a profile on each school.

Peterson's also provides SAT or ACT tips, helps you manage all your college applications online, and enables you to exchange info with other members. In addition, you'll find test prep and financial planning downloads, job and career planning sections, and certification classes.

You can use other sites, listed below, to look into specific types of education and financial aid, but when you're ready to pick your school, this is the only site you'll need.

ScholarStuff—Higher Education

● http://www.scholarstuff.com/

ScholarStuff gives you fast access to undergraduate and graduate school listings by state, country, or field of study. We recommend this site for getting quick, concise information on academic institutions, without having to sign up for complete school search and study programs like those offered by Peterson's. Drill down through selection pages, and you'll be taken to the college website of your choice or to the e-mail of the admissions office. ScholarStuff is also filled with information on, and links to, sites for financial aid, test preparation, student travel, fraternities and sororities, and even data on one of the most important aspects of higher education, spring break. There are also student chat and contest areas for those who want to hang out after class.

Virtual Campus Tours

● http://www.campustours.com/

Two of the determining factors in choosing a college are location and environment. Most students have to be amenable to the place itself or their educational experience will be less than pleasurable. These issues make trips to campuses one of the first priorities for choosing the right college.

Are you ready for the Gothic architecture and lung-freezing winters you'll have to endure at the University of Notre Dame in South Bend, Indiana? How about the southwestern spaces and scorching September days at Arizona State University? Fortunately you can take a "virtual campus tour" courtesy of CampusTours.com. Think of this site as a "try before you buy" option.

Colleges are listed here alphabetically in a matrix that shows you their online offerings in a variety of media. Each hallowed hall of learning has a checklist from which you can opt to take a virtual tour, see webcams of the campus, view an interactive map, watch Shockwave video clips, look at photos, or take a QuickTime virtual reality tour of the college. Note: You jump to each college site from within CampusTours, so you have to hit your browser's Back button to get back to the main site.

[teaching & learning]

Maricopa Center for Learning & Instruction (MCLI)

● http://www.mcli.dist.maricopa.edu/tl/index.html

What if you want to put together a complete curriculum for learning? Maybe you've always wanted to be able to discuss the history of philosophy or hold your own in a debate on macroeconomics. How about learning the rudiments of writing for professional publication? Or brushing up on your geography skills? There's always a nagging suspicion that we could stand to be a little better educated or informed in certain areas. But you're not a college professor, so assembling a comprehensive course in, say, English studies might as well be Greek to you. The potential is appealing, though, when you think about it.

The MCLI site acts as your student adviser, pointing out available courses and where to find them. Hosted by the Maricopa Center for Learning and Instruction in Arizona, this site provides categorized links and summaries of online courses from a huge variety of sources, including colleges, universities, and web-based tutorials. To qualify for inclusion here, the courses have to be available entirely online. At last count, there were 640 courses offered in 40 categories from archaeology to zoology, with business, law, economics, journalism, mathematics, chemistry, art, and almost every other college-level discipline you can think of.

To get started, select a course of study from the pulldown menu and add keywords (for example, Chemistry, then keyword Analytical). The site shows you all the URLs that can give you full instruction in that area. So pick a course and complete one a year. No one says you have to stop learning just because you're not sitting in a classroom. And unlike those early morning classes that seemed less inviting than sleeping in, you can schedule your web courses whenever you want.

WestEd DLRN

● http://www.dlrn.org/

Welcome to the twenty-first century, where even an education can be found on the Internet. At least, that's the goal of the Distance Learning Resource Network, a federally funded distance education program. The U.S. Department of Education maintains dlrn.org for primary and secondary students (grades K–12), adult learners, and educators. There is a searchable database and library of courses and available resources, including live Internet classes and listservs. Educators who want to develop their own internet courses even have access to online course design tools. Online doesn't mean you are completely alone—here's a toll-free telephone help line, e-mail information, and online forums.

This site has sections on the Distance Learning Program, trends and issues in distance education, and an interactive community with announcements and message boards. The online library includes newsletters and journals, background reading resources, and archives. Visitors can find links to various distance learning programs across the country as well as information about home schooling.

[financial aid]

FastWeb

● http://www.fastweb.com/

Whether it is field of interest, state of residence, or student affiliation, surely you'd be open to any kind of scholarship. FastWeb can help. This site can provide scholarship information from almost any school and in any discipline. FastWeb offers a directory of some 600,000 scholarships offered by schools around the country, searchable via institution and course of study. To search for scholarships, you have to register at the site and create a student profile, but you have to do that whenever you apply for a scholarship, anyway. Consider it on-the-job training.

FinAid

● http://www.finaid.org/

According to the College Board, the 1998–1999 average total yearly cost for students attending public colleges and universities was $10,458, and for private colleges and universities, $22,533. If these numbers make you realize that you might be a little short in your bank account when the kids go off to college, beeline it to FinAid. This site has everything from college cost calculators (which is where we got these figures) and savings plan calculators to loan estimators that will help you figure out where all that money for Junior's and Muffy's education is going to come from. Comprehensive sections describe the various types of financial aid, grants, and student loans, supplanted with downloadable forms for applying for financial aid. You'll also find online college applications, admissions tests, and data on jobs and internships.

This site is beneficial to both parents and students, who can review their needs and how to get the money to meet them. A bit of scholarly advice: Focus your eyes on FinAid today or start paying through the nose tomorrow.

[general education]

Education World

● http://www.education-world.com/

Appropriately titled, Education World boasts more than 115,000 site links, and this commercially funded site is much more than just a resource database. Education World generates a large amount of original content that's useful for all educators, such as the Books in Education area, which reviews new teaching titles. Original articles on such topics as curriculum and lesson planning also are available, as are reviews of other Internet education sites. A Financial Planning section provides tips, facts, and tools specifically for educators.

The site's search engine gives quick results via more than 5,000 categories and offers advanced search techniques. Among the database's features are the World School Directory, which includes everything from Montessori schools to universities, alumni publications, and online schools. The World Resource Center provides links by country and by state to education resources on the Internet, including museums, education organizations, and government resources.

An extensive searchable education employment listing is also available here, as well as sign-up opportunities for Education World's three mailing lists: the Weekly Newsletter, the biweekly Ed Jobs, and the monthly Education Reviews. And every week, to show that web education can be creative and engaging, Education World designates an institution with an outstanding website as Cool School of the Week; past winners are archived.

[gifted]

The Gifted Resources Page

● http://www.eskimo.com/~user/kids.html

Everyone likes to think that their children are gifted and talented. But only some can be clinically proven to be so. They are anomalies; and quite frankly, most schools don't know how to address the needs of these budding Mozarts or Einsteins. That's where gifted and talented programs come in.

This single-page site is intended to be a convenient starting point for gifted students, their parents, and educators to access gifted resources. This site contains links to all known online gifted resources, enrichment programs, talent searches, summer programs, mailing lists, and early acceptance programs, including CTY, EPGY, CTD, NRC/GT, TIP, RMTS, ERIC, NCSSSMST, Odyssey of the Mind, and many, many others. It also contains links to several years' worth of TAG (The Association for the Gifted) mailing list archives and contact information for many local gifted associations and government (mostly state) programs. For people involved with prodigies this is the best place on the web to point them in the right direction.

[special education]

Council for Exceptional Children (CEC)

● http://www.cec.sped.org/

The Council for Exceptional Children (CEC) is a nonprofit association that supports special-education professionals in an effort to improve educational outcomes for individuals with exceptionalities. Its website supports CEC's mission with a thorough presentation of the organization's resources. The colorful homepage has listings by category, such as CEC Career Connections and Publications & Products, and presents legislative news, teaching anecdotes, and changes in public policy.

Perhaps most useful here is the Site Index button found at the bottom of the page, which takes you to a more straightforward map of the site. One useful resource is the CEC Job Bank, where users can view job postings, educator resumes, and a catalog of special-education consultants, trainers, and expert witnesses. There are also instructions on how to submit resumes and post jobs. Detailed links to the Foundation for Exceptional Children and the National Clearinghouse for Professions in Special Education are included, while a News and Press Releases section includes updates on professional development and videos from conferences, among other things. Finally, there are numerous opportunities to learn about professional standards and accredidation, as well as how to become a member of CEC and take advantage of its benefits.

Special Education Resources on the Internet

● http://seriweb.com/

If you work in a field related to special education, or are someone with special-education needs, Special Education Resources on the Internet (SERI) is a great place to start searching for useful information. This simple link service, hosted by Hood College, presents myriad resources all reached via 22 category headings on the homepage. The categories are wide-ranging, from professional concerns such as Associations & National Organizations and University-Based Information to more general areas including Parent & Educator Resources. There are practical sections such as Disability Products and Commercial Sites, as well as areas specific to special education, such as Mental Retardation, Vision Impairment, Autism, Attention Deficit Disorder, and Gifted and Talented.

Learning Disabilities, a page of more than 30 links (many with short descriptions), is the point of departure to sites including the National Center for Learning Disabilities and a publication by the U.S. Department of Education called *What Is Meant by Learning Disabilities*. Parent & Educator Resources takes users to more than 60 additional sites, including the Sibling Support Project, the National Parent Network on Disabilities, and the Resource Sites for Parents of Special Needs Children.

[studying abroad]

Online Study Abroad Directory

● http://www.istc.umn.edu/

Here's an idea: Why not travel the world while you're in college—and get credit for it? A ton of schools offer international study programs in just about every nation on the planet and give you course credit while you're there. But you have got to find the schools that offer such programs first. No problem. The Online Study Abroad Directory (OSAD) is here to help. OSAD is a service of the International Study and Travel Center (ISTC), a not-for-profit student organization at the University of Minnesota, and it has created a database of the schools that have international studies programs.

Schools from Yale (studies in Berlin) to Long Island University (studies in Tibet) are represented; their offerings cover language courses, religion studies, international law, and many more. Type in a region of the world where you'd like to study and up pop all the schools with programs in that country. Or you can search by university or area of academic interest. A course curriculum and contact names are provided. There is also a searchable database of scholarship opportunities available for the intrepid and even the prodigal student.

[teaching]

AskERIC

● http://www.askeric.org/Virtual/Lessons/

Do you have questions about education but don't know who to ask? Just AskERIC! AskERIC (Educational Resources Information Center) is a federally funded website sponsored by the U.S Department of Education, Syracuse University, and Sun Microsystems. Visitors can submit questions and receive a quick (within two days) and personalized response by e-mail, complete with a list of database citations and links to other sites that can help you. Visitors can search archives, sign up for mailing lists and newsletters, and join discussion groups. AskERIC presents "Education Information with a Personal Touch."

The Virtual Lesson area has over 1,000 lesson plans submitted by United States teachers. The plans may be searched using the AskERIC search engine or browsed by subject (arts, math, social studies, and more). There are plans for grade schools (K-12), vocational education, higher education, and adult education. We checked the Philosophy section and found lesson plans for children and adults: Ben Franklin's Philosophy Clock is intended for grades 3 to 5, and Plato's Allegory of the Cave is for adults. Visitors can look up and submit lesson plans, and even learn how to create lesson plans. This site is an excellent place to share information about education.

Thematic Units for Primary Grades

● http://www.libsci.sc.edu/miller/Unitlink.htm

Thematic units are the classes or courses that make up the elements of home schooling, just like credits in college. A single thematic unit outlines a complete theme as part of a larger course of study, such as the study of orchestral instruments in a music course or the review of Romantic poets as part of English literature.

Many such courses are available online, although most are for sale (it's like selling an instruction book) or for trade. In contrast, this online collection of thematic units can be used free of charge for home schooling of kids in grades 1 to 9. All units conform to generally accepted curriculum standards and cover an eclectic set of topics, from ancient Egypt to whales.

College of Library and Information Science
CLIS 523/759 Materials for Early Childhood

Thematic Units For Primary Grades

The Following Thematic Units were prepared collaboratively as a Course Assignment for CLIS 523/75 1998, and 1999. Each unit is based on appropriate children's literature and addresses an across-the-cu Resources and nonbook materials are also included in each unit.

Students have given their permission to post these units on this web site for nonprofit educational pur individual authors when using these units in your classroom, media center, or library program. If you the instructor, Elizabeth Miller emiller@sc.edu.

Click here to go to the format used to write the following Thematic Units.

Last updated May 5, 1999

Ancient Egypt

China

[vocational]

Vocational Education Resources

● http://reach.ucf.edu/~voced/mainresources.htm

If the idea of spending four years sitting in a classroom sounds about as appealing as spending that time sitting in a dentist's chair, maybe you're the kind of person who prefers technical or vocational training. If so, skip all the college and university sites and head to Vocational Education Resources. This site is a page of links to vocational and technical resources on the Net, comprising a general information resource, a listing of various vocational curricula around the country, links to "school to work" sites, financial aid data, government and international info on vo-tech, and career and training resources.

ENTERTAINMENT

[collectibles]

Cards and Coins
Collector-Link

● http://www.collector-link.com/

Once upon a time, collecting coins and sports memorabilia was either relegated to kids who spent their allowance or grown men who had too much time on their hands. No more. Today, collecting these items is a pursuit not to be taken lightly. There are auctions, shows, online sites, conventions, and all the trappings of big-time commerce. There are lots of spots on the web that service this market, but this one is a card and coin collectors haven. Collector-Link provides links to websites for all kinds of card and coin collecting, especially those of the sports variety. Yet it also serves as a fully featured collector's stop, with chat rooms, mail lists, newsgroups, items-wanted postings, etc. There are also links for memorabilia, autographs, and supplies.

Collector-Link takes a unique approach to offering its wares—which range from coins and baseball cards to debit and phone cards. Using a specialized search engine, users can specify a search term, select the type of filter (i.e., sport, nonsport, autograph, memorabilia), ask for links starting with a specific letter, and even specify the date the item was added to the Internet. Having done this, users are given an exhaustive list of links to match their criteria. This well-thought-out website with attractively designed pages and colorful graphics takes a huge amount of the searching drudgery out of collecting specific items. As mentioned in several of our major league sports categories, Collector-Link exemplifies the kind of sports-card collecting that is offered on the Net.

Curioscape

● http://www.curioscape.com/

Curioscape is the emotional equivalent of visiting an antiques fair. Instead of going to some rural countryside market or a reconverted barn, you get to traipse through the digital stalls of cyberspace. There are loads of these antiques and collectibles sites, but Curioscape is an invaluable antiques and collectibles directory for Internet users. Here you can buy collectibles, browse, or just learn about the kinds of things people collect, which is the way people tend behave when attending antiques or collectibles shows.

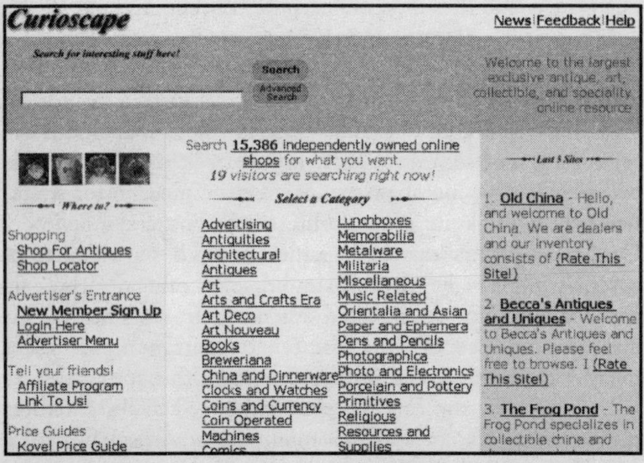

Viewers can locate specific items of interest by using the search engine at the top of each page or by browsing through some 30 categories that are arranged in a Yahoo!-like fashion. The categories alone indicate the size of this online bazaar: In addition to standard offerings such as dolls, toys, and glassware, Curioscape features paper and ephemera, vintage clothing, and classic machinery. The Resources category is impressive with subcategories and links to education, publications, price guides, and more. This site can direct you to the National Milk Glass Collectors Society as well as sources for antique Japanese furniture. Under Events you'll find fairs, shows, and swap meets. There are links for new sites, 100 hot sites, classifieds, networking, and contacts. There are also Top 20 Topics and Top 20 Items links, and discussion groups for collectors of almost everything, from sneakers to Barbies and baseball cards to Pez dispensers and Studebakers. Sites that are as broad in scope as Curioscape make one realize that there is an awful lot of stuff in the world—and that each piece of it probably has a potential buyer.

[comics]

Comic Book Resources

● http://www.comicbookresources.com/

Anyone who spends time wondering whether the Spider-man movie is ever going to get made, or who still agonizes over the introduction of another new Robin into the *Batman* series, will find this site as comforting as the Fortress of Solitude. Comic Book Resources is the ultimate comic book rest stop, covering topics like new characters, hot animators, classic reprints, film versions of comics *(Blade, Spawn, X-Men)*, and industry news from Marvel, DC, and their ilk. There are also links to other comic book sites, including auctions and online sales, as well as downloads of theme songs from TV shows based on comic books. Comic Book Resources is even designed like a comic book (kudos to the webmaster) and has its own online radio station. No offense to the paper and print people, but try getting that out of the pages of your latest newsstand purchase—with or without superpowers.

Grand Comic Book Database

● http://www.comics.org/

Larger than the largest store! Able to search thousands of titles with a single keystroke! Grand Comic Book Database (GCD) is not superhuman but its goal is: to create a database that categorizes information on every comic book ever published. Five years deep, it boasts 30,000 entries and estimates it's 25 percent of the way through the American market. GCD knows there's a long road ahead, but its creators, who claim to have no commercial objectives, are counting on comic fans, hobbyists, and collectors to help generate database content. So if you're trying to figure out what your cryosealed *Lobo's Back* is worth these days, you'll have to go elsewhere. The

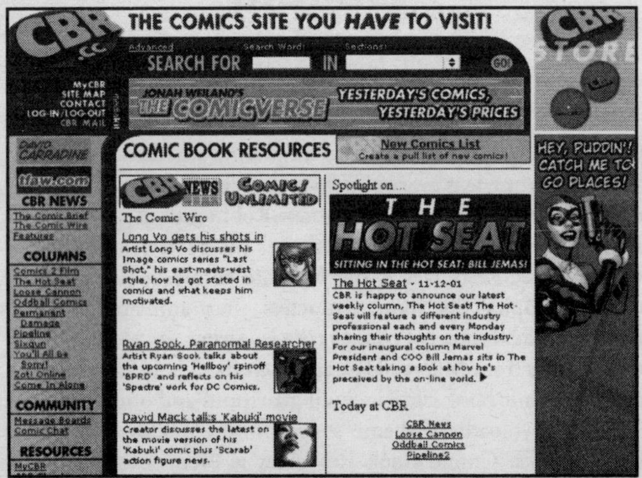

cells in GCD's search engine allow reality dodgers to find comics based primarily on the information you find in the magazine masthead; that is, date, title, publisher, writer, and artists. You can even search by character appearance. Excelsior!

[dance]

Dance Directory
Sapphire Swan Dance Directory

● http://www.sapphireswan.com/dance/

Clogging, Chinese dance, English country, Greek and Irish dance, and zydeco. That's just a small sampling of the dance styles included in the substantive Sapphire Swan Dance Directory. An index under Dance Styles is where you'll find links for countless web-based dance genres and resources. The Other Dance Links section lists books, schools, job links, and regional guides for those who take their dance more seriously.

Dance Links

● http://www.dancer.com/dance-links/

This exhaustive directory of dance links will make your head swirl more than Ginger Rogers's gowns did when she danced with Fred Astaire. Fancy footwork in all its permutations is covered here: ballet and modern dance companies; resources for flamenco, tap, and jazz; performance listings (with a link to Ticketmaster); dance publications; dance organizations; university dance; dance schools; and dancers' pages. Clicking on any one of these hyperlink categories will waltz you to an abundance of links to trip the light fantastic around the world.

Cyberdance

● http://www.cyberdance.org/

Events, auditions, competitions, research, newsgroups, bulletin boards, chat lines, articles, magazines—if it relates to dance news, you'll probably find a link to it on Cyberdance. This single page has more than 3,500 links to dance news and information, making this dance directory a must-visit for dancers. Those who can't—or won't—dance but like to watch can find a number of dance performance links for cities across the country.

Ballroom Dance Resource

● http://www.ballroomdancers.com/

This site makes your computer a dancing machine, courtesy of its dance lessons, which feature waltz, foxtrot, Latin dances, and swing and hustle variations. Each lesson includes links to a history overview, basic figures with detailed instruction, video clips, and other dances. Now you have absolutely no excuse not to get out there and cut a rug next Saturday night.

This is one of the best sites in the dance category; it's interesting to look at, learn from, and, well, dance around. Its wide range of categories include a Dance Lesson of the Month, technical tips, glossaries, resources, dance partner search ads, links to other sites, costumes for sale, clubs and teams, and more. Shall we dance?

Competitive Dance
Dancescape

● http://www.dancescape.com/info/index.html

Dancescape treats competitive dancing seriously. It is an information center that covers competitive ballroom dancing as well as dancing as a sport. And there's a lot to report: news on dance competitions around the world, calendars of events, organizations, business directories, personals, shopping, and much more.

Country Music Dance Network

● http://www.cmdn.net/

Those who like to do their stepping out on wood floors scattered with hay will find data aplenty at the Country Music Dance Network. The self-proclaimed "Best Country Dance Site on the Internet" has a depth of information more common to scientific sites than to those devoted to nighttime pastimes. Country-western dance enthusiasts will find dance news, events, resources, and chat areas as well as a directory of featured dancers and musicians.

The site search engine allows booted barroom dancers to search by type of dance, steps, counts, dance level (beginner, advanced, etc.), and artist name. Dance lessons are—need we say—of the step-by-step variety and include counts, number of steps, the choreographer's name, and suggested music. Dance terms are defined, and there is info on floor etiquette, most requested dances, concerts, and world events; plus there are classifieds, trivia, and a weekly list of top 20 music hits. A free subscription to the site's newsletter—published twice a month—is available for delivery online or via snail mail. As far as we're concerned, if country dancers can't find it here, it isn't on the Net.

Tap Dance
Tap Dance Homepage

● http://www.tapdance.org/tap/taphome.htm

The toe-tapping world of Jelly Roll Morton, Bill "Mr. Bojangles" Robinson, and Savion Glover comes alive at the Tap Dance Homepage. Tap into this site for a wealth of information and resources for dancers and fans. Divided into Events, Reference, and Support, the site covers tap steps, places to tap, and tap in film. Online video and audio clips are available, along with a calendar, history, associations, news, and supplies sections.

Tap steps are "typed out" as notational diagrams adapted for display on the Net, so you can learn them on your own. Then, to see how it's really done, go to the Sight & Sounds of Tap section and download short recordings of tap dancers.

[food and beverages]

Beverages Direct

● http://www.beveragesdirect.com/

Having trouble finding Reed's Spiced Apple Jamaican Style Ginger Brew? Craving O'ssipi Vanilla Cream and can't find it in your local supermarket? Beverage Direct is on the case—so to speak—to enable you to stock up on those hard-to-find nonalcoholic beverages.

The site is divided into Products, Recent Arrivals, Product Search, Customer Service, Shopping Basket, and Checkout, among other categories. You can search for your favorite libation by category or by keyword, then order online, by fax, or by phone. If you want to be on top of the latest and greatest liquid refreshments, you can track new beverages by visiting the Recent Arrivals section, where there are photos and descriptions of new items in stock. And if you don't find your drink of choice anywhere on the site, e-mail the company and it'll try to find it for you.

Beer
Beer Info Source

● http://www.beerinfo.com/vlib/contents.html

There is enough information about beer, breweries, homebrewing, and beer-related organizations and publications on this site to herniate a Clydesdale. Want to find Tsingtao Beer's website?

Listed here. Beer festivals in Kentucky? Listed and linked here. The two dozen categories on this page cover the obvious and even the obscure, with links to beer-related screensavers, distributor websites, beer-of-the-month clubs, and beer-by-mail offerings. From the search page enter any word, say, "Budweiser" or "barley," to receive lists of sites or articles containing your search term. Incidentally, the Beer Info Source is part of the WWW Virtual Library Project; this site was developed by John Lock, who works—ironically—for a soft drink company.

Center for Food Safety & Applied Nutrition

● http://vm.cfsan.fda.gov/list.html

If you have concerns about food safety or want to know how the government compiles information about food and nutrition, this is the place. The Federal Drug Administration (FDA) maintains this website for the Center for Food Safety and Applied Nutrition. The site is a comprehensive information resource for consumers, industry, and health professionals. Facts about food safety and nutrition, cosmetics, and even imports and exports are included. There is a search engine (by title and keyword), a question and answer page, and an online help desk with links to other sites. The site is full of information about every aspect of food, nutrition, and cosmetics. Food safety programs, FDA documents, and current news stories are also featured.

Chocolate
The Chocolate Alliance

● http://www.chocolate-alliance.com/

If you are a chocoholic who needs to share your passion, why not join The Chocolate Alliance, a club where members can indulge, communally, in "all aspects of the chocolate experience?" Membership is free, so leave your guilt offline while you explore the history of chocolate and info on growing beans; read through books and magazines; buy products and supplies direct; peruse recipes, classifieds, news, and events (such as a chocolate festival in Perugia, Italy); and learn how chocolate affects your health and how to take care of your chocolate.

Cocktails
Cocktail Club International

● http://www.cocktailclub.com/main.shtml

You know this is a site for the serious cocktail set from its subtitle, which reads, "Please don't drink and drive. Go home. Get drunk." There is a blenderful of data here for the casual tippler and the pro alike. Using the search engine, you can get a recipe for whatever you're in the mood for—or for whatever you happen to have in the kitchen. Just plug in your alcohol of choice, as well as the brand and any other comestibles you might have around. We plugged in "vodka," "Absolut," and "pepper" and were rewarded with a recipe for this Cajun martini: 1 oz. Absolut Peppar Vodka, 1 oz. Absolut Citron Vodka, 1 dash hot-pepper sauce, 1 olive, and a hot pepper sliver (no seeds). Pour Absolut Peppar Vodka and Absolut Citron Vodka into shaker with ice and shake. Pour into martini glass, add olive and pepper sliver, and float hot-pepper sauce.

There are hundreds of other delectable cocktails to be found here, sure to satisfy all tastes. You can also get nonalcoholic drink recipes, look up definitions in the Drink Dictionary, visit the online store to buy goodies, join a discussion group, or send a CocktailMail to a pal. Best of all, you can send an eDrink to a friend, including a drink recipe and the cuddly message of your choice (such as "You, me, and *Melrose Place*!"). Bottoms up!

Coffee
I Need Coffee

● http://www.ineedcoffee.com/

Connoisseurs will tell you that drinking coffee is not a vice, but a necessity. Catering to that attitude is the I Need Coffee site, where you can learn to perfect your coffee-brewing technique, roast your own beans, use a French press, and pull the perfect shot of espresso. Then, while sipping that perfect cup of java, you can contemplate the history of coffee, check out one of several tutorials, read articles, and peruse recipes, or read through editorial columns and essays that explore the rich, full blend of coffee-related writing, from fiction to research to whimsical opinion pieces. And if you need more, go to the site's directory for an impressive list of other Internet coffee resources with brief descriptions of what is offered: roasters, cafes, publications, merchandise (such as coffee jelly here—who knew?), plus equipment links to manufacturers and sellers.

If you're involved in the coffee industry—or just can't get enough coffee info—you may also want to stop by the National Coffee Association at http://www.ncausa.org/.

Exploratorium: The Sweet Lure of Chocolate

● http://www.exploratorium.edu/exploring/exploring_chocolate/index.html

Chocolate is more than a food but less than a drug for many people, and the Exploratorium explores the passion, the history, and the science of chocolate. This cool educational site will intrigue chocolate lovers of all ages. It includes a video tour of a chocolate factory that would make Willy Wonka salivate, audio presentations from chocolate "experts," and articles on everything chocolate (audio and video require RealPlayer). You can either move through the site as you read a book, page by page, or select

Exploring Online. Be sure to check out the Bibliography page for links to a variety of helpful and occasionally unusual chocolate sites.

Tea
The Tea Council

● http://www.teacouncil.co.uk

A few hundred years ago, Americans unceremoniously tossed British tea off of ships in Boston Harbor. The effort waterlogged the tea, presumably making it worthless. The Brits, unfazed, remarked that it would still be strong enough for Americans to drink. But Americans by and large stopped drinking tea, opting instead for an even more watered-down version of tea's competitor, coffee.

Times have changed. The popularity of tea, especially in America, is on the rise. There are now more than 1,500 teas in the world, from green and black to Darjeeling and Earl Grey. This British site explores every aspect of the leafy drink, including the history of tea, the pairing of tea with food, teas around the world, how tea is made, and tea and health. It also features an online directory, which lists a gargantuan number of companies in

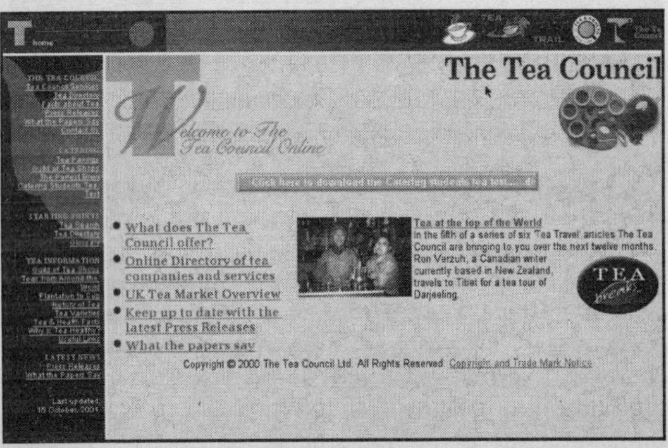

the tea trade, including blenders and packers, importers and exporters, brokers and traders, tea gardens and agents, and many more. We're not ones to make predictions, but our tea leaves tell us that this site should provide enough inspired reading and information to float any tea lover's boat. Even if it's in Boston Harbor.

Wine
Wine Spectator

● http://www.winespectator.com/

"Remember when 'red with meat, white with fish' was all you needed to know? It's no longer so simple. Food and wine today are more complex than ever before, and so are the variables associated with pairing them. That said, it is possible to

recommend a range of wines that are likely to work with a given type of food, and that's what we've done here." So promises the Wine Spectator, the site for hard-core oenophiles. Industry News will keep you up to date on controversial wine laws and bills, wine ratings will help you make your next purchase, and winery and wine-country travel info will help you incorporate your love for the grape into your next vacation.

Most visitors to the site, however, will use the search capability to find recommendations for the right wine to go with salmon, steak, or the ubiquitous Thanksgiving turkey. You can either enter the food you're serving to retrieve an appropriate list of wines, or pick a wine and get a list of complementary entrees. Complete dinner menus are also included here, making this a comprehensive site for everyone who enjoys wine.

[gossip]

E!-online

● http://www.eonline.com/

From the diary of Madonna's baby to the truth behind nude celebs on the web to famous feuds to the salaciously sniping "The Awful Truth," it seems that there is a never ending stew (spew?) of information to wade through at this site. This whole thing oozes gossip. And we do mean ooze. Putatively a media sister to the E! cable channel, this site purports to give you an inside look at Hollywood. This is easily one of the most jam-packed sites that you'll come across on the web, with two dozen stories and news roundups on the front page alone. Navigate at your own risk; you may never dig your way out.

The New York Post

● http://www.nypostonline.com/gossip/gossip.htm

Americans have a bizarre love of celebrity gossip, and nowhere does it reach a higher level of social import than in New York. Most New York papers peddle dirt, secrets, and plain old innuendo, but *The New York Post* reigns supreme. The paper's website offers its famous `Page Six` column, which is one of the only gossip columns that celebs check to make sure they're covered. The site is rounded out by two other gossip mongers, Neal Travis and the antediluvian Liz Smith.

[horror]

Horror is a concept, an emotion, something that inspires fear, dread, repulsion—and often nervous laughter. Its manifestations range from the eerie and shocking real events of the world around us to pop culture screamfests in the guise of movies and books.

On the Net, horror takes every form imaginable and, trust us, some forms unimaginable. There are horror sites designed to entertain (much like movies), but there are also sites meant to horrify simply by pushing the audacity level to its limits, in the hope that visitors will react with revulsion—or perhaps with voyeuristic thrill.

The sites in our horror category cover everything you can expect to find on the Net, from the entertaining to the excruciating. We give ample warning signs along the way (one of the reasons these sites made our list), so pay attention. As with the haunted house on the dark hill outside of town, don't turn the doorknob unless you're prepared to go in.

The Asylum Eclectica

● http://asylumeclectica.com/

For anybody, and we do mean anybody, made squeamish by the horrors that can be part of real life, we advise you to skip this site and head over to someplace safe, like Disney.com. Asylum Eclectica is the ultimate location for horror of the truly creepy, eerie, and unspeakable kind. The opening page beckons you

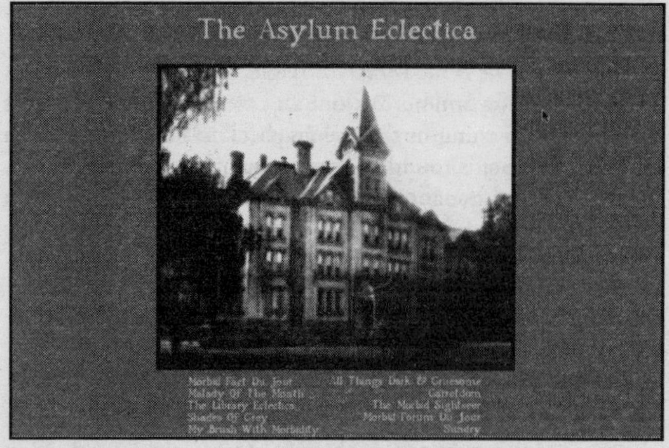

with an illustration of an old asylum, then warns you away with posters that look as if they were stolen from the carnival of the absurd.

Ten primary categories are all twisted in their own peculiar ways. All Things Dark and Gruesome leads you to sites of the medical mutation, autopsy, and postmortem kind. This section is not recommended for the faint of heart, the overly pious, the easily upset—or the easily irritated. Reciprocal Links is a list of strange sites that share the same ethos of darkness as Asylum Eclectica does, be it animated skull gifts or morbid photography. Finally, Sundry leads you to some literary and photographic self-indulgence on the part of the webmaster.

Asylum Eclectica presumes that all things horrible are fair game for inclusion, be they in writing, photography, news, or factoids. Despite the luridness of much of this site's content, it is often hard to turn away.

Gothic.net

● http://www.gothic.net/

Gothic.net is a hybrid horror 'zine and guide to gothic resources on the web. Boasting impressive graphics culled from Egyptian mythology, the site uses hieroglyphs as icons to force you to "excavate" for the good stuff. The featured horror writing on Gothic.net is worth a visit each month.

Horror Online

● http://www.horroronline.com/

$ Lon Chaney Jr. metamorphosing into the Wolf Man. A German shepherd metamorphosing into the Thing. John Hurt's chest cavity metamorphosing into the Alien. If these are the kinds of cinematic moments that you live for, then Horror Online is the kind of site that will send chills through your spine.

Serving as a guide to horror and as an entertainment medium, this site covers films, TV, books, and music. There are some 1,200 movie reviews here in a section called the Vault, which not only reviews movies but links the actors in them to other horror movies. The table of contents lists all the data contained on the site, from the *Alien* movies to a review of goth fashions. An events calendar alerts you to dates for upcoming movie, video, and book releases, as well as for horror conventions. You'll also find news sections, features, video clips, feedback, and a place to shop for horror-related merchandise. All of these are interrelated and take the form of reviews, interviews, or stories about a particular offering in the horror genre.

And, of course, there are video clips of classic horror movies, from *The Creature From the Black Lagoon* to *The Wolf Man* to modern classics like *Shocker* and *The Thing*. These are viewable in Flash 5 and Media Player and link directly to the movies'—and the site's—owner, Universal Studios, which can claim a lock on a graveyard full of the horror movies released in the twentieth century.

[humor]

Jokes
Demotivation Posters
Despair, Inc.

● http://www.despair.com/

[$] How's this for inspiration? A beautiful photograph of a lone golf ball on a barren sand dune, accompanied by the statement "Futility: You'll always miss 100 percent of the shots you don't take, and, statistically speaking, 99 percent of the ones you do." Hardly inspiring, we admit, but wickedly honest.

There is something wonderfully dead-on about this site, which ostensibly sells posters and calendars. The humor is a takeoff on much of the empowerment collateral so popular in business these days, and Despair, Inc. targets its audience with

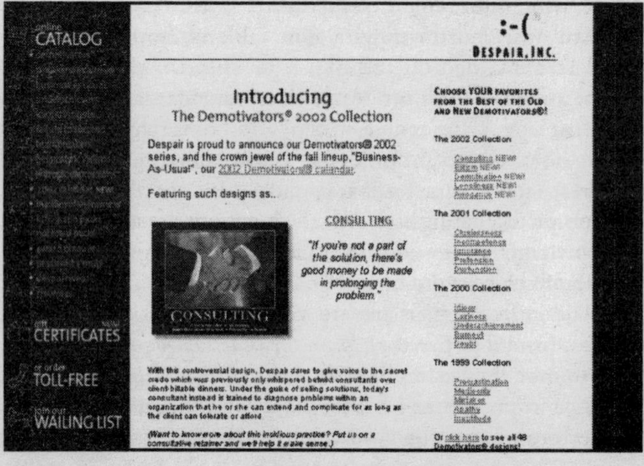

its "revolutionary tools for pessimists, underachievers, and the chronically unsuccessful."

You've seen the originals in card shops or corporate office lobbies: breathtaking scenes of gently rolling hills or waves, punctuated with motivational subheadings like "Persistence: Success Is Measured in Small Steps" or "Focus: Take Time to Visualize Your Dreams." These are all well and good, but you will get more mileage—and more laughter—out of these parodies. You'll find a photo of a runner with his head in her hands and the caption "Failure: When Your Best Just Isn't Good Enough" and our favorite, a striking photo of lightning erupting from a thunderhead with the slogan "Pessimism: Every Dark Cloud Has a Silver Lining, But Lightning Kills Hundreds of People Each Year Who Are Trying to Find It." Brilliant. A faster-loading version of these posters can be found at http://www.cs.wustl.edu/~schmidt/demotivation.html.

The Humor Database

● http://www.humordatabase.com/

This may not rank as the world's most important database, but it could be the funniest. Nowhere else on the web will you find traveling salesmen, blonds, rednecks, politicians, lawyers, Monica Lewinsky, and Bill Gates all represented on the same site. You can search by 18 different types of jokes, from comedy routines and limericks to "your mama," then by dozens of categories, from blonds and business to religious and tasteless. Then you pick a rating that ever-so-smartly mirrors the motion picture rating code. All these options are activated with pulldown menus, so you know what you're getting into. You can also search by keyword or author.

Users can add their jokes to the list, vote for best and worst, and access ratings based on recent access. For such a huge site, the response time is impressively quick. This site also makes use of split screens so you can keep selecting joke categories in the top section while viewing the results in the bottom section. The site claims it was started as a high school project in 1995. Could be true; it takes a real high school sense of humor to create something this outrageously funny.

The Onion

● http://www.theonion.com/

The Onion produces the most consistently funny content on the web today. In the guise of a real newspaper, the Onion takes sharp satiric aim at politics, business, religion, and everyday life. Regular "columns" from a bunch of habitual losers and infographics seemingly culled from *USA Today* only sharpen the jabs. The paper version of this site is a staple of college campuses, which is about the only place you can find it. Thus the web version has created interest in the publication outside the hallowed halls of academia, much to the delight of people who remember when *National Lampoon* was actually funny.

The overall site is well laid out, using a lot of doctored color photos and phony charts. Jump-back buttons take the reader directly back to the main headlines for any given issue. Though loading time can occasionally be a problem, especially with big

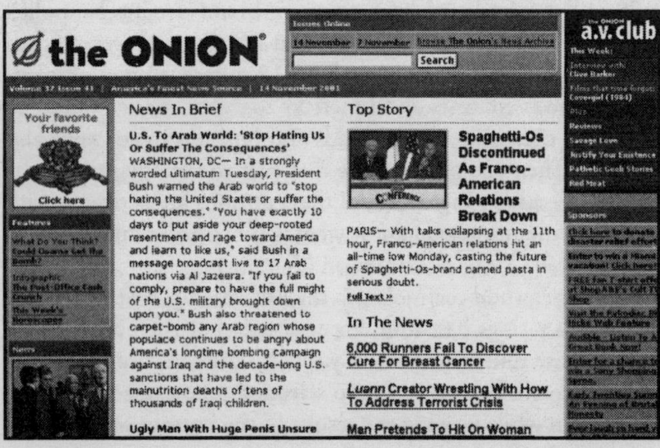

the ONION®

Search

a.v. club

Your favorite friends

Click here

News In Brief

U.S. To Arab World: 'Stop Hating Us Or Suffer The Consequences'

WASHINGTON, DC— In a strongly worded ultimatum Tuesday, President Bush warned the Arab world to "stop hating the United States or suffer the consequences." "You have exactly 10 days to put aside your deep-rooted resentment and rage toward America and learn to like us," said Bush in a message broadcast live to 17 Arab nations via Al Jazeera. "If you fail to comply, prepare to have the full might of the U.S. military brought down upon you." Bush also threatened to carpet-bomb any Arab region whose populace continues to be angry about America's longtime bombing campaign against Iraq and the decade-long U.S. sanctions that have led to the malnutrition deaths of tens of thousands of Iraqi children.

Ugly Man With Huge Penis Unsure

Top Story

Spaghetti-Os Discontinued As Franco-American Relations Break Down

PARIS— With talks collapsing at the 11th hour, Franco-American relations hit an all-time low Monday, casting the future of Spaghetti-Os-brand canned pasta in serious doubt.

Full Text »

In The News

6,000 Runners Fail To Discover Cure For Breast Cancer

Luann Creator Wrestling With How To Address Terrorist Crisis

Man Pretends To Hit On Woman

articles, the results are well worth the wait. New issues are posted every Wednesday, and the four most recent issues are archived. An additional archive site, searchable by topic, guarantees laughs of the decidedly politically incorrect variety.

[magic]

All Magic Guide

● http://www.allmagicguide.com/

Having trouble with your sleight of hand? Need to know how to hide birds, balls, and babes? Then pull this URL out of your hat and spend some quality time delving into the realm of magic. The All Magic Guide seems primarily filled with ads for how-to books and supplies, but do some snooping and you'll find it has quite a bit more up its sleeve. For starters, it's a great place to find tour schedules and club itineraries of popular magicians, and it offers hundreds of links to their personal sites. If you're looking to track down a performer or a trick you've seen, this is the place.

But the real trick to the All Magic Guide is knowing where to find the best stuff, which is nearly hidden—as are all magicians' tricks. You'll need to spend some time here with both eyes wide open. In the Arcade, dozens of routines are explained in detail. You can start out simply, say, with Neato Card Location, or dig deeper to learn other tricks of the trade involving rings, coins, and cup-and-ball illusions. For sleight-of-hand tricks, go to Ask Mr. Magic.

The site also provides a number of resources such as the Conjuror's Lexicon and the Card Encyclopedia, to help you better understand the terms and techniques commonly found in magic books. The Magic Table provides a 3D walk-through of the items on a magician's table; you can magnify, spin, or overturn the items to see where they hide those birds, balls, or babes. Various versions of the history of magic are also available, as well

YAHOO! ALSO LISTS: [magic]

- **http://allmagic.com**
- **http://magictheater.com**
- **http://www.teleport.com/~jrolsen/**
  Hocus Pocus Palace: Site contains two self-playing magic tricks, where the computer is the magician and you are the audience.
- **http://www.magic-interactive.com**
  Magic-Interactive: with games, tricks, history, and more.
- **http://www.truemagic.com/**
  True Magic: covering card magic, close-up magic, magic links, games and tricks, and sites about Houdini and David Copperfield.
- **http://www.linkingpage.com/**
  White Rabbit: the Linking Page-database of magic.

---

as prepublished tips from famous masters including Houdini and T. Nelson Downs. Unfortunately, the site doesn't reveal how to saw your assistant in half, but it does offer sage advice on how to address an audience and why you should avoid copying someone else's act.

[modeling]

Model.net

- http://www.models.net/

Yeah, yeah, yeah, we've heard all the jokes about how modeling isn't really work. We have no first-hand experience—unfortunately—but you try making thong underwear look comfortable while standing in front of a camera crew. Modeling isn't as easy as it looks, which is why so many people who think they should be models aren't. For those who have the right stuff, and you know what we mean, Models Net-

YAHOO! ALSO LISTS: [modeling]

- **http://www.model-online.com/**
  Catwalk
- **http://www.cyberus.ca/~clique/**
  Clique Magazine: eye into the world of professional modeling. Includes information on models, photography, and fashion.
- **http://www.e-model.net**
  e-Model.net: information and resources for aspiring models.
- **http://www.glamourcon.com/**
  Glamourcon:a celebration and marketplace of pin-up art and glamour past, present, and future.

work International's (MNI) Model.net is an online resource for models and prospective models. It features directories of modeling agencies, photographers, and children's modeling agencies, with links to cosmetics companies, fashion events, and magazines and TV networks that regularly employ models. The site has a variety of career-aid components, such as links to magazines, an advice component called HowToModel.com, books, and a fashion-specific search engine.

Individuals looking to get into modeling can join the Model.net's online portfolio (for a fee), which provides page space for pertinent information and photos, as well as a listing in MNI's worldwide directory. A similar service is provided for fashion photographers. Now, there's a job that sounds easy.

Supermodels Online

- http://www.supermodels-online.com/

When Cindy Crawford's name pulls up nearly 30,000 matches on Alta Vista, it's a no-brainer that there is substantial interest in those individuals who make their living as supermodels. To fulfill this interest, plenty of websites are devoted to exploring the topic. The Supermodels Online site is a repository of information about these genetic lottery winners from various media (i.e., magazines, websites). The site keeps tabs on individual super-

models' websites, interviews, and lives in general. There are extensive links to sites for these models, with categories for Latin supermodels, rising stars, and male supermodels. The commercial aspects of supermodeling get their own pages, from magazines to modeling agencies to cosmetics companies and fashion designers. Though the design of the site makes it easy to get lost, depending on your feelings about supermodels, ultimately, you might find yourself in heaven.

[movies]

Buying
Reel.com

● http://www.reel.com/

Looking for the entire *Land Before Time* collection—including those released straight to landfill—on video? How about eclectic, not-stocked-in-stores cult items like *Caligula*? You can get them all in one virtual video store, Reel.com. A gem of a site for movie buffs, Reel.com has a huge inventory of videos, DVDs, and laser discs. And from its attractive, colorful homepages, using a reasonably quick search engine, viewers can find their favorite films with ease or choose from suggested picks from Reel.com's online critics. You can search by title, actor, director, or genre, or plug in your favorite flick and the search engine will find you a list of similar titles you might also like.

How good is Reel.Com? We tested it by plugging in the name of British actor Roger Livesey, a talented but minor film star from the 1940s through the 1960s. Half expecting to receive the usual message "Your search produced no results. Try again," we were delighted to get a list of 11 movie titles, each accompanied by its principal actors, director, date, and length. By clicking on a title, we could read a short synopsis of the story line and find out the price and availability.

Reel.com also features special sales, used videos for sale, and other bargains to attract your attention. You can also read reviews of current movies not yet out on video. In all, Reel.com is the place to go to build your video library.

News
Ain't It Cool News (AICN)

● http://www.aint-it-cool-news.com/

Is Spielberg really doing another World War II flick with Tom Hanks? Is Hollywood serious about making a big-screen version of *Family Affair*? Is the acting really that bad in the yet-to-be-released action flick with Sly Stallone? All the inside scoop can be found at this one small site. Like his cyberworld counterpart Matt Drudge, Harry Knowles has leveraged his Ain't It Cool News (AICN) website into a one-man force of nature. A self-proclaimed geek, Austin-based Knowles started compiling bits and pieces of information about upcoming films and posting them on his website. Before long, actual movie-biz insiders started feeding him prerelease info.

Today his website is both feared and admired by the bigwigs in the movie industry. For example, his negative commentaries on then-unreleased *Batman and Robin* and *Godzilla* are widely cited as having impacted those movies' performance at the box office. And AICN revels in its insouciance. It is a mishmash of information thrown together seemingly at random: reviews, user forums, movie gossip and news, a museum of movie arcana, more movie news, Harry's World (a look at the man and his universe), and some info on videos and DVD. This is the kind of site that defined the Wild West mentality (and we're not talking about the movie) of the earliest do-it-yourself-and-take-on-the-world websites.

IFilm

● http://www.ifilm.com/

Independent film has been on the upswing in recent years, with partial thanks due to advances in technology. Digital cameras and desktop editing software have made filmmaking a more realistic pursuit. And the Internet has made independent film a more widely exposed commodity. To that end, IFilm is the largest online library of feature and short films. Over 80,000 flicks, searchable alphabetically, by genre and by star, are available on demand, with viewer ratings to help you make your selection. For the independent filmmaker, the site is linked to resources such as the Hollywood Creative Directory and Script-Shark. More mainstream offerings, however, include current box-office standings and the always useful movie theater listings, pinpointed by zip code.

The Internet Movie Database (IMDB)

● http://www.imdb.com/

At IMDB you can go from looking up *Star Wars Episode I: The Phantom Menace* to Liam Neeson as Qui-Gon Jinn to *Schindler's List* to Steven Spielberg to *Jaws* to the classic line

"You're going to need a bigger boat" in less time than it takes to read about it. And you can do this on into infinity. Sounds like artificial intelligence, and that's how it began life. The Internet Movie Database may be the best site on the Internet. Period. Regardless of your interest in movies or TV, the IMDB has managed to take full advantage of the capabilities of the web in a way that connects you to a seemingly infinite amount of interrelated facts and data using a very straightforward and effective series of links. Plus, it has a nice short URL that you can remember and type in faster than you can bookmark it.

The premise of the site is simple: Everything you need—or would want—to know about movies and television shows is here. With nearly 200,000 titles available, the IMDB is more comprehensive than any number of combined print references you could explore. As mentioned, the site began as an intelligent research project in the United Kingdom and has now become one of the most visited sites on the web.

The IMDB has a straightforward search engine; you just type in the name of either an actor or movie and the site does the rest, opening up multiple universes of possible information gathering (or fun seeking). If you type the name of a movie into the search box, all the data relevant to that movie, and we do mean all, comes up on a single page. Actors, character names, director, shooting locations, trivia, technical credits, gaffes, quotes, budget, awards, costume designer, and on and on and on.

What's more is that these credits are all hyperlinked within the IMDB. Talk about six degrees of separation: If you want someone else's opinion on movies, you can hyperlink to reviews from different magazines, critics, newspapers, and so on to get the "professional" take. In some cases, there are nearly a hundred of these. You'll also find ratings from the users of the site as to how good—or, even better, how bad—these movies are.

The search function is the primary feature of the site, but there are plenty of other components: a box-office monitor, which tracks the top films of the week; a new-release schedule, for theaters and video release; a tasteful update on stars who have

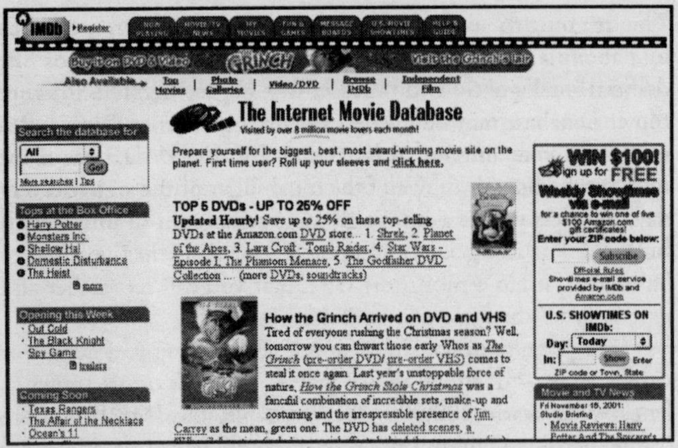

fallen off the media radar screen or are not quite as visible as they used to be (a gentle "where are they now" treatment for performers such as Lee Majors of *The Six Million Dollar Man* and *Big Valley* fame); some translated sites (German, Italian, and French); and a daily update of news from the entertainment business.

Ultimately, one of the most impressive things about this site is its continual updating of both content and design. Someday, when the web can handle the bandwidth, we fully expect this site to offer photos of every actor, as well as movie clips. In the meantime, the IMDB has put together the most impressive and well-organized site we've ever seen. It should be a model for other information-driven sites. Bookmark it, Dano.

UPCOMINGMOVIES.COM

● http://www.upcomingmovies.com/

Want to see into the future? Well, UpcomingMovies.com lets you do just that (almost) with previews of movies that will be released in upcoming months. Previews include information about the cast and crew, as well as plot information and commentary.

The site features a searchable database, and previews are sorted by date, title, director, writer, actor, studio, and genre. The site doesn't focus only on the future, though—it includes a list of top current movies and reviews. Visitors can get a feel for what other people are interested in; the site also provides a list of the most visited previews. With the motto "Tomorrow's Movies Today," UpcomingMovies.com is the perfect site for true movie buffs.

Variety

● http://www.variety.com/

Variety is the bible of the entertainment industry and has been since long before the likes of Leonardo DiCaprio were born. This site offers the daily edition (not to be confused with the weekly update edition), and it contains much of what is in the paper version, notably front-page stories, reviews, and industry news (the area in which the magazine excels). Box-office figures, TV programming concerns, corporate intrigue, and industry execs are also all part and parcel of the content. The casual reader will have to get used to the publication's heavy use of industry jargon, but there are provisions for that: If they need help, visitors can use the site's "slanguage" dictionary.

[music buying]

CDnow

● http://www.cdnow.com/

$ Running all over town trying to find that old Supertramp album on CD or the newest release from Godflesh may be an exercise in futility in a world where music stores stock flavors of the month and best-sellers. Save your bus fare, gas money, or subway tokens—not to mention your sanity—and visit CDnow. This is one of

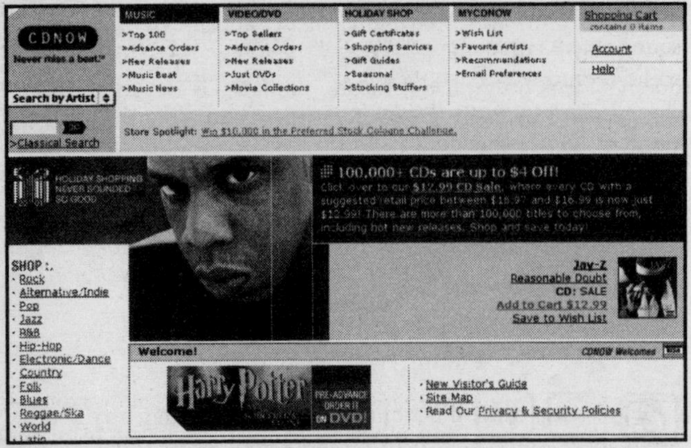

the Internet's largest music retailers, offering a wide range of musical styles and audio formats for music buyers, as well as home videos and DVDs.

The site's homepage has detailed offerings in a variety of music genres, each of which takes you to a page of features, reviews, specials, picks, and news related to that style. There's a new shopper's guide, special reward programs, and My CDnow, which allows registrants to create a musical portrait of themselves so that CDnow can make suggestions according to individual tastes (e.g., "If you like Alice in Chains, you'll love Drain STH"). The site's front-and-center search engine makes it easy to hunt for music by artist, album title, song title, record label, movie title, and actor, in English as well as other languages.

If your musical interests extend beyond purchases, you'll want to link to informational sites such as *Billboard* magazine and MTV, as well as to the respected all-star Daily Music News reporting service. Many artist listings contain near-complete current discographies, as well as import CDs, and many CD listings offer the chance to hear snippets of tracks from the album.

CDnow is more than happy to help fulfill your gift-giving needs, too, with gift guides and gift suggestions. Music recommendations are also offered from the site's editors so you can sound track your "grooving '70s party" or your "seduction scene"—and, yes, Barry White is recommended.

Other sites with the same motif, and commercial motivation, as CDnow include CDuniverse (www.cduniverse.com/), Music Boulevard (www.musicboulevard.com/), and even the big stores themselves, including Virgin (www.virginmega.com/).

Make Your Own
Mp3.com

● http://www.mp3.com/

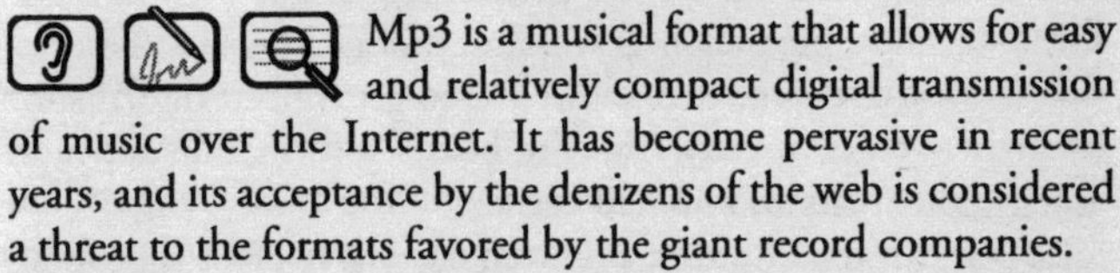

Mp3 is a musical format that allows for easy and relatively compact digital transmission of music over the Internet. It has become pervasive in recent years, and its acceptance by the denizens of the web is considered a threat to the formats favored by the giant record companies.

Mp3.com boasts of being the "ultimate source for digital music downloaded from the Internet," but what's most impressive about the site is its efforts to educate and inform the world about the resources and technology behind the music it offers.

The site's homepage offers just as many links to hardware, software, and Mp3-related news as it does to the music itself. More than 100,000 downloadable songs are grouped by genre, artist, and region, and a search engine allows you to search by those variables as well as by software, song, or news. The site also provides extensive resources for artists who want to sign up and make their music available.

As in the "real world," Mp3.com has created its own charts and popularity sections for the music it offers. Every Thursday, the site posts its Top 40 lists of songs, genres, and artists by position and number of weeks on the chart. Music on the Top 40 in recent weeks ranged from that of ex-Byrds frontman Roger McGuinn to environmental soundscape artists Ghost in the Machine to a performance of Chopin's Prelude #13.

But if compressed music just isn't your thing, there are other incentives to visiting this site: You can hear a 45-minute summary of daily news from the *New York Times* or, if that bums you out, opt for sketches from a number of featured comics.

Pollstar—The Concert Wire

● http://www.pollstar.com/

Pollstar is the trade magazine for the concert industry, but its website provides a wealth of information on live performances that both fans and music-business professionals will find useful. The site's best feature is a search engine that allows you to get concert information by artist, venue, or city (the site boasts information on more than 3,000 artists and 30,000 events).

You can read features from the current issue of the weekly magazine, as well as news on specific concert tours and artists. Audio samples accompany a profile of the week's HotStar, while a Top 50 lists the artists whose tour itineraries are most requested on the site. Under any listing, a click on the city will bring up a list of all upcoming concerts there; a click on the venue does the same by concert hall. Gigs & Bytes provides music news, with embedded links from and about the Internet, while the Gossip page shares bits of inside dope on artists and tours.

Finally, a Hyperlinks page connects you to other music-industry resources, under headings such as the Agents, the Promoters, the Radio, and the Record Labels. *Pollstar* is an invaluable resource for anyone who regularly gets out to see and hear live music performances.

[music genres]

Blues
The Blue Highway

● http://www.thebluehighway.com/

Reportedly, all the old bluesmen had hellhounds on their tails and were always expecting to meet Satan at the crossroads as comeuppance for living lives filled with wicked women, whiskey, and wild times. For a more well-rounded look at the blues—one of America's greatest indigenous forms of music—and its history, set out for the Blue Highway. A real labor of love, this is the ultimate guide to the blues on the web. It's filled with biographies of great bluesmen like Robert Johnson, B.B. King, and Muddy Waters and articles on the evolution of the blues.

To sample the blues emanating from New Orleans to Chicago, access the site's huge archive of sound files, radio broadcasts, and record-label samplers. Then share your thoughts on message boards, or in the chat room named Muddy's Cabin.

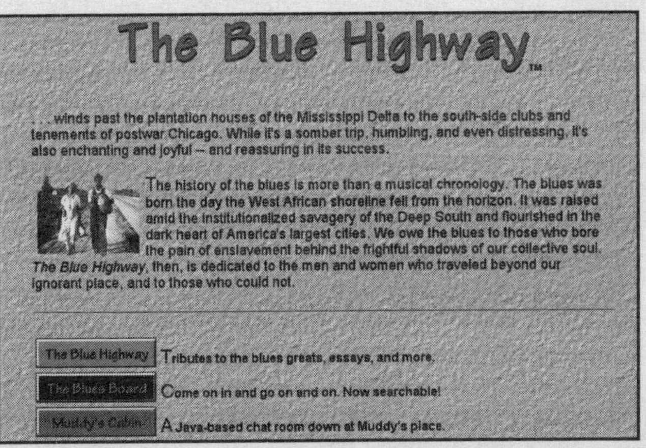

The Blue Highway™
. . . winds past the plantation houses of the Mississippi Delta to the south-side clubs and tenements of postwar Chicago. While it's a somber trip, humbling, and even distressing, it's also enchanting and joyful – and reassuring in its success.
The history of the blues is more than a musical chronology. The blues was born the day the West African shoreline fell from the horizon. It was raised amid the institutionalized savagery of the Deep South and flourished in the dark heart of America's largest cities. We owe the blues to those who bore the pain of enslavement behind the frightful shadows of our collective soul. The Blue Highway, then, is dedicated to the men and women who traveled beyond our ignorant place, and to those who could not.
The Blue Highway
Tributes to the blues greats, essays, and more.
The Blues Board
Come on in and go on and on. Now searchable!
Muddy's Cabin
A Java-based chat room down at Muddy's place.

And don't forget to scour the listings of blues-oriented radio shows around the country and check out the shopping section and numerous links.

The developers of this site have created an essential roadhouse on the information superhighway for blues lovers the world over. In fact, the Blue Highway has been awarded the Blues Foundation's "Keeping the Blues Alive Award" for blues on the Internet.

Classical
Classical Net

● http://www.classical.net/

Classical Net does not only cater to classical music lovers; it encourages the uninitiated too: "Though classical music appeals to many people, the diversity, complexity and even the mystique of 'Classical Music' can be rather intimidating. Granted, there is much to know and much to learn concerning this music, but the encouraging thing about this art form is that you can enjoy what you are hearing without knowing exactly why."

Classical Net is dedicated to sharing this genre of music with novices, as well as to serving as a resource for more knowledgeable listeners. A beginners' section explains the difference between the periods such as baroque and classical and presents a huge directory of recommended recordings to get newbies started (starred selections are considered part of the "basic repertoire" that every classical music lover should own). The site also has extensive appendixes on composers, opera, classical labels, mail-order catalogs, and societies, plus plenty of links and instructions on how to build a CD collection.

Ethnic/World Music
International Music Archives

● http://www.eyeneer.com/World/index.html

Not so long ago, to Americans, world music was something that musicians such as Peter Gabriel and Paul Simon played. They had little or no experience with music outside of Europe or the Americas, so the forays of these pop stars into African rhythms seemed daring and alien. In fact, these artists were simply incorporating music that the rest of the world was already familiar with.

Now that Americans have started listening to world music in earnest (*world music* being a term that incorporates anything outside our national boundaries, it seems), there is huge demand for new and ever more intriguing sounds. The International Music Archives meets that demand by creating an "educational resource providing extensive information about the music of our planet." The site provides fascinating and well-researched information on the music of distant cultures by offering four ways to look for data: via Music of the World, Instruments of the World, Profiles of Artists, and What's New.

Music of the World leads to six geographic categories: Africa, North Africa/West Africa, East Asia, South Asia, Southeast Asia, and Europe. Each of those leads to a page describing the music of the area with photographs. Instruments of the World has instrument descriptions for four regions: Africa, East Asia, South Asia, and the Americas, with photographs and sound files for many, including the Laotian mouth-organ, a bizarre-looking collection of wooden tubes and gourds that sounds, well, just like an organ. Profiles include biographies of a handful of internationally known musicians, such as the Master Musicians of Jajouka and Ravi Shankar, with links to related sites. What's New leads you to current events in the music world from around the globe.

Industrial
Industrial Nation

● http://www.industrialnation.com/

Two pile drivers making love during a car wreck—forever; that's the sound of industrial music. It throbs with mechanical and metallic rhythms that mirror the cold feel of machines. Those who appreciate music as an assault weapon will be drawn to this site, which houses data on all aspects of industrial music and links to several hundred band sites, from Godflesh to Pitchshifter to Nine Inch Nails, as well as to industrial labels like Earache and Metal Blade. News, tour dates, radio stations with industrial playlists, online broadcasts and listening sources, and 'zines are also listed. Let the doom begin.

Jazz
Jazz Online

● http://www.jazzonline.com/

Predominantly a series of album recommendations, Jazz Online surveys strong new releases from a variety of jazz and jazzlike musicians. Most of the albums are new or recently remastered and—surprise!—available at Amazon.com. Selected records, such as those found in Hot Picks, are described glowingly and accompanied by cover art, plus biographies, interview-based pieces, or track listings. Any review, artist Q&A, or article that has been featured on the Jazz Online site is searchable in the site's database.

The Jazz Online developers make it their business to educate music fans about their genre. Ask the site's expert, the Jazz Messenger, about an artist and he'll give a brief historic overview, plug a few key albums, and sometimes even play you a clip. Jazz 101 contains helpful information about various jazz styles and their leading proponents, and the Starter Kit is a discography of some 45 high-profile jazz albums that newcomers should appreciate from the first track. Hard-core jazzers may want to look for sites on their faves (among hundreds for Miles Davis, John Coltrane, Dizzy Gillespie, and the like), but Jazz Online is a good place to check for reviews and some general information on hand-picked new releases.

Metal
BNR Metal Pages

● http://welcome.to/bnrmetal

How many notable heavy metal bands have there been since Black Sabbath and Led Zeppelin created the genre in 1969? Would you guess 30, 40, 50, maybe 100? Try thousands (you must have forgotten about Ministry, Misery Loves Company, My Dying Bride, and many others). Many of them are profiled on the BNR Metal Pages. Created by a head-banging college student—who states with abandon that over 70 billion people have accessed his pages since they were created in 1962—this witty site is essentially a massive musical database. Each metal act gets a capsule biography and discography, plus member lists and links. The site also features a variety of top ten lists as compiled by the webmaster, including best metal albums. Anyone with a fondness for listening to skull-crushing riffs and using such terms as *thrash, speed, death,* and *heavy* will find silent solace at this site. Metal health, indeed.

Opera
OperaBase

● http://www.operabase.com/

Consider this site "opera central," as it contains enough information to fill the girdle of a 300-pound mezzo-soprano. In other words, this category-killer site marks the end of your web-based opera searching (or, to paraphrase Yogi Berra, "the fat lady has sung"). Included on OperaBase are several powerful search engines that dig through vast archives, notably a database of 40,000 opera performances (use any combination of date, composer, title, location). Another database locates schedules for singers, roles, conductors, and composers; and still another is a includes 500 opera houses and festivals. No matter where you are or where you might be traveling, OperaBase will help you locate performances of the operas you love.

OperaBase brings down the curtain with hundreds of links,

articles, discographies, reviews, and more. And a section on opera history will help you expand your knowledge. This site, offered in seven languages, is essential viewing for opera buffs everywhere, and you don't need to bring your opera glasses.

OperaGlass

● http://rick.stanford.edu/opera/main.html

OperaGlass is "an opera information server on the World Wide Web." It includes detailed information on more than 1,400 composers, 250 operas, and numerous librettists. There are also links to synopses, librettos, discographies, reviews, opera companies, calendars of events, pictures, and more.

For true aficionados, OperaGlass presents the librettos in the original language. So if you're trying to figure out what Ramades is saying to Aida in Act 4 of Verdi's famous opera, you'd better be fluent in Italian—or head over to Babelfish (see our review under TRANSLATIONS).

Rap

Original Hip-Hop Lyrics Archive

● http://www.ohhla.com/index.htm

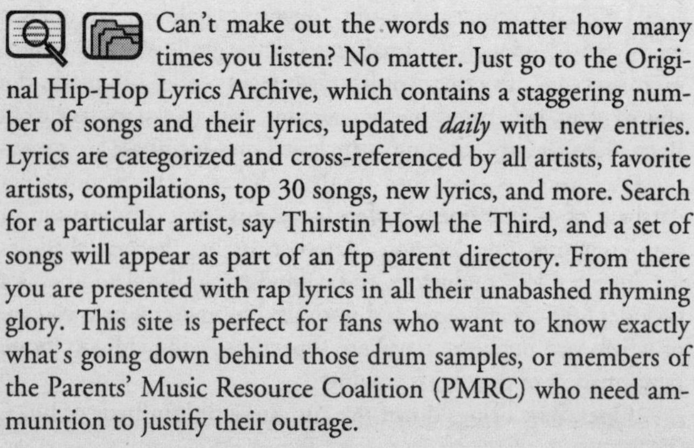

Can't make out the words no matter how many times you listen? No matter. Just go to the Original Hip-Hop Lyrics Archive, which contains a staggering number of songs and their lyrics, updated *daily* with new entries. Lyrics are categorized and cross-referenced by all artists, favorite artists, compilations, top 30 songs, new lyrics, and more. Search for a particular artist, say Thirstin Howl the Third, and a set of songs will appear as part of an ftp parent directory. From there you are presented with rap lyrics in all their unabashed rhyming glory. This site is perfect for fans who want to know exactly what's going down behind those drum samples, or members of the Parents' Music Resource Coalition (PMRC) who need ammunition to justify their outrage.

Rock and Pop

History of Rock 'n' Roll

● http://www.history-of-rock.com/

Rock 'n' roll was created by a host of people influenced by a variety of musical genres, including the blues and New Orleans jazz. But did you know that a lot of the earliest rock 'n' roll was produced in a building in midtown Manhattan where songwriters were paid to sit at desks and pianos and churn out hits? Tidbits like this can be found at the History of Rock 'n' Roll, a site devoted to the first decade of "the devil's music," from 1954 to '63. The site gives a good overview of the genre's early days, with a lot of space devoted to black spirituals, European folk music, blues, jazz, and gospel. The site nicely documents how rock grew into a distinctly American blend of musical and cultural influences. But there's no denying the irony when you read that a black rhythm and blues artist in the late 1940s might record a song only to have a white artist cut a similar version a few years later and have it called "rock 'n' roll."

The site features a section on the electric guitar and the early guitar "heroes." The "essential listening" guide to early musicians and recordings that are worth seeking out covers such important early events as rockabilly, the '50s instrumental wave, Brill Building pop, and girl groups like the Supremes and Martha & the Vandellas. Anyone who thinks that rock 'n' roll was thrust into the world pure and fully formed by the likes of the Beatles and the Rolling Stones would do well to spend some time soaking up the rocking reality offered at this site.

Yahoo! Rock and Pop

● http://music.yahoo.com/rock

Can't remember who sang "Silent Lucidity," that power ballad from a few years back, or the name of the third King Crimson album? Wondering if there's a new Goo Goo Dolls album out? For information on your favorite rock or pop act (or any rock or pop act), this Yahoo! site is a must-stop on the web. You can get reviews, artist news, chart info, feature articles, audio clips, and links to relevant sites (including Yahoo!'s music-related auction pages). You can even tune into Yahoo! Radio to hear hot new artists or "chat" with the star of the week.

To enjoy the site in full, you must become a member, but once in, there are many places to keep music enthusiasts happy for hours. Members can visit artist fan pages (such as Garbage, Jimi Hendrix, Red Hot Chili Peppers, or Smash Mouth) and visit and leave messages in musical Communities that cover electronica, punk, classical, metal, and other genres.

To test the search engine, we plugged in the name of the legendary but somewhat obscure '70s rock band Thin Lizzy (remember their 1976 hit, "The Boys Are Back in Town"?). Amazingly, this Yahoo! site delivered a complete discography for the group. When we clicked on an album title, we were provided with a thorough annotation for the album, a song list, and a detailed listing of the band members and the instruments they played. Suffice it to say, this search engine is powerful and useful, the ideal complement to a comprehensive site for rock and pop music information.

The Knowledge

● http://www.theknowledge.com/

Have you ever heard of Fatboy Slim? How about Dog Toffee? If you love their music (or want to learn more about it), then The Knowledge is the perfect place for you. The site is split into two categories: dance music and alternative music. Each page features information about music news and concerts, the groups and their members, music labels, and reviews. Visitors can shop for merchandise, sign up for special offers and exclusive music news, and read profiles of music acts and albums. They can also customize electronic postcards and flyers to send to their friends. There is even a game to test your knowledge of alternative bands and music. Check out the charts and see where the "music's @!"

[music education]

Datadragon

● http://datadragon.com/education/

Don't know the difference between a bass and a bassoon? Think Van Halen is a popular classical pianist? Don't know a G clef from a G string? Spend half an hour visiting this virtual music school and soon you'll be talking sharps and flats, trumpets and trombones like an amateur musicologist.

The Datadragon "school" begins with a look at the different classes of instruments—woodwinds, percussion, strings, and brass. Clicking on Strings takes you to pictures of the violin, viola, cello, and bass. Click on any one of these produces the sound of that instrument on your computer. Next, the site walks you through the rudiments of music notation, with an introduction to time signatures, notes, rests, and clefs. Then you can explore the differences in styles of music in the Genre Sampler. Jazz, rock, classical, Celtic, country, and blues are all covered, and each includes sound clips and links to popular artists (for example, the Rock area has a downloadable sound clip of Van Halen's "Jump").

The site is designed to appeal to all age groups, so you can teach Junior about Gershwin while Grandma learns more about Stevie Ray Vaughn.

Guitar Galaxy Educational Sites

● http://www.guitar.net/

Back when every kid wanted to be the next Jimmy Page, Eric Clapton, or Jeff Beck, the only way to do it was by playing their records over and over until the grooves wore out.

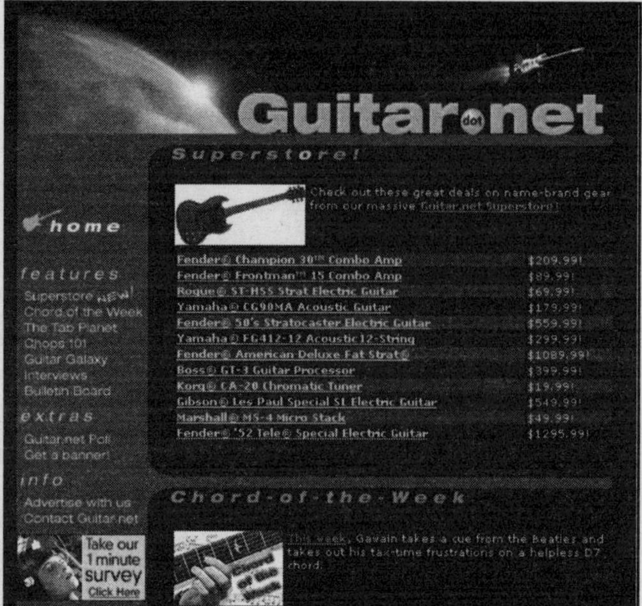

Now there are websites that will teach you how to play like the masters—for free. This component of Guitar Galaxy lists more than 100 sites that offer different types of guitar instruction. You can learn how to read tablature and play power chords or how to develop an acoustic finger-picking style and mimic the fret-burning prowess of Steve Vai, Joe Satriani, or Eddie Van Halen.

Another excellent site for guitar instruction is Guitar.com (http://www.guitar.com/), which also features musician interviews and reviews of guitar music. Those who want to further explore the styles of the guitar greats should check out the Legends of Rock Guitar (http://www.newquist.net/guitarlegends.html).

Stagepass

● http://www.stagepass.com/

The web has a huge number of resource sites that provide musical instruction online or offer books, videos, magazines, and CD-ROMs for sale. Finding them is easy when you use this section of the Stagepass site. This immense page of links will take you to more than two dozen guitar-instruction sites; another two dozen keyboard sites; more than a dozen vocal-instruction pages; seven mandolin sites; a similar number of bass, banjo, and harmonica sites; and several dozen drum sites.

[music equipment]

Harmony Central

● http://www.harmony-central.com/

Are you a "gearhead?" If you don't know what that means, you're probably not. But if you do, you're probably a musician who's really into gear: guitars, amps, keyboards, effects, drums, and every other piece of musical hardware under the sun. Moreover, you can't get enough of it. That's what Harmony Central is counting on. This site is "gear central," covering many new musical instrument products with reviews, press releases, columns, digital-music info, and so on. For example, if you're a guitarist, you can go to the Guitar department, where you will find music tablature to play; software to download (chord finders, tab makers); links to newsgroups, manufacturers, and guitar magazines; and plenty of reviews of brand-spanking-new guitar gear.

Site visitors can write their own reviews and post them online. For instance, you can go to the Fender section, check out the '62 Telecaster Reissue, and read several reviews from people who actually bought this guitar—including how much they paid. Throughout this site are amploads of good and useful information for musicians. We suggest you put Harmony Central in your browser's list of musical favorites right away.

Intermusic

● http://www.intermusic.com/

This one's for the players, not just their listeners. Broken down into equipment categories, Intermusic, a site developed in Britain, is primarily made up of articles on technique and product reviews of guitars, amps, keyboards, drums, and other musical advancements. A quick tour of the site uncovered an interview with former Rolling Stones guitarist Mick Taylor, a review of several electric and acoustic guitars, and such feature stories as "Miking Acoustic Instruments," "Selling Merchandise," and the enticing "Rock & Roll Hotel Guide." You can also join discussion forums or post a classified ad to look for bandmates or sell that ratty old drum set.

[music instruments]

Instrument Encyclopedia

● http://www.si.umich.edu/chico/instrument/

The world of musical instruments is broad indeed: guitar, bass, and drums. Then there is the bouzouki, balalaika, banjo, bassoon, bandore, bass clarinet, and, of course, the bell—and that's just the B's. For more than a soundbite of the universe of instruments, stop in at the Music Heritage Network's Instrument Encyclopedia. This is an enjoyable and intelligent look at musical instruments from every corner of the planet, divided into four categories: Percussion (Idiophones, Membranophones), String (Chordophones), Wind (Aerophones), and Electronic (Electronophones).

Jump to the String section, for example, and you'll see a list of about 20 types of instruments, from guitar and harp to violin and ud. Under Ud (or Oud) is the following annotation: "The ud (or oud) is one of the most important instruments in Arabic and Islamic musical communities. This short necked, fretless instrument is a direct ancestor of the European lute. Its name literally means 'bent twig,' or flexible piece of wood. According to some oral histories, the ud is thought to have been created by a descendent of the biblical figure Cain." Once you've digested this info, you can download a short audio clip to hear what an ud sounds like. Search out other instruments by clicking on a large map of the Earth to find out which musical tools exist in any region. This site plays everyone's kind of tune.

[music news]

Music news used to be an oxymoron. Long considered a stepchild of the Hollywood entertainment business, music got short shrift from magazines and reviewers. Today, with the music business helping to drive the movie business via sound tracks and huge corporate mergers, music now gets plenty of coverage. At last count, there were several dozen music news sites (many of which are part of magazine or newspaper sites), the best of which are reviewed here.

Billboard

● http://www.billboard.com/

Billboard is the music industry bible, the publication that keeps track of what's selling and what's not. This is, of course, not to be confused with what's hot and what's not. *Billboard* is a place you go to get the facts; and unless you're in the biz, that about covers it. At its site you can get the Top 100 album listing from the Billboard 200. Other weekly charts include Top R&B Albums, Top Country Albums, Top Internet Album Sales, and Top Singles in different genres. There is also a news section, an update of new releases, a Top 100 radio broadcast section (in conjunction with Broadcast.com), and some historical data. A membership service is available, which gives subscribers access to the full editorial content as well as archived material.

MTV onLINE

● http://www.mtv.com/news/

MTV revolutionized television—whether you like it or not—so it is no surprise that it was one of the first television channels to become a major presence on the web. From the site's earliest days, it has offered music news and interview clips (transcriptions and video), and it continues to move forward to keep a lock on what's truly hip and what is horrendously uncool.

The site is notable for its use of RealPlayer video news clips, along with a substantial amount of archived news items, both text-based and video-based. The main news section includes Headlines, Music Features, Video Newscast, Music Charts, Cold Storage, and more. Artists featured in the articles are linked to other sections of the site, including the Gallery, which features all the stories that MTV has ever done on that artist, including video excerpts of interviews. The Video Newscast section features MTV interviews, and Cold Storage is an archive of old news and old shows, especially video clips, from the past few years.

The site contains all the music news and video you could want, but you can also find non-news-related items, such as band listings, chats, and so on. And note: There are various links to MTV Xclusives on AOL, an arrangement that makes sense since the guy who runs AOL used to run *MTV*.

[music searches]

The All-Music Guide (AMG)

● http://www.allmusic.com/

How much do you really know about particular bands or their albums? How much do you really want to know? You can put these questions to the test by visiting the All-Music Guide, the definitive site on all things involving recorded music. The paperback edition of this guide is more than 1,000 pages in length, and the site matches that number in bits-and-bytes content. As of this writing, there were 516,168 albums referenced here, 476,373 people mentioned, 51,800 biographies, and 852 music styles. In rock alone, there were more than 203,000 entries, and more than 1,900 comedy albums. Now, that boggles the mind—1,900 comedy albums, that is.

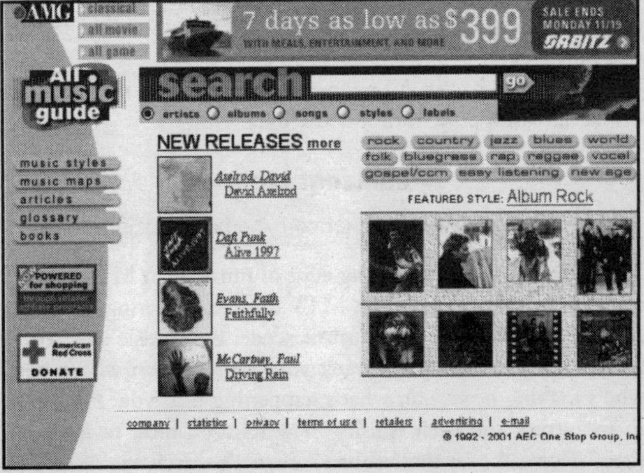

This site takes the notion of six degrees of separation to a whole new level, including links between bands and artists and their style of music and their record labels. A simple search box allows you to explore by artist, album, song, style, or label. Take a band like Black Sabbath: Look them up and you're presented with an entire page of data that looks like a thick government report. You find out they were formed in 1969 in Birmingham, England. Their genre is rock, but they fall under the styles of hard rock, heavy metal, and British metal. Sabbath albums have been released by seven different labels over the years including Warner Bros., IRS, and Castle. And they have a URL link. Then you get a full biography of the band with links to individual member bios. There are "music views" about the band's history, the band's early influences, a list of artists playing similar music (or spun off from the original band), "music maps" that trace the history of music and where Sabbath fits in, a complete discography with ratings and hotlinks to album stats and reviews, compilations on which the band's work has appeared, cover versions by other bands, and a bibliography of books written on the band. On the way out, you can complete a fun survey on the band that is used to help keep the AMG staff up-to-date. And for grins, you can view all this info in French, German, Spanish, Italian, and Portuguese.

AMG also has an All-Classical component to the site, with similar jaw-dropping numbers and data.

sonicnet.com

● http://www.sonicnet.com/home/index.jhtml

No one is more on the cutting edge of music than MTV, so it is no surprise that sonicnet, an MTV-affiliated offering, is on the cutting edge of the Internet music scene. Free music newsletters live up to their name by giving you the scoop on what's new, who's making news, and what's happening near you. Find links to the artists and their music—new releases, bios, reviews, fan sites—from all over the web via sonicnet's search engine. It's all condensed in one place, and it's all about who and what you like. Download music, see videos, enter contests, and don't forget to subscribe to get customized e-mails about *your* favorite artists. Because, after all, there *is* an "I" in music!

[mystery]

MysteryNet

● http://www.mysterynet.com/

Do the names Philip Marlowe, Miss Marple, Hercule Poirot, and Nancy Drew cause you to tremble with the anticipation of pursuing leads in a mysterious crime? Do you always try to beat the finest fictional sleuths before the last page arrives? Do you anxiously await the new book from your favorite mystery author? If so, you'll get caught in the MysteryNet. The Online Mystery Network is an interactive site that encourages frequent visits and participation through interactive whodunits, chat rooms, and communities. Topics and areas of interest include online minimysteries, book reviews, polls, events, and interviews. MysteryNet also entices comebacks by offering of first

YAHOO! ALSO LISTS: [mystery]

- **http://www.overbooked.org/mystpage.html**
  Book Links—Mystery
- **http://www.geocities.com/Athens/5544/**
  Criminal Element, the: annotated guide to mystery fiction sites.
- **http://www.idsonline.com/userweb/cwilson/mystery.htm**
  Mysterious Strands: monthly reviews and links to authors, mystery resources, character-based sites, bookstores, and groups for mystery lovers.
- **http://www.multimania.com/polar/**
  Polar Web: dedicated to mystery literature (in French and English).

chapters from new mystery novels, daily interactive mysteries, profiles of great mystery writers and characters, and TV listings for upcoming mystery-based shows. So tarry no longer. The night is cold and dark, and a dead body has just been found in the old estate on the hill. . . .

[regional]

Yahoo! Get Local

● http://local.yahoo.com/

The boss is sending you on a business trip to Edina, Minnesota. The guys want to make a road trip to see some aging rock band perform at a bar in Port Aransas, Texas. Your family is having a reunion in De Kalb, Illinois. Sounds like you need an Internet guide of local and regional info sites that allow you to quickly check out the goings-on wherever you're going.

Yahoo! Get Local is the most complete source for finding most of what you need in a particular locale. To access it, scroll to the bottom of the Yahoo! homepage. Either click on an individual listing or enter a zip code to get information on a specific locale. The result will be a Local Web Directory, listing Business & Shopping, Health, Community, News & Media, Education, Real Estate, Employment, Recreation & Sports, Entertainment & Arts, Travel & Transportation, and local Yellow Pages. You can drill down into these or use the search box to look for something specific. For instance, under Entertainment & Arts, Restaurants leads to Cuisines, which leads to websites for specific restaurants in the region. You'll also find news, lodging info, and coupons to use locally. A Highlights section links to local movies and their show times, as well as to maps and directions. Below that is a graphic of the day's weather with a link to a five-day forecast. And a Scoreboard gives the stats on sporting events in that city over the past two days. At the very bottom of the page is a list of nearby cities, with links to each. Do you really need any more information?

[restaurants]

How could restaurants and the Internet be compatible? The Internet confines you to your computer; restaurants require you to get out of the house. The Internet is available immediately; at restaurants, you usually need to reserve a table or wait in line. The Internet is about sight and sound; restaurants are about taste and smell. Nevertheless, the fusion has begun.

Thousands of restaurants have websites, most of which describe decor, cuisine, location, and price. These sites give potential diners a chance to check out the bill of fare before sitting down, and usually help restaurateurs generate good mailing lists. Our sample sites address the dining experience from completely different directions. ZagatSurvey gives you the opportunity to plan for an optimum restaurant visit. Until you can get food via modem, this is the only way to integrate dining into your webworld.

ZagatSurvey

● http://www.zagat.com/

In most major cities, the ZagatSurvey (called simply Zagat's) is respected for its no-holds-barred ratings of thousands of restaurants. The guide is based on customer satisfaction as measured by extensive questionnaires, short reviews, and numerical ratings. These are then compiled into a system that ranks restaurants based on food, decor, service, and cost. The Zagat website duplicates many of the features of the guide, and currently contains more than 17,000 reviews in about two dozen cities (the printed guides are available for 40 cities worldwide).

Once you've selected a city, you can search for a restaurant by name or search through Zagat lists titled Top by Food, Top by Service, Top by Neighborhood, and so on. The search results provide the basics on the restaurant, including the part of town it's in, the type of cuisine it serves, and the numerical ratings given in the printed guide. There's more: A more specific search allows you to select restaurants across several categories. Click on the area of town you want, type of cuisine, or time of day, and so on. Your research is then narrowed further by neighborhood, cuisine type, and hours of operation. Once you've made your final selection, the site confirms your request: "I am looking for a restaurant in the East Eighties that serves Hungarian cuisine." The results are then listed alphabetically.

The Zagat site enables you to be more experimental than you can be just consulting the print, because you can mix and match categories to find exactly what you want. That's the beauty of the web. As of this writing, membership to the site is free (you do have to sign up), but Zagat states that it plans to charge in the near future. But you'll get what you pay for in the form of complete reviews with maps, discounts, eligibility to vote for upcoming guides, and more.

[romance]

Romantic Times

● http://www.romantictimes.com/

Torn bodices and corsets, rippling male pectorals; corporate greed, double-crosses, and steamy sex with sultry strangers. Welcome to the world of romance novels—specifically their home on the Net. The Romantic Times—and isn't this what every romance novel promises?—offers a passionate look at the stories, the authors, and the readers who make romance the

● **http://www.geocities.com/Athens/8774/ring.htm**
Romance Reading Ring

most popular form of fiction in America today.

There's so much here, the heart of every romance fan will surely pound. You can search for information on specific books by their authors or—perhaps more important—by their pseudonyms. For example, did you know that shockmeister Dean Koontz is romance novelist Leigh Nichols?

The site also reviews and rates books, then leads you to Barnesandnoble.com if you have to have them right away. Budding romance writers can tap into information on agents, publishers, and manuscript evaluation. Readers can join clubs, spend time in forums, and—not surprisingly—get the between-the-covers story on various cover models, notably Mr. Romance Novel poster boy himself, Fabio. There is a guide to romance booksellers, which includes a section where those booksellers can get tips for increasing store traffic. Rounding out the site is a sizable list of author web pages and profiles, convention schedules, and half a dozen message boards (one of which is a bawdy joke area). Oh, and did we mention that there is an entire section devoted to Fabio *products*? Stop by and swoon away.

[science fiction]

The Sci-Fi Channel

● http://www.scifi.com/

Are you a Trekkie? Space cadet? Jedi wanna-be? Then hop aboard your space shuttle and cruise over to the Sci-Fi Channel's website, which contains news and info for science fiction lovers all over the known galaxy. Along with the network's weekly listings, you can visit pages devoted to specific shows, among them these favorites: the original *Star Trek*, *Quantum Leap*, *Highlander*, *Mystery Science Theater 3000*, and others. The Star Trek page, for example, has news, message boards, crew and cast listings, and episode-by-episode annotations. (For the 1966 episode titled "The Man Trap," the text

reads: "Facing a checkup of isolated research scientists on Planet M113, McCoy is already uneasy about meeting his onetime flame Nancy, now Mrs. Robert Crater. But she and her archeologist husband resent the visit by Kirk's crew, and even more so when a string of murders leaves behind corpses with oddly mottled skin. . . .") Just the kind of detail die-hard sci-fi fans love.

Naturally, there's a store at the site, where you can buy all the merchandised goods that show the world your sci-fi connections. This site makes no apologies for its "geeks only" audience—indeed, according to the Sci-Fi Channel, the geeks will surely inherit the Earth, as well as Mars, Pluto, Venus . . .

Star Trek

● http://www.startrek.com/

There is something symbiotic about the legions of *Star Trek* followers and the Internet. Arguably, the earliest *Star Trek* sites were among the first heavily traveled

(Trekkies also dominated early incarnations by the names of Prodigy and CompuServe and parts of the ARPAnet).

Much has changed for *Star Trek* since the days when Dr. McCoy had to make the professional distinction between being a doctor and a bricklayer. Since its ill-fated beginnings 30 years ago, *The Next Generation*, *Deep Space Nine*, feature films, books, and conferences have ensured that *Star Trek* has continued to go where no man has gone before. Today Paramount Pictures owns the franchise and the official website.

It has a suitably futuristic design, built with frames, with links back to each of the *Star Trek* properties. Everything from episode guides to video clips are here, with categories such as Starfleet Academy, Earth Support, Cast Biographies, Hall of Fame, and others. A site map helps the new visitor traverse all the iterations of the show (this is called a briefing area). An enhanced site, which is viewer-selected and requires various plug-ins, has more bells and whistles—literally—including animated buttons, 3D panoramic views of some pages, and streaming audio. The dedicated Trekkie will find a lot to explore. The only thing missing is a link between William Shatner and Priceline.com.

Those who feel that Paramount has included too many corporate or Borglike overtones can opt to go to TrekList at http://www.treklist.com/ for a fan-driven site that links to roughly 300 *Star Trek* websites. TrekList takes on the entire universe of *Star Trek*, and the links are cross-referenced in categories ranging from fan clubs and conventions to humor.

Star Wars
Your Daily Dose of Star Wars

● http://www.theforce.net/

This just in: Crew members for the prequel-sequel *Star Wars: Episode II* have begun moving to Australia to begin set construction for the new movie. You might not think there'd be enough daily information to fill a *Star Wars* website, but you'd be wrong. In addition to departments devoted to all things *Star Wars*—comics, books, collecting, games, trivia, humor, events, interviews, discussions, and about 20 more—this site has plenty of daily news about what has become the *Star Wars* franchise. You'll get the lowdown on new versions of toys available at fast food chains, be there for the unveiling of new comic books, read announcements of TV and magazine interviews with past and present *Star Wars* stars, and, last but not least, be among the lucky to view movie trailers. This is a serious, almost businesslike site, which belies the source of its content—a sci-fi movie.

[television]

Entertainment Tonight

● http://www.entertainmenttonight.com/

For those who can't get enough of their favorite stars or who missed today's episode of *Entertainment Tonight* on television, there's EntertainmentTonight.com on the internet. The site, aka ETOnline.com, has information about celebrities, music, television, and movies. There are feature articles, movie reviews, Reuters headlines, and top ten lists for TV shows and video sales. Actually, there seem to be top ten lists for everything related to entertainment. There are picture galleries of your favorite stars and even juicy tidbits of gossip about them (e.g., who violated the "no white after Labor Day" rule!). New album, video, and big-screen releases are also featured.

Who wouldn't want the complete *Godfather* series on DVD? Check out the contest area for a chance to win cool prizes like videos, CDs, T-shirts, and posters. The folks at ETOnline seem to care about what you think—there's an area for those over 13 to submit e-mail. There's a search engine, and visitors even have the option to personalize the site. Be careful! The site includes so much information that it is easy to get carried away and miss the real show on television.

Mighty Big TV

● http://www.mightybigtv.com/

Miss an episode of your favorite show? Well, never fear, MightyBigTV.com provides recaps of almost every series (with the exception of half-hour sitcoms) on network television or cable. For those who want a fresh approach to TV programming, MBTV provides a summary of each show along with tongue-in-cheek commentary about everything from the plot to the actors' make-up. From drama *(The West Wing, ER, The Agency)* to reality shows *(The Real World, Survivor, Popstars)*, MBTV lives up to its "Television Without Pity" motto with a take-no-prisoners approach to TV critiques.

The website includes archived recaps of the shows and a forum area for visitors to post notes and comments. Visitors who fill out an information form will be updated via e-mail when new recaps are posted for their favorite shows. Viewers can even grade each episode and see what others think about it. There's a Freebies area with screensavers, computer monitor wallpaper, and electronic greeting cards and a Sound Off! area where polls answer burning TV questions (what *was* the best '80s domestic sitcom?). The Of Interest area includes a FAQ section, along with information about the writers and other miscellaneous items. All in all, MightyBigTV.com is a mighty good place to go for television show recaps and a daily dose of humor.

Sitcoms Online

● http://www.sitcomsonline.com/

Did you know that *Mork & Mindy* was a *Happy Days* spin-off? You do now, and you'll know a lot more TV trivia when you spend quality viewing time at Sitcoms Online. This site contains links to just about every sitcom from

YAHOO! ALSO LISTS: [television]

- **http://www.slip.net/~scmetro/tv.htm**
  Entertainment Network News Television: links to all networks, favorite current and past TV programs, sitcoms, TV industry news, listings, '60s and '70s, and latest TV entertainment news.
- **http://www.teleport.com/~celinec/tv.shtml**
  Internet Television Resource Guide: extensive UsENET list and links to web pages of past and current shows, actors, magazines, plus other TV-related sites.
- **http://www.parrotmedia.com/**
  Parrot Media Network: find contact details, including phone and fax numbers, and lists of leading personnel, for every TV station in the U.S.
- **http://www.geocities.com/Hollywood/9275/television.html**
  Television Links
- **http://www.gebbieinc.com/tvintro.htm**
  Television on the Web: station directory.
- **http://www.thetvshow.com/**
  TheTVshow.com
- **http://www.geocities.com/tokyo/1264/tv.htm**
  TV on the Web: links to networks and cable channels.
- **http://www.tvradioworld.com/**
  TvRadioWorld: worldwide radio and television broadcasting directory.
- **http://www.webovision.com**
  WebOvision
- **http://www.xplore.com/xplore500/medium/television.html**
  Xplore Television: Statistics say most people watch 40 hours a week! Xplore Television has all the best TV sites, from A&E to *The X-Files*, to help you view selectively and intelligently.

---

the 1960s to the '80s, some of them classic hits, others obscure footnotes in TV history. The site itself features in-depth looks at a handful of those shows, including *Happy Days, Mork & Mindy, Please Don't Eat the Daisies, Silver Spoons, The Hogan Family, Different Strokes, Gimme a Break, Courtship of Eddie's Father, Hello Larry*, and *Webster*. The *Mork & Mindy* page, for example, features a complete cast list, an MPEG of the theme song, a collector's guide to memorabilia, and an episode-by-episode breakdown of shows. In addition to other bits of trivia there's an indispensable Where Are They Now Guide for this and all the other shows on this site. You get not only extensive Robin Williams and Pam Dawber filmographies but also detailed info for minor characters like Mindy's dad, Frederick McConnell, played by Conrad Janis, whose acting credits go back to the 1940s. If you need some Internet action to supplement your Nick-at-Nite sitcom cravings, this is the place to do it.

TVBarn

● http://www.tvbarn.com/

Looking for television headlines and news? TVBarn (brainchild of TV critic Aaron Barnhart) has a fresh approach to TV programming guides. Headlines of stories related to television are grouped in two categories: those compiled or written by the TVbarn developers and those compiled by Yahoo! TV. Headlines feature breaking news such as the Top 20 prime-time TV programs and commentary about the "dumbing down" of television. Show hirings and firings are noted, and site visitors have the option of posting their favorite headlines that aren't listed. New articles appear daily and are archived as they become outdated. There is an area devoted to critics and reader mail. The site has no graphics so all Internet users can view its contents easily. There's no eye candy here, but once you get used to that you can focus on the content (and there's lots of it).

TVbroadcasters.com

● http://www.tvbroadcasters.com/

Once upon a time, there were only three television networks in the United States. Today there are nearly 100. Odds are you can't name more than a dozen of them. TVbroadcasters.com, can, and does, from ABC to WTBS, in alphabetical order. This site provides a link to every television network and station website in North America, as well as to many international broadcasters, such as the BBC and Japan's TV Asahi. But even with all those links, you know what? There's still nothing on.

tvtattle

● http://www.tvtattle.com/

Simplicity and thoroughness make tvtattle a boon for anyone seeking television-related news. Defining itself as a "weblog of tv news and criticism," tvtattle manages to cull information from all over the web into an easily digested list of clickable headlines. A clicked headline takes you to the full article on its original site. tvtattle's content runs the gamut from articles about specific shows to those about the nature and quality of television programming in general. Interviews, lineup changes, reviews, even obituaries—if it has to do with television, you'll be able to find it through this site. With new entries every Monday through Friday, it's the one site you'll need for all your up-to-date TV news. And in case you just can't get enough, tvtattle offers an exhaustive list of other entertainment links too.

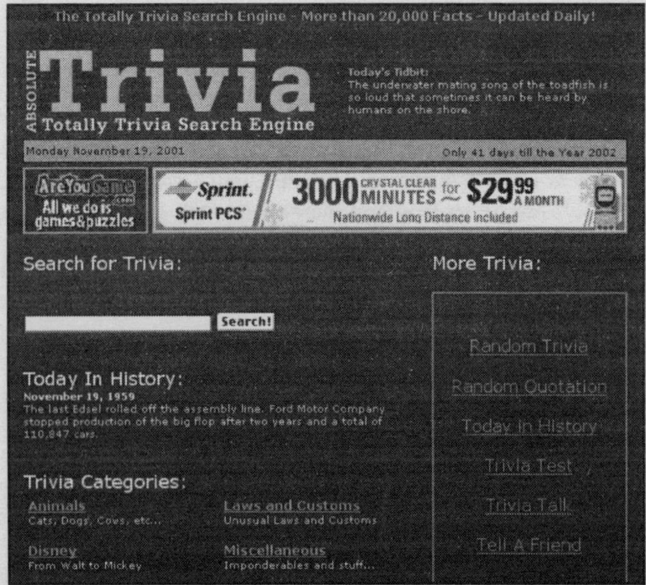

Schedules
TV Guide

● http://www.tvguide.com/

I Love Lucy reruns are on somewhere all the time. You just have to know where. The TV Guide site will make it easier to find. Type in your zip code, and the search engine responds with the name of your local cable carrier. Then type in a date and you get a full schedule matrix of the shows that are on (or available) in your neck of the woods. Each show that appears is hyperlinked, and when you click on it, you get a short description of the show and the times it typically airs. You'll never have to miss another episode of Lucy and Ethel's high jinks.

[trivia]

Absolute Trivia

● http://www.absolutetrivia.com/

Did you know that at the outbreak of World War I, the American Air Force consisted of only 50 men? Or that a bolt of lightning can strike the Earth with a force as great as 100 million volts? Or that Aerosmith's hit "Dude Looks Like a Lady" was written about Vince Neil of Mötley Crüe? Sounds like Absolute Trivia. Clearly intended for cubicle-bound employees with way too much time on their hands and for the truly trivia-addicted this entertaining site is packed full of intriguing, albeit completely useless, information—perfect for the information age websurfer. Lists of trivia are categorized as follows: Entertainment, History, Technology, etc., as well as Trivia in History, Random Trivia, and the highly addictive Trivia Quiz, plus others.

[webcams]

Around The World In 80 Clicks

● http://www.steveweb.com/80clicks/index.htm

This site gives new meaning to the term "armchair traveler." Right now, we're looking at Moscow's Red Square in the middle of the night. A few lights are on, and not a single guard is in site. Of course, thanks to the presence of a Kremlin webcam, we're sitting in New York while we're doing this. Seeing live shots—day or night—of places in far-off lands gives the Internet an additional degree of immediacy that can't be gleaned from books or television. No other medium comes close to the sense of being there, in a virtual way.

This site compiles 80 webcam sites from around the world into a virtual slide show. Webmaster Steve Fuchs has culled the best city cameras from around the world to form an Internet travelogue that almost defies description. Every webcam to

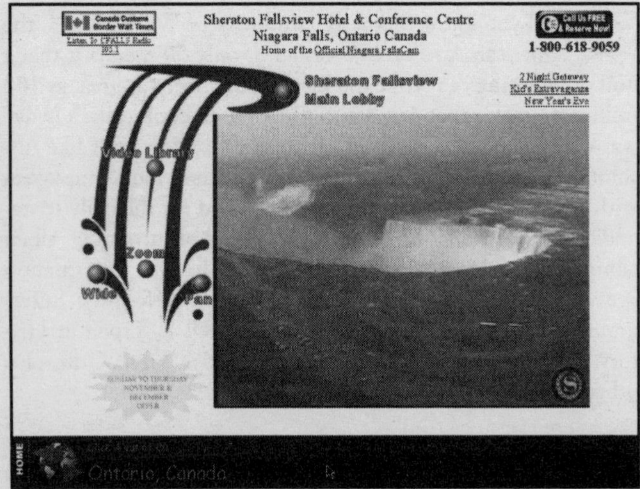

which this site links has its own set of guides, tools, quality of images, and descriptions. But note, while some cameras can be operated in near real time by the viewer, others update infrequently, with days seeming to pass before displaying a new image. Still, Fuchs has captured the best of the best, and images such as New Orleans's Bourbon Street and Paris from the Seine are almost enough to satisfy your wanderlust until you can get there in person. Almost.

GOVERNMENT

The United States government is allegedly the largest producer of printed information in the world. This is not surprising when you consider that the current tax code alone requires a stack of paper several feet tall. While the government publishes almost everything it does in some form or another, ironically, the populace it serves never reads most of it. Think about it: How many people actually have the time or the interest to read the Congressional Journal*—those pearls of wisdom spewed forth by our elected officials—every working day? Nevertheless, it gets published—every working day.*

The web may change this process in a number of ways, from cutting down government paper materials to making government itself more interesting. The web is an excellent forum for getting all this information in front of American citizens without having to kill an entire forest. And, impressively, the government has created uniformly good sites. Some, of course, are better than others, but as a group, government sites are well designed, contain search engines, and are easy to navigate. In short, government web pages more often than not contain all the elements that make for informative and interesting sites, quite an accomplishment given the rather dry nature of their subject matter.

We've compiled the most often used and most popular (yes, it's an oxymoron) government sites here, with special emphasis on those that have truly useful information.

[national]

Central Intelligence Agency (CIA)

● http://www.cia.gov/

The fact that this site exists at all is a testament to the power of the web. After all, who's more secretive than the spooks at the CIA, and what is more open than the Internet? Granted, most of the information here is of the name, rank, and serial number sort: who they are, what they do, why they're important, which organizations are part of the U.S. intelligence community, and what job openings they have. But two parts of the site make it notable. The first is the Electronic Documents Retrieval page, which allows you to look at certain CIA documents as part of the Freedom of Information Act. You can search for specific documents by keyword or document title and the engine retrieves a possible list of hits. From there you can view the original document, which was scanned from the paper copy and processed using optical character recognition (OCR). Another part of this section is the Popular Documents Collection, which includes reports on the Bay of Pigs, the capture of Gary Powers and his U2 spy plane, UFOs, and various other high-visibility episodes in our nation's recent past. But be prepared to see a lot of blacked-out text.

The second, and most unusual, feature of this site is its Homepage for Kids. No kidding. This section attempts to give a

Y! tip

When looking for government agencies like the Department of Justice, you can oftentimes get straight to the source by typing in the name of the agency or its abbreviation with .gov attached in place of .com.

lighthearted history of the agency, using some kitschy graphics to describe the cool things that the CIA does (at least the ones it can talk about). Now, other government agencies, including the FBI, have excellent kids' pages. But in this case, suffice it to say that any kids' page that begins with the words "You are entering an official United States government system, which may be used only for authorized purposes. Unauthorized modification of any information stored on this system may result in criminal prosecution . . ." is not going to be a barrel of laughs. Must be a cloak-and-dagger thing.

Congress.org

● http://www.congress.org/

How does your congressperson rate with the Christian Coalition? What does the League of Private Property Voters think about him or her? You can find out at Congress.org.

This site is a joint venture of two firms specializing in communicating with Congress: one a public affairs strategist, the other a publisher of congressional directories. As such, it is something of a clearinghouse for all things congressional. It has many of the features of both the Senate and House of Representatives sites, such as member directories and tools for writing to members, but Congress.org also has all the pertinent listings for the Executive (White House, cabinet posts) and Judicial (Supreme Court, etc.) branches, as well as information on state governors. A ticker at the top of the homepage identifies upcoming votes and session items in Congress.

The big find here is the Scorecard section, a voting records database of members of Congress as rated by a variety of national associations. It uses a drill-down methodology, enabling you to find out just how a particular senator or representative from a given state voted on any bill how those organizations rated him or her. If you're interested in government but inclined to skip the actual homepages of Congress, this is the place to spend your quality browsing time.

Department of Defense (DOD)

● http://www.defenselink.mil/

The DOD has always been on the cutting edge of multimedia due to its far-reaching recruitment campaigns and tie-ins with movies such as *Top Gun*. The department has applied that same awareness to this site, which features cool videos and virtual postcards.

The Department of Defense has under its command the army, navy, air force, marines, Coast Guard, National Guard, and reserves, and though these military organizations have their own websites, it's more efficient to access them from DefenseLink, where they're all in one place. The unique aspect of the site is how it integrates information that spans the services, using News, Multimedia, Publications, and Questions categories to do so. The last two categories are self-explanatory. The News section is extremely large and contains up-to-the-minute information about activities in all the armed forces (this information is also archived), as well as the full text of press briefings. The best part of the site is the Multimedia section, which features sound clips and video files (RealPlayer G2 is required) of training exercises conducted by the various groups. The Multimedia page also boasts a variety of cool photos that can be used as virtual postcards and sent via e-mail.

You'll of course find promotional material on the site, as well as links for writing to troops stationed overseas. A Sites of Interest box on the homepage taps directly into web locales that address concerns, such as Veterans Info, Gulf War Illnesses, and Reunion Calendars.

Department of Justice (DOJ)

● http://www.usdoj.gov/

The Department of Justice doesn't conduct the daily criminal investigations, as the FBI does, nor does it host the daily arguments and discussions that occur on the floor of

Congress. Consequently, its site is a bit more serene than these other government sites. But, like most government sites, it contains a wealth of unexpected information.

The most useful content here has to do with cases the DOJ is pursuing. Found under the What's New & Hot section, at the time of this writing, they included insurance fraud cases, computer crimes, youth violence strategies, and the antitrust case against Microsoft. But there are 11 categories in all pertaining to the department and its activities. In addition to What's New, these include Archive, Publications & Documents, Freedom of Information Act, Employment Opportunities, and Fugitives & Missing Persons. Much of the content on the site comes from the FBI and the Drug Enforcement Agency (DEA), and is repackaged for graphic consistency here.

The DOJ's kids' section is a modified version of the one found on the Federal Bureau of Investigation (FBI) site and is presented just as nicely (it also includes Internet do's and don'ts).

Federal Bureau of Investigation (FBI)

● http://www.fbi.gov/

The dark days of the FBI under the leadership of the infamous J. Edgar Hoover are still the stuff of tell-all novels, TV movies, and the occasional tabloid gossip column. But as far as the new FBI is concerned, those days are gone, and this site serves as a part of the agency's ongoing makeover. There is so much cool stuff here that it's impossible not to be impressed by what this branch of law enforcement does.

The main areas here are Press Room, Library and Reference, Most Wanted, and FBI for Kids. The information has a lot of depth, something you might not expect from an agency that is associated with law enforcement. Major Investigations is an archive of case descriptions from the relatively recent past, including the Unabomber and TWA Flight 800 investigations. The FBI Library is a collection of journals published by the FBI, including *Forensic Science Communications* and *Terrorism in the*

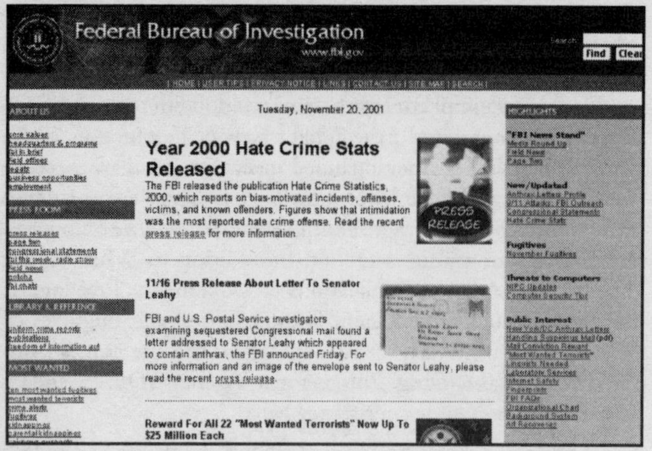

United States Report. Most Wanted (of which the 10 Most Wanted is a subset) contains lists of a variety of fugitives, from parental kidnappers to dangerous criminals; the 10 Most Wanted page then shows pictures of the fugitives, along with their vital statistics.

Speaking of statistics, also here are the Uniform Crime Reports (most in pdf format), the annual reports that get a plethora of media attention when they announce crime statistics for various regions around the country, everything from hate crimes to number of law enforcement officers killed and assaulted.

The FBI devotes a large amount of its web real estate to its employment opportunities, which are fairly diverse (from special agents to laboratory scientists). The Laboratory page should keep *Silence of the Lambs* fans happy for hours, as it details cases the lab has worked on (such as the Unabomber), complete with photos.

Ironically, the site really shines where it describes what the FBI does and how it does it, something that used to be verboten in the old days. More interesting is that this is done in the Kids & Youth homepage. Despite being targeted at kids, its discussion of a wide variety of techniques, from DNA testing to the use of chemical-explosive-sniffing dogs, makes for fascinating adult reading—even for those people who hear it all on the nightly news. Divided into learning sections for different grade levels (kindergarten through fifth grade, sixth grade through senior year of high school, and parents' and teachers' resources), a wealth of crime-related data of both the prevention and detection kinds is offered and will keep visitors mesmerized. The language is easy to understand, and the graphics are nicely done. This section of the FBI site might be one of the best kids' sites on the web—it could give the FBI a whole new image.

Federal Emergency Management Agency (FEMA)

● http://www.fema.gov/

FEMA is the organization that comes to town when the local economy gets reduced to nothing by floods, famine, fires, and other acts of nature. The list of possible disasters and dangers at this site, from tornadoes to winter driving, is extensive to the point of being nearly unimaginable; it even includes volcanoes and tsunamis. Each disaster/danger topic jumps to a text site that explains the best ways to prepare for a related emergency situation and how to deal with it once you've found yourself in such a situation. FEMA also has recommendations for community preparedness (see the listings under Disasters Info.). The front page is laid out almost like a newspaper, with news blurbs about recent disasters and how they were dealt with, both on a local and a national level.

FedNet

● http://www.fednet.net/

Imagine C-SPAN online and you get an idea of what's in store for you here. FedNet provides live webcast coverage of debates and hearings from the Senate and House floors. After each event has concluded, FedNet offers access to the archived event through a subscription service. Note: The events are streamed over the Internet, so RealPlayer is required to view the proceedings. Debates, press galleries, and hearing coverage are all available, for both the Senate and House. Click on the desired event, then sit back and watch the show. It's not quite the same as watching Comedy Central reruns on the web, but it just may be more educational.

FirstGov

● http://www.firstgov.gov/

Want to know more about state or federal government? Try FirstGov, the official website for searching the U.S. Government. The site is a partnership between public and private federal agencies; its global mission is "to connect the world to all U.S. Government information and services." In doing so, this page becomes a portal to over 47 million pages of government information and services. There are links to federal and state government websites, complete with a search engine. Visitors can also browse by topic and organization. There is a section on top news stories, links to transactions, forms, services, and even room for feedback. There is a customer satisfaction survey and links contacting branches of the government. If the goal is to create a seamless, electronic government, this website definitely helps.

Freedom of Information Act (FOIA)

● http://www.usdoj.gov/foia/other_age.htm

The FOIA site is a subset of the Department of Justice site, but it is important enough to warrant mention on its own. The popular misconception is that the Freedom of Information Act applies only to secret or spook agencies such as the CIA, NSA, and FBI, where people might want to get their hands on the nefarious data that the government has been compiling on them. Wrong. Every agency of the federal government, from the Department of Labor to the CIA to the Farm Credit Administration has to comply with the FOIA. And every website maintained by these agencies has an FOIA section. Of course, finding this section isn't always easy—unless you have this particular handy-dandy set of links in front of you. This DOJ page lists every FOIA page by category (Federal Agencies or Federal Departments) and then alphabetically.

Just so you know, the Freedom of Information Act (FOIA), which can be found in Title 5 of the United States Code, section 552, was enacted in 1966 and provides that any person has the right to request access to federal agency records or information. Upon receiving a written request for them, all agencies of the United States government are required to disclose these records, except for those protected from disclosure by the nine exemptions and three exclusions of the FOIA. This right of access is enforceable in court. If you want information from the government, you can get it here—presumably without ever having to step inside a government building.

House of Representatives

● http://www.house.gov/

There is an adage that says something to the effect that "People who love sausage and who respect the law should never watch either one being made." This site helps make watching the latter a lot more palatable. This website is probably the only place where you can get information on the House of Representatives without some media spin attached to it.

Here you can get reams of data and links to member offices, committee offices, organizations, task forces, commissions, House operations, a House directory, media galleries, and a search engine for the entire site. A tally of roll call votes lets you see how your congressperson really voted, and another section lists issues currently on the House floor. Plus you'll find a weekly and annual congressional schedule, committee hearing schedules and oversight plans, and even reports issued by specific committees.

There are also surprisingly useful links that allow you to write directly to your representative and access basic documents of U.S. law, and you'll find more than 8,900 links to law resources on the Net. And you can connect to Thomas, the excellent site maintained by the Library of Congress that contains information about the U.S. Congress and the legislative process. There you can search for updates on bills by topic, bill number, or title. Finally, the site contains the last three years of the *Congressional Record*, as well as committee reports, for those inclined to review such things.

The IRS (Internal Revenue Service)

● http://www.irs.gov/

Welcom to the Digital Daily, a page claiming: "Printed daily and it's free! And you don't have to recycle!" The design is that of a hometown newspaper circa 1950, with bold colors, kitschy graphics, and self-effacing pronouncements. This is retro information in the digital age, and, well, it actually works. You're aware it's the IRS underneath it all, but you get the sense that the agency is actually trying to improve.

There are dozens of components to this site, such as taxpayer advocates, employment opportunities, and tax info for businesses, but the two sections that will matter most to the average taxpayer are the Help and Forms sections. Help offers tips on understanding your tax notice and answers frequently asked tax questions. It also offers Taxi (short for TaxInteractive), an online 'zine for understanding taxes—why you pay them and where they go. Most important at Help, though, is Tele-Tax, an online version of the phone response system the IRS has set up to be more interactive with its "customers." There are 18 categories in Tele-Tax. Select one, say, Tax Credits, and you're led to another list, where you can choose, for example, Child Tax Credit. The next page then defines the child tax credit and allows you to print out the appropriate form for figuring the credit. If that's not enough for you, you can download the entire publication on child tax credits. This is pretty helpful, all things considered.

The Forms section contains more than a dozen different forms, plus instructions and publications that can be downloaded. You'll also find fill-in forms for use on your computer and forms from previous years (in pdf format). Overall, the IRS has done a good job supplying the taxpaying public with substantial amounts of usable information on the web. This doesn't mean you have to like the organization any more than you used to; it just means that it's trying to be more neighborly—at least in the virtual sense.

Senate

● http://www.senate.gov/

The Senate is the high-visibility component of the legislature, and its website reflects that status. After visiting this site, you'll think that senators have achieved the status of rock stars. It has everything you'd ever want to know about the Senate and its members but stops short of selling posters and CDs. This is a beautifully designed site, which outclasses most government sites and makes that of the House of Representatives look downright primitive. Easy to navigate, enjoyable to view, and worth a look for its insight into the legislative process, the Senate site succeeds on almost every level.

Categories include Senators, Committees, Legislative Activities, Learning about the Senate, Visiting the Senate, and Contacting the Senate, plus Search. You can connect with senators by selecting their home state from a pulldown menu, and the Quick List provides links to committee hearing schedules and yesterday's activities on the Senate floor. The current calendar of

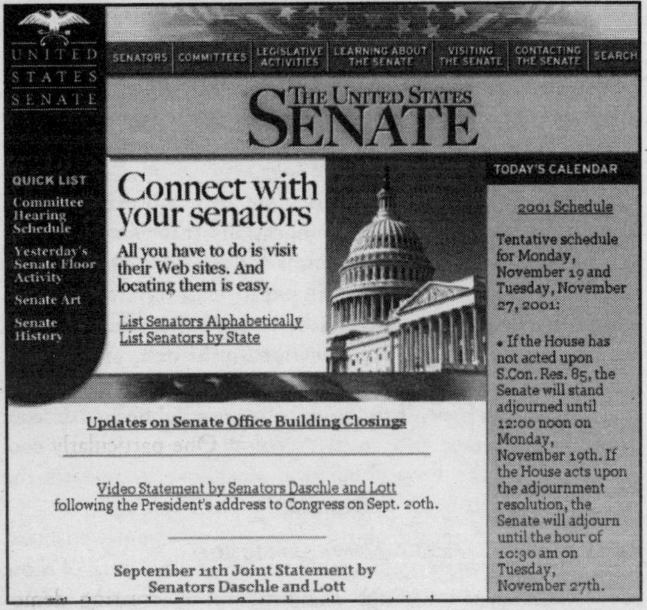

events is available, as are direct links to committee members, a list of nominations, and an index of roll call votes. In the bottom left is a bill search, where you can find out the status of bills by number or keyword.

The Senate is proud of its history, and the site displays this pride in a number of sections including This Week in History and Senate Art; here you can read about myths and legends, with samples of the latter (revealing, for example, whether the Senate's exquisite crystal chandelier ever hung in a brothel). This site is a really nice combination of history and modern practice, which elevates it above the potentially dry subject matter of making laws. More important, the contents and layout of the Senate site are an indication that at least some of our tax dollars are going to worthwhile projects.

The U.S. Census Bureau

● http://www.census.gov/

Talk about your tax dollars at work. Graphs, charts, press releases, Acrobat files, research papers—you name it and it's probably here. It's called Helping You Make Informed Decisions and they aren't kidding. The site is so deep as to be awe-inspiring. (When was the last time you heard that word used to describe a government agency?) The alphabetical index alone has hundreds of topic areas, from At Home Workers to Zip Code Statistics. A link on the homepage takes you to the most recent leading economic indicators, which then takes you to a briefing room filled with a dizzying array of data. You know all that stuff you hear on business radio about "new home starts" and "advanced retail sales"? All of it is in here in living color. One particularly cool component is the U.S. population clock, which updates the number of people living in America every five minutes.

The main categories on the front page are People, Business, Geography, Special Topics, and News, and within each of those are category-specific headings (for instance, creating demographic maps in the Geography section). Additionally, a pull-down menu allows you to view statistics relative to a particular state, and you can look at the preparation for the Year 2000 Census. The comprehensiveness of this site suggests that is intended for use by corporations, state and local agencies, and academic researchers, but it is fascinating for anyone to actually see all this data in a context that can be pored over and understood.

United States Postal Service (USPS)

● http://www.usps.gov/

The post office did something right. After serving as the butt of numerous jokes, it has the last laugh with this useful and easy-to-manage website. For those of us who can't stand the thought of waiting in lines, the site provides search engines for finding zip codes and matching zip codes to actual addresses; there's also a fairly sophisticated rate calculator for all types of letters and packages and an online store.

White House

● http://www.whitehouse.gov/

This is a very public look at the White House; you aren't going to get any behind-the-scenes scoops on goings-on that may lead to the next Watergate or Monicagate. This site serves primarily as a repository for White House press briefings, radio addresses, and presidential accomplishments. Most of the information here is the actual text of speeches and press secretary statements, as well as archives (you can look up, say, "impeachment" in the press briefing room and find every mention made of it since 1994). The History of the White House area contains excellent information on past presidents, a floor plan, and a look at pieces from the building's art collection.

There is plenty of info about White House events—galas, presentations, and the like—including some history of the fabled house. There is a list of recent presidential appearances and statements, as well as doings by the vice president and the first families. You can also—allegedly—e-mail the residents directly from here.

[international]

The web is the first medium in the history of the world to break down barriers to the exchange of information among all countries on the planet. A person in one country can view sites hosted from another country at any time, day or night. No other medium—not even TV—can claim that kind of reach.

The two sites we've chosen to include here offer a window to the world beyond our political boundaries. This level of communication hopefully will raise the level of understanding among the peoples of the world.

CIA Factbook

● http://www.cia.gov/cia/publications/factbook/

No one knows the ins and outs of a foreign country like its spies. And that pithy little fact makes this one of the best sites on the web for doing research on any country in the world. You want electricity consumption per capita? You want annual birthrate? You want the name of the deputy defense minister in charge of information? How about number of television sets, length of navigable waterways, or railroad gauge? It's all here. This is hard data at its finest.

A map accompanies each country, and a set of buttons lead to data on People, Geography, Government, Economy, Military, Transnational Issues, Communications, and Transportation. There is also a history of the Factbook and some additional reference maps. Perhaps the CIA agents should spend time at

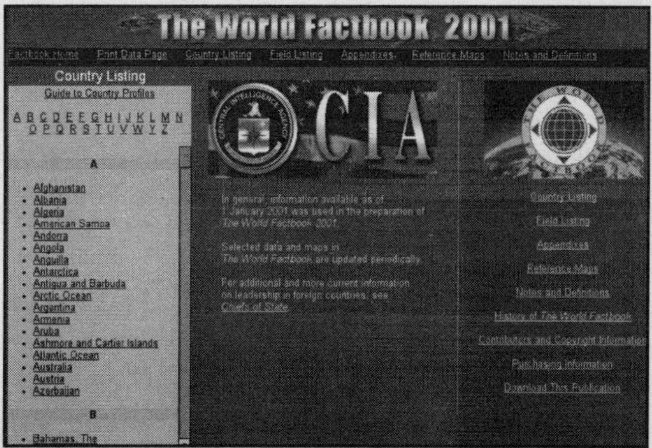

this site; they might be a little better prepared for some of those unexpected regional crises.

The Electronic Embassy

● http://www.embassy.org/

The Electronic Embassy bills itself as "a resource of and for the Washington DC foreign embassy community." But the site is enjoyable for nonpoliticos as well. The main page lists recent events and contains an events calendar and a press release clearinghouse. The site has an alphabetical—and searchable—list of every embassy in Washington, all with links. Click on one to get a brief overview of that embassy, including its location and e-mail address and a link to is website. Visiting this site is like being able to hobnob with all the foreign diplomats in Washington without the political headaches.

[law]

ACLU

● http://www.aclu.org/

The objective of the American Civil Liberties Union is to make sure no one—but no one—infringes on anyone else's civil rights. From separation of church and state issues (for example, towns displaying Nativity scenes at Christmas) to the death penalty (executing convicted murderers), the ACLU takes on 19 legal-cum-social issues. Each has its own section that explains the ACLU's work in that area. There is also information on upcoming ACLU events, its history, advocacy, motions, and how you can join. Whether it's police practices, prisons, or privacy, the ACLU site will keep you up to date on how well—or how poorly—civil rights are being protected in the United States.

law.com

● http://www.law.com/

Shakespeare was perhaps the first to suggest killing all the lawyers, but law.com is one aspect of the legal profession that even old Will would have approved of. This site is a "portal to the law," covering a lot of legal resources. The Law Guides section has information for the public (including a self-help guide described in Nolo.com), for businesses (guides, forms, etc.), for professionals (lawyers, paralegals, judges, etc.), and for students (prelaw, undergrad, etc.). The Services area has a law dictionary, a lawyer search, and free e-mail. The Information center contains links to specific legal sites, such as U.S. courts, cases, law schools, associations, and research areas for professors and judges.

The Self Help guide is for businesspeople, consumers, and lawyers who need a shortcut to specific legal information, more than 400 topic areas are available from a pulldown menu, addressing such issues as accidents and zoning laws (it may be the largest pulldown menu listed in this book). This shortcut will take you to definitions, general information, related websites, and publications; it will even provide you with downloadable forms when appropriate.

Finally, in addition to providing "real life law news," law.com links to resources that cover topics such as representing yourself in court, terminating the attorney-client relationship, and suing an attorney for malpractice. (The latter link is right above an area called For Your Enjoyment so don't get them confused.)

Lawinfo

● http://www.lawinfo.com/

Need someone to testify that you're criminally insane? Want an expert who can prove that those weren't your fingerprints on the murder weapon? Let's face it: You can't pick these people out of a phone book, so you need Lawinfo. This site is a Yahoo!-style index of professionals and services in all areas of the law. In addition to the obvious—a section on finding attorneys—you search for expert witnesses, private investigators, trial consultants, process servers, court reporters, and others. Lawinfo also has a chat area, a consumer help section, and free e-mail.

Lawyers.com

● http://www.lawyers.com/

There are lawyers, and then there are lawyers. Most handle such mundane tasks as wills and trusts and transfers of ownership—fill-in-the-blank kind of stuff (see Legaldocs). These you can find in almost any office park or suburban business complex. But when you need someone who specializes in criminal law, product liability, or land use and zoning, you're going to have to look a little more carefully. Start by going to Lawyers.com, which features a search engine that lets you look for attorneys by city, state, country, and area of specialty. Plug in a problem area and the city in which you need the lawyer and you'll retrieve an alphabetical list of lawyers who handle that kind of work—along with a profile of each firm and its partners. You'll also find tips on hiring a lawyer and how much lawyers charge, plus 12 questions to ask your lawyer.

Legal Documents
Legaldocs

● http://www.legaldocs.com/

Next time it seems that all your lawyer did is fill out a form and then charge you enough to make the payment on his or her Mercedes, go to Legaldocs. This is a database of legal documents you can fill out yourself. There are both free docs here (living wills, automobile insurance claim forms, promissory notes, demand for payment letters, etc.) and documents downloadable for a small fee (estate plans, powers of attorney, employment contracts, etc.). You might save enough money using this site to make your own Mercedes payment.

Delphion Intellectual Property Network

● http://www.delphion.com/

Search for most any device or subject you can imagine—thumbtacks, twin-engine planes, Malibu Barbie—and Big Blue's Intellectual Property Network will list the patent number, date issued, and title of relevant inventions past and present. The Network allows searches and views of patents from the United States, Europe, and Japan, as well as applications published by the World Intellectual Property Organization. The info offered throughout is official, voluminous, and generously detailed. Especially neat are the Detailed Views, where you can see the actual documentation of a registered patent and the drawings that show every element used in the construction of an item. Ever on the lookout for good ideas, IBM also offers personal links and the chance to call attention to your invention for licensing opportunities.

Finally, deep within the dark recesses of this site is the fascinating and occasionally hilarious Gallery of Obscure Patents. Don't miss the Gravity Powered Shoe Air Conditioner or the handy combo Bird Trap/Cat Feeder.

Nolo.com Law for All

● http://www.nolo.com/

The man who represents himself in court may have a fool for a client, but at least he won't be paying attorney's fees. And he can save even more money by going to the Nolo.com Law for All, a veritable treasure trove of data that provides basic legal information to anyone who wants it. This excellent virtual law firm has plenty of tools to help would-be barristers: a legal topic finder (alimony, bankruptcy, divorce, partnerships, patents, etc.), a library of articles for each topic, a legal dictionary

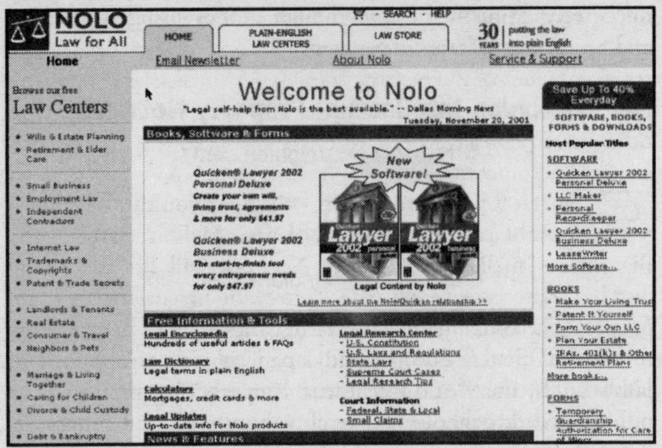

and encyclopedia, consumer news, and free legal forms. And more than 500 general questions are answered in a law FAQ.

A clever advice column, Ask Auntie Nolo, deals with unique—and often quirky—personal matters ("My neighbor's tree is blocking my view of the city lights" and "My landlord is double-dipping by charging me late fees"). Perhaps most important is the joke section, with chuckle categories ranging from Lawyers in Love (What do lawyers use for birth control? Their personalities) to Lawyers in Hell (What do you get when you cross a lawyer with a demon from hell? Another lawyer). If you find yourself needing to visit this site for legal reasons, at least you'll be able to laugh about it.

Patents.com

● http://www.patents.com/

The law firm of Oppedahl & Larson LLP has established this web service to inform all the Edisons-to-be about the nuts and bolts of patents, copyright, trademarks, and trade secrets. The site is also valuable as a portal to other Net resources for career opportunities, on how to obtain books on intellectual property, and on how to contact the government organizations that register new inventions. The firm is interested in teaching inventors how to protect their legal rights, and to that end, it shares what other inventors have been through by reviewing the circumstances and outcomes of actual trials.

Virtual Law Library

● http://www.law.indiana.edu/v-lib

This component of the Virtual Library (see the entry under LIBRARIES) has links to legal sites maintained by law schools, libraries, government organizations, private firms, publishers, and other law-related organizations. Those doing in-depth research will want to check out the impressive list of legal search engines (including a Spanish-language version), as well as the list of links by topic. This particluar V-Lib site is maintained by the Indiana School of Law at Bloomington.

[military]

Jane's

● http://www.janes.com/

Interested in navy ships? Combat fighters? Tanks? Fans of military hardware should make Jane's, "the world's leading source for global defense, geopolitical, transportation, and law-enforcement information," their number one stop on the web. Jane's print counterpart has been the place where warriors go for data on weapons and warfare—whether their own or the enemy's.

To access much of the info on this site, you need to log in, but once you're in, you're privy to a world of information about everything from armaments to military consulting to job openings in the defense industry. Jane's even branches out into general transport, to include airplane and rail consulting. There are books and magazines, too, and weekend warriors can engage in cyberwar, using Jane's Combat Simulations. And for a reality check, a weekly news feature updates major military conflicts around the world.

Special Operations
Special Operations Web

● http://www.specialoperations.com/

Special Operations groups take on the most daunting and dangerous, military tasks. There are only a handful of these Special Ops units in the United States, namely the well-known SEALs, Rangers, and Delta Force as well as the lesser known Night Stalkers and Chemical Biological Incident Response Force (CBIRF). This site covers them all extensively, serving as a portal for the Special Ops world.

Even if you aren't interested in the military, this site covers an enthralling—albeit dark—corner of our world. Each Special Ops unit has its own section with detailed information, articles, links, and member info. Broader general sections address such topics as history (betcha didn't know Special Ops were used in the Revolutionary War), specialties (from laser target designation to sharpshooting and sniping), weapons, schools (where you go to learn how to do this stuff—if you survive the training), literature, associations, an In Memory area, and humor ("Never draw fire—it irritates everyone around you," "Never forget that your weapon was made by the lowest bidder"). It's nice to know that people who do jobs that would kill most people appreciate a good laugh.

Veterans
Department of Veterans Affairs

● http://www.va.gov/

This is the main site for the Department of Veterans Affairs. It provides information on benefits, facilities, medical programs, statistics, current VA procurement contracts, and legislation. Veterans can get detailed, downloadable data on their benefits and do research on the programs that are available to them. The search engine is a must here: The site is more than 2,000 pages deep.

War
The War Page

● http://www.aylic.com/War/war.html

The War Page is a full-scale site for war aficionados, with links to a variety of broad areas covering war history, books, downloadable games, weaponry, and more. You can spend hours here cruising from site to site, either sampling a variety of past and present conflicts or pursuing a single point of inquiry, be it the Second World war or the recent events of September 11.

The section that sets this site from the rest of the web's military pages is War Literature. Included here is Tennyson's "Charge of the Light Brigade," commemorating that fateful charge of British cavalry during the Crimean War. You'll also find "Dulce et Decorum Est", a gripping WWI poem that author Wilfred Owen included in a letter to this mother (Owen was later killed in action, a week before the end of the war). Among its powerful lines is this description of a gas attack on the front lines of France:

Gas! GAS! Quick, boys!—An ecstasy of fumbling
Fitting the clumsy helmets just in time,
But someone still was yelling out and stumbling
And flound'ring like a man in fire or lime—

Dim through the misty panes and thick green light,
As under a green sea, I saw him drowning.

[politics]

Politics and the web have had a symbiotic relationship that no one could have ever foreseen. Politics is the great voice of the people, and the Internet is the new stage from which political sentiment can be pronounced. On the web, anyone can—and it seems that everyone does—have access to forums that let them express their political ideas without fear of censorship, filtering, or reality checking.

Whether someone chooses to join an established forum or create their own political web page, the outlets for political discussion and grandstanding are endless. You want to talk to like-minded Republicans about how careless the Democrats are with the taxpayers' money? Want to join Democrats in slamming the Republicans as uncompassionate serfs of big business? How about a frank chat about nominating Liberace's remains for president? No area of political discussion is too big, too small, too urgent, or too mediocre to find a voice on the Internet. It's like a virtual soapbox, and you can stand on it for 24 hours a day.

But we really don't want to discuss politics. We leave that to you, and to that end, we offer the following websites, without regard to political orientation. About the only thing we argue is whether these websites serve the needs of their constituents. That's as politically incorrect as we get.

Democrats
Democratic National Committee

● http://www.democrats.org/index.html

The party who counts among its members Al "I invented the Internet" Gore has crafted a straightforward site that downplays its "tax and spend" image (after all, it takes money to build a website). The Democrats have opted for a more serious approach, filling the site with facts and mission statements.

Lots of space is devoted to the Democrats' accomplishments and the party's ideological distinction from the GOP. But like the Republicans, the Dems put news and issues front and center on their homepage, with the requisite criticism of the GOP's various candidates and motives in the Spotlight section. Topic areas include Newsroom, On the Issues, Voter Outreach, State Parties, and About the DNC. No videos or audio is available, but there is a full contingent of archived press releases from the organization.

Republicans
Republican National Committee

● http://www.rnc.org/

     Home of the Grand Old Party, George Dubyah, Dan "Potatoe" Quayle, and tax cuts. Contrary to its rep as the party *not* for regular people, this is an extremely well-designed and user-friendly site. Ostensibly, this helps to underscore the tag line here: "The official website of America's new Republican majority."

Libertarian
Libertarian Party

● http://www.lp.org/

Are you a Libertarian? Don't automatically answer "no." The Libertarian Party encourages you to rethink your answer using a cool little test. Billed as the "world's smallest political quiz," it takes about 15 seconds to fill out. Based on your answers, the site gives you a profile, complete with graph, of where you fit in the political belief spectrum. It's an interesting exercise.

Other parts of the site proclaim "Pro-Choice on Everything," "End the War on Drugs," "Stop Internet Censorship," and "No More Income Tax." These take you to various policy articles. There are also sections dedicated to Libertarian Party activities and to Philosophy/Positions, Membership Info, Directories and Lists, Official Documents, History, and News & Announcements.

Political Commentary The Nation (Liberal)

- http://www.thenation.com/

National Review (Conservative)

- http://www.nationalreview.com/

The New Republic (Liberal)

- http://www.thenewrepublic.com/

The Weekly Standard (Conservative)

- http://www.theweeklystandard/

These four magazines are known for their political agendas; indeed, they are the flag bearers for their respective platforms. Their columnists, and the articles they write, are among the most provocative published to a national audience, and hopping between their websites is a case study in American opinion and politics.

In general, their websites are stripped-down versions of the print versions, but with the bite intact. But each contains unique sections providing an additional reason for visiting the digital edition.

National Review (NR), William F. Buckley Jr.'s long-running conservative organ, links current news to other publications, notably the *New York Times*, Reuters, and Slate in a section called The Vibe (which will not in anyone's lifetime be confused with the rap magazine of the same name). Its web-only section is called Websclusives. The site also keeps track of media appearances by its staff members.

If NR's content is just a little too old-school for you, head over to the *Weekly Standard*, a slightly more modern mag that also publishes most of its content online.

The *New Republic* calls itself the "journal of arts and politics." Its website draws a fine line between the parts of the magazine make it to the web and those that don't. The publisher is apparently still struggling to decide how to generate revenue from its Internet audience that wants it all for free.

The *Nation*'s site is more extensive than those of the other three magazines, primarily because it promotes the work of the Nation Institute in addition to offering online articles. The *Nation*'s Internet presence is further set apart by RadioNation, an audio commentary presented by the magazine's editors. The site also has a web-only section called Special Issues and features a discussion forum for its visitors.

Political Resources on the Net

● http://www.politicalresources.net/

Is there a king of Thailand? Which world leaders can still claim absolute power? To which political party does Tony Blair belong? The answers to these and other global political questions can be found at Political Resources on the Net. This site provides "listings of political sites available on the Internet sorted by country, with links to Parties, Organizations, Governments, Media and more from all around the world." That claim in and of itself is impressive; the fact that it delivers all this is even more so. The level of information contained on this site, given the content, is mind-boggling in its detail and scope. Nothing on the web compares to it for providing information about global politics and policies.

The primary component of this Italian-based site is a large color-coded world map on the homepage. Click on any continent (e.g., Asia) and a new page with the flags of all the nations in that continent appears. Click on a flag, say, Bhutan, and you get links to the CIA Factbook (see our review under INTERNATIONAL), Elections in Bhutan, *Kuensel* (Bhutan's national newspaper), the Bhutan national website, the V-Lib entry for Bhutan, the Bhutan National Tourism Corporation, and Governments on the World Wide Web.

You can also search for info via numerous classifications: European Union, country initial, elections around the world, parties around the world, parliaments around the world, political databases on the Net, and an electoral calendar.

[trademarks]

Trademark Information

● http://www.uspto.gov/web/menu/tm.html

Nike's swoosh. Apple's Macintosh. The U.S. Post Office and "Fly Like an Eagle." The Budweiser Clydesdales. The *New York Times* and "All the News That's Fit to Print." These are all trademarks, and as you already know, we live in the era of trademarks. Even the Chrysler Building is trademarked, for some arcane reason.

Maybe you need to trademark something, too. First you need to know how to do it, and that takes a little research. For starters, keep in mind that a trademark is "a word, phrase, symbol or design, or combination of words, phrases, symbols or designs which identifies and distinguishes the source of the goods or services of one party from those of another." Then you can find out who owns which words and phrases by searching this site's database (for example, Disney has 499 trademarks; Microsoft has 518, including "kid-friendly"). If no one has registered your pet phrase or design, then you can get instructions on registering and securing it as a trademark. You can even check its status online while you wait to make your mark on an unsuspecting world.

HEALTH

[advice]

Go Ask Alice

● http://www.goaskalice.columbia.edu/index.html

The conventional wisdom in pop culture is that you can "go ask Alice" anything and "she'll know." With a nod to Lewis Carroll and the Jefferson Airplane, it's quite possible that this Alice *can* answer everything, as long as it regards health. No subject is off-limits; you'll see questions on eyelid twitching, steroid use, faking orgasms, self-mutilation, and more. Alice tackles it all and does it with a grin. Questions are submitted via the site to Alice (the pen name of the Columbia University Health Education Program), then categorized by topic: Relationships, Sexuality, Sexual Health, General Health, Emotional Health, Fitness and Nutrition, Alcohol, Nicotine, and Other Drugs. Look through the hundreds of archived questions for Alice's frank and funny answers on all health concerns—some more pressing than others. For those with serious and seriously private concerns about their mental and physical health, this website is a real wonderland.

[age reduction]

Real Age

● http://www.realage.com/

Are you 30 years old but feel 70? Maybe you're 50 and feel 19. This site attempts to help you determine your real age, then helps you live "younger." Developed by Dr. Mike Roizen, the chairman of the Department of Anesthesia and Critical Care at the University of Chicago's Pritzker School of Medicine, this site helps you learn your actual—as opposed to chronological—age, based on a personality profile you fill out online. Now, we can't validate Dr. Roizen's claims, but certainly there are days when we feel a lot younger—and a lot older—than our chronological age. As baby boomers age, it may be worth finding out if you are turning into your parents or morphing into a Gen-Xer.

[aromatherapy]

Aromaweb

● http://www.aromaweb.com/

The smell of lemon, lavender, and sage is supposed to relieve stress. The scent of chamomile and patchouli is supposed to calm and relax you. While aromatherapy certainly hasn't been endorsed by all the medical associations in the country, many believe there is value in its use. This site addresses some of the most interesting aspects of the subject, with a long listing of articles and recommended books, along with links to answers for questions such as "What is aromatherapy?" and "Is all the hype true?" Diving deep into the subject, including glossaries, measurements, and oil summaries, at this writing the site spans some 60 pages. There are also links to other aromatherapy sites and recipes for creating aromatic blends. The site is so good you can almost smell it.

[children's]

Kid's Health

● http://kidshealth.org/

The human body is incredible—so incredible, in fact, that it often leaves us—particularly kids—puzzled. Our anatomical universe calls out for some explanation, and this site meets the challenge, because it has anticipated kids' questions and put them in a menu. Forget the embarrassment of asking; whatever your age, the Kid's Health site has the answers.

The site is divided into three sections tailored to parents, teens, and kids. The Kids section deals with everyday illnesses and injuries (nosebleeds, bug bites, chicken pox, etc.), as well as hurt feelings and coping with death. Teens can enter their section to look for answers to questions they may be too embarrassed to ask their friends or parents (everything you wanted to know about puberty, or why does a doctor have to touch my testicles?). Parents get answers on how to deal with kids' problems at every age, from teething to temper tantrums to discussions about alcohol and sex. This is an essential site that everyone in the family can use, just not all at the same time. Sort of like the bathroom.

[dentistry]

DentalGate

● http://www.dentalgate.com/dent/

We tend to think of our teeth only when something goes wrong. If they're working and they're white, that's all we care about. If we get a toothache or suddenly start getting weird stains on our pearly whites, then we worry—and, of course, treat it as an emergency. For those not on their way to an all-night dentist, DentalGate serves as a more relaxing and informative place than your average dentist's chair to spend time. From activator appliances to vestibuloplasty, the site has links to hundreds of resources on all aspects of teeth and dentistry. By the way, DentalGate is part of the Guide.com sites for medical specialties, including CardioGuide and OrthoGuide. These sites are reviewed in this book under MEDICINE.

A similar, though more general, dental health site is Dental Related Internet Resources (http://www.dental-resources.com/). An index of information for and about dentists and dental services, it provides good links to sites addressing general tooth care, tooth whiteners, and dental products from floss to toothbrushes.

[dermatology]

DermGuide

● http://www.dermguide.com/

Physical beauty is—so they say—only skin deep, and this could be your skin's best friend on the web. Links here connect you to information on hundreds of disorders in dozens of specialties including bacteriology and virology. Two search engines dominate the site, one for finding dermatology sites and the other for finding dermatology data within Medline. FYI, DermGuide is part of the Guide.com sites for medical specialties, including CardioGuide, OphthoGuide, and OrthoGuide. These sites are reviewed in this book under MEDICINE.

For general info on dermatology and common skin disorders, go to Infoderm (http://www.infoderm.com/). You'll learn that people over 85 almost never get dandruff, and that fingernails grow faster than toenails. The site also has serious data on skin conditions from acne and rosacea to growths, cancers, and viral infections, among others. In addition to photographs and recommended treatment, you can also scan the site's Dermfinder database to find a licensed professional in your area.

[diet and nutrition]

In a society increasingly concerned about the effects—both positive and negative—of the foods we ingest, a common question is "Who do you trust for info?" Doctors are a good place to start, but let's face it, most of us are loath to make an office appointment for a heart-to-heart discussion on the merits of broccoli versus brussels sprouts. Food packaging offers data of a sort, but it hardly qualifies as a road map for healthy eating. Books, magazines, and newsletters also offer information, but it never seems to be exactly what you need, especially when you're mixing and matching food types and meal plans.

Expanding on all of those sources, the Internet offers numerous sites comprising diverse forms of information on food, nutrition, and dieting. Of course, many have ulterior motives (they want you to buy into their nutrition programs) or are promoting personal opinions, so, to get you on the right track, the entries listed here come from recognized sources.

Advice
Mayo Clinic Health Oasis

● http://www.mayoclinic.com/home?id=SP2.5.1

The Mayo Clinic is arguably the nation's best-known medical and health facility, and now it has extended its reputation for high-quality patient care to the Internet. The advice section of the Mayo Clinic's megasite is called Answers from Mayo Clinic. Here you can "ask a dietician" questions or browse through a huge archive of questions and answers pertaining to diet and nutrition (questions are archived for searching). Also featured is Mayo's input on weight management, vitamins and supplements, and food compositions.

There's also a book review section. This site is the next best thing to checking in and getting your nutritional needs on track.

Dieting
Cyberdiet

● http://www.cyberdiet.com/

Do you know how many calories your body can use efficiently when you sit at your computer and surf the web all day? Do you know your target heart rate? This informative and amusing site has the answers to these and many other questions related to dieting and nutrition planning.

Cyberdiet tackles nutrition topics in sections titled Get Started, Eat Right, Exercise Smart, Feel Good, and Community. A section for diabetics offers an impressive amount of information, and the foods section database categorizes and labels most of the foods you eat. There's also a teen forum.

For those struggling with weight control, Cyberdiet will help you review your lifestyle and to make the proper adjustments in your diet. Fill out a personal nutritional profile and find out how you should be eating and exercising. Then determine how to eat right every day with a daily planner. Cyberdiet also specifies diet plans—for vegetarians, for those over 50, and more. Of course, the site includes recipes and recommendations for exercise. Anyone trying to get a handle on their love handles should put down that ice cream sundae—right now—and devour the information on this site.

General
American Dietetic Association (ADA)

● http://www.eatright.org/

"Your Link to Nutrition and Health" is the tag line for this outstanding site, which is the homepage of the American Dietetic Association. There is info for both professionals and consumers here, divided into several categories including Healthy Lifestyle, Meetings & Events, Press Room, and Knowledge Center. The main features are a nutrition Tip of the Day and Nutrition Resources. The latter contains detailed information separated into consumer and professional categories, with interesting articles, fact sheets, food guide pyramids, and features for specific groups of people (children, elderly, etc.). Professionals can review position papers and articles from the association's journal, participate in classifieds, and find employment opportunities and info on upcoming meetings/conferences.

For a nominal fee ($1.50 and up), ADA sells its brochures and papers on numerous nutritional subjects, including feeding overweight children, sports nutrition for children, food allergies,

vegetarian and low-fat lifestyles, and HIV/AIDS information. And if you need more, call the hot line to get a referral to a registered dietician listed with the organization's nationwide network.

Guidelines
Food and Nutrition Information Center (FNIC)

● http://www.nal.usda.gov/fnic/

This site from the United States Department of Agriculture deserves mention for its sheer volume of data—it contains more than 12,000 pages of nutritional data, with a scope to match. Content covers the personal—for example, how to properly nourish school-age children—as well as the political—organizations dedicated to feeding the homeless population.

To meet the needs of its diverse audience, FNIC contains food pyramid guides, a Consumer Corner, food compositions, dietary guidelines, FNIC Resource Lists, dietary supplements, healthy school meal plans, research, studies, and an A-Z Topic Guide. Professionals can select text links to FNIC databases for educational and training material, and the layperson can get the calorie and fat count on favorite foods. Finally, FNIC includes several government databases related to food, foodborne illnesses, and nutrition education.

[disabilities]

The areas of disability and disorder are too complex to address comprehensively in this section. What we've done is to take a careful look at the dozens of categories that fall under the topic to identify the sites that do the best at covering them broadly. For instance, spina bifida affects newborns and is very well handled by the March of Dimes site, which we have reviewed here under Birth Defects.

A fine line is drawn between some of these entries and those under the Disease heading (blindness can be caused by disease, for example). We make the distinction by including here those that can be regarded as preexisting conditions. We included sites of the support groups, care-giving organizations, and national societies dedicated to serving these populations.

Americans with Disabilities Act
DOJ ADA Homepage

● http://www.usdoj.gov/crt/ada/adahom1.htm

The Americans with Disabilities Act (ADA) was written to ensure that disabled people receive equal treatment in this country. This site serves as a significant resource for finding out just what this law covers and addresses. Categories include Search, Index, What's New, Technical Assistance Materials, Enforcement, Technical Assistance Program, and Certification. There is also news and an extremely robust search engine (called Glimpse) that scans documents in the ADA archives, where visitors can retrieve both text and pdf versions of many of these documents.

Amputees
Amputee Online

● http://www.amputee-online.com/

$ Amputee Online is the definitive web resource for information, support, and supplies for amputees. The site serves as a portal for these features: Amputation Online magazine, Website (a subsection of the overall site that covers amputee issues and concerns), Mailing List, Shopping Mall (adapted clothing, tools, books, etc.), Business (prosthetic and amputee-related businesses), and Personal (individual sites). The site also has a strong sense of humor—the magazine contains a section called Amplaff.

Attention Deficit Disorder
National Attention Deficit Disorder Association (ADDA)

● http://www.add.org/

Not so long ago, Attention Deficit Disorder (ADD) was considered hyperactivity or lack of self-control. Today it is a recognized disorder, with concomitant data, much of which is available on the Attention Deficit Disorder Association's official website. First, the ADDA is described, followed by specifics about the condition (research, treatment, family issues, support groups, etc.). A Features section includes interviews, personal stories, myths, and more. A Bookstore completes the site.

Autism
Autism/PDD Resource Network

● http://www.autism-pdd.net/

This site consolidates innumerable web resources dealing with autism and the related pervasive developmental disorder (PDD) into a single site. In addition, it mixes frank discussion and medical info with practical advice and exchange of ideas. The front page alone is an encyclopedic collection of topics and links arranged by topic. These include sections for adults with disabilities (how to look into college admissions, job accommodation, family assistance, etc.), children with disabilities, effective communications, helpful articles, More to Do (a huge set of links to online medical and professional resources), estate planning and special-needs trusts, and a state-by-state resource search. There are also links to Diagnosis & Testing, Treatments, Special Education, and a host of related services and information.

Birth Defects
March of Dimes Health Library

● http://www.modimes.org/HealthLibrary2/portal.htm

This is the Health Library component of the March of Dimes. This "library" includes a Catalog, a Resource Center, Fact Sheets, Public Policy Studies, and Birth Defects Information. The Fact Sheets section contains data specifically related to pregnancy, illnesses, screenings, and so on. It also has extensive information on specific birth defects and genetic conditions from cerebral palsy and Down's syndrome to congenital heart defects and PKU (phenylketonuria).

Using its robust search engine, you can also scan news releases, library information, core documents, and the sections of the site. Note: The main March of Dimes site can be reached by deleting everything after .org in the URL.

Blindness
American Foundation for the Blind

● http://www.afb.org/

This site is primarily a collection of hotlinks to resources for the blind: information resources, fact sheets, talking books, journals, a guide to toys for blind or visually impaired children (an excellent site in its own right), and advocacy groups. An audio collection contains speeches from various forums (RealPlayer G2 required).

Children
Internet Resources for Special Children (IRSC)

● http://www.irsc.org/

Covering a wide range of issues and topics that concern disabled children, this site is as comprehensive as a medical text. The disABILITY section, in particular, contains important data that runs from the technical to the supportive and on to the inspirational. There are more than three dozen links leading to information on adaptive clothing, brain injury, autism, dwarfism, online magazines, inspirational prayers and quotes, and therapeutic humor. These in turn jump to pages with more links to sites that address specific facets of a particular illness or condition.

Unfortunately, some of the pages on this site are out of date, and parents of children with special needs must evaluate what they read with care. We hope this important resource is not left abandoned on the side of the information highway.

Down's Syndrome

● http://www.downsyndrome.com/

This site is both a support service and an information center about Down's syndrome. The primary topic areas include Organizations Worldwide, Parent Matching & Support Groups, Family Essays, Events & Conferences, FAQ, Inclusion & Education Resources, the Toy Store, Our Brag Book, Medical Articles, and Healthcare Guidelines for Individuals with Down's syndrome. There are also four external links listed on the homepage: Down's Syndrome, Health Issues (medical essays), Family Village (an online global support community), Disability Solutions (a publication on developmental disabilities), and Woodbine House (publisher of the Special Needs book collection).

At the time of this writing, a site with the URL http://www.downsyndrome.org/ was under development, with the promise of providing information from medical professionals, plus a family and patient message board.

Dyslexia
International Dyslexia Association

● http://www.interdys.org/index.html

Dyslexia is a disturbance of the ability to use language, causing sufferers to scramble words and numbers. This superbly designed site presents information about dyslexia via these departments: About Dyslexia, Research, Technology, Legal & Legislative, Bulletin Board, Press Info, Conferences & Seminars, and others. Each of these sections contains a single page with either a series of articles or a list of thoroughly profiled resources (which in turn are hyperlinked). All the material is comprehensive and well-written.

Family Issues
Family Village

● http://www.familyvillage.wisc.edu/index.htmlx

Family Village is one of the first places that other sites in the DISABILITIES section link to. Upon entering, the reason for this becomes obvious. This straightforward site uses a small-town motif to guide visitors to the Library, Coffee Shop, Hospital, Shopping Mall, Post Office, House of Worship, School, Recreation & Leisure, Community Center, Bookstore, University, and Information. Clicking on any of these "buildings" leads to other pages with more extensive resources. Recreation & Leisure, for instance, leads to a page that includes Air Travel Rights, Cooking & Nutrition, Mobility Resources, Sailing, Wheelchair Sports, Wish Granting Foundations, and many more.

The primary function of Family Village is to facilitate communication among those who work and live with the mentally retarded or disabled and those afflicted. To that end, it has numerous chat and discussion areas, as well as links to media and professional resources.

Learning Disabilities
LD Online

● http://www.ldonline.org/

LD Online is devoted to informing its visitors regarding all aspects of learning disabilities. A dozen categories provide helpful information on coping with or overcoming learning disabilities. The What's New section highlights recent research in the field; Audio Clips offers sound bites from experts; the ABCs of LD and ADD offers basics about learning disabilities; Bulletin Boards and LD Chat give parents, teachers, and students a place to share their experiences; LD In-Depth has material from leading organizations and professionals in the field; Ask the Experts offers opportunities to communicate directly with experts; Where to Find Help is a comprehensive listing of national and state organizations, agencies, online resources, and more; the LD Store is the place to order PBS videotapes and recommended books related to learning disabilities; the LD Calendar is a comprehensive listing of events on the Internet (e.g. state and national conferences); Talk Back is an online survey; and First Person contains essays on first-hand experiences in meeting the challenges of learning disabilities.

In addition, the site offers the LD OnLine Newsletter, a free, electronic "paper," and KidZone displays artwork and stories by young people with learning disabilities (along with information to help students understand their learning disabilities). Finally, there is a search engine for looking up articles on a particular learning disability or articles by specific authors.

Paralysis
Cure Paralysis Now

● http://www.cureparalysis.org/

The hundreds and hundreds of links on this site lead to others, from those reporting on interesting research to a monstrous database of abstracts, all relating to efforts to cure paralysis. The topics range from therapies and clinical trials to prospects for cures. Maintained by Greg Winget, whose goal is to "hasten that inevitable day" when paralysis is cured, this site is a powerful support system for that effort.

Paralysis Support Groups

● http://neurosurgery.mgh.harvard.edu/paral-r.htm

Spine & Peripheral Nerve Surgery Information Links

● http://neurosurgery.mgh.harvard.edu/lnkspine.htm

This page from Massachusetts General Hospital/Harvard Medical School is a comprehensive list of support organizations for people who suffer from spinal cord injuries, stroke, or paralysis. The organizations hotlinked to their sites include the National Easter Seals Society and the American Association of Spinal Cord Injury Psychologists and Social Workers. There is also information regarding contacts and short descriptions of some of the groups.

A comprehensive page of links regarding treatment and surgery is found at the sister site, which has more than a hundred links to paralysis-related scientific and surgical information.

Resources
Assistance Dogs
Assistance Dogs International (ADI)

● http://www.assistance-dogs-intl.org/

ADI promotes standards of excellence in the training, placement, and utilization of assistance dogs and educates the public about these "best friends." Data describes the three types of assistance dogs—guide, hearing, and service—followed by leads to photos and training standards. There are also member lists and links, events, and news, plus a public-access test that outlines the functions a dog must perform in order to become a certified assistance dog.

The Disability Barn

● http://www.accessunlimited.com/links.html

The Disability Barn is a single page of more than 2,000 links divided into 22 categories, ranging from chat and children to statistics and sexuality. These links lead to books, discussion groups, personal homepages, travel services, and many others. This site is dedicated to those living—fully—with disabilities, as opposed to probing the depths of medical research.

[disease]

If the Internet can be said to have any underlying social or moral benefit, it is most likely in the area of providing information on medical issues, diseases in particular. In an age of technology where new treatments and new procedures are developed on a daily basis, those in need of information about diseases constantly wonder whether their doctor, primary caregiver, or HMO is aware of all the treatment options. At the same time, people with a disease do not always want to be limited to, or even follow, the treatments prescribed by their doctors or HMOs.

The medical and academic communities, as well as concerned individuals, have been rigorous about putting vast amounts of medical, research, and treatment data on the web. Support groups, as well as proponents of alternative medicine, have also embraced the web, using it not only to establish communities, but also—in many cases—to question the established thinking or practices of the medical community.

Regardless of the underlying purpose, the Internet has become the single largest reference source on the topic of disease, and certainly the most interactive. Such is the importance of the web that it can contain information on every disease ever catalogued. Unfortunately, there are more diseases that we could ever hope to categorize in a single reference work. The sites in this section provide excellent information on some of the most prevalent, preventable, and disturbing diseases of our age.

American Heart Association

● http://www.americanheart.org/

Be warned: If you take on more significant meaning for those who decide to take the American Heart Association's "What's Your Risk?" test at this site, you may not like what you learn. The good news is, though, it also tells you where to focus your preventive care.

The site offers much to learn about maintaining a healthy heart. The Heart and Stroke A–Z Guide is a directory of information from congestive heart failure to Thallium stress tests. Here, you can look at "biostatistical" fact sheets with graphs and data based on populations (baby boomers, women, Hispanics), risk factors (cholesterol, smoking, obesity), and miscellaneous

(cardiovascular procedures, leading causes of death). Under Family Health, you can learn how to change your lifestyle to prevent or manage heart disease and stroke, talk to your doctor about your concerns, and learn which risk factors you can change. In Your Heart, bone up on CPR techniques using detailed instructions and illustrations and learn what the warning signs of a heart attack are. Sections on Stroke (Prevention, Treatment, Recovery) and Science and Professional (Publications, Research, Statistics) round out the site.

American Social Health Association (ASHA)

● http://www.ashastd.org/

Sexually transmitted diseases (STDs) are often the most socially stigmatized—making the ability to access this information from the privacy of one's computer a major benefit of Internet health sites. Individuals dealing with problems relating to STDs, or simply interested in getting more information, will find an abundance of data here. There are informational articles that explain how to talk about STDs to your partner, myths and misconceptions, and the right way to use a condom. There's also a Q&A and a Sexual Health Glossary, which defines medical and scientific terminology relating to sexual health and STDs. Support Groups, STD news, and links to important hot lines are other pluses of the site. And the Did You Know? section lists scary and thought-provoking facts (such as one in five people in the United States has an STD; STDs—excluding HIV—cost about $8 billion each year to diagnose and treat). The ASHA also compiles news and resources from a host of specialized organizations and government agencies and features them on its site.

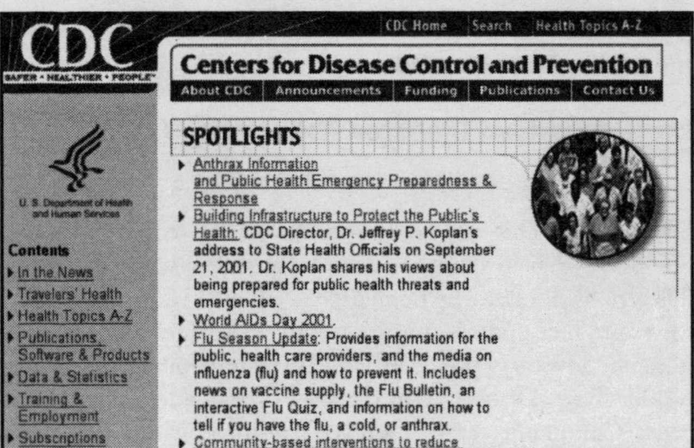

Centers for Disease Control and Prevention (CDC)

● http://www.cdc.gov/

Only on the CDC website can you research African Sleeping Sickness and dog bites at the same time. The CDC, an agency of the U.S. Department of Health and Human Services, is perhaps best known to the public for its handling of epidemics and other disease emergencies (see INFECTIOUS DISEASES). On the web, however, the CDC finds a much wider audience, by providing a wealth of information applicable to all aspects of daily life. Sections include Travelers' Health, General Health Information, News Items, and Data & Statistics. The Health Information section alone is mind-boggling; it covers such disparate topics as cancer, bioterrorism, Rocky Mountain Spotted Fever, child abuse, and animal and insect bites. Each has a related fact sheet or a focus document prepared by the CDC, with links to other sites for additional information. Particularly useful is the Traveler's Health Information section, which offers reference materials to international travelers, including geographic health recommendations, updates on disease outbreaks, immunization requirements, and food and water precautions.

American Diabetes Association (ADA)

● http://www.diabetes.org/

This site represents the ADA's commitment to help diabetics live to the fullest while managing this serious disease. The homepage is jammed with text links to news, product updates, nutrition info, magazines and journals, research, advocacy, providers, and Internet resources. Headings include Basic Diabetes Information, Type 1 and Type 2 Diabetes, Community and Resources, Healthy Living, and more. Other sections offer an African-American program, cooking and recipes, books, and shopping. For the newly diagnosed, there are articles for understanding lab tests. The site also provides professionals with up-to-date information and access to councils, journals, research, education, and clinical practice. Advocacy and legal issues fill a sizable amount of space here as well. There is even data on pets with diabetes.

A unique component of this site is that users can customize it to suit individual needs and interests. The process is easy and allows users to view the latest information from the ADA that's most important to them—every time they enter the site.

Leukemia & Lymphoma Society

● http://www.leukemia.org/

This comprehensive set of pages from the Leukemia & Lymphoma Society focuses on diseases such as leukemia, lymphoma, myeloma, and Hodgkin's. Each is treated individually on its own set of pages that describe the disease and discuss relevant areas such as new cases, deaths, signs and symptoms, treatment, and survival rates. A Patient Services section directs readers to family support groups, patient aid, and outreach programs, and the Chapter Finder locates various Leukemia & Lym-

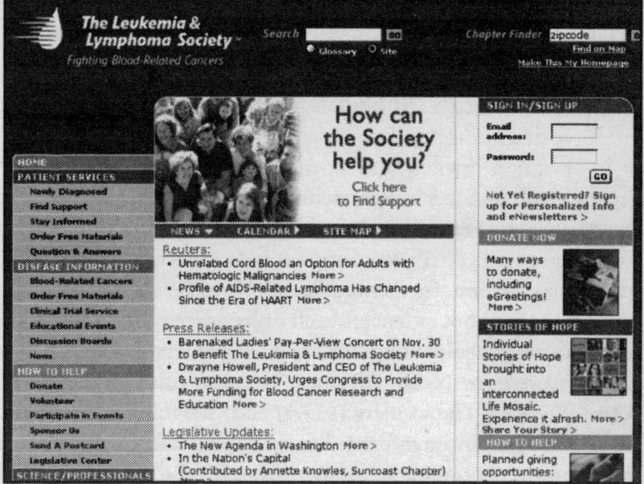

phoma Society chapters. The site also offers educational materials free of charge and features a long list of links to related sites.

National AIDS Treatment Information Project (NATIP)

● http://www.natip.org/index.html

The goal of NATIP is to provide HIV-infected individuals and their caregivers with easy-to-understand clinical information. The site is divided into four categories: Clinical Manifestations, Opportunistic Diseases, Therapeutics, and Miscellaneous. Within these categories is information on some 60 topics covering related illnesses and treatments, such as respiratory and visual problems, bacterial infections, and lymphoma, as well as treatments, including Ritonavir, Zidovudine, CD4 cell count, and viral load testing. Most of the documents are located on the NATIP site itself, though a link leads to related materials posted elsewhere on the Internet. Much of the information here is also available in Spanish.

National Cancer Institute (NCI)

http://www.cancer.gov/

The objective of NCI is to shed light on the various forms of cancer. To that end, it includes some 200 pages of information divided into three sections: Patient, Healthcare Professional, and Basic Researcher. In the Patient section, the categories are Treatment, Complementary & Alternative Medicine, Screening & Prevention, Cancer Genetics, Supportive Care, Information for Ethnic/Racial Groups, and What You Need to Know about Cancer. Each drills down to specifics, with high levels of detail, and grants access to numerous journals, articles and reports. National Cancer Institute employs two databases: Physician Data Query (PDQ) and CANCERLIT to help locate current cancer information, including clinical trials, fact sheets on cancer topics, and information from the *Journal of the National Cancer Institute*, as well as links to other websites. Each database has its own search engine.

The site also has recent news updates on treatments, studies, and drugs. .

National Center for Infectious Disease (NCID)

http://www.cdc.gov/ncidod/

E. coli, *Streptococcus*, parasitic, flesh-eating—names like these make us never want to leave home. But the best way to allay such fears is to educate ourselves, and the CDC is the primary source of data on these diseases. Its Infectious Disease component enables you to search through infectious disease topics, publications, and training programs and use the search engine to look for specific topics within the NCID site. You can also review current and past issues of the *Emerging Infectious Diseases Journal*, which tracks and analyzes both new and reemerging infectious diseases issues.

Other areas include information on AIDS, STD, and TB research; arctic investigations; bacterial and mycotic diseases;

hospital infections; parasitic diseases; scientific resources; and more. A travel link takes you to the Centers for Disease Control's travel information page, so you know where not to travel. About all this site doesn't provide are the cures or the protective suits.

Project Inform

● http://www.projectinform.org/

Project Inform can be considered a companion to the NATIP site listed above. Project Inform's mission is to provide inspiration and information for people with HIV. The key areas are women's HIV/AIDS treatment, a national hot line, and a section on advocacy and public policy. Audio-video files (found in a file index indicated by an open-book icon) provide presentations from the group regarding issues such as antiviral therapy and AIDS research.

The site also has news and current events, and, as with NATIP, much of the content is available in Spanish. There is a lot of information about this nonprofit organization, including its mission; how to join, donate, and volunteer; and its outreach and education programs.

[drugs]

Drugs come in many forms: legal, illegal, prescribed, over-the-counter, liquid, powder, tablet, capsule, herbal, banned, approved, experimental, medicinal, synthetic, natural, and then some. The following sites can shed a little light on what many drugs actually do, divulge government policy about their use, and educate about their dangers.

Drug Education
Druguse.com

● http://www.druguse.com/

The official title of this site is D.R.U.G.S., an acronym for Don't Risk Using, Get Smart. Its purpose is to educate users and potential users to the dangers of popular—and hence widely available—illegal drugs. Run by a reformed delinquent and ex-addict, the site aims to provoke conversation about drug use by serving as a resource for hard facts and anecdotal data. Highlighted by stories by addicts and infrequent users who have seen the wrong side of drugs, D.R.U.G.S. also has surveys, kids links, discussion forums, and a surprisingly complete description of street drugs, their origins, effects, and legal status and classification.

Office of National Drug Control Policy (ONDCP)

● http://www.whitehousedrugpolicy.gov/

Historically, the U.S. government has spent huge amounts of money in the twentieth century combating various types of controlled substances: demon rum and bathtub gin in the 1920s, LSD and marijuana in the 1970s, and crack and so-called designer drugs in the 1990s. How successful has this war been? Well, you'll get the government's take on it on this site, where the White House outlines its rationale behind decades of spearheading the American war on drugs. This is a no-nonsense site,

Y! tip

Browsers now come with facilities that allow you to find "related" or "similar" sites to the one you're viewing. These can be helpful for doing quick comparisons of sites that address the same subject.

with lots of reports, sections on law enforcement, treatment options, prevention and education, and links to the National Institute of Drug Abuse. The deleterious effects of drug abuse are chronicled in dizzying detail, in formats from text reports to slide-show presentations.

Drug Policy Reform
DRCNet (Drug Reform Coordination Network)

● http://drcnet.org/

Remember that money we mentioned in the above site that the U.S. Government has spent on combating drugs? Well, many people believe that the Feds would have been a lot more productive if they had simply flushed that money down the nearest toilet. Drug use and abuse has been an aspect of the human condition since there has been a human condition, and many argue that trying to legislate such behavior only fosters violence and wastes money on ineffective policing and draconian prison laws. Instead, they argue, we should look at treatment options and stop the war on drugs, because it's resulting in too many casualties.

This site bills itself as the central Internet resource on drug policy reform, and it does bring a lot of supporting data to the table. It has links to the world's largest online collection of documents about drugs and drug policy, a weekly online newsletter, a reformer's calendar of events, and a huge archive of articles detailing how current drug policy falls far short of the mark. Some of the most intriguing features cover the militarization of the drug war, the epidemic of drug-related AIDS, and a scathing look at the D.A.R.E. program and its accomplishments—or lack thereof. DRCNet is sponsored in part by the Drug Policy Institute.

PDR.net

● http://www.pdr.net/

PDR.net, which originated from the classic medical text the *Physicians Desk Reference,* is a website devoted to supplying healthcare information for just about everyone. Physicians, pharmacists, nurses, and consumers can find educational and informative resources relevant to all phases of medicine and health care. Physicians can find links to medical journals and publications and latest medicine and drug news. Consumers can take advantage of the Getting Well Network; resources include information about drugs, doctors, and general health updates. Information normally available only to physicians is now available for consumers in a clear and understandable manner, not in medical jargon. Medical news is provided by Reuters and there is even a search engine and a FAQ section. Created by the Medical Economics Company, PDR.net lives up to its moniker as a "Leader in Interactive Healthcare for Medical and Drug Information." And it costs and weighs a lot less than the actual *Physician's Desk Reference,* which is, of course, available here for purchase.

[emergencies]

Emergencies are, by their nature, huge rips in the fabric of our otherwise nicely structured lives. You hope they never happen, and because they rarely do, you never plan for them. Then, when they strike, you look frantically for assistance, diving through books and first-aid guides, or maybe first-aid kits, medicine cabinets, and ultimately the phone book. A better way to prepare for emergencies is to spend some time poring over these emergency sites. Then bookmark them—now. In an era of cable modems, these pages will be faster to get to then your big book of first-aid facts. Remember: Timing, as they say, is everything, whether you're dealing with a broken finger or the onset of Armageddon.

Emergency and Disaster
National
FEMA

● http://www.fema.gov/library/lib07.htm

No matter where you live, you're in the way of some kind of natural disaster or seasonal natural disturbance. Live along the eastern seaboard? You've got hurricanes. The West Coast? Earthquakes. The Southwest? Monsoons. The Northeast? Blizzards, searing heat, and power outages. The Midwest? Tornadoes. Pick a place and there is bound to be some relative of Mother Nature who has a bone to pick with you.

The Emergency and Disaster page of the Federal Emergency Management Agency (FEMA) site has a large selection of files and documents devoted to preparing you to deal with regional emergencies. Emergencies described here start at the really local level, like your kitchen, and fact sheets list hazardous materials and tell how to keep food and water pure in an emergency. The disasters get broader and worse, covering hurricanes, landslides, tornadoes, and volcanoes. Then FEMA even goes beyond the realm of natural events to the truly scary man-made crises, which include nuclear power plant disasters and terrorist situations.

You'll find plenty of preparedness documents at the site, explaining how to create a family disaster kit, make checklists for emergency events, and get your finances in order. Some of these documents contain photographs, and there are several audio and video files. Our recommendation: Don't wait until the flood waters start seeping into your second-floor bedroom to visit this site. Know in advance what you're up against by spending some quality time with this page next time you have a sunny day to spare.

Emergency Preparedness
The EPICenter

● http://www.theepicenter.com/

Billed as an "emergency preparedness information center," the EPICenter is a simple site that provides helpful tips and access to products so that you can be ready for almost any natural disaster. In addition to checklists and articles, plans for such emergency systems as solar power and water purification, and background information on various potential disasters, the site offers RealPlayer recordings of radio programs and a wide range of supplies that run the gamut from all kinds of flashlights and first-aid kits to MREs, the "meals ready to eat" used by the armed forces.

The EPICenter offers a host of links grouped according to topics such as volcanoes and earthquakes and includes the Tip o'da Week and an archive of past tips. And on a lighter note, there's a page with games and links to "fun things to do while waiting for disaster"; this page encapsulates the EPICenter's apparent goal: making emergency preparedness fun.

[exercise & fitness]

Most people need more than a little motivation to begin exercising. The thought of beginning a fitness routine can be intimidating—where to begin? The abs? The glutes? The love handles? The sites below will help make you sweat and take off the pounds. They range from serious weight lifting of Arnold Schwarzenegger proportions to the meditative benefits of yoga. Best of all, nobody's going to see you in your workout spandex while you're starting out, and you don't have to pay for a monthly membership

General Fitness
Shape Up America

● http://www.shapeup.org/

How much weight do you really need to lose? For that matter, do you need to lose any weight at all? (Believe it or not, there are people in this category.) Stretch your knowledge at Shape Up America, a site that provides visitors with the latest information on safe weight management, healthy eating, and physical fitness.

The site boasts some cool interactive sections. In Cyberkitchen, you can "order" meal plans tailored to your lifestyle by creating a profile of yourself and your physique. Enter your weight, gender, activity level, height, and age and Cyberkitchen uses the information to estimate a daily calorie goal. It even allows you to specify a daily fat limit. The Body Mass Index (BMI) lets you look at your own current physical condition and determine how much fat you might be carrying around. Select your height and weight, and a customized chart and rating will tell you if you might be at a level where you can encounter health risks.

Shape Up America has a library with full-color brochures on living well, plus a section for health professionals. The Support Center talks about the difficulties of weight management, and offers practical solutions. Don't just sit there—shape up.

Workouts
Fitness Online

● http://www.fitnessonline.com/

You want to look and feel better? You want to lose weight? You want to eat better? Add muscle? Find out how at Fitness Online. Offering a full range of workout information, tips, and dieting, Fitness Online can address your individual needs via tailored data in its various categories. You create a personal profile with your goals to direct the site to find articles and data that relate to these criteria.

In addition, there are analyses of diets ranging from Weight Watchers to the Zone. There are advice columns from various experts, including workout pioneer Kathy Smith. Content is provided by a variety of magazines, including *Shape, Men's Fitness, Muscle & Fitness, Fit Pregnancy, Natural Health*, and *Flex*, all published by Weider.

Aerobic
Turn Step

● http://www.turnstep.com/index.html

Maybe you're not a fan of doing aerobics with two dozen other people—all in better shape—watching your every move. Well, you can formulate *your own* "class" at this site. Pick your own workout moves from more than 5,000 aerobic patterns; you can search by pattern (body sculpting, step, slide, etc.) or look at the featured patterns of the month to vary your routine. There is also an aerobics dictionary and a list of recommended aerobics music selections. Unfortunately, the site cannot provide an instructor to help you stick to your regimen and make you "feel the burn."

Running
Running Online

● http://www.runningonline.com/

Running Online is sort of an oxymoron, since one of the things you can't do online is run (at least until virtual reality kicks in). In lieu of that, you can get tons of information online about running, at Running Online—the site that has it all. This is a single-site search engine and browsable directory for running enthusiasts of all levels, ages, and interests. As with other category-specific search sites listed in this book (ScubaSearch, Femina, Bibliofind), the categories here have been screened by the site's editors to provide interested visitors with the best sites. The astounding number of running categories include Clubs, People, Colleges, Publications, High Schools, Races, Indices, Records, Marathons, Software, Media, Stores, and Training.

Run the Planet

● http://www.runtheplanet.com/

For travelers or visitors who need to get out and run while they're on the road, this site serves as a guide to running anywhere on the planet. Run the Planet is a huge database that provides runners and walkers with information on where to run or walk in the main cities of the world. It offers descriptions of courses and parks and recommendations on where to spend quality jogging time in places like Paris, Rome, New York, and many more. There is also a running dictionary in different languages, a list of who's who in running, a T-shirt trading post, data on marathons, quotes from runners, and even an audio welcome-to-the-site message available in a various languages. Run the Planet is hosted by Neri Editore, the publishers of the Italian running magazine *Podismo*.

Seniors
Aging, Exercise, and Depression

● http://www.coolware.com/health/medical_reporter/exercise.html

Currently, there are 31 million people, or 12 percent of the total U.S. population, age 65 and older. The Census Bureau anticipates that 62 million people, or almost one in five Americans, will be age 65 or older by 2025. Though we cannot stop the aging process, we can make it a healthier, happier one by exercising. This site is a short treatise on why seniors should exercise. Too many people feel that as they get older, chronic illness, debilitating disease, and moving in slow motion are part and parcel of the aging process. Not true, and this page sets out to debunk those myths, such as "Older people shouldn't exercise, because it might hurt them or use up what little strength and vitality they have left" and "Even if exercise won't hurt, it can't possibly help. By the time someone is 60 or 65, the damage has already been done and can't be reversed anyway, so why bother?" The message of this site is "Use it, don't lose it." This site is presented by the Rose Medical Center and Cigna in Denver, Colorado. For actual exercise regimens that seniors can engage in, we recommend checking out the other sites in this section.

Walking

Racewalk.com

● http://www.racewalk.com/

Race walking is a combination of running, racing, and walking. Though it is an excellent, simple form of excerise, there's a right way and plenty of wrong ways to do it. Racewalk.com, the official race walking homepage of United States Association of Track and Field, provides all the information you need to start or improve your walking program (whether for competition or fitness). In addition to discussing the benefits and how-to's of race walking, the site posts events in the walking community and links to walking resources.

Yoga

Yoga Anand Ashram

● http://www.santosha.com/

Yoga Paths

● http://www.spiritweb.org/Spirit/Yoga/Overview.html

Yoga Site

● http://www.yogasite.com/

To the uninitiated, yoga practitioners may resemble human pretzels. This ancient form of excerise—a philosophy, really—is the focus of the Yoga Anand Ashram site a guide to yogic postures and meditation, illustrated graphics, and instructional texts. The texts are transcriptions of meditations by Gurani Anjali at Yoga Anand Ashram. They cover the essential yogic topics: Kriya yoga, Svadhyaya (self study), and Maya (illusion). Step-by-step instructions are shown for more than two dozen postures, including Akarna dhanur-asana, Bhadda kona-asana, Parshvakona-asana, and Vriksha-asana. The site also features yoga philosophy, vajra books, a moksha journal, and an area for feedback.

If yoga to you is a lifestyle, not just a form of excerise, a lifestyle, Yogic Paths is the site for you. This site focuses on the study of the Vedic texts and lessons that form the basis of yoga, which is a complete course of spiritual study and pursuit. There are hundreds of pages on yoga here, from lessons in each of many different traditions, to history and resources on the web. Subject headings include Yoga Paths, Karma Yoga, Bhakti-Yoga, Original Kriya Yoga, Astanga Yoga, Siddha Mahayoga FAQ, the Living Tradition of Sahaj Marg, Sahaja Yoga, the Quan Yin Method, Agni Yoga, Mantra Yoga, Yantra Yoga, Tantra, Laya Yoga, Yoga lessons, and Miscellaneous Yoga Information.

For broader information on all things yogic, stop in at the Yoga Site, positioned as an "eclectic collection of yogic connections." Its purpose is to facilitate education about yoga and its traditions, more so than to describe positions. There is a diverse set of sections here, including a teacher directory, a yoga style guide, yoga retreats, teacher training, publications, newsgroups, yoga organizations, and a posture page.

[first aid]

First Aid—Skill for Life

● http://firstaid.eire.org/Firstaid_index.html

"The life you save may be the life you love." From this sobering introduction, the First Aid—Skill for Life site takes you through the proper treatment procedures for more than 50 different emergencies, large and small. This site is set up to help you during an actual emergency and guides you through the process of dealing with a variety of accidents and occurrences, ranging from splinters, sprains, and stings to spinal injuries, shock, and burns and scalds (the difference is that the latter is caused by wet heat). Information like this can make all the difference in a critical situation.

Each of these categories gives you a crash course—time is of the essence, obviously—in identifying the signs and symptoms, followed by the quickest and most prudent course of action. In some cases, the treatment given in the first few minutes determines the outcome. This site, based in Ireland by the way, should be browsed and bookmarked, if only so that you become familiar with the types of emergencies you may encounter.

Mayo Clinic First Aid & Self-Care Guide

● http://www.mayoclinic.com/home?id=SP5.6

Did you know that if one of your teeth gets knocked out and cannot be replaced in the socket, you should immediately place the tooth in milk, your own saliva, or a warm, mild saltwater solution? Or that human bites can often be more dangerous than animal bites because of the types of bacteria and viruses living in the human mouth? Simple emergency information like this can go a long way toward helping you survive a lot of crises, and this Mayo Clinic site brings the full bearing of the institution's respected medical reputation to handling emergencies.

The Mayo site differs from the First Aid site just described in that it takes a more specialized approach to emergencies (spinal injuries, arm fractures, sprains, and dislocations are all listed under Trauma, for instance). It also provides information on the medical diagnoses behind each emergency (e.g., poisoning is the ingesting, inhaling, or injecting of any substance that interferes with the body's normal function). Some of this information may not be exactly what you want in the heat of a dire situation, but Mayo does deliver the goods when you find the First Aid listing under each topic (such as tick bites, foreign objects in the eye, head trauma, resuscitation, etc.). Moreover, in many cases, the Mayo site offers .avi videos on specific treatments that you can download and review.

[general health]

Health
General
Healthfinder

● http://www.healthfinder.gov/

Food safety. AIDS. Medicare. Tobacco. All are national health hot buttons. You can now click on this U.S. government site that can retrieve authoritative data on these and other health topics. Developed by the Department of Health & Human Services, Healthfinder is a portal site that provides reliable consumer health information. The site's search engine leads to online publications, databases, support groups, and health-related websites selected by the agency. You'll also find news categories for different age groups, ethnicities, and families and data on quality medical care.

HealthAtoZ

● http://www.HealthAtoZ.com/

Imagine having a medical assistant residing in your house to keep track of your family's health records and medication. That's HealthAtoZ, a site that acts as your personal organizer for all things health-related. The site's E-Mate feature will schedule e-mail reminders of important medical appointments; keep track of your daily diet and exercise; maintain your family's health and immunization records; record

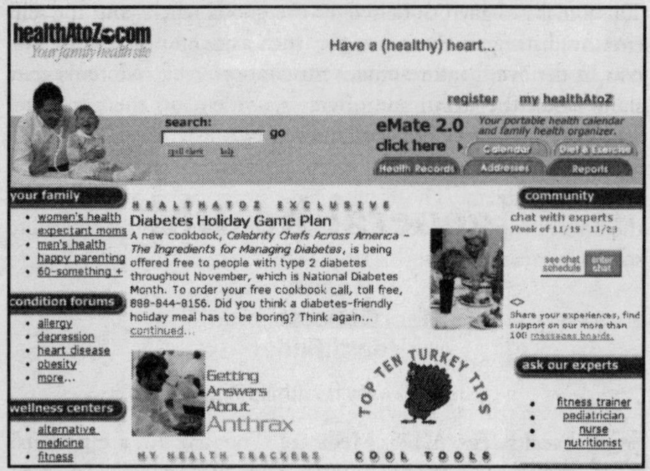

and retrieve your doctor's and local hospital's phone numbers (along with directions); keep an accurate record of your medications, refills, and supplements; and determine how your lifestyle and daily habits affect your daily and long-term health. Not bad for a free service.

Of course, like all good health sites, HealthAtoZ has plenty more to offer. There are nearly 40 Condition Forums that serve as support communities and information resources, on allergies and asthma and sleep disorders and stroke and everything in between. The site's search engine leads you to more than 50,000 professionally reviewed sites, and the homepage features health and medicine updates, news, and a weekly poll.

Healthcare Issues
Employer Quality Partners

● http://www.eqp.org/

People would get better healthcare if they knew what they were entitled to and—just as important—what they could demand.

This site is designed to help employees, employers, and the self-employed navigate the maze that is our nation's healthcare system. A series of online guides gives people the questions they should ask their healthcare providers, and it alerts them to issues regarding when they can see a doctor, how extensive their coverage is, what their personal responsibility is, and how to handle a coverage problem. Those who have ever had a problem with their healthcare plan, or are joining a new plan, would do well to schedule some time on this site.

Health Economics

● http://www.healtheconomics.com/

For a truly global view of health sites on the Net, click on Health Economics. It categorizes much of the web's health content into a dozen sections: Associations, Consulting/Service, Databases, Education/Universities, Employment, Government, Journals & Publications, Libraries, Miscellaneous Links, Pharmaceutical & Biotech Companies, Pharmacy Resources, and Questionnaire/Performance Assessment. While this search site considers itself the "professional's guide to health economics resources on the Net," any smart healthcare consumer will consider this the place to start when looking for second opinions.

HealthWorld Online

● http://www.healthy.net/

If you're one of those people who doesn't like to go to the doctor for anything short of major invasive surgery, this site could become your favorite medical destination. A veritable online cornucopia of medical advice and self-care on hundreds of conditions from athlete's foot and anorexia to warts, whooping cough, and wounds, this site gives you basic information on what your affliction is, what might have caused it, what can be done about it, and what you should be doing to fix it.

The stylized design of HealthWorld resembles the map of a college campus. Each of the buildings is labeled by its respective functions. There is a Health University, a Library, a Nutrition Center, a Clinic, a Marketplace, and several other scenic stops. There are also plenty of other general-purpose and consumer health-related "locations" here.

The Library, the Health Clinic, the Association Network, and the Professional Center are the pages for getting more technical medical information. At the Health Clinic are two pull-down menus, one for Health Conditions and one for Emergency & First Aid. The Health Conditions menu has more physical ailments than we could count, ranging from the routine (coughs, cold and flu, cuts) to the serious (pneumonia, hepatitis, chemical poisoning, rheumatism), to the debilitating (multiple sclerosis, prostate cancer, epilepsy), and even the puzzling or annoying (bad breath, flatulence, canker sores, dandruff, jock itch). The content for each of these varies; some have full text descriptions of the condition and recommended paths to recovery, others are research papers addressing the topic, and still others are downloadable audio presentations on the condition (some in this last category must be purchased and are identified by a Premium button).

The Emergency & First Aid section has a similar pulldown menu, but it addresses more urgent medical situations including animal bites, electric shock, frostbite, head injuries, and seizures. Choosing one of these puts you in a section of text information about what to look for, what to ask, and what to do in emergency situations.

One cool aspect of both these sections is a logic diagram that charts a course of action for you to follow, starting with a basic question. If the answer is yes, you follow the chart one way; if no, you go a different way. At each new point you answer another question until you get to an appropriate solution. For instance, under electric shock, the first question is "Has the person

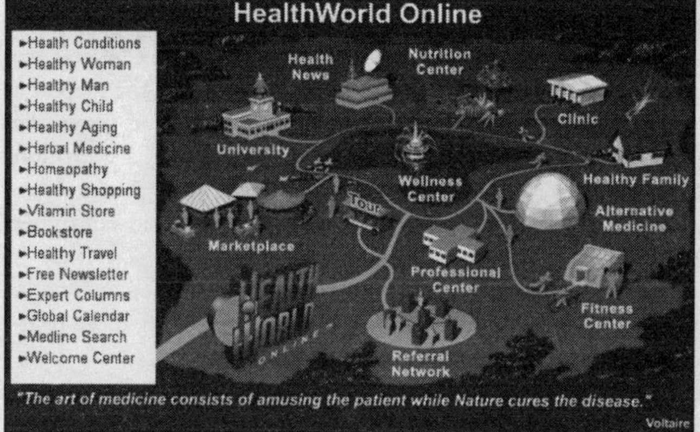

received a shock from a high voltage wire?" If the answer is yes, the next stage of the diagram is "seek emergency care" and "give first aid" with instructions how to administer that aid. If, on the other hand, the answer is no, you proceed to the next part of the chart, which asks, "Has the person been struck by lightning?" If the answer is yes . . . and so on. Great feature.

The library has a Medline search; medical reference journals, newsletters, interviews and columns; and a collection of audio tapes for sale. The Professional Center is geared more toward integrative health care, homeopathy, and natural and alternative medicine and features columns as well as a professional referral menu.

As great as this site is, remember that a doctor is still your best first line of inquiry. Besides, spending too much time on this site might turn you into a hypochondriac. But, if you use it wisely, it can turn you into a well-informed keeper of your own body.

[internet medical guides]

Cardiology—CardioGuide

- http://www.cardioguide.com/

Dentistry—DentalGate

- http://www.dentalgate.com/

Dermatology—DermGuide

- http://www.dermguide.com/

Neurosurgery—NeuroGate

- http://www.neurogate.com/

Ophthomology—OpthoGuide

- http://www.ophthoguide.com/

Orthopedics—OrthoGuide

- http://www.orthoguide.com/

Urology—UroGuide

- http://www.uroguide.com/

Each of these sites is designed to search for information specifically related to its name (CardioGuide searches for cardiology, for example). Although they are different sites with different URLs, they all have the same layout, containing two search engines and an index for browsing. The first search engine scans the web for all information related to a term you type in. The second search engine scans Medline within the category you've chosen, trimming all the available journals down to those that are related (for faster results). If you type "cataracts" into the OphthoGuide search box, for instance, the first engine will return every web reference to cataracts it can find. If you do this in the Medline search engine, only ophthalmologic journals are returned, which gives you more focused results, faster.

There are also browsing sections in each category, where you can drill down for more general information, or at least be pointed to more specific data. These indexes include Specialties (in Cardiology, this includes areas such as Catheterization, Cardiovascular Research, Transplantation, etc.), Education (from board reviews to residency), Disorders (listed alphabetically), and Organizations. The Disorders category in each guide is immense, in some cases covering hundreds of different areas—all hotlinked to sites on the web addressing those particular disorders.

[massage]

Massage Therapy Central

● http://www.qwl.com/mtwc/

Let's make one thing clear: Massage therapy is not a euphemism for "illicit sex." Massage Therapy Central is a site for serious practitioners of massage therapy and its application in medical and therapeutic situations. It contains a user's guide to massage therapy (stressing the importance of hiring a licensed therapist, the value of massage as a drug-free healing art, etc.); a global directory of massage therapists; resources such as schools, organizations, and healthcare groups; and articles and research literature. There are also networking sections for professionals, an index of massage techniques and methods, and an analysis of massage as portrayed in the media.

Illustrated Guide to Muscles and Clinical Massage Therapy

● http://www.danke.com/Orthodoc/

Ever wonder why your hand falls asleep when you hold your arm over your head? Prefer to have your carpal tunnel syndrome treated without having your tendons sliced by a surgeon? The answers are here in a kaleidoscopic page of information ranging from muscles and massage to pain and posture. Dozens of sections on the site include an animation of how muscles work, articles on tendonitis and bursitis, massage treatments for various types of pain, and discussions on posture alignment and common injuries such as carpal tunnel syndrome (with illustrations). The site has a complete massage therapy section, with information for everyone from children to dancers.

[medicine]

Only three areas on the web are so pervasive that they have their own dedicated networks: medicine and health, financial services, and leisure and entertainment. What's notable about medicine in particular is that though many sites are dedicated to the professional, their owners claim that a huge percentage of the visitors—in some cases as much as half—are laypeople looking for information.

One of the reasons we've included so many medical sites is the recent widespread availability of medical information that formerly was regarded as the private domain of physicians since the days when leeches were used to cure hangnails. But thanks to the Net, everyone can access this material and be better informed about their health, their illnesses, and the information that doctors tell them. Now there is no reason for anyone not to understand what's happening—or could happen—to their body (of course, some things aren't knowable; we're trying to be general here).

That said, one caveat: The web shouldn't serve as a first or even a second opinion if you're in need of medical attention. That's why doctors and hospitals exist. But the Internet can be used to help you help yourself, to get data on areas of medical concern without a prescription. With all this in mind, we've included some resources designed for consumers, others designed for doctors, and even those that straddle a middle ground, especially in the area of alternative medicine.

Alternative & Complementary Medicine Center

● http://www.altmed.net/

This part of Health World Online uses the same excellent features as its parent to address specifically what most of us consider alternative medicine. There are two areas here: The first is made up of types of medicine designated by the World Health Organization as traditional medicine, but referred to as alternative or complementary in the United States. The areas include Acupuncture, Homeopathy, Ayurvedic Medicine, Naturopathic Medicine, Chiropractic, Osteopathy, Herbal Medicine, Traditional Chinese Medicine, and Alternative & Complementary Therapies.

The second area is made up of therapies currently considered to be "unconventional" in the United States. For all their unconventionality, there certainly are a lot of them: Aromatherapy, Biofeedback Training, Bodywork & Somatic Therapies, Chelation Therapy, Detoxification Therapies, Energy Medicine/Bio-Energetic Medicine, Environmental Medicine, Expressive Arts Therapies, Fasting, Flower Remedies, Guided Imagery, Integrative Dentistry, Mind/Body Medicine, Nutritional (Orthomolecular) Medicine, and Qigong (Chi Kung) & Taiji (Tai Chi).

Martindale's Health Science Guide

● http://www-sci.lib.uci.edu/HSG/HSGuide.html

Martindale's is a slickly packaged index of links to medical and health resources across the web. It covers nearly two dozen "centers" including Brain & Neuro, Chemistry, Dental, Nursing, Nutrition, Cardiology & Pulmonary, and, of course, Otolaryngology, Otorhinolaryngology & Ophthalmology (don't ask; go to the site and look it up). These centers are the launch points to extremely long pages of links with innumerable quantities of data. Well, that's not exactly true; webmaster Jim Martindale has counted them. According to his tally, the links on his site lead to more than 61,700 teaching files, more than 131,700 medical cases, 1,235 multimedia courses/textbooks, 1,625 multimedia tutorials, 4,160 databases, and thousands of movies (audio-video files).

The Merck Manual

● http://www.merck.com/pubs/mmanual_home/content.htm

The Merck Manual is the medical textbook most widely used by healthcare professionals around the world, so we thought it would be a good place to start your journey into web medicine. Officially known as *The Merck Manual of Diagnosis and Therapy*, this site is based on *The Home Edition*, which transforms medical jargon into commonly used English while retaining all of the vital information about diseases, diagnosis, prevention, and treatment.

Although the web version is composed only of selected extracts from *The Home Edition*, it does contain the complete sections on the heart, infections, the eye, and gynecology and obstetrics, along with the complete table of contents, a full guide to medical terms, and a list of contributors. The section on the heart can be viewed with Adobe Acrobat Reader, which approximates the way the book looks in print. Of course, the actual print edition can be purchased here, too.

The URL listed here is for the table of contents, which provides you with all the links to the online text. *The Manual* site is fairly standard HTML gray, and except for the noted Acrobat files, is straight text. (Note: the Merck.com/ site is quite good. It features a host of issues related to health and wellness.) All in all, this site may end up being the model for companies that want to put their retail products online without giving away the entire store.

Wellness Web

● http://www.wellweb.com/

The Wellness Web is equal parts medical journal, professional contrarian, traditional and homespun sage, and researcher. The site presents information on a plethora of medical topics from incontinence and impotence to cancer and cholestrol. Along the way it presents data about drug dosages and compliance and treatment options and research; tells how to select a healthcare provider; reports on dozens of illnesses and conditions; and offers tips about healthy lifestyles, clinical trials, community health programs, and complementary treatment alternatives and options.

What sets this site apart is that it presents more than one view of the news and breakthroughs, particularly in the alternative medicine category, where there's information supporting—and debunking—the health benefits of various vitamins and supplements such as garlic and chromium picolinate. You want another opinion? You'll get it here, as pro and con on every topic are presented one after another.

This is also a place to come and share ideas, and where clinical trial participants discuss their medication and experiences in open letters to the Wellness Web. The best example of this is the Pain Management section, a no-holds-barred look at the dilemmas facing patients and doctors in maintaining quality of life.

But the site's main goal is to inform, and its primary concern is for the individual patient, not a group of case studies. The following excerpt from the site's mission statement says it best: "Some widely accepted conventional practices have yet to be proven effective, and when quality of life is considered, some even leave the patient worse off from crippling side effects. On the other hand, although many—probably most—alternative practices haven't been scientifically studied, they may add to quality of life even if they aren't effective for the condition they're prescribed for." If you want technical data for all things related to medical conditions, you might want to start with other

> **Y! tip**
>
> There are times when you will not get any response from clicking on a hotlink. Sometimes this is because the link is dead, or the problem could be that your browser didn't register the click. Always try connecting least one more time before giving up.

sites reviewed in this section, but if you want to approach it as a daily experience, bookmark the Wellness Web.

[men's]

Men's Issues VL

● http://www.vix.com/pub/men/index.html

As one page within the Virtual Library—billed as "the oldest catalog on the Web"—the Men's Issues page provides easy access to information and links on topics that all men should realize are important issues, from the difficult-to-discuss such as domestic violence and battered men or false-rape reports, to the more universal, such as physical and mental health, and fatherhood.

There is both an alphabetical subject index and a hierarchical topical index at the site. And, displaying a bit of humor amidst very serious subjects, the index is described with the words "Of course it's hierarchical. It's a guy thing." The Periodicals Option of the Men's Movement button leads to a listing of more than 45 magazines, with links to their websites; the Men's Health button leads to articles and links on such issues as sexual addiction, suicide, AIDS and HIV, and diet. The Paternity heading in the Single Dad Index leads to a dozen articles related to the issue.

[mental health]

Everyone experiences anxiety, whether just before making a speech, asking someone out on a first date, buying a car, or rushing to meet a deadline. But these are minor forms of anxiety; anxiety of a more serious nature can be crippling, preventing sufferers from getting on with their lives. According to the National Institute of Mental Health, anxiety disorders are the most common type of mental disorder.

Anxiety

Anxiety Disorders

● http://www.nimh.nih.gov/anxiety/anxiety/index.htm

This site from the National Institute of Mental Health is designed to provide information on anxiety disorders, panic disorders, obsessive-compulsive disorder, post-traumatic stress disorder, phobias, and generalized anxiety disorder. Each is given its own section, which describes—in a conversational tone—the disorder, its effects (what it feels like), the possible causes and treatment, and where you can go for help. The help category has a long list of associations and organizations, as well as contact and online data. The site also has a news section and a library, plus a link to the main NIMH web page.

The Anxiety Panic Internet Resource (tAPir)

● http://www.algy.com/anxiety/index.shtml

TAPir is a self-help network dedicated to helping people overcome debilitating anxiety disorders. The site is divided into sections that include Anxiety Disorders (agoraphobia, social phobia, anxiety in children), Newsletter, Bulletin Board, Support (online discussions, alternative approaches to treatment), and Store (books and links). Lengthy and well-written articles delve into each of these topics, with further data available via links to professional and research organizations.

Internet Mental Health

● http://www.mentalhealth.com/

Internet Mental Health tackles a tough subject with a succinct approach: "Our goal is to improve understanding, diagnosis, and treatment of mental illness throughout the world." Impressively, the site does just that. The Disorders section has descriptions, diagnoses, treatment, and research findings on the 52 most common mental disorders, listed alphabetically from acute stress disorder to Tourette's syndrome. This same group is also cross-referenced by category, from anxiety to substance-related disorders. Under the Medications heading is information on many prescribed drugs, according to "pharmacology, indications, contraindications, warnings, precautions, adverse effects, overdose, dosage, supplied, and research."

The site includes an online Internet Mental Health magazine, as well as a huge number of links to other websites related to specific mental disorders. And it gives students and future mental health professionals an early start on their research; the Help section offers advice under the Helping Students with Projects heading. There are also links to more than 20 Internet search engines to guide users who are unable to find the information they require at Internet Mental Health.

Mental Health Net

● http//mentalhelp.net/

Mental Health Net is a comprehensive site for both the layperson and the professional, providing some 9,300 indexed resources. Features here range from What's New and Lighten Up! (a humor page) to Disorders & Treatments, Professional Resources, and a Reading Room. There are Community and Services subsections, as well as topic-specific buttons. The Sleep Problems section leads to a large listing of web resources, newsgroups, a mailing list sign-up opportunity, and other resources, including an area of products for sale.

Mental Health Net also provides a valuable Clinicians Yellow Pages, with a search engine that allows users to choose from more than 1,200 listed professionals according to geographic and diagnostic information. The Reading Room features articles, expert advice, chat and support forums, and Mental Health Net's monthly editorial. A subscription service updates enrollees twice monthly, and the Metapsychology bookstore lets you to search for titles on-site or at Amazon.com. About the only thing this information-packed site can't do for you is prescribe medication.

[organ transplants & donors]

Organ Donation

● http://www.organdonor.gov/

Each day approximately 55 people receive an organ transplant, and 10 on the waiting list die because not enough organs are available. That simple statistic is the reason this site exists. People refuse to donate their organs primarily due to fear, misconception, or lack of information. Organ Donation goes to great lengths to provide the information that it hopes will help people make the decision to donate. To that end the site is packed with facts and figures, FAQs, myths, public affairs, and legislative issues.

Agreeing to organ donation is a simple process: You can become a donor simply by signing the back of your driver's license. If you want something more formal, you can download a donor card in .pdf format from this site (under the Sign Up link).

TransWeb

● http://www.transweb.org/

In spite of all the medical advances in this arena, the transplanting of organs still sounds like the plot of a sci-fi movie, circa 1950. But transplanting—the activity that follows organ donation—saves thousands of people's lives a year. This site covers all the philosophical and some of the medical issues of organ transplantation, as well as a few of the more esoteric ("How many are waiting?" and "Can I reach my donor's family?"). Sections include Real People, Q&A, Top 10 Myths ("Which religions oppose donation?" and "I heard about someone whose kidneys were stolen; is that true?" Sorry, urban legend lovers, not true), News, Reference Desk, On-Location, and the Transplant Journey. The last set of pages is an illustrated journey through the transplant process, handled very tactfully. You follow Amy, a transplant recipient, along every step, from finding out that a transplant is necessary to the donor process to the operation. Each segment is clarified by simple pictures that lay it on the line.

The multimedia segments here include videos, most notably relating to the "Nicholas Effect" (the international response to the donation of organs by a seven-year-old murder victim named Nicholas Green) and audio moments from the World Transplant games. The value of organ donation is exemplified in the lives of transplant recipients.

An entire section of the site is dedicated to the discussion of xenostransplants and xenografts, which are organ exchanges between different species. A link to the National Institutes of Health database on xenotransplants is included, along with article links to other media discussions of the topic.

[pregnancy]

Infertility
International Council on Infertility Information Dissemination (INCIID)

● http://www.inciid.org/

The stated goal of this site is to provide infertile couples with immediate access to information they need to find the best available medical and psychological treatment. To that end, it succeeds very well. INCIID's site features several dozen fact sheets on topics such as infertility and testing information, reproductive technologies, surgery options, legal and insurance issues, and others. It also contains transcripts of INCIID events and seminars, nearly 50 message and support boards, and a glossary, plus industry updates on companies that provide infertility products and services.

Midwifery
American College of Nurse-Midwives (ACNM)

● http://www.acnm.org/

Since the 1980s, midwifery has been making quite a comeback. Midwives serve as doctor, nurse, counselor, administrator, and paramedic all in one. At ACNM.org, you can read articles on the benefits of using midwives, get information on pregnancy—and not getting pregnant—learn about midwives who participate in managed healthcare, and search for a licensed midwife in your area. And if you're interested in becoming a midwife, you'll find links to accredited programs, certification boards, and financial aid.

Miscarriage
FertilityPlus—Miscarriage Resources

● http://www.fertilityplus.org/toc.html#miscarriage

Miscarriage is a physical and emotional trauma. In its aftermath, it is often difficult to understand what happened and whether it's possible to stop it from happening again. This site addresses many such sensitive issues, from testing to grief support. The primary sections offer information on recurrent pregnancy loss testing and a medical dictionary of terms associated with pregnancy and miscarriage. There is also a comprehensive listing of online newsgroups, mail lists, medical websites, support groups, and memorial pages. This site is just one small component of the FertilityPlus website, which provides information for people who are trying to conceive.

Prenatal Care, Diagnosis
Prenatal Diagnosis Homepage

● http://www.stanford.edu/~holbrook/

Percutaneous umbilical blood sampling and alphafetoprotein screening aren't exactly terms that roll off the tongue; what they are are important tests for at-risk pregnancies. This site is a source of discussion on these and other prenatal diagnostic tests. Hosted by an associate professor at Stanford University's School of Medicine, the site features detailed explanations—and images—of tests ranging from the familiar (ultrasound, amniocentesis) to the not-so-familiar (chorionic villus sampling). It outlines the procedures and details the benefits and risks associated with each. Additional information is provided in the form of video clips, and there is data on specific types of disease, such as Rh, cystic fibrosis, and Ashkenazi Jewish genetic diseases.

Support
StorkNet

● http://www.storknet.org/

When you're pregnant, there are times when no one—not your husband, your friends, your mother, nor anyone else in your life—understands what you're feeling. The only person who could possibly understand is another pregnant woman. In recognition of this particular need, StorkNet has set up a community for pregnant women, where they can share their comments, their joys and sorrows, and their experiences. Divided into "cubbies," moms-to-be can get very personal information—and support—on topics such as Cesarean birth, working while pregnant, and home birthing. There are links to baby products and services, parenting journals, free electronic birth announcements, and a week-by-week pregnancy guide. The last feature tells what to expect each week relative to the development of your child and how your body will change, tidbits for dads, and inspirational thoughts. StorkNet is a superb outlet for all those times when being pregnant feels like you're carrying around more than a new life.

[psychology]

Psychology is the study of the mind, a large and nebulous world. In fact, no one actually knows how the mind works. Fortunately, some workings of the mind can be studied, and when necessary, treated by mental health professionals. These sites take a look at a wide variety of psychological issues, each set up to help you "take a look at yourself" (to quote about a thousand pop songs). But don't start diagnosing yourself—or your friends—with the information you find here; you might drive yourself crazy.

The Phobia List

● http://www.phobialist.com/

Terrified, but you don't know of what? This site is about putting a name to your fears. Literally. The Phobia List is exactly that: a long index of hundreds of fears by their names, from bibliophobia (fear of books) to gnosiosphobia (fear of knowledge). If you look long enough, you'll probably find something you can be afraid of here. Our favorites? Coulrophobia (fear of clowns), scriptophobia (fear of writing in public), and, of course, hippopotomonstrosesquippedaliophobia (fear of long words).

Psychology Web Resources

● http://www.psych.neu.edu/facllinks/

For a serious study of psychology, this list of links from Northeastern University is the best on the web. It categorizes every-

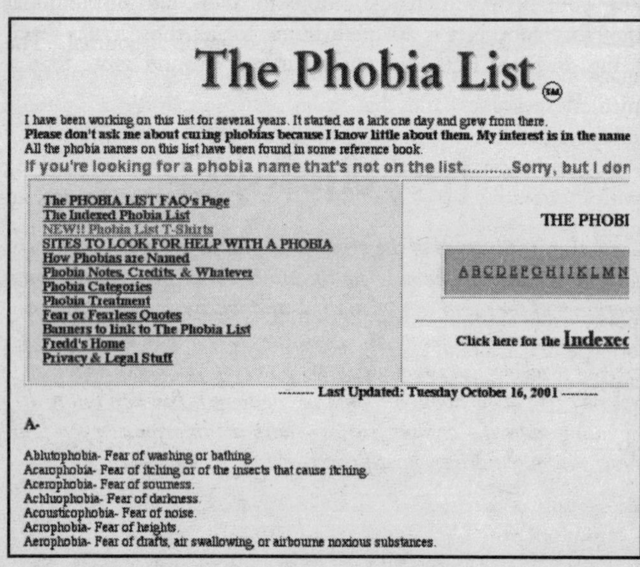

thing in a table of contents under the main headings Abnormal, Behavioral Neuroscience, Clinical, Cognition, Developmental, Language & Speech, Organizations, Perception, Personality, Psychology of Women, Research, Social, and Statistics. Within these you get such psych specifics as personality disorders, sexual dysfunction, substance abuse, and so on. The links jump to a variety of sites, primarily research, academic, and governmental institutions, although plenty are topic-specific, too, such as schizophrenia.com.

[resources for professionals]

The Lancet Interactive

● http://www.thelancet.com/

This is the web version of *The Lancet*, a widely recognized and respected medical journal. The magazine is written so that it can be read across a wide array of medical specialties, and this makes its information a bit more understandable to the general populace as well.

The Lancet Interactive site contains the current issue, along with information supplements, back issues, discussion groups, an arcade (jobs, conferences, contacts, etc.), and guidelines for submissions.

The primary points of interest are in the current journal, which contains medical news from around the world (as well as policy issues affecting medical care and treatment), editorial pieces, original research, and case reports. Professionals will dig into every aspect of this journal (it is, after all, one of their primary sources of information), while patients and those interested in healthy living should scan the Contents at a Glance. A recent issue covered such diverse topics as recovering from strokes and the benefits of vitamin A. The site does require registration, but it's free.

Medscape

● http://www.medscape.com/

Want a medical website that caters to medical professionals *and* consumers? Try Medscape, a health-related website that includes searchable databases. For professionals, there's a specialty spotlight area that has links to more than 30 specialty websites (everything from Pertussis and itchy rashes to childhood anxiety are covered here). There are links to Medline, medical journals, conferences, and pressing medical news. There are professional web pages for students, nurses, and pharmacists, and other webpages devoted to things like managed care and business aspects of medicine. There's even an instant poll (when will there be a cure for Parkinson's disease?).

The consumer health section includes information about drugs and nutrition, health news and tools, and related articles. Allergies, women's health, and depression are some of the many issues that are presented in this section. There's an instant health poll, a daily news story featured in the Daily Byte section, and a section titled Ask an Expert (ask a question or see what others are asking). The CBS HealthWatch library section lets you browse and access 48 topic centers and other consumer medical resources. You can browse and search for health-related books in the Marketplace area.

Mental Health InfoSource

● http://www.mhsource.com/

The key concept to remember when visiting this site is mental health, rather than mental illness. Brought to you by the same organization that publishes *Psychiatric Times*, the Mental Health InfoSource is a perfect example of a professional resource that is easily accessible by—and useful to—the general public.

The Disorders section is a main component of the site.

Those covered include Alzheimer's, anxiety and panic disorders, eating disorders, obsessive-compulsive disorders, post-traumatic stress disorders, sexual disorders, self-destructive behavior, and many more. These topics lead to Ask the Expert columns, Healthier You articles (which contain descriptions, symptoms, possible treatments, and recommendations for obtaining professional help), features from *Psychiatric Times*, and related websites.

The Ask the Expert columns are numerous, including Mental Health Experts, Medical Experts, and Bipolar Experts. The Write Brain is the site's online 'zine, which features art, poetry, and articles. From the site, you can search for mental health professionals near you, or follow any of the 600 links that lead to other mental health resources on the web. The site offers plenty of resources for physicians, primarily in the area of continuing education, not surprising since the site is run by the Continuing Medical Education (CME) organization.

Priory Professional Journals

● http://www.priory.com/

If you require a contemporary view of oral opioids or want to explore the fine points of "Sedation of Phobic Dental Patients with an Emphasis on the Use of Oral Triazolam," this is your kind of site. Priory is a publisher of online medical journals, which it offers free of charge to all visitors. Each section of the site is devoted to a particular journal and specialty, making each its own mini-site. They include General Practice, Family Practice, History, Medicine, Anaesthesia, Pharmacy, Psychiatry, Chest, Dentistry, and Veterinary. Like most medical journals, these adhere to a submission and review process for doctors and researchers wishing to submit articles or papers.

The Patient's Page explain the importance of certain procedures to the layperson (e.g. flossing bridgework, noting allergic skin conditions in dogs), and links lead to more consumer-oriented sites. Priory also has job postings for professionals across these specialties.

Vesalius Graphical Medical Resource

● http://www.vesalius.com/

Not everyone needs images of the dorsal view of the brain stem. But then, it's not every site that has the content of Vesalius, which, not coincidentally, includes a dorsal view of the brain stem. For those who need anatomical images, the site is the surgical equivalent of a portrait studio.

The Vesalius site is a repository of anatomical and surgical images that are meant to be used for education and reference by physicians. A lot of these are original illustrations, while some are photographs and radiological images, and others are storyboards and QuickTime and Shockwave video presentations. These images are free to all users (subject to a condition of use), but you must register on the site to partake of them.

The basic images cover a dozen categories including Pediatric Surgery, Head, Heart, Vascular, and Musculoskeletal. The animated sequences show surgical procedures, such as a cross section of the anatomy of the heart, and the transparencies display layered images of anatomy, such as the axillary lymph node dissection and pediatric laparoscopic nephrectomy.

And you thought you'd never find those images anywhere.

[safety]

eSafety

● http://www.esafety.com/esafety_cfmfiles/

Childproofing a home goes beyond putting a gate in front of the stairs to ensure that Junior doesn't take a two-story tumble. It involves being vigilant about the entire home environment, from fire and window safety to protecting against carbon monoxide, germs, poison, even house paint.

The Safety homepage has an extensive list of child products that have been recalled as well as national safety alerts. Areas of interest run from the easy-to-address—"Should we be concerned if our sitter smokes?," "Are antibacterial soaps better than regular soaps"—on to the more difficult—"At what age should parents teach their children about the dangers of strangers?" and Children and Firearms. There is also a test called Can Your Kitchen Pass the Food Safety Test? Take it—and be prepared not to pass.

The site features a live chat room, a reader's poll, and a search engine. ESafety.com is maintained by the Parenthood-Web, which is reviewed in our PARENTING section.

[sexuality]

It used to be that there were two places you could learn about sex and sexuality: from your parents (not the preferred choice) or on the street (not always the best choice). Today, sex and sexuality are still private matters. So the Net, with its anonymity, offers better options: searchable data about sex that can be accessed at any time, without embarrassment or discomfort.

These sites address concerns that people have about their sexuality and sexual practices. They range from raw data to a virtual panoply of sexual information, advice, and tips. Choose the one that's right for you.

Advice
Dr. Ruth

● http://www.drruth.com/

She put frank talk about sex on the map, and now Dr. Ruth Westheimer is on the Internet. In her inimitable style, she answers your questions, addresses the touchy topics (sex with a friend's wife, middle-aged dating, losing one's virginity, etc.), and provides daily sex tips for getting the most out of your sexual relationship (two recent ones were titled "Wrestling" and "Another Tongue"). Die-hard fans, those who need to hear that distinctive voice, can listen to audio clips (as if you can't hear her voice inside your head already).

FYI, this is part of the ever changing Time Warner Pathfinder site, so areas of this particular page are subject to change.

Birth Control
Ann Rose's Ultimate Birth Control Links

● http://www.ultimatebirthcontrol.com/

"Diaphragm—it's not the part of your body that controls breathing." "It's gotta be the morning after—or at least within 72 hours [for emergency contraception]." These are just two of the headings that lead you to information and links on all forms of birth control, including female contraception, male operations, and abstinence. Delivered with a humorous but serious tone, host Ann Rose guides you through the myths and the realities of preventing pregnancy, telling you which work and which don't ("withdrawal—yeah, right" and "hormonal injections—a shot in the arm every three months sounds good to me"). Each section leads to a variety of other sites on the web, notably professional institutions and health organizations. And those still too embarrassed to go into a drugstore and ask for contraceptives from a pharmacist can link to online contraceptive retailers.

Gay and Lesbian
Gay.com

● http://www.gay.com/

While serving as a portal for the gay and lesbian community on the web, Gay.com acts like other genre-specific search sites do: It filters information on the web for the use of its core community. In this case, Gay.com offers a huge amount of indexed data tailored to the interests of gays, with sections that include A&E, Travel, Pride, Relationships, News, Family, Finance, Health & Fitness, and HIV life. There are also city guides, events calendars, gay radio (which requires RealPlayer), news from *The Advocate*, chat rooms, and shopping areas.

Society for Human Sexuality

● http://www.sexuality.org/

This site is for "sex-positive" people and is devoted to the appreciation of myriad consensual forms of relationships and sexual expression. The Society for Human Sexuality, which claims to have almost unlimited online disk space, has filled its site with guides and reviews of videos, sex toys, erotica, and matchmaking services. But that's just the teaser. It also features learning sections devoted to a wide range of sexual interests, from erotic talk and flirting to more exotic pursuits such as swinging and polyamory (also known as "responsible non-monogamy"). These topics are addressed in extensive essays and linked to books, newsgroups, and FAQs. There are also guides to sex resources in various cities, a guide to erotica, and a library index for those who want to go to bed with nothing but a good book.

[sleep]

SleepNet

● http://www.sleepnet.com/

Do you have a sleep disorder or know someone who does? Do you keep your partner up all night with your snoring? Do you feel groggy and tired during the day? If so, you may have a sleep disorder, and SleepNet just might be your first step toward catching some decent ZZZ's. According to the intro, "About 40 million Americans suffer from sleep disorders such as narcolepsy, sleep apnea, restless legs syndrome, and the insomnias. Most are unaware. Each year, sleep disorders, sleep deprivation, and sleepiness add an estimated $15.9 billion to America's health-care bill. The consequences of sleep disorders, sleep deprivation, and sleepiness are significant and include reduced productivity, lowered cognitive performance, increased likelihood of accidents, higher morbidity and mortality risk, and decreased quality of life."

SleepNet links all the information about sleep disorders on the Internet in one place. There are forums on insomnia, children's sleep, narcolepsy, and sleep apnea, which includes snoring (interestingly, this can be a symptom of a serious disorder called obstructive sleep apnea, which requires treatment by a specialist). There's even a little quiz to help determine whether you have sleep apnea. SleepNet should be a welcome relief for those interested in taking their sleeping habits—good or bad—a lot more seriously.

[stress]

Stress Management and Emotional Wellness Links

● http://imt.net/%7Erandolfi/StressLinks.html

Ah, yes . . . stress. It threatens to turn us into either exploding balls of human rage or tightly wound bundles of jangled nerves. Trying to reduce stress in all facets of our lives has become a national obsession, and the objective of this site is to help everyone take that first step toward releasing the weight of the world from their shoulders.

Take it easy while you browse through links to helpful articles and sites about stress and stress reduction in these categories: Relaxation Techniques, Situational Interventions, Stress & College Students, Emotional Self-Help Links, Professional Organizations, Physiology & Disease, Stress in the Workplace, and Commercial Vendors Selling Products and Services. Our favorite section is Stress in the Workplace, which links to articles for professionals, to related websites (such as WorkingWounded.com/), and to articles for laypeople (with titles like "Surviving Downsizing" and "Information Overload Syndrome"). Other linked sites are devoted to stressful occupations, such as Police Stress and Medical Doctor's Stress. Did you think you were the only one whose job stressed you out?

[support groups]

Exploring Your Health

● http://www.pfizer.com/kpw/explore/support.htm

If you've never ventured into the world of online support, this is a good place to start. This simple site outlines the three major types of online support (chat areas, newsgroups, and mailing lists) and discusses how you can participate to meet your support needs. Wisely, it also addresses the risks of online interaction and provides links to respected and authoritative sources on the web.

Self-Help Sourcebook Online

● http://mentalhelp.net/selfhelp/

The Self-Help Sourcebook Online was created to serve as a starting point for exploring support groups and networks throughout the world. To find support groups specific to your area of concern, enter a term into a search box or choose from a list of hundreds of topics available on the homepage, from Acidemia to Waldenstrom's Macroglobulinemia. Once you've chosen a topic, you're taken to a list of organizations that deal with that problem, with information on each group, as well as contact data and online information. Several help sections are available to assist you in navigating the site, and there's an area for finding local self-help groups.

Alcohol

As we all know, alcohol is a legal, easily obtainable and addictive drug, and the one that takes a higher toll on the health of the general populace than other illicit substances. Thus there are more support organizations for the treatment and support of alcohol abuse than for any other kind of substance abuse. There are government-funded, national nonprofit organization, and locally sponsored treatment programs, many of them with a strong web presence.

Alcoholics Anonymous

● http://www.alcoholics-anonymous.org/

No alcoholics support group is better known or more trusted than AA. And now the organization's website helps the public decide privately whether joining AA is right for them. Visitors address 12 questions only they can answer. And the AA Guide for Newcomers asks additional pointed questions. The AA site also devotes sections to teens and to health professionals. Other features include a list of AA offices, the Grapevine newsletter, and an open letter to the media about the importance of maintaining anonymity at AA. The site is also available in French and Spanish.

National Institute on Alcohol Abuse and Alcoholism

● http://www.niaaa.nih.gov/

The part of the National Institute on Alcohol Abuse and Alcoholism site that is designed to be used by professionals is known as the Alcohol and Alcohol Problems Science Database. It contains more than 100,000 records and is the largest online resource covering all aspects of alcohol and alcoholism. Other useful sections can be used by people suffering from the disease. Among these are a drug thesaurus, sections on the chemical effects of alcohol, discussions of pharmacology and toxicology, and data on diseases related to alcoholism.

Caregivers
Family Caregiver Alliance

● http://www.caregiver.org/

Disease takes its toll not only on the afflicted individual, but also on those who care for the sick. It takes an astonishing amount of personal strength and resolve to help someone cope with severe illness, and usually the caregivers, too, suffer but must keep their struggles concealed.

The Family Caregiver Alliance site seeks to provide an outlet for caregivers, who wrestle with their issues day in and day out. It serves as a resource center for caregivers in all types of situations. Sections of the homepage include a News Bureau on care-related issues; a Clearinghouse of research, fact sheets, statistics, and diagnoses; a Resource Center with online services and work/eldercare information; Interviews; and Public Policy Initiatives. Most important, the site grants access to an online support group where members can post a message, share their thoughts, or ask for help 24 hours a day.

Child Abuse
Child Abuse Prevention Network

● http://child-abuse.com/

Child abuse is not new; throughout history, and in all cultures, children have been the victims of cruelty from the unintentional to the heinous. Yet it is only in recent years that the public and professional communities have begun to address the effects of this behavior. The Child Abuse Prevention Network provides information to professionals on child abuse and neglect, and serves as a hub for numerous organizations involved in trying to identify and prevent child abuse. These include SAVE (Survivors and Victims Empowered), the Family Life Development Center at Cornell University, the Family Advocacy Programs of the U.S. Army, and more.

Numerous sections at the site address all aspects of this

problem, including Where to Report Child Abuse, Survivor Issues, and Shaken Baby Syndrome. And a variety of articles and links deal with specific issues ranging from kids who kill to the Child Abuse Quilt Project.

Co-Dependency
Co-Dependents Anonymous (CoDA)

● http://www.codependents.org/

National Council on Codependence

● http://nccod.netgate.net/

Co-dependency is defined as needing others to validate one's self. In the late 1980s and early 1990s, co-dependent support groups became increasingly widespread as the condition was finally given a name and was recognized for the its connection to other personal problems ranging from depression to addiction.

These two sites address different aspects of co-dependency. CoDA's mission is to help people break free of codependent relationships and address their problems so they can form normal, healthy relationships. Like AA, CoDA relies on a 12-step (and 12-tradition) program and support from other members. The program is laid out at the site for the benefit of those who might want to become CoDA members and includes lists of meetings, news and events, and literature available online.

In contrast, the National Council on Codependence serves more as an information resource, detailing the various signs of co-dependency (low self-esteem, pleasing behaviors, relationship issues, etc.), listing sources for educational material, and providing links to other websites.

Mental Help Net (MHN)

● http://www.mentalhelp.net/poc/center_index.php/id/5

"Cheer up." Too often, that is the response of others to someone who is clinically depressed. But depression can stem from chemical imbalances or be rooted in severe mental health problems and are not curable by a change in attitude. Alarmingly, it's estimated that 20 percent of the population will suffer some form of depression in their lifetimes.

Mental Health Net's Depression page has comprehensive sections on symptoms, treatment, research, online resources and support, and organizations that can help. A conscientiously designed support site, this one provides information that will help individuals and determine whether they should seek treatment and shows them where they can get that treatment.

Divorce
Divorce Online

● http://www.divorceonline.com/

Divorce often leaves one or both partners emotionally devastated, and the comeback rarely begins in singles' bars, as clichés would have us believe.

Helping the newly single begin again, Divorce Online offers free articles and information on the psychological, legal, and financial ramifications of divorce. Advice is given on dating before and after the divorce, divorce from a child's perspective, and single-parenting skills . A section is devoted to psychological difficulties caused by the breakup of a marriage, featuring articles on all aspects of divorce. The site also features a chat area—called He Said, She Said!—for people going through or just completing divorces.

Domestic Violence

National Coalition Against Domestic Violence

● http://www.ncadv.org/

To victims of domestic violence, seeking help can seem like a catch-22. Yet getting help is the only way to end the torment. For those in domestic trouble, this site offers resources ranging from local organizations to suggested reading. It also details the steps to take to get help, from personal safety plans to getting legal assistance. Promotional materials such as T-shirts and bumper stickers are sold to help spread the word that there is help available for this societal scourge.

Eating Disorders

Traditionally, anorexia (self-starvation), to bulimia (binging and purging) were thought to affect only emotionally unstable teenage girls, but more recent research indicates that even adult men suffer from eating disorders. Typically, eating disorders are symptomatic of other problems such as abuse or depression.

ANRED (Anorexia Nervosa and Related Eating Disorders)

● http://www.anred.com/toc.html

The ANRED site comprises comprehensive technical information on eating disorders, offering definitions, statistics, warning signs, psychological complications, and treatment and recovery options. Organized like a book, with chapter titles and subheads, the site covers more than 100 issues. ANRED also addresses the unique eating problems caused by athletic training. Everything on the site is written in easy-to-understand language, to benefit as wide an audience as possible.

Eating Disorders

● http://www.something-fishy.org/

The quirky name and the flashy graphics at this site are a front for more than forty categories full of serious data on bulimia, anorexia, overeating, self-perceptions, and cultural issues. Something Fishy delves into the causes, symptoms, preventions, and cures for all forms of eating disorders in the form of lengthy articles and essays. This site also has links to dozens of organizations that deal with specific eating problems.

Harvard Eating Disorders Center

● http://www.hedc.org/

The Harvard Eating Disorders Center combines information on eating disorders and their causes with technical details and a research orientation. The organization's mandate is to increase public awareness of eating disorders while advocating for health policy initiatives and funding research into the causes, prevention, and cure of eating disorders. The site also lists major events and resources that focus on the study of the problem and includes a "Do I Have a Problem?" evaluation for those concerned about their relationship—or lack thereof—with food.

Narcotics
Narcotics Anonymous (NA)

● http://www.na.org/

Though less well known than AA, Narcotics Anonymous has been around for more than 50 years. The NA's charter mandates that narcotics addicts face their addiction, with the support and assistance of other addicts. This site highlights all of the efforts of the NA organization, from its phone-line help to events and news. It also has a huge library of basic information, ranging from worldwide studies about narcotics addiction to how to start an NA meeting.

Sexual Addiction
Sex Addicts Anonymous (SAA)

● http://www.sexaa.org/

Though mostly treated as a joke in society, uncontrollable sexual appetites are problems that can have devastating consequences, jeopardizing careers and home lives. This organization seeks to provide support for those with this disorder. In addition to defining terms, the site offers a profiling questionnaire and information on SAA's 12-step programs. You can also use the site to find an SAA meeting near you or to attend online meetings. And be sure to read The Plain Brown Wrapper, the group's free newsletter.

Smoking

The insidious power of nicotine addiction is no longer debatable. Even people suffering from emphysema or lung cancer are known to be unable to quit. And despite laws banning smoking in most public places in this country, along with the ongoing public outcry against tobacco companies and "smoke-outs," smoking continues to be a national health issue of major proportions. Fortunately, support for those trying to or wanting to quit is now widely available, as these websites attest.

Quit Smoking Support

● http://www.quitsmokingsupport.com/

If you can't quit cold turkey, log on to the Quit Smoking Support site and hook up to thousands of links to sites that will entice, cajole, or scare you into stopping smoking. The Notables section alone should stop you from lighting up when you read the names of hundreds of famous people who were able to quit smoking only by dying.

The site is divided into Yahoo!-like categories that feature quitting-smoking tools, weight and dieting links, a teen-smoking section, self-evaluation questionnaires, tobacco in the news, discussion groups, inspirational letters, and more. These lead to information resources both on and off the site, which comprise a broad spectrum of support data. Quit Smoking Support is maintained by webmaster Blair Price, who claims he hasn't smoked since he started this site. Now, that's inspiring.

QuitNet

● http://www.quitnet.org/

QuitNet is a community-based site to help people stop smoking. It features forums moderated by trained counselors, real-time chat rooms, a personal mailbox for each user, buddy lists, and advice tailored to each member. Smoke-free hopefuls register and create a personal profile that lets the site's staff customize guidelines for them. A Where You're At tool will help you determine where you are in the process of quitting, and a Why Do You Smoke? questionnaire will clarify some of the underlying reasons why you smoke.

The site, hosted by the Boston University School of Public Health, also features an online library, daily news related to tobacco and nicotine addiction, and links to other web resources.

[suicide]

Alarmingly, the suicide rate has been on the rise in recent years, and the impact on survivors' families is devastating. Unlike with disease or accidents, the survivors of a suicide often wonder "What could I have done to prevent this?" This site aims to answer this question—before it is too late. In some cases, recognizing suicidal symptoms and taking action can help save a life. It is important for people feeling suicidal, as well as for those around them, to be aware of changes and events that may be precursors of suicide.

The web offers a new form of suicide prevention, one that ensures even greater anonymity than hot lines, and one that is there 24 hours a day, with no one logging your call.

American Association of Suicidology (AAS)

● http://www.suicidology.org/

This nonprofit organization is dedicated to the understanding and prevention of suicide. The group's members include mental health professionals, researchers, crisis intervention centers, school districts, crisis volunteers, and survivors of suicide. The AAS site offers info about the warning signs of suicide and data on suicide in various segments of the population. There are also resources for people feeling suicidal and for survivors of suicide.

American Foundation for Suicide Prevention (AFSP)

● http://www.afsp.org/

The AFSP is involved in all areas of suicide awareness, from support for research to publicizing the magnitude of the problem to promoting professional education. The site has numerous articles about specific aspects of suicide under these category headings: Assisted Suicide, Neurobiology and Suicide, Depression & Suicide, Survivor Support, Youth Suicide, Suicide Facts, and Suicide and AIDS. Note: The group is opposed to assisted suicide and so has a number of articles relating to Dr. Jack Kervorkian.

SAVE (Suicide Awareness/Voices of Education)

● http://www.save.org/

SAVE has a large number of articles that address a wide variety of suicide issues, including misconceptions about suicide, what to tell children when the worst has happened, elderly depression, hospitalization, students and depression, and many more. A valuable feature is the option to e-mail (anonymously, of course) the text of these to someone in trouble.

[women's]

Estronaut: Women's Health

● http://www.womenshealth.org/

Women's health concerns differ from men's across the board, from the way they recover from hangovers to the way they achieve orgasms. Estronaut recognizes that and revels in the detailed exploration of women and their bodies, with nary a gender crossover to be found. The site targets adolescents, women of reproductive age, those in midlife, and mature or postmenopausal women. Sections include Sex (problems, positions, sexual response), Gyny (female organs), Looks (hair, skin, plastic surgery), Eat (nutrition, weight control), Mind (psychology, relationships), Body (everything but female organs), Healthcare (getting what you need from doctors and insurance), and Move (sports, fitness, exercise).

All sections contain articles that cover the spectrum of concerns, from mammogram results and how much calcium women really need to antidepressants and tips on dodging your doctor's receptionist so you can go straight to the source. Estronaut has a

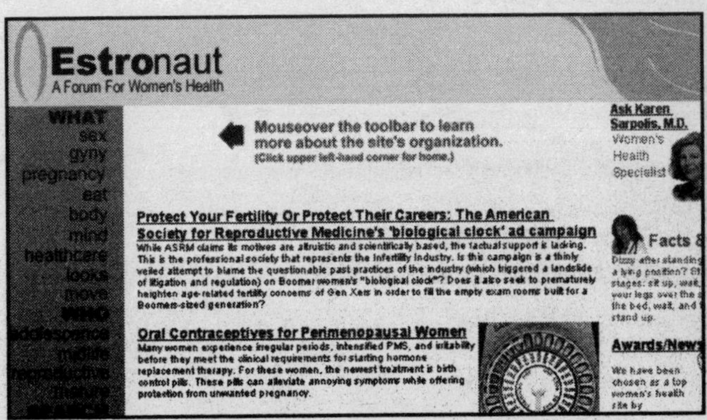

huge archive of information, and women of all ages will want to get familiar with their health by getting familiar with this site.

New York Times—Women's Health

● http://www.nytimes.com/specials/women/whome/index.html

What better way to get thorough and accurate reporting on women's health than from the "paper of record?" The *New York Times (NYT)* has one of the great websites on the Internet, and its women's health pages make it even more notable. In addition to news stories (culled from articles that have been featured in the paper), there are comprehensive guides to some 29 topics of concern to women. These include aging, osteoporosis, ovarian cancer, depression, cosmetic surgery, and many more. On selecting one of these, the user is taken to a different section of the "paper," where articles, facts, books, and web resources are presented on a full page. A Special Edition features articles and insights by *NYT* writers, and a data page looks at statistics related to disease, mortality, and chronic conditions. Finally, an annotated list of 100 health sites that specifically address women's health is given. This site is so full of exceptional health data that you'll wish it could be delivered to your doorstep every day.

NEWS & MEDIA

[books]

Books and the Internet are strange bedfellows. On one hand, they compete for your eyes and time. After all, if you're reading a book, you're not surfing the Net, and vice versa.

The Internet has become a popular place for doing research, finding quality information, and doing some good old-fashioned reading. Which popular medium used to fit this description? Books. Conversely, the sale of books—through Amazon.com—was the web's first success story and arguably launched the whole notion of retail. So there is a symbiotic relationship, a lot like that between shark and lampreys. Only it's not yet clear in this case which are the sharks and which is the lamprey. This symbiosis is strengthened because of two apparently coincidental yet complementary factors. One is that books, as a category of information, are the best-indexed and best-catalogued entities on the planet; even people aren't tracked as carefully as books. The other is that the Internet has proven to be a near perfect repository for storing and accessing indexed and catalogued information.

It took more than a century after the invention of the printing press for books to be considered items that the general public could own. It took another two centuries for the invention of the paperback to make books a truly mass-market commodity. Proponents of all things technological claim that one day we will download books onto our computers from websites and paper will disappear. There is already a strong movement under way to do this with college textbooks, which are big, bulky, and expensive and go out-of-date quickly. We believe that this could happen within the next ten years; thus, it may take less than 20 years for the Internet to change books from a paper to a digital medium. You read it here first.

The book sites listed in this section are those that are already creating a bridge between how we've dealt with the book for the past several centuries and how we'll deal with it in the very near future.

Bookworm

● http://www.kidsreads.com/

Are your kids passionate about Harry Potter? Scared silly by R.L. Stine? Then a big green worm, named Booker T. Worm, may help turn their interest into an educational experience. Children from 6 to 12 years old (and older) will enjoy the six sections of the site: Reading Club, Free Newsletter, Cool Stuff, Meet the Authors, Wish List, and Write to Us. Within these, kids can join a reading club and set up their own goals for each season and chart their progress. They can also look up favorite authors and learn a little bit about them. The Cool Stuff content is straightforward: Kids can search for books on cool and favorite subjects. A unique feature of the site is the ability to build a wish list of books for personal use or one that can be e-mailed to relatives and friends. A search engine and an index allow you to select books by reading level—from age six to young adult.

From *Sweet Valley Junior High* to Dr. Seuss to *The Magic School Bus*, Booker T. Worm encourages children to love the written world, in a site especially created just for them.

On-line Text
ibooks inc.

● http://www.ibooksinc.com/

Isaac Asimov. Irving Wallace. Arthur C. Clarke. Raymond Chandler. These are the names of great modern authors whose works usually cost you a pretty penny—unless you go to ibooks. At that site, they're free, which is not a term you'll often hear at your local bookstore. Ibooks has taken classic works by twentieth-century authors and put them on the web, free. If you like them, read them online. If you want more, order the books here. And unlike at that bookstore on the corner, you can browse and read 24 hours a day, every day of the year. The concept is great, but the price is even better.

ipicturebooks.com

● http://ipicturebooks.com/

ipicturebooks.com is the number one source for children's e-books from major publishers including Little, Brown and Co., Farrar, Straus & Giroux, Henry Holt, Millbrook Press, Bank Street, and Random House. Here you will find free and inexpensive classic, out-of-print, original and full sound/animation enhanced titles with popular characters like Toot and Puddle, Shrek, Barney, and Wishbone. Ranging in age appropriateness from zero to ten, the ever growing titles list has hundreds of works including those from Caldecott Medal-winning illustrators and celebrity authors like Jane Goodall, Dolly Parton, Joni Mitchell, and Paul Simon. You can browse titles by age, themes, or author, as well as create custom children's e-books. Like its sister webiste, ibooks inc, ipicturebooks.com enables you to enjoy inexpensive children's e-books on any device—PC, Macintosh, desktops, laptops, and even wireless handhelds.

Reviews
New York Times Book Review

● http://www.nytimes.com/pages/books/review/index.html

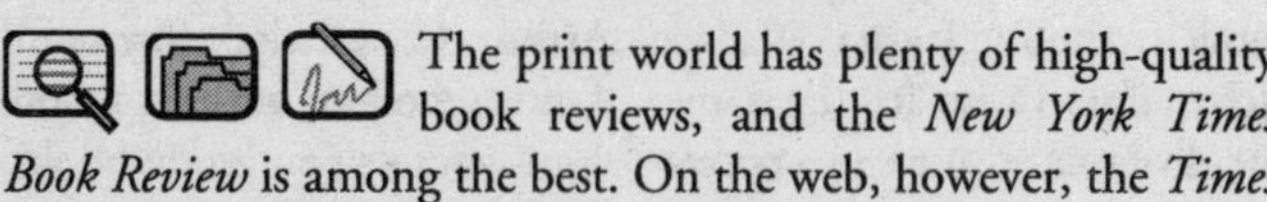

The print world has plenty of high-quality book reviews, and the *New York Times Book Review* is among the best. On the web, however, the *Times Book Review* stands alone.

Though this site is part of the main *New York Times* website, it seems self-contained given that it is devoted to a Sunday supplement, the *Book Review* section. On the main page, reviews are listed by title and include a quick summary of the review. Even better, there is a link to the first chapter of every book listed in the review, so that readers can get a true sample of the work in question (not possible in print due to space limitations).

There are more than a dozen primary reviews, segmented by Cover Story, Nonfiction Reviews, and Fiction Reviews. The site also offers Daily News & Reviews, Expanded Bestseller Lists, Book Forum, a search engine for looking through an archive of book reviews, as well as Books in Brief, New & Noteworthy Paperbacks, Children's Books, Letters, and an editorial. This site serves as the perfect bridge between literature online and literature in your lap.

[journalism & media]

Broadcast
TV Rundown

● http://www.tvrundown.com/

Back when TV was still considered a bastard child of journalism, people used to get their news from newspapers. Television still struggles with its image, especially now with the proliferation of newsmagazines of dubious credibility, but the fact is, most people get their news from TV. If you're looking for information in any way related to television journalism, TV Rundown on the web is the place to start. This massive resource has listings and information for all interested parties, whether you're a professional looking for a job (head for TV Jobs and its thorough catalog of links), a student considering a TV journalism career (click on TV Careers for advice and resources), or a viewer with an opinion (try Viewers Views, where you can take part in polls and read about polls at many news organizations). The gigantic homepage has a useful site map along the top and a type-in-the-box search engine way down at the bottom.

In between, you can find teaser stories, links to news services (ABC, CBS, CNN, NBC, and PBS) case studies, and links to various TV commentators, reporters, critics, and observers. The Quick Links to Television Stations button can take you literally anywhere in the country where TV is broadcast. And if all these electronic connections to electronic media are just too much to deal with, you can subscribe to the print version of *TV Rundown* (published 50 times a year since 1981), the contents of which are archived on the website.

[magazines]

Since the advent of the web, magazine publishers have been struggling to learn how to straddle two media: print and digital. Though they make much of their revenue from subscriptions, more frequently readers want—and expect—the mags to post at least part of their content on the web (not to mention their archives) free of charge. In a sense, this forces these publications to compete with themselves.

This conundrum has not yet been fully resolved. Many magazine publishers have launched versions on the Net, while others are trying mixed formats, granting only subscribers to the print editions access to their sites. Still others have opted to post only subscription information on their web pages.

The mags included here represent the best of the general interest and business weeklies on the web, and they don't require payment to view them. If you're wondering how they can make any money doing this, the answer is not yet known. Ultimately the web's information providers will have to create a model for deriving revenue from the use of their data—whether via online subscriptions, pay-per-visit, access-by-minute, or perhaps a telephone model (general charge per month, with exceptions for long distance).

Thousands of magazines are available on the web, and we've included many of them as special interest publications in their respective categories in other sections of this book. But we predict that special interest and niche magazines in print form will be a thing of the past by the year 2005, and general interest publications will disappear by 2010. And you can print that.

The Magazine Rack

● http://www.magatopia.com/

If you like to browse the newsstand and randomly select a magazine, then you'll enjoy the Magazine Rack. The homepage is designed to mimic a rack of mags; it displays the

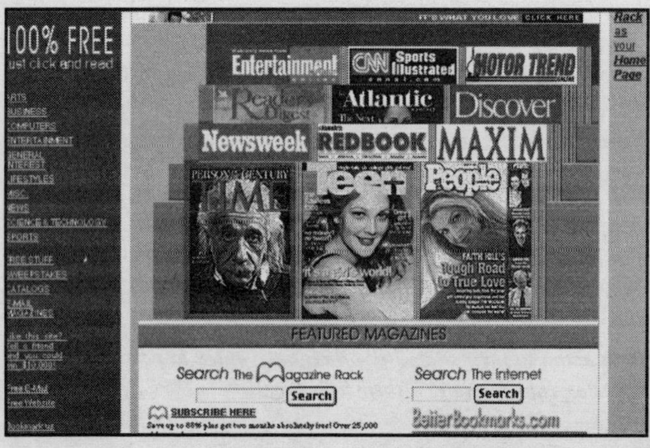

covers of current issues. You click on the one you want and jump straight to its site. If you want a specific type of magazine, such as entertainment, science and technology, or sports, click instead on a listing to see magazines in that genre appear on the rack.

The beauty of this layout is that you can browse magazines you might not ordinarily buy. We thumbed through the current issue of *The Robb Report*, for instance, as well as this month's *Q* magazine—two more dissimilar magazines do not exist on the face of the planet. The site features hundreds of magazines across the broad publishing spectrum, just as at a regular newsstand.

The Economist

● http://www.economist.com/

The *Economist* is a must-read—make that a must-bookmark. No, it doesn't have the typical newsstand appeal or celebrity focus of most American mags, but it is perhaps the best source for world news and analysis. The online version features much of what's in print, including Science & Technology, Finance & Economy, and People. Hopefully, this site will encourage a wider readership.

To get beyond the top stories and into the archives you must sign up and use a password. Thereafter, you'll receive e-mail every week that tells you about the upcoming issue. As with other newsweeklies that have transitioned to the web, some of the graphic content has been stripped out, but the *Economist* preserves many of its charts and graphs and animates some illustrations to grand effect.

Forbes

● https://www.forbes.com/

Readers are unlikely to find a more information-rich site than the Forbes homepage, known as the Digital Tool, which contains dozens of articles, editorials, links, forums, and more—before entering the site.

The Digital Tool serves as the hub for the Forbes online world. You can access all the Forbes publications (*Forbes Magazine*, *ASAP*, *FYI*, others), as well as numerous business elements from the homepage. There is a Stock Quote box, a Toolbox (calculators, calendars, etc.), departments (Technology, Convergence, Startups, E-business, etc.), business centers, forums, online columnists, cover stories, and the Media Center (which takes you to webcasts and Forbes-sponsored audio-video forums—which require RealPlayer or Media Player). Fans of other Forbes publications will want to jump to the subsites that serve as homepages for those mags, notably the *Eponymous* mag and *ASAP*, its technology sister. The search engine for the site looks up data across publications—meaning you don't have to specify that you're looking up, say, digital cash, in *ASAP* as opposed to *FYI*. You can also register for an e-mail newsletter, send stories to friends, and generate print versions of articles.

The Digital Tool pages are always visually engaging and informative, with volumes of new information posted weekly. At last count, the site reportedly contained more than a thousand pages.

Time

● http://www.time.com/

Some would say *Newsweek* is the yin to *Time*'s yang: they represent two sides of the American viewpoint. Of course, they both have their pluses and minuses, depending on your perspective. *Newsweek* prides itself on its political coverage, while its science coverage can hardly be considered authoritative. *Time* delves deeper into American culture, but perhaps at the expense of more thorough political coverage.

Both, however, have made the transition to the web in fine style. Both are free, and you don't have to wade through the print versions' multitude of advertisements to get to the meat of the issue.

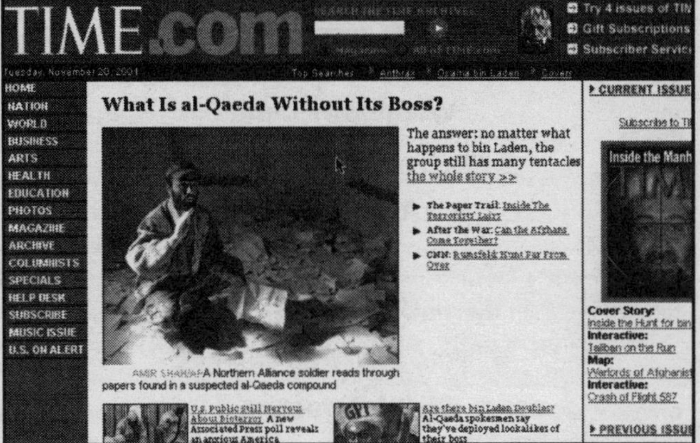

Newsweek has reproduced most of the mag online, including Perspectives, Periscope, Conventional Wisdom, its political coverage, and Cyberscope. And clicking on Daily News Info on the homepage certainly beats waiting until next week to read about this week's news. Unlike the print version, however, there are few photos or graphics (except for Perspectives). There is also an international edition and special online issues.

In contrast, the *Time*'s site is more commercial, featuring books, links, *Time* for Kids, *Time* Digital, Boards & Chats, Archives, Daily Update, and—finally—the magazine itself. A portion of the paper version is presented in a table of contents, with this notice: "For the full content of this week's issue, check out the magazine archive next weekend when it goes online." A nice feature of *Time*'s website is that the current week's articles contain links to others on the same topic in past issues.

[news]

Worldnews.com

- http://www.worldnews.com/

ABC News

- http://abcnews.go.com/

CBS News

- http://www.cbsnews.com/

CNN Interactive

- http://www.cnn.com/

FOX News

- http://www.foxnews.com/

MSNBC

- http://www.msnbc.com/

For breaking news, for a number of reasons, the web is better than TV. To start with, there aren't many TV sets at the office. For another, many of the national news websites pick up TV video feeds and put them on the web, and those websites can link to other related data during a crisis or special report (such as government reports on terrorism a history of stock panics, etc.), which adds significantly to the value of the information.

These sites from the major news networks are intense, up-to-the-minute affairs. Like their television counterparts, all have feature stories front and center, with "segments" on international and national news, business, sports, weather, technology, entertainment, and health. There are also polls, surveys, and reports on interesting—though not necessarily pressing—topics. Each site also has tie-ins to its respective interests: MSNBC to

NBC's *Dateline* and *The Today Show*; ABC to ESPN, *20/20*, *Nightline*, and *World News Tonight*; CBS to Marketwatch.com; CNN to Time Inc. and CNNfn; and Fox to its Sports and Marketwire sites. At the end of the day, which one you choose depends on which news you usually watch.

Newseum

● http://www.newseum.org/

The fall of the Berlin Wall, Watergate, and the moon missions—all of these were news stories that made history in the twentieth century. The Newseum site has compiled the news stories that captured—and in some cases prompted—these historic events.

Newseum is an actual museum, yet online it is accessible to everyone—especially kids. Capsule write-ups, complete with photos, describe the current exhibits at the museums, as well as online exhibits, such as those mentioned above. Kids can follow the Adventures of Chip Tracer: Cyberjournalist, in search of the truth behind the stories. Teachers can visit the Classroom and pick up curricula on various topics for their students, such as "How to Become a Reporter" or "A Walk to Freedom," about the civil rights movement. This is a great site for exploring how news and the media affect our society and the way it is recorded for history.

Personalized News
My Yahoo!

● http://my.yahoo.com/

The Daily Me. That's the title of the feature that gives you only the news that interests you, not all the other junk that clutters the daily reports. Regardless of the medium—TV, radio, print media, Internet—segments of the news interest everyone. Maybe you want only sports news. Or just financial updates. Or how about entertainment and breaking news, but no sports? Perhaps you care about only one topic—say, the current political climate in Kuala Lumpur.

The Daily Me, up and running at My Yahoo!, allows you to create a single news page that displays only those sections that you want on it, whether they be international headlines, technology news, or weather reports and sports scores. You can select 20 different modules (Essentials, References & Tools, Travel, Personal Finance, Shopping, etc.) and place them on the page in

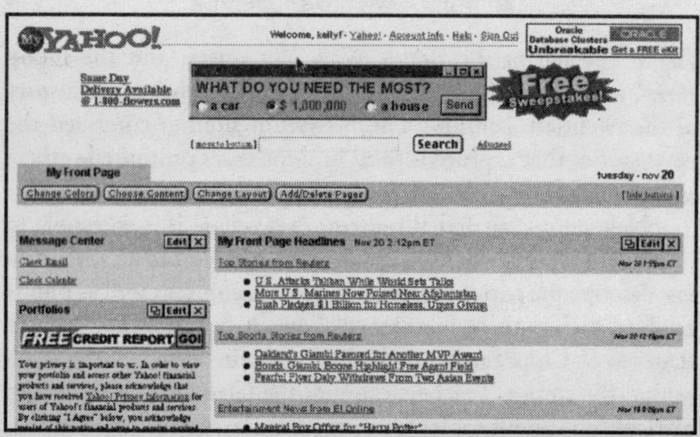

any configuration that makes sense to you. My Yahoo! also lets you add weather from different cities and create an area where you can view your favorite stocks, updated every 20 minutes. Other site conveniences include a calendar section (with which you can create an online organizer), dates of upcoming record and movie releases, a place for your bookmarks, e-mail, Yellow Page, searches, calculators, and on and on. We have yet to find a better place on the Internet that serves so many of our interests simultaneously—and all from a single page. Yahoo!.

[newslinks]

Newspapers.com

● http://www.newspapers.com/

Newspapers.com breaks up publication categories into more specific areas, such as religious and classified advertising publications. This is helpful if you need to seek out printed information in a particular specialty.

[newspapers]

Despite the fact that the Internet competes directly with newspapers, there are hundreds of newspaper sites on the Internet. Most are very good in that they are online versions of their printed parents, plus they feature links to sites of local interest, including events, museums, services, and restaurants. Many of them have similar formats and often link to the same comic strips and syndicated columns.

There are also impressive sites for many local newsweeklies, papers that tend to have more of an arts and music, as well as an investigative and political, orientation than their daily counterparts. These papers, usually called alternative weeklies, often break local stories that ultimately become part of the national agenda. Among the best are the Dallas Observer *(www.dallasobserver.com), the*

Denver Westword *(www.westword.com), the* NY Press *(www.nypress.com), and the* Boston Phoenix *(www.bostonphoenix.com). These papers also feature links to syndicated columns that are (still) considered alternative or underground, such as the cartoon "Red Meat" and Dan Savage's advice column.*

Two national newspapers stand out, however; their stellar sites match their reputations: the Los Angeles Times *and the* New York Times.

The *Los Angeles Times*

● http://www.latimes.com/

The *LA Times* has a much more local and regional bent than the *New York Times* and, not surprisingly, devotes more space to entertainment. Its international coverage is sparse, relatively speaking, but that's not the reason most people read the *LA Times*. It devotes more space to cultural events and trends (many of which are nurtured in Southern California) than any other major daily, and its Calendar section is a must-read for keeping up with serious commentary on American pop culture and cultural shifts.

The site is extremely easy to navigate because it uses a variety of pulldown menus that guide the reader. There are two ways to view articles: as full-length scrollable pages or as smaller segments that continue from page to page—more in line with what you'd expect in the paper version. More than most newspapers, though, the *LA Times* has adapted its content to the structures and hypertext capabilities of the web, as opposed to simply generating a digital version of the printed copy.

The *New York Times*

● http://www.nytimes.com/

If any site should be a required bookmark on the web, it's this one. The *New York Times* is a primary source of daily information for much of the

United States and the world, and the online version provides most of it—for free.

The top headlines are featured in a day-at-a-glance front page (actually two front pages: Quick News and Page One Plus). Each headline has a capsule summary that helps you gauge how much time you really want to spend reading a particular article. Of course, everything is a click away, as opposed to several dozen pages away. More article headlines can be viewed within particular sections (Politics, Arts, Cybertimes, etc.).

As part of a venture with careerpath.com, the site has a very good job search section that takes you through the classifieds by title. An additional benefit is that the online version is put up shortly after midnight EST, usually by 1:00 A.M. This means that West Coast readers can have the next day's *Times* well before midnight and be reading tomorrow's news tonight. Such is the wonder of the breakdown of time on the web.

Online viewers who prefer the look and feel of the actual paper can download a complete jpeg of the front cover. The *New York Times Magazine* (a Sunday supplement) finally joined the rest of the paper when it went online as part of the site in mid-1999.

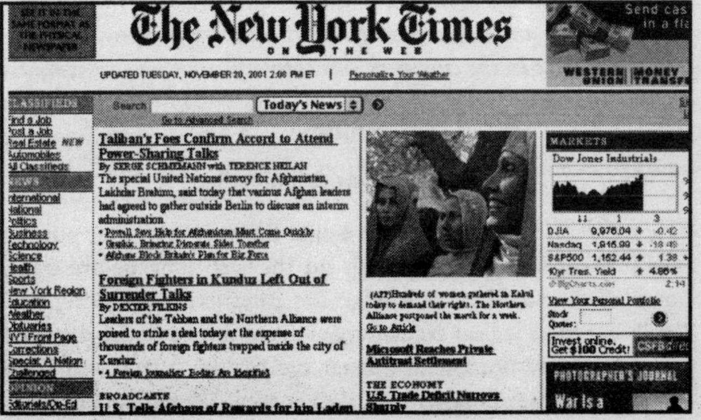

The New York Times
ON THE WEB

UPDATED TUESDAY, NOVEMBER 20, 2001 2:06 PM ET | Personalize Your Weather

Search Today's News

Taliban's Foes Confirm Accord to Attend Power-Sharing Talks
By SERGE SCHMEMANN with TERENCE NEILAN
The special United Nations envoy for Afghanistan, Lakhdar Brahimi, said today that various Afghan leaders had agreed to gather outside Berlin to discuss an interim administration.

Foreign Fighters in Kunduz Left Out of Surrender Talks
By DEXTER FILKINS
Leaders of the Taliban and the Northern Alliance were poised to strike a deal today at the expense of thousands of foreign fighters trapped inside the city of Kunduz.

BROADCASTS
U.S. Tells Afghans of Rewards for bin Laden

(AFP)Hundreds of women gathered in Kabul today to demand their rights. The Northern Alliance postponed the march for a week.
Go to Article

Microsoft Reaches Private Antitrust Settlement

THE ECONOMY
U.S. Trade Deficit Narrows Sharply

MARKETS
Dow Jones Industrials

DJIA	9,976.04	-0.42
Nasdaq	1,916.99	-18.48
S&P500	1,152.44	1.39
10yr Tres. Yield		4.86%

View Your Personal Portfolio
Stock Quotes:

PHOTOGRAPHER'S JOURNAL
War Is a

Many people stack up issues of the *Times* for weeks, intending to get to them each and every day, and feeling guilty when they don't. In cyberspace, you can let the *Times* do the storage for you. A basic search engine allows you to scan the day's articles, as well as a 30-day archive, which is also searchable. For a fee, the newspaper will give you access to a full year's worth of articles. Or sign up for the premium subscriber's service, which has "diversion" offerings such as the famous crossword puzzle. Finally, the site offers a direct link to many daily political cartoons, as well as to the "Dilbert" and "Doonesbury" comic strips, which the paper version doesn't—and might never—do.

The site does require a sign-up, as well as a password (which you need to remember). However, it is a worthwhile trade-off.

[online 'zines]

Online magazines were part of the first wave in moving our culture from one dependent on paper-based information to one that relies on digital information. Online 'zines have no paper counterpart; they were born and nurtured in the digital environment. As such they tend to take a digital age perspective on news, politics, celebrities, reviews, and so on. This translates to cutting-edge design, a tendency toward acid-tongued commentary, more confrontational points of view, and less concern for political correctness—all of which you'll see in the entries in this category.

Salon

● http://www.salon.com/

Salon staked out e-zine territory early on, putting news and opinion on the web long before traditional mags would acknowledge the Internet. And taking web sensibility to its logical extremes, Salon combined outrageous and piercing observations with a keen eye for the nuances of news events—and the idiosyncrasies of the people who make the news.

Salon is segmented much like a daily newspaper: Arts & Entertainment, Books, Comics (including the wickedly funny "Story Minute," by Carol Lay), People, Politics, News (analysis, pundits, and links to news sources), Technology, and Business. There is an area for chat and discussion, and you can also get printer-friendly versions of each page.

Slate

● http://www.slate.msn.com/

Slate has taken lumps since its founding: It wanted to charge for viewing, and it was under the control of Microsoft, so it was soft on Bill Gates—things that Netizens fear as signs of Armageddon.

But Slate survived, primarily because it has incorporated other media into its site. Particularly noteworthy is the Briefin' section, which offers a quick review of the cover stories in other weekly magazines—from the *New Yorker* and the *Economist* to *Vogue* and *Time*. Links are given, where appropriate. There are also features, 24/Seven (editorials from the past few days), movie reviews, and columns (Chatterbox, Strange Bedfellows). Membership is primarily for e-mail and discussion access.

[photojournalism]

Digital Storyteller

● http://www.digitalstoryteller.com/YITL/index.html

Interesting concept: Ten photojournalists keep an online diary of their assignments, giving visitors a Behind the Viewfinder tour of their daily challenges. This isn't a warm and fuzzy page devoted to wildlife photography; the subject matter is the gritty, real-life sort that fronts our newspapers and newsmagazines every day.

On July 23, 1999, for example, ace photographer Mark Hertzberg uploaded a dramatic report to the site, along with several compelling photos. There had been a double murder just two blocks from his house. When he heard the news, he raced to the crime scene and began shooting pictures as the police captured the suspect. Here is a snippet: "[Suspect Arthur] Vine spit at me twice as I photographed police taking him away. The crowd of gawkers cheered the police when the door was shut on Vine in the prison transport van. It turns out that Vine had been hiding in a space under the bridge two blocks from our house . . . which means that when I went on my daily early-morning bike ride, I was riding right over his hiding place."

The rest of the site is filled with similarly powerful stories and photos. You can follow all the submissions or just the adventures of a single photojournalist. Whichever route you choose, once you start reading these regular submissions, you will quickly begin to understand the immediacy and power of both photojournalism and the Internet.

[print]

Pulitzer Prize Site

● http://www.pulitzer.org/

The prestigious Pulitzer Prize is one of the most coveted awards in American arts and letters. There are four primary tracks: the current year, Archive, History, and Resources. The current year leads to a listing of the most recent awards, which now include 14 journalism citations; seven letters, drama, and music awards; and a special award to honor Duke Ellington in the centennial year of his birth.

The Archive provides an award listing by year, a type-in-the-box search engine, and a full-text archive of the winning works from the past several years. This History section provides—what else?—a history of the prizes, a short biography of Joseph Pulitzer, the man behind the prize, and a summary of the administration and rules for the prizes. In Resources, visitors learn how to contact the Pulitzer organization, and are provided with links to three related sites: the Columbia University Graduate School of Journalism, that school's Center for New Media, and its bimonthly publication, the *Columbia Journalism Review*.

Perhaps most important, glory seekers can find the guidelines and application forms here as well. In this case, though, there's a bit more involved than just entering your e-mail address and waiting to see if you've won.

Reporter.org

● http://www.reporter.org/

The image of reporters used to be of daring men and women pursuing stories in desolate parts of the world, meeting nefarious contacts under the cover of darkness and writing their stories on beat-up typewriters as the dawn approached. Today, it's more likely their resources would include sites like this one. Provided by Investigative Reporters & Editors, "the premier grassroots network for journalists of all kinds from around the world," Reporter.org is largely a listing of resources for journalists, journalism educators, and the public.

The site's homepage contains listings, links, and descriptions of journalism-related programs and organizations around the world, ranging from the National Association of Black Journalists to the Science Journalism Center to the Global Beat, a resource service for global journalists writing on international security issues. Its Resource Center contains more than 10,000 investigative stories, while its search engines combines the resources of a dozen similar organizations. Other informational areas include the Beat Source Guide, which contains useful informational links grouped by area of reporting such as Environment or Transportation. News on the Net lists other news resources on the Internet, everything from the Weather Channel to myriad daily newspapers across the United States. Finally, users can head to the site's virtual Coffeemaker and gain access to various journalism mailing lists to interact with peers or even learn how to establish and maintain a mailing list for journalism-related organizations.

[publishing]

Bookwire

● http://www.bookwire.com/

Bookwire is for publishing professionals and those who want to be. Editors, publishers, booksellers, agents, packagers, distributors, and, of course, writers will find book-related data that includes Industry News, regular features on the book publishing industry, reviews of the latest books, *Publishers Weekly*'s best-seller lists, and a weekly list of authors who will be making media appearances. There are also links to trade pubs such as *Publishers Weekly, Library Journal, Books in Print, Literary Marketplace, and Library Resource Guide*, among others.

Book writers in search of representation will find a welcome link to the Association of Author's Representatives (with no guarantees, mind you), and the Soapbox is a forum for book business discussion.

[radio]

Yahoo! Broadcast.com

● http://broadcast.yahoo.com/home.html

While writing this entry, we are listening to talk radio station KFYI in Phoenix, Arizona. So what, you might think, but we're writing this at a desk in Manhattan. Furthermore, with a click of our mouse, we can switch the station to listen to alternative radio in Boston, from station WFNX, all the while looking out at the Chrysler Building.

No, radio stations have not extended their signal output to reach listeners around the country or around the globe. Instead, they have put themselves in the hands of Broadcast.com, a website that streams live radio broadcasts, and even TV, to your desktop. Using RealPlayer or Media Player, you can select a radio station from a huge list, either by typing in a city or station call letters, even by genre. This comes in handy if all the good radio stations in your city have replaced their content with programming that you don't consider to be content at all. Now you can tune into a good station in another city and still keep up with your favorite music or talk topics.

Many programs run live, but some are archived, especially for certain popular shows, a nice feature if you missed your favorite radio program originating from across the ocean (the BBC is included here). National radio shows also run on the site, including Rush Limbaugh and Art Bell, as do sports programs. For TV buffs who want to use their computer monitors as television screens, there are music videos online, as well as a number of local and national broadcasts (both live and archived). A handy-dandy TV guide even lets you know when to tune in.

The sites use your built-in computer speaker, which is fine for listening at the office and to talk radio, but if you want to crank it, this site sounds great when you add some external speakers to

YAHOO! ALSO LISTS: [radio]

- **http://www.davemichaels.com/**
  Dave Michaels—The Radio Page: links to America's best broadcasters, information sources, and entertainment companies
- **http://kzsu.stanford.edu/other-radio.html**
  Noncommercial Radio Stations
- **http://www.radiodirectory.com/**
  Radiodirectory
- **http://www.topradio.com/**
  TopRadio.com: links to radio stations worldwide. Add your favorite station.
- **http://www.tvradioworld.com/**
  TvRadioWorld: worldwide radio and television broadcasting directory

your computer. It's nice to know that no matter what happens to your local radio station, somewhere out there is a station you can relate to and connect to via Yahoo! Broadcast.com. The world is truly a small place, and Broadcast.com makes it even smaller.

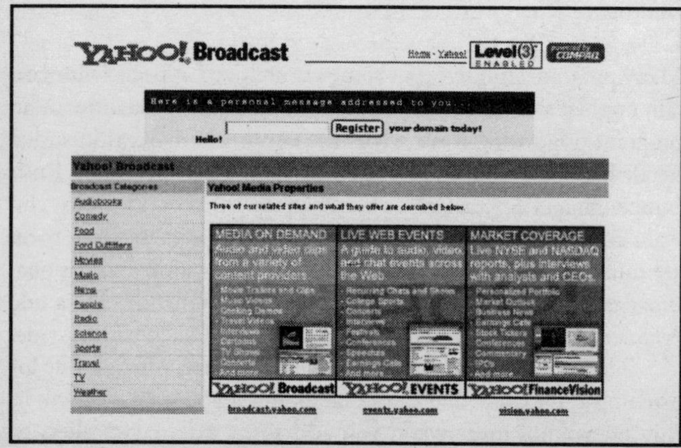

NPR Online

● http://www.npr.org/

National Public Radio is the closest thing America has to a "national" radio station. Along with three dozen other shows, its popular "All Things Considered" and "Fresh Air" are rational, intelligent alternatives to shock radio, call-in formats, boring music formats, and recycled news. The best thing about NPR online is that you can listen to audio files from its insightful hourly news and even get the live broadcast of NPR via streaming audio. Also online are news reports, profiles of the station's personalities, lists of local stations, and overviews of individual shows.

[weather]

Weather.com

● http://www.weather.com/

Unless you've been living in a cave, you already know how computers and the Weather Channel have changed our lives. Now weather information anywhere in the world is available at the click of a mouse. Go to the Weather Channel's website, Weather.com, and you can access all types of weather. You can track hurricanes and tropical storms via satellite radar, complete with their barometric pressure, maximum wind speed, and direction of movement. If you haven't tried it, we assure you, it can get very exciting.

Weather.com also headlines national weather hot spots (e.g., "A powerful system moving through the Northwest is generating strong, gusty winds from Washington to Montana and Wyoming"), but most visitors will want to pop their zip codes

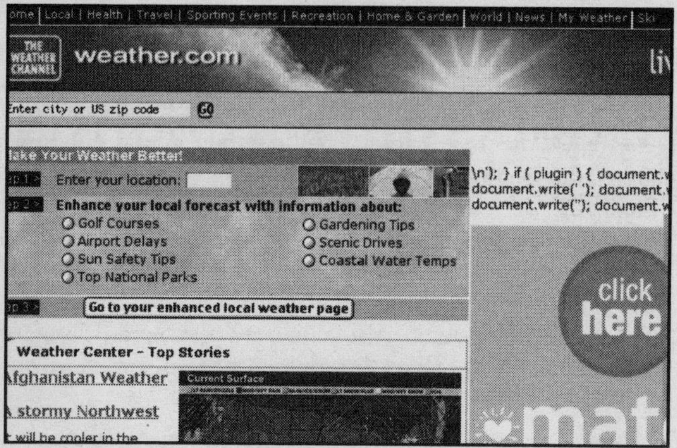

into the search engine to get a four-day forecast, which includes predicted weather, complete with current radar shots, which can be very handy if you're about to travel. This site also is a lifesaver during the winter, when storms can emerge out of nowhere and drop a foot of precipitation on your head before you even get out of the driveway. In short, Weather.com is the online equivalent of an early warning system.

RECREATION & SPORTS

[automotive]

Depending on what you read or which study you believe, buying a car is one of the three or four most stressful commercial endeavors a consumer can undertake. From experience, this strikes us as being underrated—we'd rank it higher. Car buying, especially of the used variety, has been grist for anxiety attacks and comedy sketches going back at least 50 years.

However, the method of buying cars is going through a fundamental change, driven in part by the resources of the Internet. With research materials, reviews, and accurate pricing available free online, the car buyer is no longer limited to local sellers. Since the web knocks down geographic borders, it is now entirely possible to simultaneously check dozens of different prices on a single model. The savvy websurfer can make a deal without ever stepping into a dealer's showroom. "Better living through technology" comes true at last.

Though we doubt this is the kind of "technology of tomorrow" that car manufacturers had in mind when they touted their futuristic dreams at world's fairs of bygone eras, the web and its resources may have become the best improvement to the automotive world we consumers could have hoped for.

Advice
CarTalk

● http://www.cartalk.cars.com/

The success of this tandem team of talkers defies description. These two smartmouths, Tom and Ray Magliozzi, known as Click and Clack, the Tappet brothers, talking about transmissions and transaxles became the darlings of the comic radio genre. But, not content to be just a couple of guys who bring weekly car discussions to the national airwaves (450 NPR stations) and newspapers (300 in syndication), they set up their own website. They have transferred their wry sense of humor and automotive knowledge to an impressive corner of the Internet. This is an invaluable site for car owners who want relatively straight talk on problems with their cars—before they head to their mechanics.

The best place to start delving into Click and Clack's words of wisdom is the search section, where auto owners can select topics from an alphabetized table of contents or enter a keyword or phrase. For really meaty tech talk, the Actual Car Information section contains the majority of information for car owners, namely a compendium of Tom and Ray's syndicated columns past and present. There are also articles on collision data, how the Tappet brothers identify odd noises emanating from inside cars, and a variety of other quirky areas on the site.

There is a chat area to submit your own question or to check out one of the 13 subcategories for information on everything from lemon laws to winter driving tips. In addition, there are areas where you can ask a car manufacturer a question, complain to the National Highway Traffic Safety Administration (NHTSA), get multivehicle comparisons with repair histories and problem areas, and find out what it will cost you to repair and maintain everything from a Volvo to a Chevrolet. You can also shop for a new or used car in the classifieds section. Finally, if you have RealAudio installed, you can even listen to Tom and Ray's weekly show on your computer. Too bad your local dealership or mechanic can't always be this knowledgeable—or amusing. Not bad for a couple of MIT grads.

Buying
Autobytel.com

● http://www.autobytel.com/

Autobytel takes the sting out of shopping for a car. Unlike other sites reviewed in this section, Autobytel.com is the place to go to when you've finished your research and are ready to buy. The homepage guides buyers to sections for new cars, preowned cars, car care, financing, insurance, warranties, and more. A main feature called Ready to Buy? lets you jump instantly to nearly every variety of car you can imagine, including some at the high end, such as Lamborghini Diablos and Ferraris (when you're ready to start buying cars that cost as much as a house). Here you also specify your zip code to help locate the car of your choice in your area. The site then drills down until you have specified exactly what you want and alerts you to where you can find just such a vehicle. You can even specify the configuration you want for both new or used vehicles, then Autobytel.com calculates the estimated price before you talk to a dealer. When, and if, you are ready to buy a car, you fill out a purchase request and wait for a dealer to contact you—within 24 hours.

As part of the process, you can research information on your potential purchase by pulling up reviews on new or used cars and checking trade-in values, buying and leasing options, invoice pricing and specs, and current manufacturer incentives. Even from these areas seemingly extraneous to car-buying, Autobytel.com makes it easy for you to jump right into buying mode. Say, for example, you've read a review on the site regarding a 1998 Volvo Sedan and you're ready to buy. Directly from this review you can select the appropriate link and you're on your way to lists of dealerships or used car offerings. Or, if you want to review more articles about the car, you can jump to them from within the article as well.

Last but not least, there is the 3D Virtual Showroom that allows you to rotate and view a vehicle from any angle you choose (this requires the G2 video plugin), from the comfort of your own home without anybody looking over your shoulder, asking if you're ready to "take this baby home with you."

Edmund's Automobile Buyers Guide

● http://www.edmunds.com/

New cars, used cars, road test, safety info—Edmund's, for those unfamiliar with the name, is the automotive equivalent of *Consumer Reports* for the car-buying public. The publishers of the well-known magazine have successfully applied their car-reviewing expertise to the web. You can search by type of vehicle while reading news, editorials, and road tests. Each car or truck review is presented with a photograph (a major benefit of the website) and a Vehicle Information Menu of subtopics including pros and cons, consumer comments, competing models, specs and safety features, insurance cost, standard and optional equipment, and pricing. Used car reviews include many of these same subtopics, as well as Edmund's ratings. Additionally, users can get a free Carfax lemon check for those borderline jalopies.

The road test section includes comparison tests of new vehicles, long-term road tests, and most wanted cars for the current year. Other useful features include car-buying tutorials, a loan calculator, a bulletin board, recalls, general consumer advice, and safety information.

Kelly Blue Book

● http://www.kbb.com/

Informed car buyers use the *Kelly Blue Book* to hunt down car values and pricing. This website might make the printed version obsolete. Everything you need from the famous *Blue Book* (and quite a bit more) is here. Find out what your car, truck, or van is worth; which dealers are in your area; and how to sell your car on the Internet. You'll also find the prices for new cars, as well as reviews and specification of this year's models. There are descriptions of, and links to, the best sites on the web for buying or selling your car, as well as financing and insurance links. You can even get "door-to-door" directions and maps to dealers in your area.

The information can be tailored to searches for motorcycles, ATVs, scooters, personal watercraft (i.e., jet skis), and snowmobiles. Basically, if it's a vehicle, the Kelly Blue Book site can help you find out what it's worth.

Motorcycles
Motorcycle Web Index

● http://sepnet.com/cycle/index.htm

Motorcycles have always been more than just a way to get from point A to point B. From Brando in *The Wild One* to Fonda in *Easy Rider*, bikes have become the epitome of cool. And the Motorcycle Web Index does the bike's reputation justice, partially due to its unique design. The homepage, which is really the only page, is eye-catching with a grid of 20 flashing rectangular advertisements for everything from Harley Moms to motorcycle parts.

Just below this display is a pulldown menu that leads to more than 100 manufacturers and sites for fans of particular types of motorcycles. Beneath this is another group of links for insurance, events, dealers, auctions, racing, tours, legal issues, magazines, homepages from bikers all over the world, clubs . . . you get the idea. The Motorcycle Web Index claims that it contains more than 3,000 motorcycle links, and we aren't inclined to argue with professional bikers. But, just in case there isn't a link here for that bit of motorcycle data that somehow escaped the notice of the proprietors of this site (Scorched Earth Productions), they link you to another site with all the popular web search engines on a single page. Born to be wired, indeed.

RVs
RV Tech Stop

● http://www.rvtechstop.com/

Don't like where you live? Pack up the fake lawn, tie the bikes on the back, and head out—it's that easy with a recreational vehicle. Tens of thousands of people make these mobile mansions their primary residence during the year, and RV Tech Stop serves as their link with the realities of the road.

Written by two journalists and RV experts, this site has plenty of useful information for RV owners. Recreational road warriors can get the scoop on tolls, review the latest press releases relevant to RV owners, submit questions to the webmasters, or browse through previously published articles. The selection of topics covered is impressive: do-it-yourself projects, educational and technical information, company profiles, and product reviews. But note: Viewing some of these articles requires Adobe Acrobat, which can be downloaded from this site. The links page can help you locate manufacturers or get information on travel, weather, and road conditions. Other link areas include RV-oriented organizations, alternative energy, and electrical systems.

Trucks
Truck World

● http://www.truckworld.com/

From custom 4x4s to street trucks to monster trucks to NHRA and NASCAR truck racing, this site caters to everyone who has any relationship—on any level—with trucks. Animated photo icons point readers to 25 different areas for truck-related information. Within these areas are even more categories and topics, making the site some several hundred pages deep. There are links relating to news, event coverage, and promotions, while metacat-

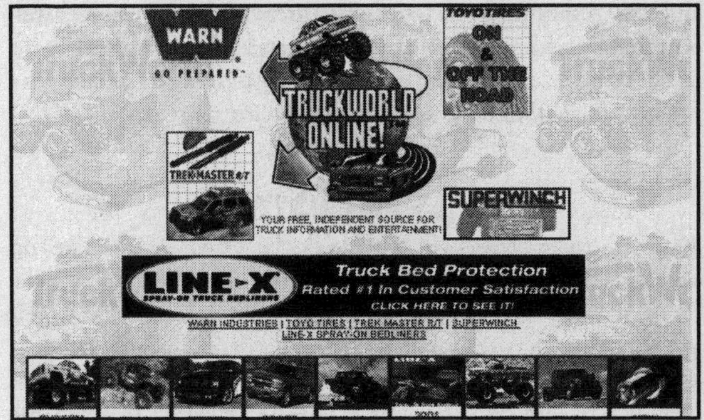

egories include truck tests, shows and events, readers' rides, travel and adventure, golden oldies, reader mail forum, and classified and catalog guides.

Even in the details, the site never lets up on its "all trucks all the time" theme. The How-to technical section illustrates a variety of topics ranging from the obscure to the obvious, including bushing technology, electrical basics, differentials, brake installations, and a three-part series on rebuilding a Chevy engine. The Clubs and Associations section is impressive, with a tremendous number of links to group sites in every state in the country as well as international sites. There are also calendars of events, coverage of road events and trade shows, road reviews, and contests.

World Motorsport

● http://worldmotorsport.com/

This online directory and search engine about everything related to motor sports is a racing fan's dream. The directory includes categories of everything from motorcycle racing to ice racing, NASCAR to tractor pulling. Links to racing clubs, news and media, and suppliers and companies are all included. There is a section that includes latest news and a forum for site visitors to post and view responses to various topic threads. Visitors can feel empowered by adding or modifying links and submitting sites to be listed in the directory. The website is easy to navigate and chockfull of information for the discerning motor sport fan.

[aviation]

Landings.com

● http://www.landings.com/

Landings, believe it or not, are the easy part of flying; it's knowing when to take off that really determines whether you succeed or not. This site has both ends covered and gives private and recreational pilots a category site of the first order. Designed to cover the gamut of aviation issues from flight planning to modifying aircraft to medical concerns for flyers—and addressing them on both the professional and the amateur level—Landings.com offers the most data any aviator needs. It doesn't matter whether that aviator is interested in only single-engine planes, helicopters, gyrocopters, ultralights, or balloons: Each has its own section here.

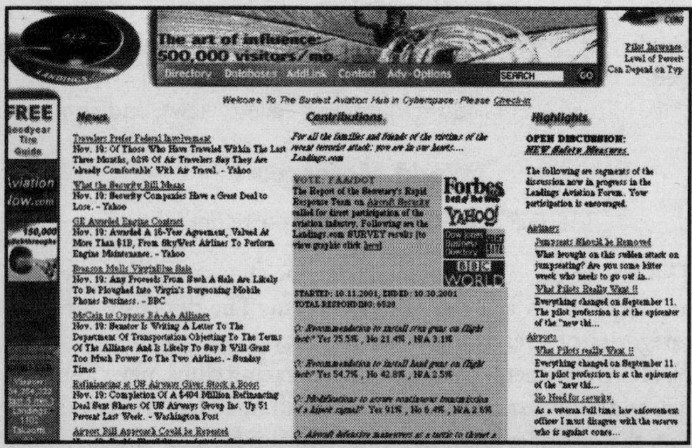

YAHOO! ALSO LISTS: [aviation]

- **http://www.airaffair.com/**
  Air Affair
- **http://www.ameijer.demon.nl/airlinks.htm**
  Arjen's Aviation Links: huge, sorted list of aviation sites
- **http://www.ugamedia.com/asr2.htm**
  ASR: Aviation site register offers you thousands of links to aviation sites worldwide including USAF, warbirds, air force, aviation magazines, display teams, airshows, and aircraft sites.
- **http://www.aviationaccess.com**
  Aviation Access: links to aviation and airline information, organizations, research, etc.
- **http://www.dreamland.co.uk/aviation**
  Aviation Jumpstation: thousands of links
- **http://sportflyer.com**
  Sport Flyer's Internet Resources: comprehensive listing of sites for recreational flying, general aviation, ultralights, and kit planes.
- **http://www-logistics.aetc.af.mil/**
  USAF AETC Aircraft Maintenance Analysis: large collection of AETC aircraft images, WWW lists, and information about 2R0 Maintenance Analysts
- **http://www.sky.net/~wings/**
  Waypoint #1: aviation links from Commercial/Military to Aviation R&D and Area 51 links

---

So much information is crammed on the homepage that you might think you're looking at the control panel for a 747. The top of the site hightlights info on essentials such as flight planning and equipment sales. The middle section includes monthly news and articles, some of which are first-person reports, while the bottom—called the Aviation Directory—provides links to more than 50 specific areas within the site, ranging from forums on medical data (pilot fatigue, diabetes, etc.) to airport searches to calculators for measuring distances between airports. All pilots should consider adding this site to their preflight checklists.

[boating]

Boat Trader Online

● http://www.boattraderonline.com/

If you are looking to chart a course on the high seas or just to buy a kayak, this site is a good place to start. Boat folk will find everything here, from racing to charters, weather, financing, new and used boats for sale, info on fishing, organizations, brokers, dealers, insurance, instruction, repairs, manufacturers, and publications.

When diving into sections such as Boats for Sale, a whole new set of searchable criteria results, which allows you to scan through the database very quickly. A commerce section called Site at a Glance lists how many boats are for sale on the site (an impressive 63,440 at the time of this review), the number of brokers/dealers, boating events, and boating links (equally impressive at 3,140). It's very likely that boat enthusiasts could explore the entire web-based boat world from this site and never have to, uh, set sail.

[camping]

CampNet America

● http://www.campnetamerica.com/

Ever had one of those times when you planned a camping trip by consulting a travel guide only to find out that the "campsite in a great location" was located right next to the busiest highway in the state?

To make sure you never have scary camping adventures like that again, CampNet America comes to the rescue. Beating out all the other camping sites that let your mouse do the grunt work, this no-frills site is a great collection of links to sites dealing with every aspect of camping. To get started, use the campground and public parks locator maps, find addresses, and browse links to travel clubs and associations. Then outfit yourself by linking to RV and tent manufacturers and dealers, outdoor supplies dealerships, and log cabin rentals. Finally, make sure you're prepared for anything by checking out the links to general travel sites, a route planner, and *USA Today*'s weather site. At the end of your day, head over to the Virtual Campfire forum to exchange campfire stories and recipes. Camping may never be the same.

[cooking]

When personal computers were first sold in the early 1980s, marketers relentlessly pitched consumers on the value of putting these machines into their homes. Invariably, they cited three computer applications that would make the traditional home that much better: word processors, spreadsheets, and databases. Word-processing programs were essential for writing letters and helping the kids with their homework. Spreadsheets were the only realistic way to keep track of household finances. And databases? Well, they were . . . uh, they were good for . . . storing recipes. With that stroke of marketing brilliance, computer sales were set back for a decade.

While computers have not become the type of household appliance that one puts in the kitchen with the microwave and the coffeemaker, the Internet has brought this idea closer to reality. As searching the web becomes a pursuit to rival channel surfing on TV, more information gleaned from the Net will be used for household endeavors. Maybe now the recipe database that was supposed to drive sales of the IBM PC Jr. or the Apple Lisa will reside on the Internet with little concern for the actual hardware.

If the cooking sites on the web today are any indication, the providers of cooking information will be ready to move in and take charge once the family computer makes its way from the den into the kitchen (and it will happen, we assure you). Epicurious's 13,000-recipe database, Veggies Unite!'s 3,000-recipe database, and SOAR's nearly-60,000-recipe database are all just the tip of the iceberg. It is only a matter of time before the Internet becomes just as important a tool in the kitchen as measuring cups, timers, oven mitts, and those soon-to-be relics from a bygone era—cookbooks.

Diabetic

Diabetic Gourmet Magazine

● http://www.gourmetconnection.com/diabetic

Diets for diabetics don't have to be boring or bland, and this site's goal is to prove that. While it is actually an e-zine for diabetics, the overall focus is on food and how to eat well within a restricted diet. The site's departments include Food & Dining, Diabetes 101, a Diabetes Q&A, Healthy Living, and more. There are daily news and features, current government (FDA) news, a daily tip and recipe, basic diabetic information, and a newsletter. Then, for dealing with actual food, there are a recipe archive, a diabetic glossary, current menus, articles on reading food labels, nutrition tips, healthy eating, and a marketplace. The forum section includes links to articles on children with diabetes, doctors, cooking, medication, and help for the newly diagnosed.

The recipe search engine has an advanced search feature to search using categories of food, ingredients, and preparation methods. A menu link takes readers to a collection of menus grouped by season, theme, and food type (e.g., spring menus, peanut butter recipes, ethnic and regional dishes, and holiday menus). Diabetic Gourmet Magazine offers a free diabetic newsletter subscription if you add your e-mail address to its mailing list.

Ethnic

Sue's Recipe Server

● http://www.hubcom.com/cgi-win/recipe.exe/1$1$1

It's hard to believe that someone named Sue has come up with a site that focuses on ethnic recipes. But indeed she has. Even with a decidedly nonethnic name, this site has recipes from 45 countries and regions around the world, from Australia to Burma to Cyprus and on to Sicily and Sri Lanka. You can choose to view the listing of recipes by country or by category (soup, dessert, lamb, oysters, etc.). When a country is selected, you're presented with indexed recipes for that part of the world. Each recipe, say for crab laksa from Malaysia, is followed by an indication of the number of servings and simple, easy-to-read step-by-step instructions. The recipes all feature a helpful "abbreviations and conversions" icon that jumps to several tables with standard measurement conversions. At the bottom of the page is a set of links that take you back to look at a new country (or category) as well as similar dishes or the next dish on the list.

Other features include a group of icons for What's New, Top Ten Recipes, Books for Cooks, and a link to Barnes & Noble. The Books for Cooks section features reviewed and recommended books. At the bottom of the page there is a text link to other Internet recipe sites, as well as a place to add your own recipe, and a selection of travel articles written by the site's authors. This site gets huge kudos for its scope and simplicity in delivering such a diverse set of recipes—something you might not expect from a site named Sue.

General

Epicurious

● http://www.epicurious.com/

Epicurious comes very close to being the category-killing site for cooking on the Web. It is, quite simply, a site for people who want to cook and

eat and eat and cook. Compiled from issues of *Bon Appetit* and *Gourmet* magazines, this Condé Nast megasite has a searchable database of, at this count, approximately 13,000 recipes.

Gourmands can search by using a combination of keywords and selected terms such as cuisine, ingredients, meal, special considerations, preparation, and occasion or by specifying a category—meal type, main ingredients, etc.—and then drilling down through a host of classification options.

A recipe can be saved to a personal recipe box that organizes and stores recipes for future use and features a calendar with reminders about upcoming episodes of the *Epicurious* TV program—a clever marketing feature and a useful tool for learning new skills. Although it is a free service, you must register to access the recipe box feature.

But wait, as they say on late-night TV, there is much more. Cooking lessons, tips, video instruction (QuickTime or RealPlayer plugins are required here), metric conversion tables, a food and wine dictionary, cookbook reviews, etiquette, kitchen equipment information and guidance, kid-friendly cooking, recipe swaps and chat, dining guides, wine guides, and on and on.

The site is lovely to look at with loads of illustrations, photos, and appealing graphics. After spending time within Epicurious, you may get the feeling that the designers of this site believed there was a computer in every kitchen. It's a good reason to put one in yours.

RecipeSource

● http://www.recipesource.com/

How many magazine articles or cookbooks would it take for you to have 50,000 recipes in your kitchen? Even then, how would you be able to find a single recipe for, say, sesame chicken in all that paper? All in all, a complicated process.

But in the online world, it's very simple. Stop by Recipe Source, a welcome site in an otherwise cluttered Internet world. The homepage is essentially a search engine that claims to access nearly 60,000 indexed recipes. Just type a word or recipe name into the search box and you're off. If you're not looking for a specific dish, choose from a huge list of categories including food types (baked goods, soups, desserts, main dishes, side dishes, etc.), restricted and special diets (diabetic and vegetarian), and regional or ethnic groups (South American, Jewish, etc.). You'll get lists of recipes, or even additional categories that help refine your search. This site is especially recommended for individuals who want recipes for restricted and special diets.

With this site, you can try a different recipe every night for approximately the next 200 years, ending any complaints about having the "same old thing" for dinner.

Product Resources
Cooking.com

● http://www.cooking.com/

Need an upscale Porsche-designed coffee pot for your kitchen? How about a professional bar blender or maybe just a chef's apron? From the utilitarian to the unique, shopping for cooking supplies online at Cooking.com, you can easily stock your first kitchen or add a professional piece of cookware to your larder.

The range of product categories is impressive: bakeware, cookware, cutlery, electrics, specialty foods, cook's tools, books, and CDs. The range of individual product offerings is immense, from a $7 tin pie pan to a $360 copper saute pan. Once you've made a selection, such as a blender, you'll get lists of appropriate products, descriptions, and pricing. A small shopping cart icon in the upper right corner accumulates your items and tallies them for purchase. A big site benefit is that you can also do product or brand searches and get suggestions for gift ideas, as well as recipes and cooks' tips.

Resources
The Cook's Thesaurus

● http://www.switcheroo.com/

Don't want—or can't have—beef in your meals? Try substituting venison, turkey, ostrich, or tofu. It's info like this that makes the Cook's Thesaurus a tremendous site for anyone who cooks, offering substitutions for thousands of cooking ingredients, such as low-fat and reduced-budget alternatives and replacement ideas for not-so-handy ethnic ingredients.

The categories here are listed as food or liquid and include meat and fish, legumes and nuts, fruit, vegetables, grain products, alcohol, flavorings and accompaniments. Within each category is an alphabetized list of items with descriptions, cooking hints, and substitutions. Site compiler Lori Alden also lists her sources and useful links, getting extra credit from us for her cool choice of URL.

Vegetarian/Vegan
Veggies Unite!

● http://www.vegweb.com/

There are probably as many kinds of vegetarians as there are religious sects in the Judeo-Christian world. You have strict, sometimes totally militant, passive, and even those of the orthodox variety—the vegans. This site seeks to bring them all together and that serves all levels of the vegetarian community. And although this site is oriented toward supplying veggie-minded resources, nonvegetarian eaters may want to check the more than 3,000 ways to prepare vegetables.

Addressing all aspects of vegetarianism, sections include a recipe directory, articles, resources and tools, an interactive area for FAQs, Vegchat forum, membership, exchanges, and (honestly) veggie poetry. The recipe directory has thousands of vegan recipes, plus links to a recipe of the week, measurements and conversions, new recipes, a glossary, and substitutions. It also enables users to assemble a week's worth of menus and print out a grocery list—an extremely nice feature. There is also a nutritional analysis tool, a grocery-list maker a weekly meal planner, Internet resources, veggie shopping resources, and, perhaps most importantly, ways to live in harmony with carnivores.

[dating]

Dating Advice

● http://dating.miningco.com/msubadvice.htm

Dating Advice is a dating-specific subsite of the popular About.com site, featuring 50 forums with help for the heartsick. The forums include lots of Miss Lonelyhearts–style Q&As, some of which are hosted by syndicated pros, others by fast-and-loose know-it-alls, à la Adam Carolla from *Loveline*. Archives are maintained at most of these sites, so if you missed that article explaining how to tell her that you weren't always a man, not to worry.

Your guide at Dating Advice is one Brenda Ross, who describes herself as "a dating adviser and slightly cynical romantic optimist." She offers a summary opinion of each forum so you know where to surf, based on whether your issue is specific to marriage, teens, breakups, or anything else heartstring-related. Ross has also penned a handful of articles that are available here, and the site is rounded out nicely by chats and a free newsletter.

Dateable.com

● http://www.dateable.com/

Relate, date, and mate is the mantra at Dateable.com. The developers of this site have gone to great lengths to distinguish it from the other online dating sites, primarily through its People2People forum. This section of Dateable.com goes beyond the standard, text-driven personality profiles (read: "classifieds") available to the lovelorn; here you can send and view pictures or even send a voice greeting. So don't just tell that prospective mate that you like piña coladas and getting caught in the rain; sing a few bars and upload a picture of yourself looking great in bad weather.

Dateable.com has a variety of other resources and services including poetry, romantic stories, contests, gifts, games, and horoscopes for those seeking romance in the digital age. Oddly, there's an Online Auction, and we're not sure how that fits into the romantic picture; perhaps if you do find your one and only love, you could go there and buy him or her a *Star Trek* action figure or perhaps a 200-piece socket and drill set.

Dating Tests
Love Test and Quizzes

● http://dating.about.com/msubtests.htm?pid=2817&cob=home

The content providers at the Love Tests and Quizzes section of About.com know there are more important questions to answer in the world of dating than "Do you come here often?" and "What's your sign?" To that end, this site has compiled tests, quizzes, and surveys that could make even the editors of *Cosmo* jealous. Questionnaires deftly help differentiate between the sensitive and the cold-hearted, the needy and the commitment-phobic. "Are You a Jerk?" corners men with a true/false test that handily churns out one's "jerk quotient." The "I'm not Bitter Quiz-o-Rama" lets women know whether they're "helpmates or saboteurs" (blood sample required). "The Bimbo Quotient" helps define status in the, er, pecking order ("Were you voted easiest woman on campus? Two years in a row? By the chess club?"). And "Do You Like the Opposite Sex?" can reveal, in five easy questions, whether you've been shopping at the wrong mall altogether. And if you don't like being told you're an airheaded flirt or a latent, nose-picking man lover, there are three dozen other tests that give you the chance to get it right.

[gambling]

The Online Gambling Directory & Casino Guide

● http://www.gambling.com/

Gambling has not taken hold on the Internet in the way that, say, auctions have, but given the general populace's seemingly insatiable desire for betting money on almost anything in almost any venue (witness riverboat gambling, reservation gambling, and state lotteries), it's probably just a matter of time. Odds are that it will happen sooner rather than later.

YAHOO! ALSO LISTS: [gambling]

- **http://www.gambling-links.com**
  AnteUp Gambling Links: contains gambling-related content and online wagering sites
- **http://www.gamblingreview.com**
  Gambling Review Online: features online casinos with site reviews, gambling links, and world casino phone numbers
- **http://www.gamblink.com/**
  Gamblink.com: up-to-date online gambling news and links
- **http://www.placeyourbet.net/topsites/**
  Online Gambling Network: guide to 100 gambling sites
- **http://www.wheretobet.com/**
  Where to Bet Online: directory of Internet casinos, sportsbooks, and lotteries; also includes updated online gambling news

---

Gambling.com is billed as the "Ultimate Free Gambling Site," a gateway to the netherworld of gaming for dollars. First and foremost, Gambling.com is a link service, providing nearly 10,000 connections to every imaginable form of gaming sites, from lotteries and sports betting to horse racing and casinos, sweepstakes, and card games. By registering as a member of the site, you earn "ludos," or credits, for each visit as well as other activities, allowing you to enter contests without actually sacrificing your hard-earned dollars (although you'll sacrifice your e-mail address to the gambling gods). There are also links to sites that offer gambling tips and news, and members are able to rate the good sites (and earn more ludos), allowing first-timers to carve the mountain of links into a molehill of opportunities.

As you might expect, the site's design is pure Las Vegas: The overwhelming multitude of morphing, blinking, and flashing advertising banners make finding actual site information a gamble in itself.

[games]

Gamespot

● http://www.gamespot.com/

Like a group of marauders from Quake invading a Pokemon convention, this site pounds away at you with so much information that visitors are powerless to resist. Name a game or a game category and this superb site addresses it. From such standards as Myst and Doom to Warcraft, Hydro Thunder, and System Shock (and even Pokemon), you can get enough data to fill Lara Croft's munitions pack for the next decade.

This site also has a news section, a computer game section (divided by types of games, from action and adventure to sports and strategy), game hardware (3D, controllers, even do-it-yourself), video games (Dreamcast, Nintendo 64, PlayStation), used games at auction, and downloads. There are also sneak previews, tips and cheats, articles on the games and their designers, and discussion areas for every gnarly game on the face of the planet. You can also jump from this site to lowest-price online vendors of the games, or you can play with other people online.

For those who are interested only in online games, check out Blue's News (http://www.bluesnews.com/) for the gory details on web-based weapons and warfare.

GameSpy

● http://www.gamespy.com/

If playing online action games can be considered a form of war, then consider this collection of sites is the equivalent of briefing rooms. They'll point you to the hot Net places where you can indulge in pan-global pursuits of programmed pain. For you plebes, this means huge network servers that run all versions of Quake, Duke Nukem, Descent, Baldur's Gate, Warcraft, MechWarrior, and many more. GameSpy will also get

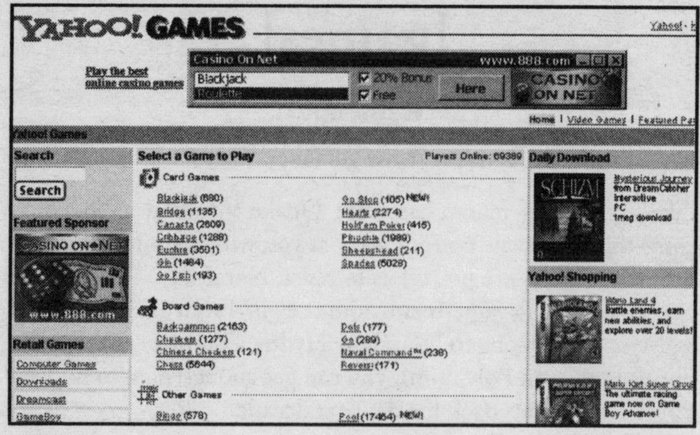

you the equipment you need for your online assaults, from patches to packs. After you've been here, you can suit up and strap yourself in. From that point forward, you're on you own.

Yahoo! Games

● http://games.yahoo.com/

If you miss playing Go Fish with your grandmother in Illinois or backgammon with your college roommate in Iowa, you can pick up where you left off by logging on to this online game site. The Yahoo! site has a strong coterie of games that include venerable card faves poker, gin, cribbage, and canasta and board games such as chess, checkers, crossword, and mah-jongg.

Log in to a game room, check out the available games (you can either watch or join), or start your own game. The games are Java-powered, which makes them look good and move quickly. Even if you just want to watch, it's fun to see invisible hands move pieces on, say, a backgammon board. But be forewarned, there may be thousands of people in a particular area at any given time, so you and your grandma might want to get your own table.

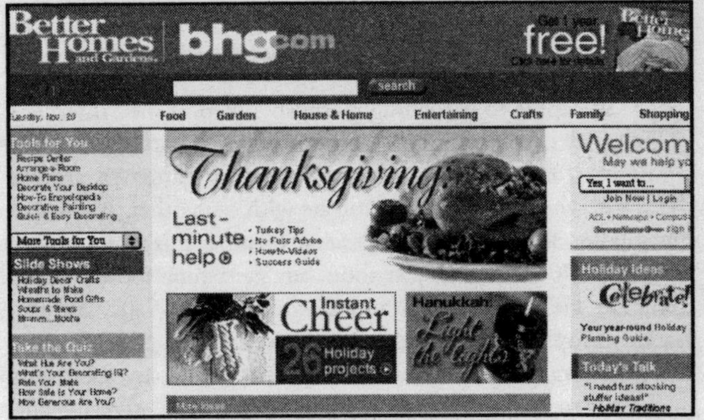

[gardening]

Better Homes & Gardens

● http://www.bhg.com/bhg/gardening/index.jhtml

We're pretty sure there is only one Pawpaw Patch on the web, and it isn't on Disney's *Jungle Book* site. It's here at the online wing of *Better Homes & Gardens* magazine, where you'll find more than a dozen layouts for various types of gardens, from a shade and nook garden to a property line bed and corner of perennials. In addition to visiting the aforementioned Patch (an online forum and appreciation society), you can chart the progress of the mag's Test Garden (which shows periodic photos taken over a season), go to the Editor's Choice section to sift through its gigantic plant database, read articles and flower show reviews, join discussion groups, and lots more. For ideas on how to arrange your outdoor space, take a stroll through this garden spot.

GardenWeb

● http://www.gardenweb.com/

Welcome to gardening glasnost. Billed as the "Internet's garden community," GardenWeb is a horticultural site whose chief asset is its numerous forums for gardeners around the world who want to communicate with each other. And we're not talking about just a few general forums; this site contains more than 90 forums on just about any gardening topic you can think of: Heirloom Plants and Gardens, Lawn Care, Shrubs, Cactus, Tropical Plants, and more. There are even pages devoted to "seed swapping," a wonderful practice whereby gardeners mail seeds to each other, which promotes botanical diversity and comradeship. GardenWeb's international reach extends to Canadian, European, and Australian visitors. Other fun features are a plant dictionary, a contest to discover a "Mystery Plant," a glossary, weather reports, and a directory of gardening organizations. No question, this site has created a vibrant and thriving community of global gardeners.

Horticulture Online

● http://www.hortmag.com/

If there *is* a way to garden in cyberspace, Horticulture Online has surely found it. Well, anyway, it has come closer than any other site to putting a garden on the web. More accurately, Horticulture Online helps you to design a garden in bits and bytes. The site (from the editors of *Horticulture Magazine*) features the Garden Planner, an interactive way for you to create your own design. Using this program, you can measure out your beds, put in plants, and more. There's even the elaborate Plant Finder: You plug in basic info (soil type, sun exposure, region, color preference, etc.) and this search engine will identify the plants that are perfect for your garden. We looked for a blue, fall-blooming flower for a Zone 6 garden with partial sun and clay soil and were referred to the Clematis "H.F. Young," complete with a color picture of the plant and a link that lets you buy that plant from a mail-order nursery.

The site also offers access to special online articles (for example, "Hydrangeas" and "Mastering the Color Palette: Pink," by English gardening expert Christopher Lloyd), back issues, and info about the staff, which includes *Victory Garden* TV host Roger Swain. You can also link to Garden.com, the big gardening retailer on the Internet. This site, especially with the Garden Planner, is quite impressive and convenient and is certain to attract gardeners in droves. A green thumbs-up for this fine site.

Hydroponics
The Growing Edge.com

● http://www.teleport.com/~tomalex/index.html

Most of the world thinks of gardening as an outdoor activity, but others know it's an inside job, too. According to the Growing Edge.com, "While a great future may lie ahead for large-scale indoor agriculture projects, the potential of indoor gardening for individual and small community projects may be even more intriguing and hold greater promise for the enrichment of society."

The Growing Edge.com is a site for indoor and hydroponic gardeners, as well as for advocates of more environmentally friendly agriculture. Here you can learn about hydroponics—the science and art of growing plants in water—and meet other indoor gardeners and garden supporters in the Community section. You can read articles from the *Growing Edge* magazine (such as "Choices for Safe Pesticides" and "Community Supported Agriculture: A New Way to Supply Food"), find local retailers in the database, get growing tips, have your questions answered, and check out the latest products for indoor growing. For indoor gardeners, this site promises to be a growth area, indeed.

The Philadelphia Flower Show

● http://www.philaflowershow.com/

Gardening is about nothing if not stopping to smell the flowers. In order to do that, you've got to visit the granddaddy of American flower shows (in fact, the world's largest indoor flower event), the venerable Philadelphia Flower Show. Information on this annual flowerfest is now online all year long at this website. You can get directions and transportation info, ticket prices, and visitor tips or shop in the Marketplace and even buy tickets online. Of course, you can also learn which expert gardeners won awards in those ever fierce floral competitions and see photos of the blue-ribbon exhibits. If you register to become a member of the Pennsylvania Horticultural Society, which produces the Philadelphia Flower Show, you can get free tickets to the show, as well as a host of other special benefits, including its acclaimed gardening magazine, *Green Scene*. But to actually smell the flowers, you have to go to the show.

Gardening Guides
Ames

● http://www.ames.com/guides/index.html

You've got a patch of land. You want to plant something on it. But what? Roses? Raspberries? Rutabagas? This site from Ames can help you plan that planting project. It is broken down into several subtopics of information: herbs, fragrance, pest-free, cut flowers, vegetables, pruning, butterfly gardening, and water gardening. Need some rationale for your plans? You'll get some homespun wisdom along with hard data, such as "Plants provide a variety of compelling scents for our enjoyment. The primary purpose of scent in flowers is to attract pollinators (usually insects) for fertilization. The flower produces scent in glands located near its petals. Insects are attracted to the scent. As they search for nectar they, at the same time, coat themselves with pollen which is carried from flower to flower, causing pollination."

You can retrieve more detailed information about fragrant plants, including soil and growing habitat. Make plant choices based on such tips as "Gardenia, freesia, and jasmine trigger memories of special occasions. Lavender turns our mind to thoughts of Grandma's house." Then learn the tools recommended for planting. This site is primarily for beginners, containing solid, useful information for the neophyte green-thumber, all handsomely presented. If gardening is a new hobby for you, this is a nice place to start.

The Virtual Library of Botany

● http://www.ou.edu/cas/botany-micro/www-vl/

A clearinghouse of links, this page is devoted to sites specializing in botany (the scientific study of plants) and general horticulture. The hundreds of sites listed here range from the general (the American Fern Society and GardenNet) to the more science-oriented (the University of California's Plant & Microbial Biology pages). Heavy stuff, indeed. Most of these sites are for hard-core gardeners and plant aficionados, but if your love of plants is all-consuming and you're fascinated by green-growing at a molecular level, this site will be extremely valuable. It is also an exceptional resource for botanists and students of botany.

[herbs]

GardenGuides Herb Guide

● http://www.gardenguides.com/herbs/herb.htm

Basil grows well with tomatoes but dislikes rue. Caraway shouldn't be planted near dill, and it will help loosen the soil in a garden. Nasturtiums will keep aphids and striped pumpkin beetles at bay. These are just a few of the tips you can learn about herbs from the Herb Guide section of Garden

Guides.com. It has info on cultivation drying and harvesting,culinary uses; feature articles and how-to stories (use windowsill herb gardens to "make an oil infusion for your hair!"); and a weekly newsletter. You can also get planting companion charts.

MedHerb

● http://www.medherb.com/

Herbal medicines in general don't go through the rigorous approval of the FDA, but many herbs have been clinically tested. MedHerb provides links to such information and to resources that are relevant to medicinal herbs used in clinical settings (herbalism), regardless of the medical tradition or system. Created by *Medical Herbalism*, a quarterly journal of clinical herbalism, large sections link to Anatomy, Herb Sites, Plant Pharmacy, Herbal Journals, Photographs, Physiology, Organizations, Schools, Therapeutics, and more. There's also a newsletter that you can subscribe to for the latest on the use of herbs in all areas of medicine.

A Modern Herbal Home Page

● http://www.botanical.com/

Based on *A Modern Herbal*, a book on herbal medicine written by Mrs. M. Grieve in 1931, A Modern Herbal Home Page explores the medicinal, culinary, and cosmetic uses of herbs, describes their cultivation, and discusses folklore about herbs. The site claims that it has data, in the form of articles, essays, reports, and reference works, on more than 800 varieties of herbs. Databases comprise the heart of the site; they contain listings of plant types, recipes, and general information. (For example, searching on the term "hay fever" generated a huge list of herbal cures, along with a list of plants that cause it.) And lest you think that all herbs are of the curative variety, an index of poisonous herbs will teach you otherwise.

Organic Gardening

● http://www.organicgardening.com/

What exactly is organic gardening? According to Organic Gardening, "Organic gardeners don't use synthetic fertilizers or pesticides on their plants. When you garden organically, you think of your plants as part of a whole system within nature that starts in the soil and includes the water supply, people, wildlife, and even insects." Indeed, this creed has become so popular that *Organic Gardening* is the best-selling magazine of its ilk, with some 750,000 readers per issue.

A laid-back sense of humor, which pervades all of this site's components, gives it charm, as it informs. To start, an almanac of organic gardening tells you what to plant and, more importantly, when. It's categorized by zone, so that you get the right advice for your region. The almanac is supplemented by an excellent Q&A called Solutions, and a down-to-earth section called Maria's Weekly Garden Thought that discusses the merits of specific aspects of organic gardening.

The Southwest School of Botanical Medicine

● http://chili.rt66.com/hrbmoore/HOMEPAGE/

If you favor echinacea over Nyquil and Valerian root over Sominex, then this is a site worth investigating. Greenhouses of information here include more than 1,000 images of plants, plus numerous text documents (in pdf format for Adobe Acrobat). You can read herbal glossaries, instructions for medical applications of tinctures (extracts, usually herbal, made with a mixture of water and alcohol), and articles about herbs to use for specific medical problems.

As the site for an herb school, a lot of the material here is for those who are interested in the professional use of herbs in medical treatments.

[hiking]

Trails and Trips
The Back Packer

● http://www.thebackpacker.com/

Incredible mountain vistas, informative trail databases, and an extremely knowledgable staff make this stylish, reader-driven site ideal for backpacking enthusiasts from all walks of life.

The Beginner's Corner provides extensive information for those just starting out, from advice on what foods to pack to trail etiquette; the Question Section solicits responses to current topics of concern (such as "How do you keep your tent looking and smelling like new?") and offers access to archived questions; Trail Talk provides chat opportunities; Gear has book and gear reviews and the option to read or place classified ads; Destinations describes specific hikes within regions; and the Trails Database enables searches for backpacking trails by state, region, length of hike, and even hike difficulty score. There is also a searchable database of backpacking articles and a long list of company contact addresses, phone numbers, and website links.

And if you're too lazy to get out of your websurfing chair, check out the Pictures page, where reader-submitted photographs will take you on a virtual trip into the backcountry.

Trail Walk (gear)

● http://www.trailwalk.com/

When going up the Himalayas, you better have the right equipment or you won't to get to the summit in one piece. This "online outdoors magazine that gives you nothing but gear—and lots of it" makes outfitting yourself for bipedal adventures an educational experience, with sections labeled Load Carriers, Clothing, and Footwear all leading to discussions of technology, styles, and specific products. The What's New section introduces the latest in hiking technology, such as "satellite navigation in a watch."

The site leads you on increasingly detailed treks through such gear trappings as footwear accessories and navigational systems. While Trail Walk doesn't offer specific products for sale, it does have order forms for several "special offers," and there are ample opportunities to link with the site's gear advertisers.

Trail Walk also hosts gear discussion forums, solicits and reprints reader reviews of specific pieces of equipment, and offers to answer any reader questions on gear. The site seems to have everything you might need in the way of hiking, but it will not do any actual hiking for you. Pity.

[hobbies & crafts]

Hobbies is a tough category to tackle because it's not always clear where to draw the line and on the web you can indulge a hobby and find resources related to it, or you can learn a new one. No hobby is left unturned online, from origami ornaments and maple furniture to glass sculptures and, yes, even wind chimes. The best of the hobby sites are listed below. (Note: Other pursuits that may also be considered hobbies—collecting, playing music, gardening, participating in sports—are found in other sections of this book.)

Art Shows
Arts & Crafts Shows

● http://www.artandcraftshows.net/

Whether you want to exhibit your artistic accomplishments at a local crafts fair or just find out when the next one is coming to your area, visit Art and Craft Shows. This site, sponsored by *Sunshine Artist Magazine,* has cataloged an exhaustive list of approximately 2,000 craft events around the United States, complete with dates and locations. For those who fall into the realm of prospective exhibitors and potential attendees of arts and crafts shows, such information is invaluable. Visitors can search the entire events database by selecting the name of the event, state, region, or approximate dates, or they can check out this week's events for their entire state. Either way, this site will ensure they never miss another fair.

Vellum Gallery of Calligraphy

● http://www.catalog.com/gallery/welcome.html

Fewer and fewer people these days take pen to paper for their correspondence, so a site like this seems particularly inspiring, reminding us of the beauty in the art of lettering. The Vellum Gallery promotes the calligraphic arts. Its site is divided into three categories: one for demonstrating techniques and tools for lettering; another featuring current and future online exhibitions of calligraphy, illumination, and related works; and a third for links to resources for calligraphers. It also has a links section with a calendar of events, gallery and artist sites, organizations and resources, manuscript libraries, and other sites of interest.

With its beautiful borders and photo illustrations, this site almost makes your computer's font library seem limited.

Ceramics

Ceramics Web

● http://art.sdsu.edu/ceramicsweb/

Making clay pots is serious work, especially, for example, when you're trying to achieve delicate shades of blue while firing clay in a kiln that could melt steel. To help potters get it right, Ceramics Web serves as an excellent resource and reference site. Developed by a group of potters at San Diego State University, the site includes articles on ceramics from around the world, glaze databases complete with "recipes", safety and health information, educational materials, software, chat rooms, and material analyses.

The highlights of Ceramics Web, though, are its electron micrographs of clay and its GlazeBase—a unique database of glazes accessible via a strong search engine where you can select a glaze name, color or surface, cone, and thermal expansion and learn how to bring them all together to create that perfect ceramic piece.

ClayNet

● http://home.vicnet.net.au/%7Eclaynet/claynet.htm#contents

ClayNet is a repository for clay-related organizations, artists, educational institutes, galleries, and discussion groups. Addressing the professional potter, ClayNet is broken down into categories that include Wedgwood, Virtual Ceramics, Ceramic Societies, and Technical Ceramics. Each category takes visitors to links that reside either on ClayNet or other websites. There is also a gallery of featured artists, complete with descriptions and photos of their works for online viewing. Finally, ClayNet features its own specialized ceramics engine called Celadon.

Jewelry

Rings & Things

● http://www.rings-things.com/PROJ1.HTM

When you look at a piece of wire, metal, glass, and a bead and see earrings, a necklace, or a brooch, you know you've got the jewelry-making bug. Rings & Things can help you indulge that creativity. The site targets artisans who make their living creating jewelry (and offers supplies to them); amateurs will also find plenty of value here. Rings & Things features bead projects for necklaces, chokers, earrings, hatpins, and other fashion items, complete with illustrated step-by-step instructions and color illustrations of the finished item. There are also links to bead suppliers, trade shows, new stuff, metals, and tips, plus a jewelry supply index.

Knitting
Wool Works

● http://www.woolworks.org/

Most knitted clothing these days comes off industrial looms the size of a warehouse. This hasn't diminished the popularity of hand-knitting. Wool Works is dedicated to providing knitters with patterns, resources, discussion, and supplies. There are links to guilds, computer resources, websites, a magazine for knitters, charities, and more. Much of the information—especially relating to knitting projects, such as afghans or baby hats—is composed of postings from fellow knitters (usually in an e-mail format). Hand knitters of all levels will also find myriad tips and techniques to help them improve their skills and keep the needles flying.

Knives
BladeForums

● http://www.bladeforums.com/

Knives—is this a hobby? Go to BladeForums, "the leading edge of knife discussion," for the answer. This site is for enthusiasts of very sharp weapons and tools, from bowie and khukuri knives to machetes and bayonets. Blade Forums has an index to knife-related information, that includes manufacturers, custom knives, training, even knife-making supplies. But to cut to the heart of the site, enter the various forums, where you can discuss general topics, industry information, automatic knives, knife exchanges, tactical and martial arts development, serrated to smooth, and loads more. To make your point, as it were, you need to register as a member.

Lace
The Lace Guild

- http://www.laceguild.demon.co.uk

The Lace Guild is the largest organization for lacemakers in the British Isles. It works both to educate the public about lacemaking, a craft that dates back several centuries, and to promote high standards for the manufacture of lace. The guild's site includes information on the organization and its membership, a brief history of lace with photos, articles from the guild's magazine and newsletter, notices on events, and suppliers. A separate section just for kids encourages the young to learn about this delicate and revered craft.

Needlecraft
Needlecraft Site on the Internet

- http://www.execpc.com/~judyheim/pages.html

No contest. Needlecraft has the most comprehensive web-based information and directions on how to use needles of all kinds to make things. Its comprehensive list of topics includes sewing, doll-making, costuming, quilting, embroidery, knitting and crocheting, lacemaking, rug-hooking, and weaving. Other sections include online needlework magazines, books for stitchers, discussion groups, relay chat channels, galleries, business sites, software for stitchers, and instructions for how to search the Internet for other craft and stitching stuff.

Quilting
World Wide Quilting Page

- http://ttsw.com/mainquiltingpage.html

The web may become the location of the world's largest quilting bee. The World Wide Quilting Page is a mammoth resource. In addition to instructions, there are sections devoted to patterns, quilters and their work, regional information on shows, exhibitions, quilting library and shopping, plus links to other quilting sites on the Internet. And the Users Pages section enables the exchange of fabric and blocks, the sharing of tips, buying, and selling—as we said, the world's biggest quilting bee.

Rubberstamping
RS Madness

● http://www.rsmadness.com/

Rubberstamping enthusiasts (and we don't mean bureaucrats) can browse this site for handy tips and information on stamps, inks, and what have you. The big draw here is the archive section of *Rubberstampingmadness* magazine, which, for example, offers 50 tips for stampers, from goof-proofing your work to fabulous finds for specific projects. The links section connects avid stampers to materials suppliers on the web.

Rug Hooking
Rug Hooking Online

● http://www.rughookingonline.com/

Rug hooking is considered by some to be America's only true indigenous folk art. Rug Hooking Online hooks up both novice and accomplished to these: What Is Rug Hooking? Articles & Patterns, Ask the Experts, and more. The site includes a brief history of the craft, an archive of some of *Rug Hooking* magazine's feature articles, free patterns for printing out, a gallery that displays readers' works, and a What's New section. The Ask the Experts link takes readers to an archived list of questions answered from experts and sorted by category.

Sculpture
International Sculpture Center

● http://www.sculpture.org/

Wood, stone, marble, clay, glass, metal, and even found objects are all the stuff of sculpture. But along with materials, sculptors require space and inspiration. Here to help is the International Sculpture Center (ISC) site, a hub for finding sculpture information on the Internet. The ISC has generated a remarkable index divided into such categories as Opportunities, Exhibitions (museums, galleries, and sculpture parks), Libraries, Discussion Forums, *Sculpture Magazine*, and more. The subdivision within these categories is even more impressive: associations, sculptors' pages, online galleries, computer-aided sculpture, foundries, biographies of famous sculptors, classroom sculpting, supplies, stone carving, partnering, researching, legal issues for sculptors, and classifieds.

Trains/Railroad
National Model Railroad Association

● http://www.cwrr.com/nmra/

Warning: This is not a simple guide to setting up a circular track under a Christmas tree. This amazing site boasts more than 3,700 links to model railroading and actual railroading sites around the globe, arranged by category. How upscale is this site? Click on Layout Tours and jump to an astounding array of websites featuring such track setups as the one of the Erie Lackawanna that's laid out in a spare bedroom of a hobbyist's home—in Sweden!

If you are into model railroading, probably you are already familiar with the National Model Railroad Association. The organization's site lists links to clubs by state and country and to hobby shops and tourist sites. Under Prototype Railroading, you can find photo galleries of, for example, specific caboose types links to historical sites related to specific railroads, even to railroad unions. The site map is more than adequate for exploration, or you can use a type-in-the-box search engine to find the info you need, whether that be details on specific parts you need for your layout or track ideas for your re-creation of an old Northern Pacific run.

Woodworking
Woodworker's Central

● http://www.woodworking.org/

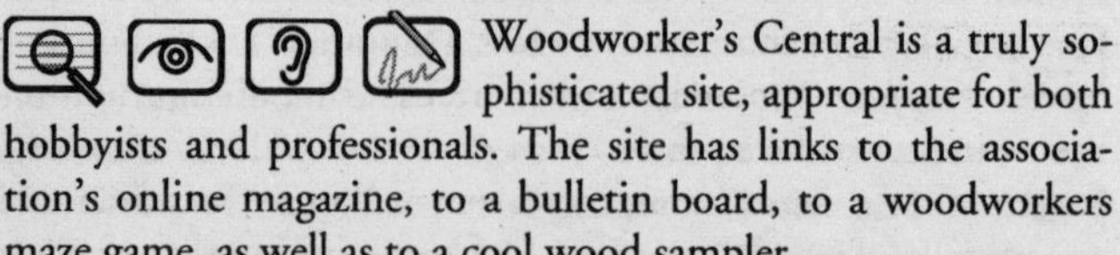

Woodworker's Central is a truly sophisticated site, appropriate for both hobbyists and professionals. The site has links to the association's online magazine, to a bulletin board, to a woodworkers maze game, as well as to a cool wood sampler.

A variety of search engines perform some great functions: Article Search allows users to specify keyword/subject, title, and author; Plan Search looks up furniture plans and ideas throughout the Internet; and Info Exchange scans archived messages from the association's bulletin board to help you locate data on a specific topic. There are also some extremely cool databases. The first is Tool Survey, a compilation of more than 1,000 tool reviews. You select the tool type you're interested in and specify the type of information you want (e.g., manufacturer, model number, age, other users' level of satisfaction), and the site locates it for you. The Accident Survey uses the same technique to retrieve real-life stories of injuries, followed by advice on what *not* to do with your tools. You can look up accidents by type of tool (drill press, chisel mortiser, and reciprocating saw are just a few of the weapons of choice), type of accident (close call, hurt but okay, need medical attention), and skill level at the time of accident. The victims give advice on how to avoid having similar abusive relationships with metal machinery.

Expanding the site is access to a teaching channel (viewable in QuickTime), where you can go for a visual lesson in specific areas of woodworking, such as sharpening a scraper plane. This site will give you a new level of respect for the art of woodworking—not to mention its tools.

[houses & homes]

Better Homes & Gardens (BH&G) Improvement Encyclopedia

● http://www.bhg.com/

For those ready to take a hammer to their house—as opposed to their heads—this home improvement site can make a whole lot of projects a whole lot less of a headache. Just type "home improvement" into the search and pages of links for different areas of home improvement are at your fingertips. Using the BH&G Improvement Encyclopedia, you can search for a special project you have in mind, then run an animated demonstration (using Macromedia's Flash plugin).

The project directions are easy to follow, even for beginners. Here's an example from shelf-building: "A simple-looking shelf unit can be a surprisingly complex project. For example, middle shelves usually are slightly shorter than the bottom and top pieces. If joints are off as little as 1/16 inch, the whole unit may look shoddy. Even getting perfectly straight cuts can be difficult, especially if the boards are warped or bowed. But when the end result is a unit custom-made for your space, it's worth the effort." Info like this makes sure you don't waste your time, or ruin your home.

Easy, accessible, and fun, this site is a good starting place for your home improvement fantasies. It might not turn you into Bob Vila overnight, but there's enough info in the Encyclopedia to ensure that you finish your project and, more important, that you do it right.

Contractors/Designers
Improvenet

- http://www.improvenet.com/

Everyone wants to improve their living space. The problem is making that renovation or redecoration project coordinate with everything else already adorning your home. For that, often you need a professional. This site puts you in touch with local pros, and you don't even have to pick up the phone book. Just describe your project in the appropriate section on this site's fairly detailed form and it will be submitted to contractors, designers, and architects in your area. Those pros who are interested will contact you; from there it's your decision as to whom you want to work with. The benefit of this site is that you get to choose from pre-screened pros, who will understand what you're hoping to accomplish. Best of all, this process is probably the only part of your plans that won't cost you a dime.

Home Fashion Information Network

- http://www.thehome.com/

If you're into interior decorating or have just bought a new home, this site will prove a useful resource. Under section headings such as Floor Coverings, Bedroom and Bath, Decorative Accessories, Lighting and Fans, Wood Furniture, and more, the Home Fashion Information Network offers plenty of articles that address these essential areas of home decor. This site treats decorating very seriously, as evidenced by this commentary on hardwood floors: "Solid hardwood floors repay a little care with a lifetime of value. When you first glimpse a solid hardwood floor, you sense richness, warmth and natural beauty. Gradually, you get to know its distinct personality—visual harmonies, the traces of history in the forest and in your home."

Each decorating area is addressed in depth. For instance, when you click on the subject of floors, you are provided with additional shorter articles, such as "Preventing Damage," "Do Your New Hardwood Floors Look Old?" and "What Condition Is Your Floor In?" These articles are supplemented with a list of manufacturer links to help you find the flooring or other home decor item you need. For nuts-and-bolts home-decorating advice, this site is better than a swatch-and-sample book.

Or you can take an entirely different tack: Build a miniature of your house and decorate that. La Petite Maison (http:// www. lapetitemaison.com/) specializes in building custom oversize model homes—complete with running water and appliances. It can also reproduce a miniature of your home. Then you can go to town decorating the playhouse before you take on the big one.

Hometime

● http://www.hometime.com/

Have a hankering for a backyard gazebo or outdoor deck? Look no further. Based on the popular cable-TV show, the Hometime site features a wide range of do-it-yourself projects, from decks, porches, and painting to flooring and gardening. And these aren't just tips—they're full-blown get-yourself-involved projects. For example, if you want to build a deck, the site gives you a 12-step demonstration, including photographs. There is also ancillary information on tools, materials, and details such as getting a building permit and determining the frost line for putting in concrete footings. If you need more, you can buy a video demonstration of the project from Hometime's online store.

Kitchen and Bath

● http://www.kitchen-bath.com/

Some homeowners are obsessed by their yards, others by furniture, and even a few by flooring. Then there's the kitchen and bath contingent, a truly dedicated group of interior designers who now have their own website. This site—dubbed "The Center of the Kitchen & Bath Universe"—contains all the info K&B lovers crave: new products, do-it-yourself projects, and lots of photos.

From a restaurant menu, you can choose to view different kinds of kitchen and bath styles. If you're interested in, say, a contemporary-kitchen look, the site displays photos of different types, with accompanying text. And if you see something you like, the Kitchen and Bath site gives you the brand name of the product, so you can ask for the exact item at your local home store. Or skip the details and just use this site as a launch for your own explorations. Either way, there is plenty of information here and it's attractively presented for kitchen and bath aficionados everywhere. This is the hot place for cool K&B data.

Repair
Home Maintenance and Repair Index

● http://www.msue.msu.edu/msue/imp/mod02/master02.html

For the king or queen whose castle needs repair, upgrading, or a royal improvement of any kind, this large, text-driven index is a must on the subject of home repair. Just click on the letter of something you're interested in and you're taken to a page listing all the relevant articles available. In the F section, for example, you can learn all about fabrics, faucets, fiberglass, fireplaces, fleas, flies, and more. If you want to learn more about fireplaces, you can scan a variety of articles on the subject. In "Cleaning Brick Fireplaces," for example, you can get the following advice, as well as step-by-step directions: "If the fireplace is to be used for family entertainment, such as popcorn popping, or marshmallow toasting, etc., it would be wise to have the brick or stone fireplace front sealed so as to resist absorption of grease or oils and smoky soot." Indeed, no one wants sooty marshmallows, so this is advice worth heeding. The rest of the site is similarly well ordered and methodical, offering no fancy graphics, just plenty of nuts-and-bolts info to make sure that everyone's home truly is their castle.

Restoration
Old House Web

● http://oldhouseweb.net/

With a focus on detail and authenticity, the Old House Web helps you turn the old homestead into a home worthy of landmark status. To that end, the site provides two distinct services for owners and renovators of old and historic houses: First, there's a library of how-to stories on various aspects of redoing houses, such as doors and molding; second, there are links providing connections to suppliers and manufacturers of products.

One of the best-developed sections of the site is Gardening, with subject listings such as Flowers, Pests, Lawns, and Groundcovers, leading to myriad links to related sites and products. The Community section displays bulletin boards and opportunities for homeowners to discuss similar problems and projects. The Store has additional links by subject area or by product. From the site you can subscribe to the Old House electronic newsletter. Finally, for inspiration and as a place to start, a section called Visuals leads to home tours and historical photograph collections, where homeowners can see how others have solved Old House dilemmas and maybe even borrow a few ideas.

Today's Homeowner

● http://www.todayshomeowner.com/

What a concept—improving your home with a click of a mouse. The website for *Today's Homeowner* magazine enables you to do just that. The site contains original content and information, as well as articles and archives from current and past issues of the publication, covering subjects such as interiors, exteriors, plumbing, and kitchens. An extensive forum area lets users discuss their own improvements or concerns with like-minded homeowners, while features such as the Backyard Gossip Poll and the Tip of the Day keep the site interesting and fresh.

Today's Homeowner has cool hands-on services on its homepage, including Find a Pro, where visitors can fill in a series of forms about remodeling projects that can then be submitted to contractors in a specific geographic area. The Interact service provides a number of useful calculators to estimate job costs; for instance, type in various dimensions of your house and you'll get a ballpark figure for an exterior-painting project. Once you've estimated those costs, use the site's numerous links that help you to spend those dollars and improve your home—all from the comfort of your chair. A free newsletter is available to subscribers—as are opportunities to subscribe to the magazine itself.

[hunting]

The Hunting Network

● http://www.hunting.net/

The big site for big game hunters is the Hunting Network. Billed as the "Ultimate Hunting Website," it gives hunters plenty to explore when they can't be out in the field.

Site headings include Hunting Net Communications (chat, message board, swap hunts, and classifieds), Legislative Alert (keeping tabs on those pesky congressmen who might be trying to restrict hunting), Featured Outfitter, Hunting News, Featured Site, Sweepstakes, and TrailCam (photos taken in the wild of unsuspecting animals). And several links connect to *Hunting Net* magazine and its contents. Hunting News has dozens of partner sites, including the aptly named WhitetailDeer.com, SportingDogs.com, and TrophyGallery.com. A search engine accesses a surprisingly extensive archive of information on just about any type of weapon or animal you can imagine—and quite a few you can't. The search button is marked Hunt Now, which is a clever metaphor.

A disclaimer at the top of every page attempts to effect a truce with nonhunters visiting the site, and though thoughtfully written, it probably won't prevent opponents of hunting from getting all fired up about this site's content.

[outdoor activities]

Great Outdoor Recreation Page (GORP)

● http://www.gorp.com/

What's your idea of an outdoor activity? Kayaking on the Orca Highway near Puget Sound? Cycling through New England? Driving through canyons in northern Arizona? Fishing the Willemoc Creek in New York's Catskill region? Whatever your interest, as long as it takes place outdoors, you're bound to come across it at the Great Outdoor Recreation Page. Fondly referred to as GORP, this is the web's category-killer for outdoor recreation.

GORP has a number of great sections, but let's start with

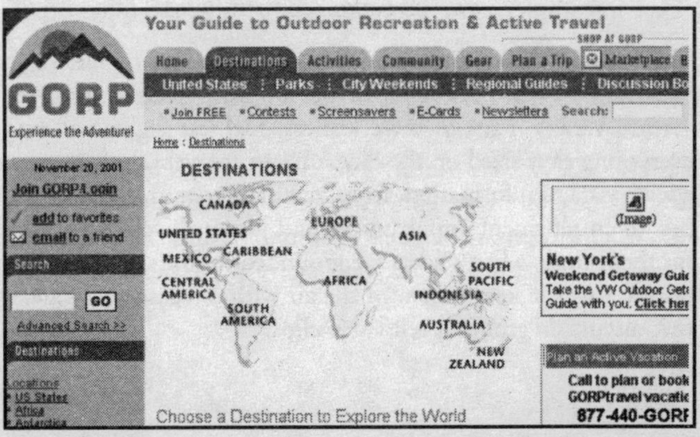

activities, which include just about everything you can do outdoors: hiking, biking, birding, skiing, snorkeling, camping, and climbing. Each of these activities has its own subsite, where you can read articles on cool trips (e.g., biking in Cairo), download regional guides, check reviews of locales and events, and get linked to other relevant resources. The Destination section describes places all over the world that offer interesting and unique outdoor attractions; Gear makes sure you're properly outfitted no matter where you decide to go. GORP even has a travel agency that will help you get to where you want to go with a minimum of hassles.

GORP also features eclectica (health articles, traveling with pets, etc.) and links to maps, books, and other media. If you're going outdoors, go to GORP first, because, unfortunately, you can't take GORP with you when you go—unless that Orca Highway has Internet access.

[paragliding]

Paragliding and Hang Gliding Sky Adventures

● http://www.web-search.com/myhom13.html

Paragliding and hang gliding are sports for which you need a lot of open space—preferably of the vertical variety. Fans of these fearless, fuel less flights will find everything they need on the Sky Adventures website. It features a wide vista of information, from manufacturers and tour operators to employment opportunities and personal web pages. And for those times when gliders are grounded in front of their computers, this site keeps them in the air with screensavers, wallpaper, discussion groups, even video clips.

[photography]

PhotoLinks

● http://www.photolinks.net/

Whether you want a photograph of Whitehall, World War II, or even famous weddings, PhotoLinks is the site for you. It contains dozens, if not hundreds, of links to photography sites all over the Internet. Within its purview are glamour/fashion, advertising, commercial photography, journalism, nature photography, and more. You can also seek information through the search engine, alphabetical lists, or a regional search feature.

PhotoLinks also offers online gallery space to visitors to post their own photographic work. Have a one-in-a-million photo that you're dying for everyone to see? Go to PhotoLinks and learn how to upload it. It might not make you as famous as Ansel Adams or Richard Avedon, but you never know. Click!

Shutterbug Magazine

● http://www.shutterbug.net/

Shutterbug Magazine is a huge print periodical with tons of info for novice and expert photographers. Likewise, at the mag's online site, visitors can bone up on the latest techniques in how-to columns, read reviews of new camera gear, or check out photos by famous photographers. There are also book reviews, a Q&A section, a calendar of events, and much more. There's even a column on digital photography, which is a particularly hot area right now, supplemented by product profiles of new digital cameras.

To get the full text on any of these stories, however, you'll need to subscribe to the magazine. Many people will click on just to scan Shutterbug's famous classifieds, which feature lots of cameras and hardware for sale by private sellers. If you're a photo junkie and need a new outlet, scroll by this site. On the Net, it's a snap.

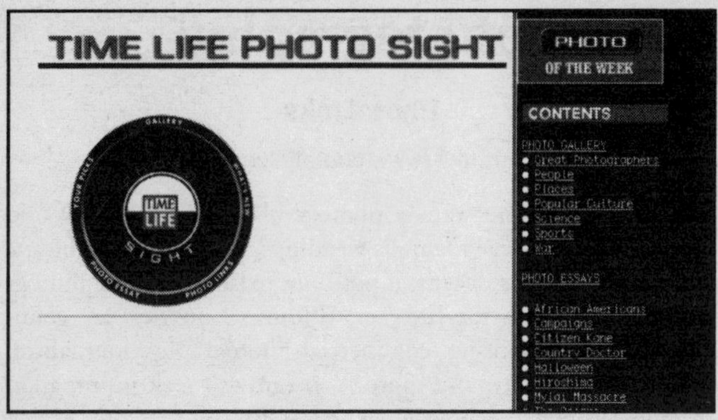

Time Life Photo Sight

● http://www.pathfinder.com/photo/index.html

If your passion or profession is photojournalism, you'll want to visit this powerful, nostalgic site that recalls the best journalism photography of the last 150 years, much of it from the pages of *Life*, *Time*, *Fortune*, and *Sports Illustrated*. The central archive holds about 20 million photographs, which are rotated on its pages as part of various collections and stories. You can see classic photos of people, places, wars, developments in science, and popular culture, as well as a Photo of the Week.

Perhaps most provocative of all, however, are the photo essays covering such diverse and compelling subjects as Hiroshima, African-Americans, and *Citizen Kane*. A startling example is the essay on the 1968 My Lai massacre in Vietnam by U.S. troops, which is both riveting and horrifying, especially in light of the recent atrocities in Bosnia and Kosovo. Accompanying Robert Haeberle's wrenching color photos of murdered Asian villagers and burning huts is a running commentary on the controversial actions of the American soldiers—including the tale of one soldier who shot himself in the foot to escape from the bloody nightmare. It's extraordinary, but one would expect nothing less from the vast Time-Life photo archive. This site is a must-see for photographers and anyone interested in the history of our culture as seen through a camera lens.

[sailing]

Sailfree

● http://www.sailfree.com/

Captain Ahab was one. Captain Hook was another. Heck, even Gilligan was one. We're talking about sailors, those people who find themselves drawn to the open sea and the vessels that traverse it. For those who feel a recurring tidal pull, Sailfree offers the web equivalent of glassy waters, a steady wind, and a full sail.

The site is designed for both old salts and those who have yet to get their sea legs. A comprehensive guide to sailing and all its aspects, sailors can set anchor here to learn about the full spectrum of navigational tools (from lighthouses to loran) or such facts as keelboats having 40 percent of their total weight underneath them. There's also an online sailing class, a dictionary (for those

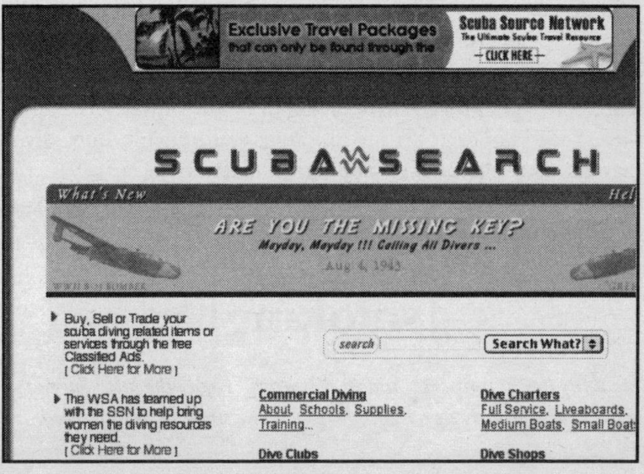

who still don't know the difference between bow and stern), an essential knots section, info on rig types (from Bermudian Ketch to four-masted barque), and descriptions of the parts of a sailboat.

There are also great links to weather info, a marina locator, race calendars, classifieds, and photos (for those currently landlocked). With so much data, Sailfree is a welcome port for all those who sail for a living or ride the weekend waves, or even those whose idea of sailing is simply a three-hour tour.

[scuba]

ScubaSearch

● http://www.scubasearch.com/

Thousands of eccentric scuba diving sites are maintained by diverse proprietors, from retired Navy SEALs to Australian reef fisherman. Since scuba diving is popular all around the world, there is only one way to wade through all of this information: Use ScubaSearch.com. Whether you're an interested amateur or longtime professional, this site will surface all the dive information you need. Somewhat mimicking the layout of the Yahoo! search site, ScubaSearch establishes categories of interest, then allows you to search through all of them via a simple search box. Want to go shark diving in Belize, or wreck diving in New York Harbor? This site can hook you up with tours, divemasters, and equipment suppliers, and tailor facts to you requirements. And it does it all in less time than it would take you to clear your regulator.

[smoking]

Smoking has its advocates and its detractors. Today the latter far outnumber the former, especially where cigarette smoking is concerned.

Fewer people, it seems, get upset over cigar or pipe smoking; indeed, in certain circles today, cigars and pipes have achieved a certain cachet. For those who believe what Groucho Marx said, that "a woman is just a woman, but a cigar is a smoke," we've got several sites where you can indulge in the flaming passion for smoking tobacco.

And lest you think we're showing partiality by not including a cigarette site, we challenge you to try to locate a pro-cigarette site on the web that actually sells or discusses product benefits. They're harder to find than smokers in a California health club.

Cigar.com

● http://www.cigar.com/

NetCigar

● http://www.netcigar.com/

Cigar aficionados spend a lot of time looking for great cigars to smoke. Good ones are easy to find; great ones are a different story. Since Cuban cigars are still technically illegal in the United States, smokers have to search for quality alternatives elsewhere. This isn't always easy, as the advice you're likely to get from your local tobacconist usually reflects what happens to be in stock.

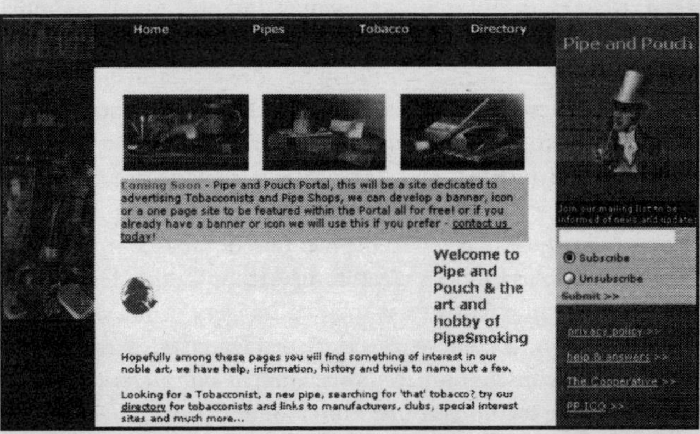

For a better selection and greater insight, get a whiff of these cigar sites. You can search for various cigar brands and buy them online, while delving into cigar-related data. Both sites are lit with links to cigar specialty stores and offer similar forums and message centers. The difference is that Cigar.com has a huge set of links catering to the world of cigars while NetCigar leans more toward providing information and articles about various stogie brands. Either way, you'll get your virtual Cohibas and Corojos in spades on both sites.

Pipe & Pouch

● http://www.pipe-smokers.co.uk

The image of Sherlock Holmes will forever to be associated with a long calabash or briar pipe dangling from his mouth. So it is only fitting that Holmes serves as something of a patron saint for the Pipe & Pouch site, a celebration of all things related to pipe smoking—of the tobacco kind. Using very British and very "proper" graphics (including a cool top-hatted icon who looks as if he just stepped off a Johnny Walker label), this site explores the history and the pleasures of all things pipes.

As you might imagine, tobaccos and pipes are discussed in great detail here, and in no time you will be able to tell easily the difference between a British flake and a flue-cured tobacco. All the site categories run down the right side of the pages and they include Tobacco (Know Your Tobacco, Reviews), Pipes (all you ever wanted to know about your pipe), the Directory (a shop search), Help (Q&A), and YesterYear (a look at how smoking began).

A full page is devoted to the mention of tobacco in Sherlock Holmes stories. Holmes's creator, Sir Arthur Conan Doyle, certainly made abundant use of tobacco imagery in his stories; 33 mention pipes, 31 reference cigars or cigarettes, 4 talk about snuff, and 24 discuss tobacconists. And to put a cap on it, the site quotes the memorable line from Holmes's case of *The Solitary*

Cyclist: "Put that in your pipe and smoke it." Other recipients of the royal treatment are Alfred Dunhill and Sir Walter Raleigh.

The entire site has a regal bearing. While luxuriating in its history pages or being instructed on how to fill the perfect bowl, you may get an uncontrollable urge to call for your slippers and robe, or at least expect that Dr. Watson will show up to help you begin your next investigation.

[textiles]

Textiles.org

● http://www.textiles.org/

They put the shirts on our backs—and clothe the rest of our world. Those who work or play with textiles keep us in stitches. This site is for both amateurs and professionals, providing links to classifieds, bulletin boards, companies, products, crafts galleries, raw material suppliers, and various directories and FAQs. Textile fans will enjoy a visit the four textile museums listed here—or at least a visit to their websites.

[tools]

Sears' Craftsman Shoptalk

● http://www.sears.com/craftsman/shoptalk/index.htm

Once upon a time, tools were not considered something you used to help you get the most from software programs and website-building applications. Tools were for pounding, pulling, pushing, cutting, carving, and crushing. For those who still need, or want, to use traditional tools— saws, screwdrivers, and so on—there is the Craftsman's Projects & Tips section of the Sears tool site.

This site has several areas you can pound away at: Tips &

Techniques (more 300 tips from Bob Vila), Project Plans (fun and interesting projects for you to build), and Workshop Advice (expert information). Most of these areas comprise easy-to-remember tips so you can glance at them and keep them in mind for the right occasion. The Maximizer section, though, has photographs and descriptions of various tools, including data on when to use them and how to determine which is best for which job.

While the site has almost every tool under the sun, there are no links to any testosterone—apparently, it oozes out of every entry.

[toys]

eToys

● http://www.etoys.com/

Betcha' just love Christmas shopping for kids—the crowds, the miles of aisles with products in disarray, jockeying for position, fighting over the last must-have-it gift every year. If you've had enough of this nightmare—and we suspect you have—get out of that toy-store line and log on to the eToys site.

A toy supermarket online, eToys stands to change the way people shop for toys in the future. You can look for goods via six product categories: Toys, Learning Toys, Collectible Toys, Shop by Age, Video Games, and Software. Color photographs, prices, and brief descriptions accompany each product display. And if you don't see what you're looking for, use the Search option to track it down. The availability of each item is shown while you're browsing so that you're sure not to be disappointed.

After you make a selection, move to the Express and Regular Checkout section; you can even request gift wrap. If anything on your list was not in stock, click on the Wish List option, type in what you're looking for, and e-mail the list with comments to your child's other gift givers. Finally, you can set up a My eToys page where you enter birth dates; thereafter, eToys will ensure that you never forget a beloved child's birthday again.

[travel]

Travel planning and the Internet were meant for each other. The travel industry has always relied on the same kind of computer networks—for making reservations and selling of hotel rooms and plane tickets—that form the backbone of the Net. Integrating those travel networks with the Net was a relatively simple process. This upgraded form of personal travel planning has made travel one of the pioneering e-commerce industries on the Internet. Travelers can now search for their tickets, view their intended destinations, and bargain for lower prices without the intervention of travel agents. Some travel sites, especially those belonging to specific airlines, post bargain fares on a weekly basis. We highly recommend visiting individual airline, hotel, and car rental sites to get information that isn't offered on the general sites and to keep track of your frequent flier programs. As you'll see here, whether your travel needs require immediate or long-term planning, the web has sites to fit everyone's taste and budget.

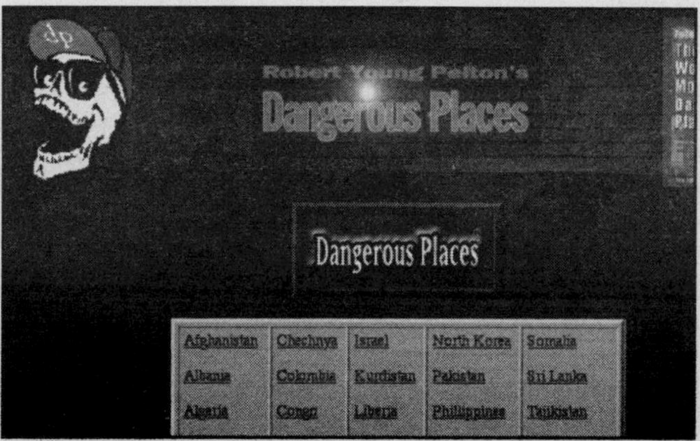

Adventure Travel
Fielding's Danger Finder

● http://www.comebackalive.com/df/index.htm

"Danger is not something you can measure, predict, or prevent. The statistics fired at you by the government are for lab rats and grad students. In the real world, danger is an electric feeling in the air, a gutlike animal feeling that something bloody is about to happen. Danger is in the bloodshot eyes of a crack addict waiting for you to leave the hotel. Danger is in the fraying rudder cables on an aging Tupelov over Tajikistan. And danger is in the eyes of a crocodile waiting for you to brush your teeth along the stream bed." So says Fielding's Danger Finder, a site for travelers who want to explore the world in tour buses that just might blow up.

Cleverly written by a group of intrepid authors led by adventurer Robert Pelton, the Danger Finder leads you to places where the locals would just as soon kill you as give you directions. Along the way, the site covers civil and religious wars, warring tribes, terrorists, thugs, subway muggers, and just plain "dangerous things."

The Danger Finder helps you explore individual countries, then tells you how to go about getting into those countries. It includes reviews of such dangerous places as Chechnya, Somalia, Afghanistan, Burundi, Cambodia, and dozens more, including, yes, the United States (with a list that includes fast-food joints, the Golden Gate Bridge, Atlanta, and Minnesota in the winter). For each country you'll find a section on getting in and getting around, its particular dangerous aspects (for example, land mines or the local water), and nuts and bolts, which is a description of currency, language, electricity, population statistics, religion, and so on. There are also maps, a calendar of dangerous days, and advice for what to do if you find yourself sick in a dangerous country. Tip: Don't get sick in Somalia. Finally, there is an adventure forum for travelers whose only fear is of glossy travel brochures, backpacker guidebooks, or Robin Leach.

Earthwatch

● http://www.earthwatch.org/

Instead of going to that theme park for the sixth summer in a row, why not do something useful or educational, such as study dolphin behavior in New Zealand or research indigenous herbal medicine in Kenya or maybe help excavate Pleistocene mammal fossils in Mexico. All these and more are available when you plan a trip with Earthwatch. The organization's mission is to bring scientists, educators, and the general public together in programs that promote a better understanding of the planet through conservation, study, and cultural exploration. To accomplish this, the site offers nonprofessionals the opportunity to join an expedition with a specific field team. But note: You pay for the privilege, just as you would with a regular sightseeing trip, but with Earthwatch, you can dig in up to your shoulders, literally.

On these expeditions travelers assist researchers to accomplish specific goals, serving as resources that many of these teams otherwise could not afford. More than 100 trips are listed on the site, covering every region of the world. You might, for example, choose to study temple monkeys in Sri Lanka or measure the impact of health education in Cameroon. No matter which package you're interested in, these are opportunities to do something unusual—and worthwhile.

Guides and Planning

Family.com—Travel Category Page

● http://family.go.com/Categories/Travel

Planning a vacation with the kids requires, well, a lot more planning. Fortunately, Family.com. is here to help. This site, run by that kid-friendliest of corporations, Disney, has put together articles and travel planners appropriate for the entire family.

You can plan your trip by U.S. region or by type of vacation: day trips, cities, beaches, cruises, and, naturally, theme parks (remember, this is a site by the house that Mickey built). This site's offerings are remarkably diverse and should satisfy everyone from stressed-out moms and dads to easily bored teens. Selecting the Southwest, for example, turned up 34 different vacation ideas, from houseboating on Lake Mead in Nevada to family dude ranches in Arizona. There are sections on getting good family deals, various exhibitions around the country, and day trips to regional festivals and fairs. And a feature article highlights a specific type of vacation, such as great learning getaways.

Fodor's Online

● http://www.fodors.com/

We had the opportunity to go to London—on someone else's dime—and were without a London travel guide on our bookshelf, so we headed to Fodor's Online, specifically its City Miniguide.

This brilliant site has 99 destinations to choose from, all in major vacation destinations from A to Z (Acapulco to Zurich). We told the site exactly what we wanted in the way of hotels, restaurants, and other travel info (such as ground transportation, telephones, currency, etc.) and it gave us districts to choose from, including Kensington, Knightsbridge, Covent Garden, West-

minster, and a dozen others. We selected Bayswater and Notting Hill Gate. From there we selected a price range (luxury at over 190 pounds) and style of cuisine. The site returned a miniguide with restaurants and hotels in that price range and area, along with detailed descriptions and contact data for each. For a hotel, we chose the Hempel, which is now our favorite hotel in the world. (The only detail not included was a recommendation on which room to stay in.) We also chose a restaurant from Fodor's recommended list, which, conveniently, was in our hotel.

Of course, the site has all the travel basics in addition to its cool miniguide, including hotel and restaurant indexes, a fare finder, a resource center, and a travelers forum. This is a fabulous travel planner that can save you hours. Make it your first stop on your next trip.

Resorts
Resorts and Lodges.com

● http://www.resortsandlodges.com/

This is the site you go to when you want/need to be pampered—or if you're wealthy enough to always be pampered. Whether you want an oceanside resort, a ski lodge, or an equestrian-themed getaway with four-star restaurants, Resorts and Lodges.com has the URL for you.

The site serves as an interactive agent for finding a resort that matches your criteria. Searches are performed in three categories: Locations (listed by regions of the world), Type of Resort (beach, casino, ski, spas, etc.), and Activity (birding, boating, diving, fishing, etc.). Select your preference and you are presented with detailed maps that show you where you can find the kind of resort you're interested in. Summaries are given of each resort, which describe the type of resort (bed-and-breakfast, country inn, etc.), cost, amenities, activities, languages spoken, on-site restaurants, and more. After a few minutes at this site, you may never go camping again.

Tourist Offices
Tourism Offices Worldwide Directory

● http://www.towd.com/

Who ya' gonna call to find the website or the phone number for the tourist bureau in Macao? The Tourism Offices Worldwide Directory, that's who. This single search page is where you can find every tourist information bureau in the world, as well as those for individual U.S. states. Simply select a location from a pulldown menu to go to a page of lists that include phone numbers, addresses, and URLs. Hong Kong, for instance, has 19 listings, including most of the international offices. Every country that offers travel and tourism data has a listing here, including a few that probably shouldn't be promoting travel. (Check with Fielding's Danger Finder, pg. 381, for more information on those hot spots.)

Services
Priceline

● http://www.priceline.com/

Most online discount travel brokers (cheaptickets.com, airtravel.net, and the individual airline sites) work in one of two ways. Either they use existing fares along with available discounts and restrictions to put together a complete, if occasionally tortuous, itinerary that matches your plans, or they take "remaindered" tickets that have not sold or were left unused because of group cancellations. Priceline sets the standard in this category. It continues to break new ground in all areas of travel, offering reduced-fare travel options for domestic and international airline tickets, hotel rooms, and complete travel packages. To state the obvious, it has become big—really big.

Priceline is for people who want to get where they're going inexpensively. In return for this service, the site asks for a lot of data from travelers, which enables it to be as aggressive as possible in getting fares that meet budget and scheduling constraints. When you enter the site, you pick a departure city, an arrival city, dates, how many tickets you need, and what you want to pay. You also include the number of stops—layovers—you're willing to make.

Now, take note: You are not going to get a $50 ticket from Boston to Bangkok, so don't even try. Priceline puts your number up "for bid" with the airlines, meaning it sees if there are any airlines that are willing to put a warm body in a particular plane in order to recoup the cost of flying with an otherwise empty seat. In order to make sure you're not way out of line (or bidding higher than the going rate on a trip), you can check on a listing of current fares. Once you've done all this, submit all the information (as well as whether or not you are willing to fly nonjet aircraft) and Priceline returns the name of the travel provider and the relevant data that matches your request—if your request can be matched.

You've got to be serious at this site, though. Credit card numbers are required up front. If you want to fly cheap, you'd better be ready to go at a moment's notice. So once you start clicking, be ready to start packing.

Travelocity

● http://www.travelocity.com/

Travelocity is like having a travel agent living in your desktop. Everything you would normally ask a travel agent to do for you can be done on this extensive site.

Travelocity has a section for creating your personal profile (much like the airlines do); once established, it automatically plugs in all the pertinent information every time you make a reservation. Convenient layouts guide you in your search for flights, rental cars, hotel reservations, vacations and cruises, and special deals. The Best Fare Finder lets you adjust your plans to save some mone, and destination and travel guides offer weather data, maps, a currency converter, and books. Various tools and articles, as well as special offers on the homepage, ensure that you'll always be an informed traveler. An e-mail component will send you info on specific flights or packages as they become available.

Yahoo! Travel

● http://travel.yahoo.com/

Traveling has gotten more complicated. Fortunately, sites like this one can take a huge amount of the rocket science out of travel planning. Icons at the top of the page let you choose the type of reservations, such as air, car, hotel, vacations, cruises, and specials. One click takes you to pages that ask for the vitals: where you need to be, when you need to be there, what you need, how much you want to spend, and so on.

For those short on time, Express Booking lets you get fares and flights to any destination just by filling in a few boxes (essentially, destination and dates). You can book tickets right there or put them on hold while you mull it over.

If you want to take a trip but aren't sure which Sahngri-La beckons, Yahoo! Travel even helps you determine where to go with a search engine defined by a number of criteria including destination, activity, and lifestyle. The site is rounded out by a group of community chats and message boards that let you share travel experiences and tips.

[sports]

More than any other kind of fans, followers of sports embody the true spirit of that word —fanatics. No matter where in the world people are located, it is sports—more than even politics—that rallies people together, if only for a few hours at a time. For instance, the soccer fans of the U.K. are known worldwide for their fervent and even violent support of their teams, while the fans of the Chicago Cubs are revered for their loyalty to a perennially downtrodden team. Tennis fans will stay glued to the courts—and their couches—for hours on end watching international matches between players whose names they may not even be able to pronounce.

For fans of everything from adventure racing to wrestling, the web has it covered. Die-hard fans will find the Net to be better than TV or radio because it operates 24 hours a day, year round. Not getting your fill of basketball during the summer

YAHOO! ALSO LISTS: [sports]

- **http://www.activeusa.com/**
  Active USA: nationwide source for thousands of participatory sports events including registration
- **http://www.allstarsites.com/**
  All-Star Sports Fan Sites
- **http://www.clubsites.com/**
  Club Sites: golf, country, yacht, city, tennis, and social clubs throughout America
- **http://www.netspace.org/users/david/sports.html**
  The Clubhouse: extensive list of sports links covering baseball, basketball, football, hockey, golf, and boxing
- **http://www.EL.com/elinks/sports**
  Essential Links to Sports: Select online resources for professional, college, and general sports information including football, baseball, basketball, and all other sports.
- **http://www.oldsport.com/search/main.htm**
  SearchSport: If it's sports, find it here.
- **http://www.sportcal.co.uk**
  Sportcal International: comprehensive online international sporting events database, updated daily to provide the latest event information on more than 180 sports up to the year 2005
- **http://www.sportfind.com/**
  SportFind
- **http://www.sportlink.com/**
  SportLink
- **http://www.SPORTquest.com/**
  SportQuest: Search for all sports, Olympic sports, water sports, winter sports, statistics & results, sports medicine, and coaching information.

break? During the dunking and dribbling droughts, go to the Internet to check out the Italian professional leagues, where you'll find some U.S. players keeping their skills sharp. Can't get international soccer or rugby coverage from your local TV stations? Head to the web, where you'll find sites for just about every league and club on the planet. And the web can augment any sports lover's regular sports habits. You can get player and team stats while you're watching a game on TV, keeping you one step ahead of the color commentators and every fan who isn't connected to the web. In some cases, you can even watch replays of the best plays on the web throughout the season or listen to the events on various web radio stations. (Tip: Keep an extra window open on your computer for sports coverage while you're surfing the Net. That way you can work and play on the same computer.) You can even get up-to-the-minute scores and stats at Yahoo! Sports (http://sports.yahoo.com/).

Web sports coverage isn't limited to the pros, either. There are thousands of college sites, fan sites, and sites dedicated to those who haven't yet signed their multimillion-dollar endorsement deals with sportswear companies—the amateurs. There are also thousands of sites for regional and city sports leagues, as well as minor leagues and farm teams. By far and away, one of the hottest areas of the Net is devoted to those pursuits of the perfect teams—fantasy sports leagues (check out Yahoo!'s offerings as part of its sports sites). If your favorite real-world team isn't cutting it this season, try to create a better one on the hundreds of fantasy games offered on the Net.

The Net will give you just about everything you can imagine from the world of sports, from live coverage and history to fan sites and chat rooms.

[badminton]

International Badminton Federation (IBF)

● http://www.intbadfed.org/

Badminton players don't seem to inspire slo-mo Gatorade commercials or their own sneaker lines. Nevertheless, badminton is an internationally recognized sport, with star players, world rankings, Olympic qualifications, and training books and videos. And the IBF is the governing body of badminton, thus making this site the hub for badminton online. All of the above topics are covered here, as are rules (presented with graphics and court diagrams) and regulations, including instructions for disciplinary action. News and interviews with current circuit stars are included, as is an international calendar of events. Now there's no excuse for missing the next IBF tournament near you.

[baseball]

As the all-American sport (at least until professional wrestling starts targeting postadolescents), baseball is a major focus of the entertainment mind-set in the United States. This obsession translates directly to the web, where Yahoo! lists more than 300 categories—not just sites—for baseball. A search of Alta Vista yielded more than 200,000 pages containing the words "baseball" and "league." We estimate that there are more than 5,000 sites dedicated strictly to professional baseball. You couldn't hit them all even if you were Mark McGwire.

Here are some tips for looking around: Many team sites are simply the club name with .com added, as in Yankees.com. The Major League Baseball site is a good hub for lots of current as well as historical data. From there, you can easily jump to teams. If there are particular teams you want more info about, a search of

Yahoo! by the full team name will bring up hundreds of fan pages maintained by fervent, and often rabid, team loyalists.

For up-to-the-minute sports news—or if you want it recapped—we recommend the Sporting News and ESPN sites (and we don't even get endorsements from them). See their listings in this book under Sports—News. For baseball collectibles, cards, and memorabilia, check our guide under Sports—Collectibles and Cards. Now, as they say, play ball.

Major League Baseball (MLB)

● http://www.majorleaguebaseball.com/

Every once in a while, it seems that professional sports organizations, especially the MLB, forget whom they're playing for—the fans. Fortunately, the online world of baseball is so fan-friendly it could make the most jaded followers forget about the seasonal player-owner squabbling. Everything a baseball fan needs is here, and there isn't an error in sight. A daily main story leads off the site, followed by a listing of that day's games. A list of the week's MVPs, some exclusive video, and a minor league report occupy the cleanup spot.

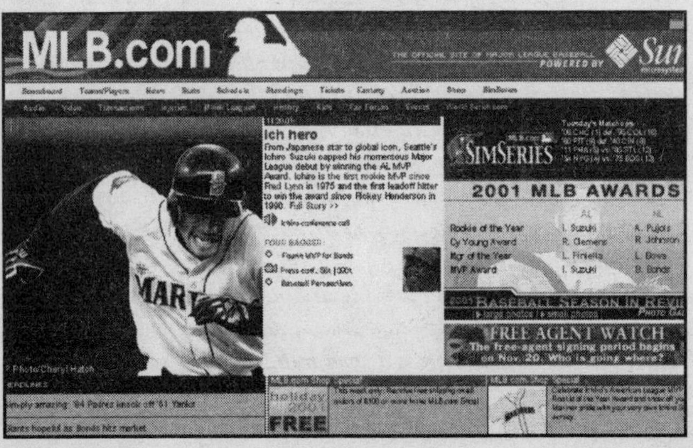

By using a pulldown menu, you can jump to a stats page of any club in either the American or the National League (it links from there to the actual team websites). Another pulldown menu takes you to information on a plethora of topics from Jackie Robinson to spring training. Then there are links to baseball history, fan forums, a merchandise store, and reference books. Fans who are sitting in front of their computers and not in the bleachers can access live audiocasts of games over the web via Broadcast.com. In a world of players' unions and salary disputes, this is one place where fans can always find what they love—pure baseball.

Fantasy Baseball

● http://www.sportingnews.com/
● http://www.espn.go.com/

There are hundreds of sites for fantasy baseball on the web. After all, where better to play virtual ball than in a virtual space? These two sites have a variety of leagues available, both free and for a fee.

[basketball]

Surprisingly, there is only one master site covering pro basketball on the web, and that is the NBA's official site. Not only does the NBA have a lock on most of the information about pro b-ball, but it also hosts all the team sites.

Though there are thousands of other basketball sites out there, overwhelmingly they are team and player sites maintained by fans, and trying to find a site that rivals the NBA's is like trying to find a power forward who is five feet tall: It's impossible. Perhaps this is a reflection of the control the NBA has over all facets of the league, or perhaps it has to do with the extreme devotion that basketball fans have to their team—and no one but their team.

For basketball news and memorabilia, check out our "Also Lists" under Sports. For college basketball, check out www.fansonly.com, *which also is profiled under College Sports.*

National Basketball Association (NBA)

● http://www.nba.com/

In fast-break style, the NBA throws data at fans unrelentingly. The front page starts with a feature story, then bounds downcourt through an interminable series of links, currently culminating in a Michael Jordan Career Retrospective. There are audio and video clips, as well as the required stats, schedules, merchandise, and links to fantasy games. There are also a chat/mailbox area, a global basketball link, history, an action photo gallery, news of the day, and career retrospectives. One unusual feature: All the team websites are hosted under the NBA umbrella, meaning that there is no "official" site at, say, www.celtics.com or www.bulls.com.

There are a stadium's worth of links here, including some to other leagues and to ESPN and ABC Sports (a joint venture with ESPN). There are more than 80 linked items on the front page alone, offering the kinds of choices normally reserved for the college draft.

Women's National Basketball Association (WNBA)

● http://www.wnba.com/

This site mirrors the NBA's, right down to the layout and the use of video and audio highlights. Thus the same positive and negative aspects apply. But it's good to see this amount of space devoted to a woman's sport, and no expense seems to have been spared (except for investing in a search engine). Everything you need to know about the WNBA is here, with updates, team info, and player stats.

[bowling]

Bowl.com

● http://www.bowl.com/

Bowl.com brings hip to the tenpin passion. With metal music blaring—as if from video games in the corner—the site's opening Flash graphics let you know you're in for more than a sleepy Wednesday night with Uncle Lou and his pinhead team. The top line on the Pro Shop page reads, "If you look cool on the lanes, people think you got game." Most elements of Bowl.com back up the claim.

Survey sidebars accompany news bits, answering such questions as "What is your favorite candy bar?" and "Should bowling be an Olympic sport?" (95.8 percent of respondents say yes). Exhaustive in its coverage of industry news, leagues, awards, and regional events, the site is laid out cleanly and never misses an opportunity to help you have a good time. In the Fun & Games section you compete against your computer to try to make it to the bar or to catch as many pins as you can without getting creamed by a bowling ball.

The site is efficient and practical as well, providing helpful services, such as a database with which to find an alley near you and a Coach's Corner where you can find a coach locally or just scam a free lesson.

[boxing]

Boxing.com

● http://www.boxing.com/

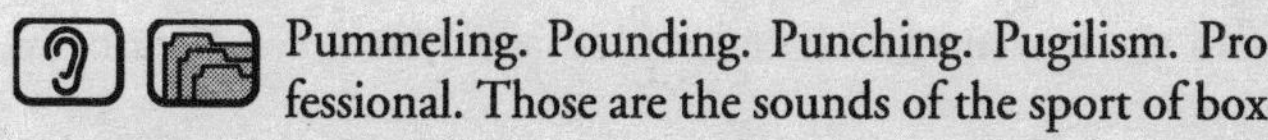

Pummeling. Pounding. Punching. Pugilism. Professional. Those are the sounds of the sport of boxing. And fans will applaud Boxing.com, where pieces on punching professionals (or is that professional punchers?) are published.

This site is designed as combination fight poster and newspaper, with information on all levels of competition and various boxing associations. Sections include Opinions, Schedules, Rankings, Results, and Merchandise. An archive of great fight moments lets you replay events starring Mike Tyson, Oscar De La Hoya, and others. This is a must-see site for fans, and it may even win a few converts. Besides, you've got to love a sport where the prize they give to half-naked guys is a belt.

[college sports]

FANSonly

● http://www.fansonly.com/

Do thoughts of Georgetown, Duke, University of Arizona, and UConn in the Final Four make you drool? Does the prospect of Notre Dame and USC playing in the Cotton Bowl send you into a foaming, hysterical rant? If the answer is yes, then clearly you are a rabid college sports fan. In practice, however, *rabid* barely begins to describe true fans of college sports, and from NCAA hoop finals and track-and-field to the Rose Bowl and hockey, FANSonly indulges these fans by offering a tailgater's worth of their favorite pastime. There are headlines and more headlines, game-day features, predictions, scoreboards, team pages, official college sites, and merchandise.

Players and coaches are interviewed throughout their respective seasons, and some of them contribute their thoughts to the Game Day Diaries. In the off-season, the sizable Recruiting section keeps tabs on all those future Michael Jordans, Derek Jeters, and Joe Montanas—as well as more than 2,600 other recruits. Finally, fans who can tear themselves away from the tube (and the live Internet broadcasts available here) can keep high-fiving or crying in their beer in FANSonly's forums, polls, or even the free e-mail that the site offers. FANSonly will either cure college-sports fan rabies or just make it worse.

[cricket]

CricInfo

● http://www.cricket.org/

The British cliché "it's not cricket" means not doing things the proper and noble way. Its namesake is a delightfully complex pursuit called, obviously, cricket. Cricket has long been the sport of gentlemen around the world—except for the United States, where no one can seem to figure out the rules. With luck, this site may begin to change all that.

CricInfo contains news, opinions, polls, interviews, chat, classified ads, and links to national cricket sites from Australia to Zimbabwe. These pages have a wry heart. They open with—we swear this is true—a poetry section. But the site's true heart lies in the section for those who understand cricket's rules, despite their own playing limitations.

[cycling]

Cyber Cycling

● http://www.cycling.org/
● http://www.cyclery.com/

Riding a bike used to be as simple as, well, riding a bike. Today, though, bikes are more complicated, and there is one for nearly every environment and terrain, with gears galore, myriad shifting options, frame styles, suspension types, and on and on. The places you can ride have changed as well; for instance, you can't ride on the sidewalks (well, you're not supposed to, anyway) in New York

City, but you can ride in the middle of the streets during its 42-mile Five Borough Tour. It all gets kind of complicated, which is why Cyber Cycling is such a valuable resource. Primarily a directory of bike links, the site is organized according to e-mail lists, directories, classified ads, events, job boards, a cyber mart and shopping, discussion forums, and links to bike magazines.

Of course, the content goes beyond just news and updates on cycle styles. Want to work in a bike shop or just find directions to one? Ride by here. Need to sell an old racing bike or looking for ideas on building a custom mountain bike? All here. For those of you who revel in two-wheel mobility, this is almost as much fun as riding with no hands.

[fencing]

Advance Lunge

● http://library.thinkquest.org/15340/home.html

An advance lunge is a fencing move whereby one fencer moves quickly forward in an attack on his or her opponent. This website addresses the sport of fencing in the same self-assured and aggressive manner. Call it being *en guarde* on the web.

Part history, part online tutorial, and part list of contacts, Advance Lunge explores all aspects of fencing in complete detail, with photographic accompaniment. The History section takes you through a time line of swordplay (there is evidence of such in Egypt as far back as 1200 B.C.), coupled with bios of fencing masters. The Tutorial pages take you through each of the fencing weapons (foil, epee, sabre) and outlines the moves that are the core of competition. In Games there are two challenges, Fencing Trivia and You Make the Call, which pit the knowledge you can pick up here against some real-world scenarios. Contacts puts you in touch with local fencing organizations, listed by state.

[football]

National Football League (NFL)

● http://www.nfl.com/

The world of Astroturf and gang tackles is transferred to the web in all its colorful glory at NFL.com. From the sport that gave us instant replays and overhead cams come the same kind of multimedia innovations via the web. NFL Films provides clips of classic highlights and plays of the week via streaming video. An especially effective aspect of this site is the use of team logos as the launch points to teams' sites. The logos are intuitively arrayed in a column, and they are much easier to deal with than any listing of cities and team names sorted by divisions or coast or whatnot. Each team link goes to NFL.com's overview of the team, and from there you can

YAHOO! ALSO LISTS: [football]

- **http://www.EL.com/elinks/sports/football/nfl/**
  Essential Links to NFL Football: resources including news, scores, games, teams, and players.
- **http://www.uic.edu/~hlee12/donlinks.html**
  Big Don's NFL links
- **http://www.geocities.com/Colosseum/Track/9899/football.html**
  Black Hole of Links: Football
- **http://www.geocities.com/Colosseum/Stadium/8975/**
  Josh Karr's Sports Web—NFL Media Directory: links to the official sites, local newspapers, and internet broadcasters for every NFL team.
- **http://www.cs.cmu.edu/afs/cs/user/vernon/www/nfl.html**
  NFL Info Web: the usual, plus links to team-specific usenet groups.
- **http://www.tdl.com/~chuckn/nfl/nfl.html**
  NFL Yellow Pages: extensive compilation of NFL links.
- **http://www.nfltalk.com/**
  NFLtalk.com: media resource.
- **http://www.arning.com/football/**
  Portals of NFL Links

connect to the team's homepage (à la www.azcardinals.com).

From there you'll find everything you need to armchair-quarterback your way through a weekend of games. The front page has easily identifiable links covering news, stats, standings, and more (the key words here are "easily identifiable," a concept that most other sports organizations seem not to be familiar with). An overview of each week of the season gives you information on the games, along with a viewers' poll, some commentary, and official NFL merchandise. Ultimately, with so much cool stuff on its site, along with really cool icons and an appreciation of simple navigation, the NFL.com site may be the best-designed professional sports site on the web.

[golf]

The days of exclusive country clubs are over now that everyone has access to this pro shop. The Internet offers tips, techniques, videos for sale, newsletters, courses, vacations, professional and amateur tours, course design, computer games, equipment, clothes, and on and on and on. And we haven't even talked about individual players or events. The best way to find what you need is to drill way down into the Golf category in Yahoo! and prepare to be overwhelmed.

The GolfWeb

http://www.golfweb.com/

We estimate that there are more than 12,000 sites on the web dedicated to golf and golfing, but GolfWeb is the best for dedicated duffers.

You get coverage of breaking news, reports on tournaments from around the world, a viewer's poll, and departments addressing the game in all its facets. Buttons link to tour data, instruction, equipment, tour pros, rules, games, and contests, as well as leaderboards for various tournaments and real-time PGA scoring. GolfWeb has the GolfWeb Course Guide, which allows you to enter the name of a course and get relevant info (greens, fees, yardage, directions to site, and course reviews.

GolfWeb is sponsored by CBS SportsLine, which also explains why you can link to stock quotes via CBSMarket Watch.com at the top of the homepage.

[hockey]

National Hockey League (NHL)

● http://www.nhl.com/

One of the most intriguing aspects of hockey on the web is the number of sites dedicated specifically to hockey fights and to fights by team. The sport itself has a huge number of sites, ranging from women's field hockey to alumni teams composed of ex-pros; there are an incredible number of team sites and individual player sites. But this great site belongs to the NHL. Its fast-moving design (literally, thanks to video feeds and tickers) does justice to the fastest sport on stainless-steel blades.

The homepage comprises a main feature, some news, and a pulldown menu of places to go, from history to chats to Q&A to player diaries. Links take you to a kids' hockey site, sponsored interactive sites, and the obligatory Merchandise section. Recent scores stream across the site in the mode of a stock ticker. Those who can't make it to the rink can listen to radio broadcasts of every daily hockey game via RealAudio (with connections provided by Nortel). Half a dozen video highlights from the previous night's game are also available.

The links to teams and players are quite good, leading you into a frame-based section that includes player stats, news, links to the official team site (e.g., www.bostonbruins.com), and more videos specific to that team. In a manner similar to that of the NFL site, NHL.com ends with a tribute link to a re-

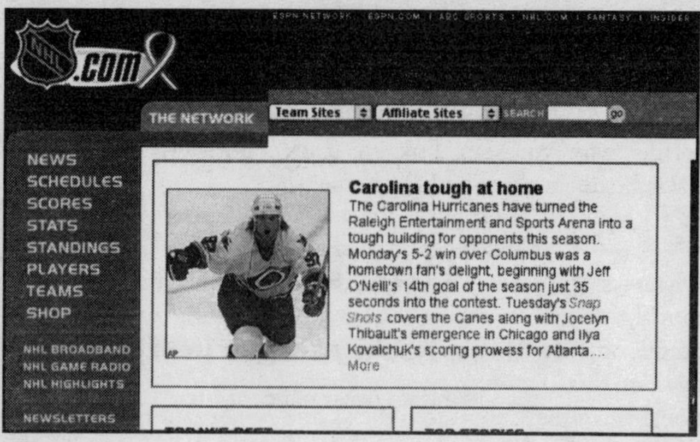

cently retired great—in this case, Wayne Gretzky. While you can't get real blood or cracked skulls here, you can get a free NHL e-mail address.

ALSO LISTS: [hockey]

- **http://www.hockeylinks.com/**
  All Hockey Links
- **http://www.geocities.com/Colosseum/2566/cdlinks.html**
  Cyber Dome Hockey Links
- **http://www.travel-net.com/~marbar/**
  Hockey Links and Sports Games: Find here all the NHL web pages on the Net and download a few great shareware sports games.
- **http://www.geocities.com/Colosseum/Loge/8745/**
  Hockey Web Page Union
- **http://mav.net/infostar/hockeycity/**
  HockeyCity
- **http://www.icepower.com/hoklinks.htm**
  Ice Power

[olympics]

The International Olympic Committee (IOC)

● http://www.olympic.org/

If you're going for the gold—or just looking for the sports equivalent—then you need to be part of the Olympics. Those of us who aren't officially on the team will have to make do with watching the coolest highlights from the events on this official site. Presented in English and French (literally side by side), this Olympian site features categories including International Olympic Committee (news and organizations), Olympic Museum (history and virtual expositions), and WADA (World Anti-Doping Agency).

Special Olympics

● http://www.specialolympics.org/

Every year, more than 1.2 million individuals compete in the Special Olympics. The official site tells you how to get involved or make a donation, then goes on to discuss specific sports, pro-

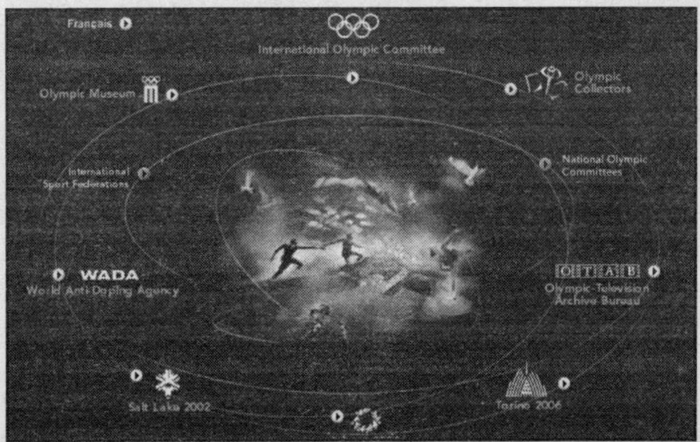

gram locations, games and competition, and corporate sponsors. The Sports section details the various events and training required by the athletes (including tips on improving participation), and the Program Locations section provides a guide to Special Olympics organizations in your area.

[polo]

The New PoloNet

● http://www.polonews.com/

The Sport of Kings and the King of Sports are the popular tag lines for polo, a sport that too many people associate with Britain's royal family, designer clothing, and cologne. It is, in fact, a hard-charging competition involving human, horse, and hardball. On the New PoloNet you can meet other polo aficionados, exchange ideas, chat with the pros, or just discuss game strategies.

The New PoloNet has a very cool navigational window that pops up to act as a remote control for this big site. There are more than two dozen "channels" to choose from, including Tournaments, Clubs, Players, Associations, Grooms, Products and Services, and Fun and History. There's even an advice column and a dating service for lovers of the ponies; this is, after all, a site that claims to be "serving the modern needs of the modern polo player."

In addition to online chat and strategy, links lead to a varied marketplace that sells tack and supplies, hay, ponies, grounds equipment, and overnight stabling. You can hire a trainer here, too. Surprisingly, more than a touch of irreverence adds spice to this site, as evidenced by a gossip column called Polo Snoop and the icon for Polo Art, which is a martini glass.

[racquetball]

RacquetWorld

● http://www.racquetworld.com

United States Racquetball Association (USRA)

● http://www.racquetball.org/

Every once in a while, we stumble upon a site that has such a great component, we wish it were employed across the entire web. RacquetWorld—"your racquetball arms dealer"—has such a component, the RacquetWorld Player Database. This section of the site allows visitors to search for players in their area: You simply enter your city and state and a list appears. Click on an individual's name and his or her profile page comes up, along with a direct link to his or her e-mail. In the process, you can add your own profile to the database. This serves as a perfect meeting place for people with similar interests living in the same area who might not otherwise get together.

RacquetWorld also has several articles on equipment tips and a huge collection of links to other racquetball sites around the world. This organization is in the business of selling equipment, so there is plenty of shopping information on the site (which, by the way, is also available in Spanish).

But if what you want is professional coverage of the sport, go to the United States Racquetball Association (USRA) site and its official site for *Racquetball Magazine*, at http://www.racqmag.com/.

[rodeo]

Professional Rodeo

● http://www.prorodeo.com/

Saddle bronc riding, bareback and bull riding, wrangler bullfighting, team roping and steer roping, calf wrestling, barrel racing, and all-around cowboy: Sounds like something out of the wild Wild West, but it's the lineup of events that comprise professional rodeo. This is the website of the Professional Rodeo Cowboys Association (PRCA), or ProRodeo for short.

ProRodeo employs a very clever device for guiding visitors around the site. You drill down into, say, the Rodeo Hall of Fame or the Record Book via a series of pop-up boxes. You'll get the inside look at the sport, its stars, Miss Rodeo America, and the rules (e.g., to score in bull riding, you have to stay on for eight seconds, without touching yourself or the bull). You can listen to rodeos across the country on ProRodeo Radio, which requires RealPlayer G2, and you can buy rodeo merchandise to wear while you listen.

One serious topic given substantial coverage on the site is the treatment of the animals. After all, rodeos would not exist without animals: calves, steers, bulls, and horses. A large animal-rights and animal-welfare section here seeks to define the difference between using animals for sport and mistreating animals. A lot of finger-pointing goes on in this section, so be prepared for some thought-provoking discussion on how we use animals in daily life—not just in rodeos, but on farms, for food, and for research.

[rugby]

Scrum—The Home of Rugby

● http://www.scrum.com/

Scrum. Great name for a website, although probably three-quarters of you have no idea what it means (okay, neither did we). The dictionary definition is "a rugby play in which the forwards of each side come together in a tight formation and struggle to gain possession of the ball when it is tossed in among them; short for scrummage." Now you know, and so you can proceed into the unrestrained and oftentimes brutal world of professional rugby. Come to think of it, the second definition for scrum in the dictionary is "madhouse." Draw your own conclusion.

Scrum.com will appeal to every true fan of rugby, what with the Daily Scrum (which is all news—and there is an amazing amount of it), World Cup data (including a countdown that begins after the last event), a TV guide, a look at the best tournaments, player profiles and interviews, Club Rugby (a look at teams by country), editorial columns, games and trivia quizzes, a bulletin board, a merchandise area called the Shopping Maul, and women's rugby—there are more than 200 women's clubs in England alone. You can receive e-mail newsletters by registering (it's free), and you can enter various contests, whose prizes include a day of training with a national team. Scrum if you dare.

[skating]

SkateSearch

● http://www.skatesearch.com/

Here's another excellent search-specific page with one point of entry. Type anything into the search box—from hockey to triple axel to judging—and SkateSearch returns every page it can find from all over the Net that meets your request. You can input really clever searches that include phrases, root words, and alternate spellings. Enthusiasts are sure to find this page helpful year-round, but no doubt SkateSearch activity really heats up during televised and national competitions.

[skiing & snowboarding]

SkiCentral

● http://skicentral.com/

Think of this site as a mountain with every conceivable shape of slope and degree of difficulty. Think you're really good, you know what you want, and you're ready for the black diamonds? Then dive into the advanced search engine and choose your destination. Prefer an energetic but more leisurely run, a green perhaps? Choose specific topics from a pulldown menu that directs you to everything from accommodations to waxing. Just want to take your time, do a few blues, and enjoy the scenery? Then meander through the index and browse at your own pace. There you'll find ski resorts (nearly 600 worldwide), ski reports (some 400 updated twice daily during the season), trip planning guides, racing (teams and results), organizations, snowboarding, news, and equipment and product links.

An entry marked simply Skiing includes the nontraditional gamut—Summer Skiing, Extreme, Heliskiing, Snowcat Skiing, Cross Country, Telemark, Jumping, Freestyle, and Disabled Skiing. All told, there are some 4,500 sites connected to this one.

SkiCentral also serves as a great jumping-off point for snowboarders, who get their own category in the index. And if you're longing for the slopes during the off-season, you can download ski-themed wallpaper and thousands of photos to remind you of packed powder every time you boot up your computer.

Snowboarding.com

● http://www.snowboarding.com/

Ready to hit the slopes in a new way? Snowboarding.com provides a comprehensive network of resources related to snowboarding. Site visitors can find everything from snowboarding camps to competitions, companies that sell equipment, and resorts. There's an area that features snowboarding news, a photo gallery, events, and links to other sites related to this as well as other winter sports. There's even an interactive bulletin board so visitors can interact with other enthusiasts. The site includes reviews of upcoming trends in the business and stories of pro snowboarders. Whether you're a snowboarder or an observer, this site is a great resource for novices and experts.

[soccer]

Major League Soccer

● http://www.mlsnet.com/

It's long been the rest of the world's most popular sport, but soccer has only recently come into its own professionally in the United States over the past decade. Scoring on that development is the official website of America's Major League Soccer, MLSnet, a well-designed and informative resource for U.S. soccer fans, replete with stories, stats, standings, and schedules of upcoming games. Team pages have schedules, rosters, statistics, game summaries, and information on getting tickets, getting to stadiums, and seating charts for venues. The History area archives statistics, game results, and season records, as well as complete roster listings and college draft results.

The Theater section replays videos of weekly highlights and plays of the week (using Windows Media Player). Youth Soccer is a kid-focused area, where kids, in Coach's Corner, can learn about the game, enter contests or enroll in soccer camps, take part in the MLS chat room, download MLS screensavers, and get involved in Fun Stuff from individual teams, such as essay contests.

There are listings of MLS job and volunteer opportunities, links to soccer media, sponsors, and other leagues, and a, well, slick Mazola Corn Oil Team of the Week profile of a youth soccer team.

The Soccer Net

● http://www.soccernet.com/

You know you've come to the heart of soccer on the web when you're greeted with headlines that shout "Fergie's Out for Charity Revenge," "The English? To Hell with Them," "Dick Slates Scared Bosses," and "Yugoslav Police Fire Shots in Air as Fans Rampage." Now, that's soccer.

Fans of international soccer will find all the information they need to stay current with leagues around the world at the Soccer Net. The site originates in England, so coverage is most thorough for the English and Scottish leagues. Buttons at the top of the homepage lead to areas devoted to England, Scotland, Europe, Global, Champs League, World Cup 2002, Extra Time, and Betting Zone. Information is often listed by individual league club. Other areas are what they say they are: Live Scoreboards, Statistics, Reports, and On the Move. A Whistleblower area rates referees. Feature stories, SportsBook Odds, and Predictions from Experts round out the site. The site is interactive, too; visitors get to display their prognostication skills each week.

The Soccer Net offers live audio coverage of select matches (requiring Windows Media Player), and a fun and challenging Find the Ball feature has viewers attempting to find a hidden soccer ball in a series of world-class match photographs.

[squash]

Internet Squash Federation

● http://www.squash.org/

Squash was invented at England's Harrow School around 1830, when the pupils discovered that a punctured tennis ball (called a rackets ball) "squashed" on impact with a wall. The outcome was a game with a greater variety of shots than in tennis and that required much more effort on the part of the players, who could not simply wait for the ball to bounce back to them.

Of such random events are international sports born. One hundred seventy years later, squash has a big website that presents data ranging from national team rankings to squash coaching jobs. The data is broken down into News, Equipment, Rankings, Rules, Nations, Calendar, WSF, and more. You can also browse through a complete history of the game or read about the evolution of rules and types of games. Search engines are available for looking up teams and scanning the entire site.

[swimming]

SwimInfo

● http://www.swiminfo.com/

SwimInfo is a site for serious swimmers, the place to keep tabs on competitive swimmers and swimming events and to work on your swimming techniques. Latest meet results are posted, as are the NCAA top 25 times, along with articles on swimmers and various aspects of swimming (goal setting, techniques, etc.). These are accompanied by links to swimming magazines, swim and dive camps, and a chat room. You can subscribe to an online 'zine here for free.

One of the best features of this site—and one you don't usually come across in sports sites—is a database called Find a Workout. From pulldown menus you pick your Ability Level (lap swimmer, master, etc.), Workout Type (sprint freestyle, backstroke, individual medley, etc.), and Workout Duration (from 20 minutes to more than two hours). Based on your criteria, the site returns a variety of workout regimens tailored to your needs.

A Swim Shop offers related merchandise, including videos, apparel, books, and posters.

Swim Links

● http://www.marcel-wouda.com/

Planning on doing some swimming on your next trip to the Netherlands? Need to follow the goings-on at Switzerland's Schwimmclub Birsfelden? Swim Links is an index of swim sites all over the world. Within each country are links to college, high school, and club teams, as well as to organizations that sponsor swimming events. When sites are selected, they appear inside one of Swim Links' three frames so you never have to leave the site. There are also links to personal pages, swim camps, manufacturers, and water polo sites.

[tennis]

Tennis.com

● http://www.tennis.com/

If you stay glued to Wimbledon, the U.S. Open, Davis Cup matches, and everything tennis, then Tennis.com might be able to serve what you need. The category-killer site has news and updates on recent pro tournaments, matches, and exhibitions, plus features on individual players (both active and retired). Additional sections cover juniors, college, and seniors tennis.

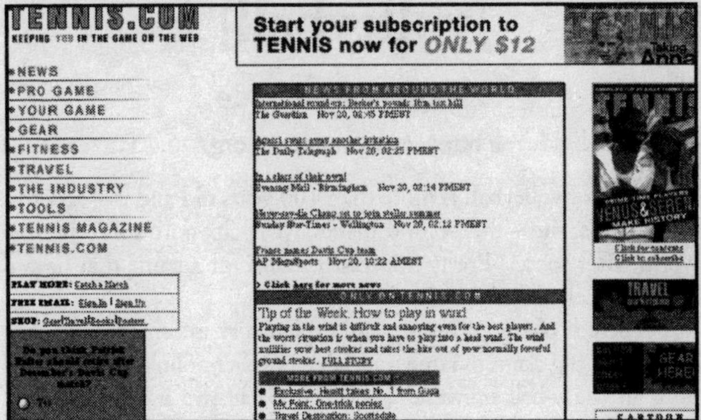

For those more interested in their own game, Tennis.com also offers instruction (with tips, drills, and analysis of various pro styles), equipment (including a gear search and gear reviews), and fitness (avoiding injury, playing in the summer sun, etc.). Using the Catch a Match service, you can find players and opponents in your area. You register your criteria, search for other players by location, date, and skill level, then hook up with them via e-mail. Traveling players can also get updates on some of the best courts and locations around the world.

Those who can't get to the courts can indulge in lots of verbal lobs and aces on one of the site's numerous forums, and armchair tennis players may want to visit the United States Tennis Association (http://www.usta.com/).

[volleyball]

Volleyball Worldwide

● http://www.volleyball.org/

The sport of volleyball is more than 100 years old and is—according to this site—the second-biggest participation sport in the world, after soccer. Pretty impressive claim for a game that began life being called "mintonette."

There is plenty of history and explanatory information on this site, but its big claim to fame is its large number of links to organizations in the v-ball universe. There are exhaustive indexes of high school, club, college, Olympic, and professional clubs and teams. A guide covers volleyball in all 50 states (Alaska has 77 girls' high school volleyball teams, for example), an international listing, a specific city listing, and a complete calendar of upcoming v-ball events.

[wrestling]

Intermat Westling

● http://www.intermatwrestle.com/

$ Intermat Wrestling is a well-researched and daily-updated resource for the fans and athletes of amateur wrestling. Hundreds of high school and college pages are available, providing info on everything from rules and regulations to job postings, coaching changes, and conference ratings. The site can also help aspiring wrestlers find camps and clinics or seek out match results and rankings of their heroes. And if their headgear was broken last time they got crunched on the mat, or they got blood all over their old singlet, a fully stocked store can make almost any wrestling merchandise available in under three clicks. Individual profiles of college recruits are also available in resume format, outlining stats such as weight, year of graduation, and wins/losses, plus comments from coaches.

Professional
The Internet Wrestling Zone (IWZ)

● http://www.prowrestling.com/

If you just can't get enough of America's muscle-bound matheads on TV, the Internet Wrestling Zone will keep you likewise pinned to your computer screen with its girth of pro-wrestling news and reviews. Top Stories report the most recent happenings at title matches between the likes of the Rock, Mankind, Kane, and Undertaker. If that's not enough, prowl through the more than 5,000 articles a day that can be sent directly to your desktop or mailbox via Personalized News. Access to the World Wrestling Federation and World Championship Wrestling pages is also provided. And on the Tournaments page, you have the opportunity to put on the black and white stripes and decide matches for yourself; votes are tabulated weekly on a long list of fantasy matches. Good thing this is all in the name of legitimate sports contests.

[sports collectibles & cards]

This category is tricky. As for all things related to sports on the web, there are hundreds of sites addressing just this one area of fan interest. Unfortunately, the e-commerce model of Amazon.com and CDNow doesn't apply here. Why not? Because, by and large, when you are buying a book or CD, you're not getting a limited edition or one-of-a-kind memento; you're getting a mass-manufactured product. With sports memorabilia, as with any other type of collectible, certain criteria make the items in question more or less valuable. Some of the elements are visually evaluated, such as condition. You want a Carl Yastrzemski baseball card from his rookie year? Great. If you're going to fork over hundreds of dollars for it, you want to make sure that it hasn't been torn in half and doesn't have beer stains on it. One thing the web can't do is allow that kind of inspection.

Y! tip

When using search engines, make sure you click on the Go or Search button when necessary. Yahoo! allows you to simply hit Return or Enter to start your search; others may not activate unless you hit the appropriate button.

Furthermore, the types of sites selling these items are as diverse as their bricks-and-mortar counterparts, where you can at least touch the merchandise. Some sites are independents; others are the offspring of big companies. Some specialize in exotic sports genres; others only offer niche items, for example, Wayne Gretsky's used skate laces. The auction sites, such as eBay, do a brisk trade in this area, and most reports are favorable. But there is no way that we can validate each and every sports site offering "certified" memorabilia on the web. So beware. Forewarned is forearmed.

What we can offer is advice: Start by going to Yahoo! and typing "collectibles" into the main search box. You'll be presented with lots of choices, so start digging, based on your needs (or, perhaps more accurately, your wants). Be prepared; do some research—know what you want and what its market price is. The web is great for doing comparison shopping, so don't feel bashful about querying every site that is selling your heart's desire. Establish your price, then use e-mail (or the phone) to get your guarantees.

We will leave you with one good site, called Collector Link (http://www.collector-link.com/). Its business is strictly cards, but it is a big and ambitious site, so it may be a good place to get acquainted with searching for memorabilia on the web.

[sports news]

The Sporting News

● http://www.sportingnews.com/

ESPN

● http://www.espn.go.com/

No, you're not seeing double. Although these two sites are owned and operated by separate companies, they could easily be twins. Both feature links to news in all the major sports leagues across the top, both have access to fantasy games and leagues, both tout their columnists (and their merchandise), both have major stories on games of the day (we've seen the same content featured at the same time), and both run headlines down a long page, covering everything from NASCAR to the PGA—everything except professional wrestling.

Just to confirm there wasn't something wrong with our sight, we ran these two sites side by side in two Netscape windows and were hard-pressed to come up with major differences. There are some minor differences, notably in the use of search engines (pulldown versus search boxes), but beyond that, these sites give you more sports than you should probably be allowed to have on any given day. Which one is better? That's like asking a New York sports fan to choose between the '57 Yankees and the '98 Yankees. And we know better than to start that argument.

[tickets]

Ticketmaster

● http://www.ticketmaster.com/

Ticketmaster has become the de facto ticket source for most major events in the United States, from concerts and plays to baseball games to the circus—the efforts of some rock groups notwithstanding. This site was recently redesigned to good effect, given that the old one was more about entertainment news and merchandise than ticket info. Each of the three color-coded sections—Hot Tickets, Special News, and Spotlight—has its own set of subsections and news.

Two search boxes—one for state, the other for events—unveil a universe of places where you can buy tickets. Once you pick a state, for instance, pulldown menus list most venues (including some dive bars that we can't believe they even found, let alone put on the list), as well as promotions and contests. The site gives you other ways to narrow the search for events, including by category, by word search, or by city and date. To top it off, there are also venue seating charts, directions to venues, even descriptions of concessions. That way you can figure out if you're getting good tickets and how close your seats are to the bar.

Even if you're not buying tickets but just want to know what's happening at a particular club or when the circus is coming to town, this site is extremely worthwhile.

REFERENCE

The web can be seen as one vast reference library, and within that library, are singular sources that address specific needs. That's what this section is all about. We've covered encyclopedias and dictionaries in their own sections; what remains are works that offer granular levels of reference information. We've included a few standard reference guides, as well as The Straight Dope, which fills in a gap left by the others.

[almanacs]

The *Old Farmer's Almanac*

● http://www.almanac.com/

The *Old Farmer's Almanac* has been a staple of American reference—and folklore—since this country was founded. Its online version maintains its homespun design and offers the same homespun wisdom as its paper parent. There are tips here for seasonal cooking, home improvements, maintaining a garden, and all sorts of endeavors.

The almanac has myriad sections: Cooking, Gardening, Homeowning, Radio Report, Specialty Products, Weather Extremes, Weather Report, and on and on. Each contains a series of articles or essays on its respective topic, with linked text that takes you directly to projects such as a specific home repair or an outdoor dinner recipe. There are also a general store and a calendar for the current month with "red letter days" (literally) that can be clicked on to learn more about important events that occured on that date. This site also has the expected entries: Today in History, Today in Weather, History, Advice of the Day, Puzzle of the Day, and Question of the Day.

[dictionaries]

Dictionary.com

● http://www.dictionary.com/

The utility of this site reminds us of a Swiss Army knife: small, but with lots of blades that deftly handle most tasks you throw at it. Dictionary.com is a quirky but powerful little site, with features that take it beyond the realm of mere defining and spelling. There are links to *Roget's Thesaurus* (which is owned by the same company), Columbia University's *Strunk's and White's Elements of Style,* and *Bartlett's Familiar Quotations.* You can also search for the meaning and correct spelling of computer and Internet terms, chemical elements, and Bible names and get info on U.S. cities and zip codes (type in the zip code, up comes the city), as well as data on the countries around the world.

The site features a word of the day, some games, and word and grammar advice from Doctor Dictionary.

Merriam Webster's Dictionary

● http://www.m-w.com/netdict.htm

The best way to look up definitions is on Merriam Webster's (MW) site. Type a word in the only available box, hit Return, and you get your definition—along with pronunciation, function, etymology, and synonyms. If you are looking for a correct spelling, the MW Dictionary offers a list of possible alternatives to the word you typed.

[encyclopedias]

In some ways, the web is a vast encyclopedia, where each site can be regarded as an entry. This doesn't make the web authoritative, mind you, since no one prescreens most of this material or its authors. That's not to say, however, that the web doesn't have authoritative reference works. In case you need a real encyclopedia, there are websites that offer access to famous and not-so-famous encyclopedias, varying widely in presentation. As a rule they are quite good when it comes to offering their texts via the web.

As an Internet user, you should get comfortable finding encyclopedic information on your computer; with the growing use of both the Internet and CD-ROMs, it is likely that the paper versions of these references will ultimately become fodder for the tar pits.

Encyclopedia.com

● http://www.encyclopedia.com/

Do you know where Bacon's Rebellion occurred? Need to learn about the XYZ Affair, but there's no time to go to the library? Whether you are writing a term paper or just want to learn quick facts, Encyclopedia.com is a great place to find information about these and more than 50,000 other topics found in the Sixth Edition of the Columbia Encyclopedia. Produced by Infonautics Corporation, the site is free to use and includes links to other information sources. Entries may be searched by keyword or phrase, and articles may be browsed alphabetically. The entries include a bibliography of texts to learn about the topics in depth. The site is a great place to learn more about thousands of topics from A to Z.

[etiquette]

In Polite Company

● http://www.epicurious.com/learn/etiquette_guide/index

Ever wonder what the proper etiquette is for eating frogs' legs? According to this tasteful site, the directions are as follows: "Frogs' legs are typically eaten with your fingers, although large ones can be disjointed with a knife and fork before they are picked up." Perfectly charming.

The In Polite Company section of the Epicurious site contains an amusing and useful database on how to eat various difficult foods. Lobster, caviar, snails, and more mundane foods are covered in this very clever site that teaches you how to eat gourmet delights without looking like a complete Neanderthal. Also included are food "fool" entries, such as Fondue, and Chopsticks, and the all-important Which Utensil to Use.

Of course, this is just the tip of the tortilla: The larger Epicurious site is filled with gallons of information for the gourmand, glutton, and plain ole obsessive food lover. Fortunately, if you're hungry, the site is cleanly laid out and attractive, allowing you to find those essential food facts in a hurry. Bon appétit!

[FAQs (frequently asked questions)]

Internet FAQ Consortium

● http://www.faqs.org/

FAQs are the equivalent of preventive medicine for newbie netizens. Frequently Asked Questions spare experts from having to answer the same questions over and over again when newcomers make their way onto the Net. FAQs are the Internet equivalent of someone handing you a sheet of paper and saying, "Read this. If you still have any questions after you're done, then you can ask me." FAQs are so popular that they now dot the entire web like pins on a wall map.

FAQ pages can be found on almost any topic area or discussion forum, providing answers to questions that new visitors inevitably ask. The problem is finding them. Yahoo! usually lists FAQs in its index of sites for a given category. But, FAQs also exist in hidden nooks and crannies of the Net, especially in newsgroups or in areas related to Internet development and standards. For those more esoteric areas, go to the Internet FAQ Consortium, where more than 3,000 FAQs are archived; there you can search for them by the name of the area that you're interested in or by scanning through category listings.

[general information]

Information Please (InfoPlease)

● http://www.infoplease.com/

Information Please claims that it has "All the knowledge you need." We're perfectly willing to forgive the hyperbole, because this site comes pretty darn close to hitting that mark. This is one of those sites where you can get lost for days. You want lists of easily confused words? Smoking-related mortality? Top 40 tourist destinations? Pulitzer Prize winners? All here. Dozens of reference works fill Information Please, including almanacs in a plethora of categories: Daily, World, People, U.S., Sports, Entertainment, Business, Society, Living, Science, Homework (References for K–12 Studies and a Kid's Almanac), a dictionary, and an encyclopedia.

All of the site categories are searchable using specialized search engines that retrieve your requested information from all areas. Within each almanac is a table of contents set up as subject boxes with summaries. For instance, the Living almanac has

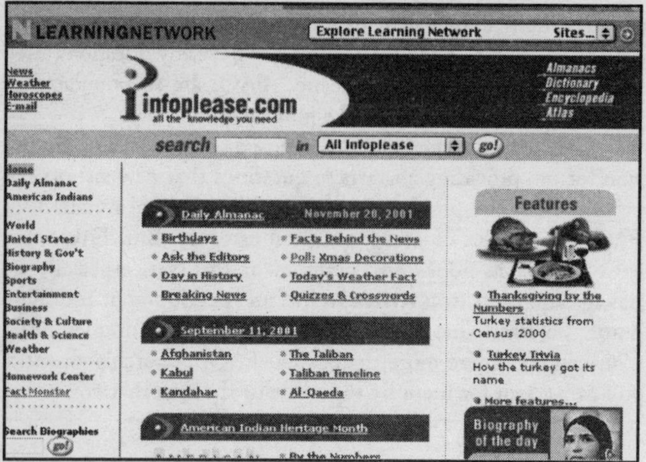

Travel, Health, First Aid, Holidays/Calendar, Writing/Language, Crossword Puzzle Guide, and a list of Current Favorite Topics, as well as Special Features (male body image, seasonal affective disorder, federal obesity guidelines, etc.). Similarly, under People, there are drill-down sections for entertainers, athletes, presidents, the Supreme Court, recent deaths, and so on.

About the only thing InfoPlease can't tell you is how much time you'll spend on this site when you really should be doing something else.

The Straight Dope

● http://www.straightdope.com/

The Straight Dope's motto is "Fighting ignorance since 1973 (it's taking longer than we thought)." It is that rarest of sites: an information source that is as entertaining as it is enlightening. Running in alternative newsweeklies for more than 20 years, The Straight Dope answers the most intriguing and

bizarre questions imaginable, with one foot firmly on the ground and one eyebrow cocked toward the sky.

The Straight Dope is written by the reclusive Cecil Adams and his doppelgänger,editor Ed Zotti. No question is too complicated or too inane for Cecil. He takes them all on: "How many people have ever lived?" "Can you barrel roll a 747 or DC-10?" "Why can't you put pineapples in Jell-O?" "Who came up with the term *Third World?*" and "Were vampires simply humans suffering from porphyria?"

This site reproduces the column that runs in syndication, updated every Wednesday. Also featured are an online archive dating back to 1994, a discussion forum for topics covered in Straight Dope columns, FAQs, merchandise, and all five Straight Dope available books for sale. We recommend buying every one. Then bookmark this site and read it every week: You'll laugh while you learn, without the use of chemicals.

[geographic navigation]

Professional
Physical Geography Resources

● http://feature.geography.wisc.edu/

This resource site put together by the University of Wisconsin's Geography Department is more than just pretty maps—though they're here too. You can find all sorts of detailed information and links to specialty pages across the web. For example, if you need weather data, in addition to conventional weather forecasts, you can also consult the Space Science and Engineering Centerfor satellite images or the CPC for "Current Monthly Atmospheric and Sea Surface Temperature (SST) Index Values.

You can also tap into these other types of geographical information: Atlas of Global Instrumental Climate Data Maps of Monthly, Seasonal, Annual Temperature, Precipitation, Pressure, and 500mb Heights; U.S. Drought Palmer Index by State or Division from NCDC; or Global and Hemispheric Air Temperature, 1854–1991. If you want to know if it's going to rain tomorrow, go to http://www.weather.com/, but if you want to look at the Trade Wind Index for the Eastern Pacific, then look no further than the Physical Geography Resources page.

[how-to]

Huge segments of the web qualify as how-to sites. Certainly, many of the sites in this book are instructional or teaching-oriented sites, whether they be for learning how to access documents under the Freedom of Information Act or figuring out how to download movie scripts.

Sometimes, though, you just need to know how to do a particular task that defies the categories of this book. Guide to Lock Picking and the Ropers Knot's Page offer instructions in skills that everyone wishes they had at one time or another.

Guide to Lock Picking

● http://www.lysator.liu.se/mit-guide/mit-guide.html

This document has been floating around the Internet for more than a decade, and has become part of Internet lore. It was created to assist MIT students to gain access to "forbidden" parts of the famed campus. (There is now a disclaimer from MIT regarding the guide.)

This is an unadorned, 10-chapter, 40-page HTML document that addresses lock types, tools, exercises, and advanced lock picking. It's probably worth noting that the first section is entitled It's Easy, while the last section is entitled Legal Issues.

Ropers Knots Page

● http://www.realknots.com/

At some point in your life, you need to know how to tie a better knot than the one you use for your shoes. The Ropers Knots Page has both an alphabetical and categorical listing (hitches, single loops, nooses, stoppers, bends, etc.) of dozens of knots, all illustrated with simple diagrams and written instructions. The site also has links to knot books, other knot sites, and knotting news. An e-mail update on knotty situations is also available.

[libraries]

We've said it before, but it bears repeating here: If there is anything the Internet resembles from our prewired lives, it is a library. Think about it: The Internet is a huge collection of sources by innumerable authors, catalogued for public perusal, with no admission fee. Sounds like a library to me.

Will the web one day replace libraries? Some predict it will. Will the Internet then become the world library? Those questions will probably be answered in the not-so-distant future. But there can be no doubt that we live in a time of transition from paper to digital ether, and it's happening faster than anyone ever dreamed, as these entries prove.

The Internet Public Library (IPL)

● http://www.ipl.org/

No, it's not ivy-covered. The Internet Public Library (IPL) is just like a bricks-and-mortar reference library, with permanent collections and shared resources. As in other online libraries, the categories here are called "collections" and are arranged exactly as in a large metropolitan library: Reference (links to sites on the web); Exhibits, Magazines & Serials (links to more than 2,000 online pubs); Newspapers; Online Texts; Web Searching, and Especially for Librarians (advocacy, news, and employment). There are also sections for youth and teen interest (Career & College, Issues & Conflict, and Dating & Stuff).

The IPL has current, featured, and permanent exhibitions—this is the most developed part of the site—which range from historical (Western composers and their music) to geographical (lighthouses of America) and include photographs and audio/video (the permanent dinosaur exhibition includes a QuickTime tour).

Two components on the homepage raise the IPL a notch above most others: a literary criticism section with some 2,500 links to critical and biographical websites and Pathfinders, a series of guides created by the IPL as starting points for research. The library is open 24 hours a day, 365 days a year, rain or shine, even on holidays. Know of any public libraries in real life that meet that description?

The Library of Congress (LOC)

● http://www.loc.gov/

The Library of Congress is one of the world's most revered reference entities, an unimaginable collection. Now much of its famous content is available on the web.

The site has seven primary sections: Collections & Services (catalogs, collections, and research services), Thomas (Congress at work; see our listing for Congress, under GOVERNMENT), American Memory ("America's Story in Words, Sounds & Pictures"; see our review under HISTORY), Exhibitions (an online gallery), Copyright Office (Forms & Information), the Library Today (news, events, and more), and Help & FAQs (general information). Together, these online library "rooms" occupy nearly 3,000 pages of the LOC website. Take off your coat and stay for a while.

Start by wandering through the library's immense catalog; look up a book using a simple word/title search. The results are immediate—much faster than in real life—and comprehensive. You'll find all the LOC's collections here, including its digital materials programs, library maps and floor plans, Acquisitions

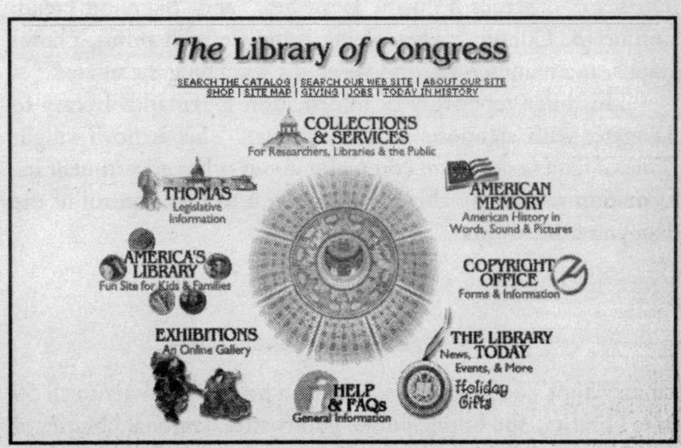

section, and much more. From here you can link to other libraries' collections (from among several hundred), services for researchers, publishers, educators, blind and physically handicapped people, and many others.

In the Research section of the Collections & Services room (okay, it's a page, but it feels like a room), check out the LOC Research Tools. This has links to online catalogs, legislative information, specialized bibliographies and indexes, full-text databases including Country Studies (see our review under WORLD CULTURES), four thesauri from the LOC, access to the Copyright Office and its records dating back to 1978, and the digitized collections from American Memory. Legislative info includes the Global Legal Information Network (GLIN), which has abstracts of national laws from more than 35 contributing countries, and Thomas, the full text of bills and resolutions under consideration in the current and past Congresses. An online index grants access to a microfilm database of documents pertaining to Vietnam POWs and MIAs, plus bibliographies on subjects from Korean books and Latin American studies to cold regions research.

Numerous gems may be uncovered deep within the individual sections, such as "Frank Lloyd Wright: Designs for an American Landscape," "Scrolls from the Dead Sea," and "Sigmund Freud: Conflict & Culture." These come complete with prints, photographs, and manuscripts. And we're just scratching the surface.

This huge repository of information is remarkably easy to navigate, with signposts at every corner. This is no Twilight Zone of data (a common complaint about other government information resources); this site allows you to take control of the data you came to find.

Library Spot

● http://www.libraryspot.com/

Library Spot's online page is, simply, a point of contact to all 50 state libraries, 380 online public library sites, national libraries of the world, academic libraries, K–12 school libraries, the Library of Congress, the National Library of Medicine, and others. It also lists links to music libraries, law libraries, medical libraries, and a huge selection entitled "Reference Desk" (dictionaries, business info, phone books, statistics, etc.).

Virtual Library

● http://vlib.org/

The V-Lib is the oldest catalog on the web, started by the acknowledged founder of the web, Tim Berners-Lee. Unlike commercial catalogs, portals, or search sites, it is run by a "loose confederation of volunteers, who compile pages of key links for particular areas" in which they have expertise. In many cases, the VL pages are the only comprehensive indexes available for particular topic areas. The pages (or, more accurately, indexes) reside on hundreds of servers around the world and are maintained at a large number of universities (for instance, Florida State hosts the Law VL, and Stanford hosts the Virtual Museum list). Each is responsible for the content of its pages, following certain guidelines relative to content, appearance, and structure. Most of these sites can be considered category-killers; at the very least, they are excellent starting points for research.

Several hundred categories get the full V-Lib treatment, from Aboriginal Studies to Zen Buddhism. As you've probably noticed, several of the entries in this book are from the Virtual Library, indicated as being from the V-Lib or part of the WWW Virtual Library.

[maps]

Thanks to the web, maps have become interactive. You can zoom in or zoom out on them to get eagle-eye views. You can shift them to the north or slightly to the south. You can get directions and street addresses, or plot a course across country, all with the click of a mouse or the spin of a trackball.

Maps, however, are more than just routes for getting from here to there; they also reveal information about the environment, political separation, and the vastness of the globe. The web does an extraordinary job of addressing all of these concepts—in addition to getting you to your vacation destination. The Internet has made maps something more than a sheet of paper that can never be refolded properly.

GLOBE Visualization Homepage

● http://globe.gsfc.nasa.gov/cgi-bin/home.cgi

Need to know what the weather was like three years ago last Tuesday in El Paso? Or perhaps you need a climatological map of your city to track rainfall for the past summer. In either case, go to Global Learning and Observations to Benefit the Environment (GLOBE). The GLOBE Program was developed to help students create and understand models for data visualization. Without getting too technical, data visualization is the process whereby raw data is converted into images such as maps and 3D images. Since most geological and space data is gathered as data points that mean nothing to the untrained eye, converting it to pictures is incredibly useful.

GLOBE takes this data and creates maps based on information recorded since 1995. Students from more than 7,000 schools in more than 80 countries contribute climate information from their schools on a daily basis, resulting in a vast database. This in turn becomes a central conduit to graphical information on observed environmental data (solid and liquid precipitation, temperature, cloud observation, features of surface water, and more). Viewers can create their own maps by choosing a category (e.g., solid precipitation, snow depth), picking a map type (contours, points, or both), a data source (satellite, weather source, etc.), map size, and date (day, month, year). A variety of map styles are available (including one in 3D that requires a plugin), and an image can be printed out and transformed into a physical cube.

Map Machine

● http://www.nationalgeographic.com/maps/index.html

This National Geographic site is a collection of hundreds of maps of all types, ranging from state to world, political to star maps. The various map types are categorized as follows: Map Machine Atlas (with statistics, facts, figures, and local maps), Map Resources (links to dozens of cartographic and political sites), Physical, Political, View from Above (satellite images with superimposed national borders), Star Chart (an interactive "map of the heavens" using Hubble Space Telescope images), and several others.

Many of these maps are thumbnail images that can be enlarged on screen or downloaded onto your computer. The best example of this capability is the Xpeditions Atlas category, which contains some 600 maps that you can print out. Simply click on the name of a region above a master world map, then drill down to go from continent to country to state. When you get where you want to go, you'll find two map versions, detailed and basic, which are ready for your printer. The world, as they say, is now at your fingertips.

FYI, the top of the main page contains a pulldown menu that leads to other areas of the National Geographic site.

Mapquest

● http://www.mapquest.com/

It's hard to know where to begin to describe Mapquest. As a geographical reference work, Mapquests boasts capability that dwarfs anything that existed in the paper-only years. Never before have people had access to the pinpoint detail that Mapquest provides—not without government clearance anyway. But because this is primarily a graphic site it's difficult to explain in text only.

Suffice it to say that Mapquest can locate any address and street in the United States and provide both a detailed map and directions for getting there—from anywhere. The phrase "you can't

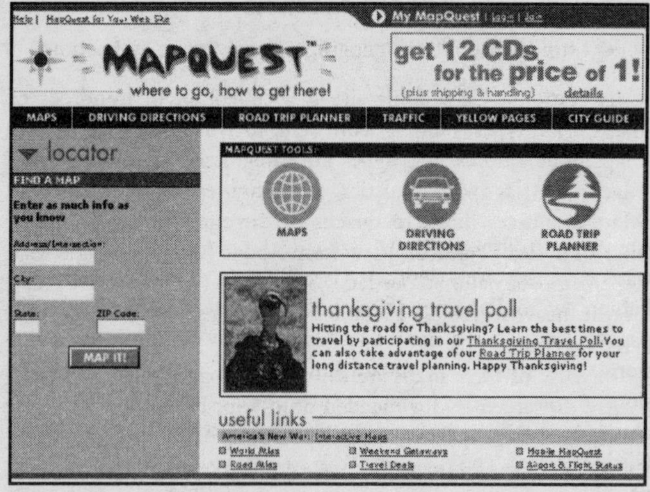

get there from here" becomes moot once you've logged on to this site. Need directions to someone's house in Alabama and you live in Arizona? No problem. It's all right here. Once a map has been generated for your query, you can manipulate it in several ways. The scalability, or zoom factor, is superb, enabling you to get bird's-eye views from different elevations. You are also able to move omnidirectionally to get more points of reference.

Mapquest is the provider of map services to the majority of Internet portals, including Yahoo!. So though the Mapquest site is the mother ship, as it were, most of its features are included in other sites.

[measurements & conversions]

Convert It

● http://www.image-ination.com/test_maker/convert.html

Are you one of those people with a burning need to convert kilowatts to horsepower, calories to British Thermal Units or degrees Fahrenheit to Rankine? If so, bookmark this incredibly useful page. Convert It is a site for technical and complex unit conversions. In addition to standard temperature and weight conversions, it also performs force, pressure, power, speed, heat, numeric conversions, and more. Enter a number into any measure space (such as Inch), press tab, and the corresponding conversion appears in a neighboring space (in this case, Millimeter). Developers Christian Ramsviks and Carl Adler have created this page of utilities that is faster than a slide rule and more comprehensive than your desktop calculator. Convert It is a site to bookmark.

Enter a number and press Tab!

Numeric formats

Decimal	Hexadecimal	Octal	Base32

Temperatures

Celsius	Fahrenheit	Kelvin	Rankine

Measures and weight

'British'(U.S.) Unit	'British'(U.S.) VALUE	SI VALUE	SI NAME
Length			
Mile			Kilometer
Yard			Meter
Foot			Meter

The Full Universal Currency Converter

● http://www.xe.net/ucc/full.shtml

You've got 10 U.S. bucks in your pocket, and you've just found yourself in the middle of downtown Djibouti. How much is your cash worth in the local market? Fortunately, you can log on to this page and find out that your single bill is worth 1720 Djibouti francs, which should cover the cost of lunch.

This page is an extremely powerful currency converter. All you have to do to perform any conversion is enter the amount and type of currency you want to convert, then pick the currency to which you want it converted. Seemingly every currency on the planet is available from a scrollable list that begins with the Afghani and ends with the Zimbabwe dollar. It's all incredibly straightforward—and nice to have when you're trying to figure out just how much you spent on that last trip abroad. The converter is maintained by Xenon Laboratories.

[quotations]

Bartlett's Familiar Quotations

● http://www.bartleby.com/99/

Thanks to Jean Bartlett, there's always an answer to "Who said . . . ?" His book of familiar quotations indexes words from authors as diverse as Chaucer, Dryden, Pope, Swift, and Newton. As part of the Bartleby Library, this site allows you to search through authors' names and their works, alphabetically or chronologically, or you can use the site's search engine to find specific words and phrases. (Note: The search engine is on the main Bartleby Library page at http://www.bartleby.com/). Heads up, though: This is the online version of the 1901 edition, so don't expect to find bons mots from the likes of Ernest Hemingway, Flannery O'Connor, or Doris Lessing.

[research]

The Argus Clearinghouse

● http://www.clearinghouse.net/

The purpose of this site is to point researchers of all stripes to quality information on the web. Argus members evaluate and rate sites, then include those that pass muster in their listing of recommended resources. Categories include Arts & Humanities, Business & Employment, Communication, Computers & Information Technology, Education, Engineering, Environment, Government & Law, Health & Medicine, Places & Peoples, Recreation, Science & Mathematics, and Social Sciences & Social Issues.

Researchpaper.com

● http://www.researchpaper.com/

No, you can't download an A-level term paper from this site. Researchpaper.com is a research tool to help you write one; it offers ideas and bibliographies to those in need of assistance on their research papers.

The motivational areas here include a chat room, an idea directory, a research center, and a discussion area. There are also sections for specific areas of study, including Art & Literature, History, Science, Business, and Society. These lead to the primary component of the site, the idea directory, where dozens of subcategories are presented, each with an impressive list of possible topic questions. Under music, for example, some of the topics include "Musical Notation in Electronic Instruments," "The Instruments of Orchestra: How the Components Have Changed and Evolved," and "The Role of Masonic Ideology in the Music of Mozart." Under each of these headings are two boxes, one labeled Ask eLibrary and the other titled Net Search. These buttons take you to two different areas of the elibrary.com website: the first to a bibliography, the second to a listing of websites that might provide additional information (via Ask Jeeves).

[style]

Elements of Style

● http://www.bartleby.com/141/

This is the online home to William Strunk Jr. and White's *Elements of Style*, still considered a bible for proper grammatical usage. Developed as part of Project Bartleby at Columbia University, the site is now called the Bartleby Library, which contains dozens of great books online. As for the *Elements of Style*, the entire book is here, so you'll never join independent clauses with a comma again.

[thesaurus]

Roget's Thesaurus

● http://www.thesaurus.com/

Synonymous with thesaurus is *Roget's*, and its companion website is the definitive source for finding synonyms. Enter your word into the lone search box and hit the OK button for a list of all the synonyms you should ever need. That's it. Oh, there are some word games here, too. It's an excellent site. Exquisite. Superb. Stellar. Superior.

[time]

The World Clock

● http://www.timeanddate.com/worldclock/

The clock on your wall is always five minutes slow. You watch is always eight minutes fast. Your computer clock is never on time. What time is it, really? This is the one and only place to find out.

The World Clock shows the current time in more than a hundred cities around the world, including Aklavik and Zagreb. Other components and features of the site let you time things more precisely, such as its capability to display only the cities you want and a calculator you can use to figure out, for example, what time it is in Leningrad if it's noon in New York. The site is

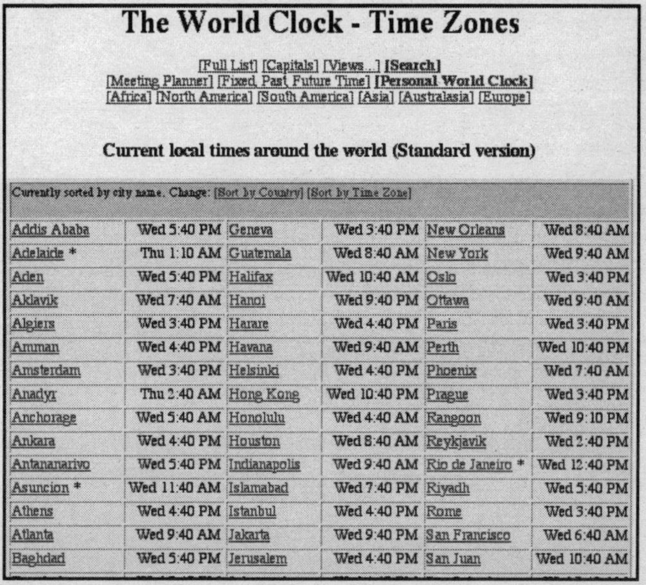

The World Clock - Time Zones

[Full List] [Capitals] [Views...] **[Search]**
[Meeting Planner] [Fixed, Past, Future Time] **[Personal World Clock]**
[Africa] [North America] [South America] [Asia] [Australasia] [Europe]

Current local times around the world (Standard version)

Currently sorted by city name. Change: [Sort by Country] [Sort by Time Zone]

Addis Ababa	Wed 5:40 PM	Geneva	Wed 3:40 PM	New Orleans	Wed 8:40 AM
Adelaide *	Thu 1:10 AM	Guatemala	Wed 8:40 AM	New York	Wed 9:40 AM
Aden	Wed 5:40 PM	Halifax	Wed 10:40 AM	Oslo	Wed 3:40 PM
Aklavik	Wed 7:40 AM	Hanoi	Wed 9:40 PM	Ottawa	Wed 9:40 AM
Algiers	Wed 3:40 PM	Harare	Wed 4:40 PM	Paris	Wed 3:40 PM
Amman	Wed 4:40 PM	Havana	Wed 9:40 AM	Perth	Wed 10:40 PM
Amsterdam	Wed 3:40 PM	Helsinki	Wed 4:40 PM	Phoenix	Wed 7:40 AM
Anadyr	Thu 2:40 AM	Hong Kong	Wed 10:40 PM	Prague	Wed 3:40 PM
Anchorage	Wed 5:40 AM	Honolulu	Wed 4:40 AM	Rangoon	Wed 9:10 PM
Ankara	Wed 4:40 PM	Houston	Wed 8:40 AM	Reykjavik	Wed 2:40 PM
Antananarivo	Wed 5:40 PM	Indianapolis	Wed 9:40 AM	Rio de Janeiro *	Wed 12:40 PM
Asuncion *	Wed 11:40 AM	Islamabad	Wed 7:40 PM	Riyadh	Wed 5:40 PM
Athens	Wed 4:40 PM	Istanbul	Wed 4:40 PM	Rome	Wed 3:40 PM
Atlanta	Wed 9:40 AM	Jakarta	Wed 9:40 PM	San Francisco	Wed 6:40 AM
Baghdad	Wed 5:40 PM	Jerusalem	Wed 4:40 PM	San Juan	Wed 10:40 AM

set to Greenwich Mean Time, which means that it isn't set to your computer's internal clock and so can give you an accurate reading any time of day. Once you bookmark this site, you'll have no excuse for ever being late again.

SCIENCE

[agriculture]

AgView

- http://www.Agview.com/

Old McDonald had a farm. And if he was smart, he would have visited AgView, an excellent starting point for information and resources on *all* aspects of agriculture. This site is primarily a powerful search and index tool covering 42 categories, such as animal production, aquaculture, organic farming, pest management, crop production, forestry, even beekeeping.

YAHOO!

ALSO LISTS:
[agriculture]

- **http://www.agrisurf.com**
  AgriSurf!: Find relevant agricultural and farming information.
- **http://www.joefarmer.com**
  Howdy Howdy: agriculture and farming search engine
- **http://www.usagnet.com**
  Internet Directory for U.S. Agriculture Resources
- **http://www.prairielinks.com**
  PrairieLinks: starting point for agriculture on the Internet; features worldwide agribusiness links

A great feature on the Net is the lists of new agricultural sites (tracked and categorized), plus a recommendation of the cool agricultural site of the month, chosen based on content, uniqueness, layout, and graphics. (An archive of previous cool sites is maintained.)

[archaeology]

Picture middle-aged men and blond twentysomething women in khaki shorts and pith helmets sitting under a brain-frying sun for months digging up dinosaur bones with tiny brushes and little tools. Or the Jurassic Park *and* Indiana Jones *versions, where, in addition to the dirt and dust, you also have to face the forces of good and evil.*

But if that's all you can imagine an archaeologist doing, then you've never encountered an archaeoastronomer or an archaeobotanist. The sites listed here take you to a variety of archaeological worlds, covering everything from research material to clothing to—if you're new to the field—how to get involved with archaeological expeditions. Tracking down the mysteries of the ancients is a truly unique experience, but it's also good to know where you can get a pith helmet on a moment's notice.

Archaeologic.com

● http://www.archaeologic.com/

Archaeologic.com claims to be the most comprehensive web directory of all things archaeological. Certainly any site that includes entire sections on archaeoastronomy (study of ancient astronomers and their technologies), archaeobotany (research of plant remains and their use in ancient cultures), and zooarchaeology (analysis of animal remains) has their bases covered.

There are two primary sections to this site: the Archaeology Portal and the Great Plaza. The Archaeology Portal is a Web directory for archaeology topics and regions, featuring thousands of links to dozens of categories arranged by topic (conservation, history, cultural heritage, and gender) and region (primarily by continent). Each category is divided into subsections containing, among others, general links, books, associations and organizations, research groups, and electronic mailing lists.

The Great Plaza is a separate directory of artifact reproductions, academic departments, booksellers, archaeology book publishers, associations, clothing with ancient designs and clothing for field expeditions, archaeological consulting firms, educational games, archaeological field equipment, fieldwork opportunities, archaeological site images, jobs in archaeology, language learning, serials, and archaeological adventure travel and tour operators. In short, everything you need to look and play the part of an archaeologist on the go.

Archaeology on the Net (AON)

● http://www.serve.com/archaeology/main.html

$ Need to know about ethnohistory and ethnographic portraits of Arctic cultures? AON, a text-only resource site that directly targets the professional, is the ideal place to begin your search. Categories here are divided into Regional (countries and continents), Resources (academic journals, bibliographies, field and research reports, maps, etc.), and General (topics such as archaeological computing, archaeometry, dendrochronology, linguistics, lithics, and underwater archaeology). The related links are presented as an alphabetical list of sites that match your interests; you can also search via a search engine box. Should you find—it's unlikely—that the websites listed here don't address your needs, more than 25,000 books are available for sale on the site.

[astronomy]

Astronomy Interactive Network (AIN)

- http://library.thinkquest.org/15418/home.html

The sky's the limit at the Astronomy Interactive Network, which takes on topics as weighty as the origin of time. Developed by three students (one college, two high school) with their well-educated heads focused above the clouds, the AIN summarizes the history of the universe as we know it. The site is a kind of *CliffsNotes*™ for budding and amateur astronomers, providing succinct descriptions of everything from the Big Bang Theory to the Heisenberg Uncertainty Principle to the launch of the Lunar Prospector. Capsule biographies of authoritative figures in the field are given, research techniques are described in depth, and the history of astronomy from 2500 B.C. to 1998 A.D. is summed up in a time line.

Embedded in the Interactive section are some terrific images, two cool games, and outstanding presentation graphics. Experts in the field may not find the information groundbreak-

YAHOO! ALSO LISTS: [astronomy]

- **http://astroplace.com/**
  AstroPlace: astronomy educational and informational links
- **http://www.astronomy.net**
  Astronomy Net
- **http://www.ncc.com/cdroms/as1/as1_sites.html**
  Astronomy Resource List
- **http://www.cvc.org/astronomy/index.htm**
  Astronomy Links
- **http://www.mtrl.toronto.on.ca/centres/bsd/astronomy/**
  Expanding Universe: Search this directory of classified sites for amateur astronomers.
- **http://www.users.dircon.co.uk/~jmwebb/links.htm**
  Pulsar's Astronomy Links
- **http://webhead.com/wwwvl/astronomy/**
  WWW Virtual Library Astronomy and Astrophysics

ing, but enthusiastic occasional stargazers will enjoy using AIN to boldly go where they've never gone before.

[biology]

Human Anatomy Online

● http://www.innerbody.com/htm/body.html

Can you find your precuneus? Do you know whether it's okay to have your jejunum showing in public? If not, check with Human Anatomy Online, a fascinating and authoritative site dedicated to getting you in touch with your innards. Brought to you by the same folks who created the Automotive Learning Online site (see our review under AUTOMOTIVE) site, Human Anatomy Online adroitly uses the multimedia format to put books like *Gray's Anatomy* on the shelf forever. See a "Cut and Surface View" of your brain, get a taste of all there is to know about your tongue, and learn every bone in the foot. Using an illustration style similar to those found in biology textbooks, the folks at Innerbody.com wisely, and tastefully, opt to give bio lessons with text,

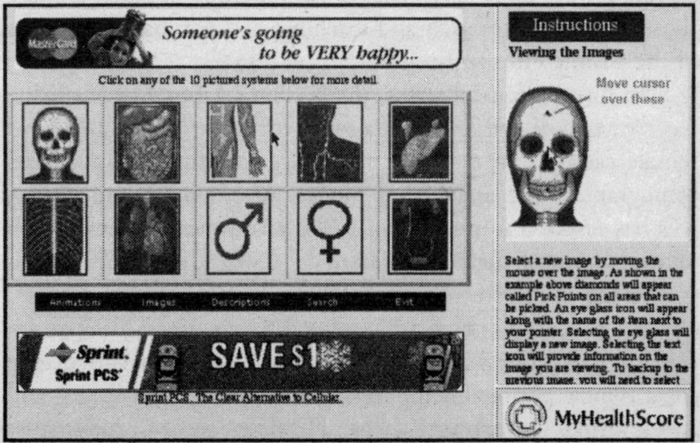

pictures, and animations rather than those live-surgery images that seem to bring out the worst in teenage boys and serial killers. The Systems pages feature details of, for instance, the endocrine system, where extensive information and microscopic views can be accessed by clicking on almost any biological point of interest. The click points are reminiscent of the game Operation, only the user is presented with meticulously documented anatomical knowledge instead of being startled when the guy's nose lights up.

All the information at this site is easy to access and encompasses all matters biological, from wounds to contact lenses to AIDS. Numerous pages are available to expectant mothers, who can see what is happening to their bodies during various stages of pregnancy. The site is useful to anyone with eyes, a brain, and a medial patellar retinaculum.

The Visible Human Project

● http://www.nlm.nih.gov/research/visible/visible_human.html

Take two human bodies, freeze them, and slice them so thin (4mm) that you get more than 1,800 pieces; then photograph, scan, and digitize those pieces to create computer graphics models for viewing every single slice or combination of slices; and use those images for research and teaching, and you have the basics of the Visible Human Project.

In more technical terms, the National Library of Medicine has created a digital image data set of complete human male and female cadavers in magnetic resonance imaging, computerized tomography, and anatomical modes. After slicing and dicing, this has resulted in more than 5,000 anatomical images, which take up about 40 gigabytes of hard drive space. Even though this is not the complete project (which you have to get on CD-ROM), the samples here are too good to pass up. This is an incredibly dense site, with downloads that, unfortunately, will clog most typical personal computers (many files—in both jpeg and mpeg formats—are over 7 megs). However, some of the smaller

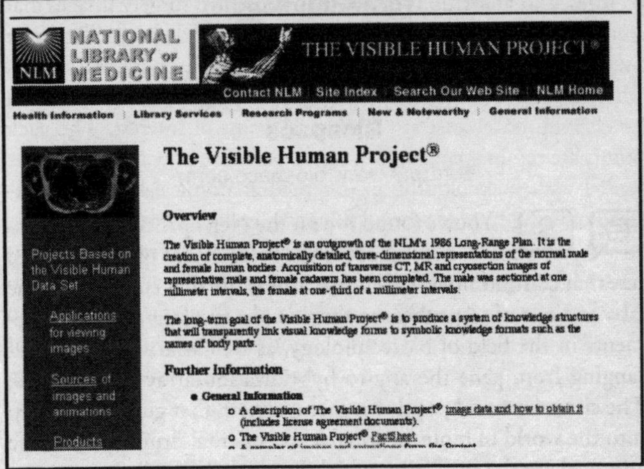

files and still photos will give you a sense of the wonders that lurk beneath our collective human skin.

The site also contains dozens of links to other sites that focus on specific aspects of the project, along with applications for viewing the bodies from different axes or in different dimensions (2D, 3D, virtual reality), as well as scientific papers on the importance and applied uses of the project.

In case you were wondering about the potentially semi-gruesome details, here they are (these aren't on the homepage): The male cadaver cross-sections came from a 39-year-old convicted murderer who had donated his body to science. The woman was a 59-year-old from Maryland who also willed her body to science. It took more than two years to find subjects who matched a set of criteria established to ensure that the bodies were as general and healthy as possible. First, two data sets were created: one of the fresh cadaver, the other after the cadaver was frozen. Then the cadaver was embedded in gelatin, frozen, and sliced from head to toe. As each layer was exposed, a color photograph was taken. Now you know.

Biotechnology
Bio Online

● http://www.bio.com/

Biospace

● http://www.biospace.com/

"You've found life on the Net," proclaims Bio Online, a resource for the biotech and pharmaceutical research communities. Of course, this is life that comes from the labs and out of test tubes, so there is plenty of data on advancements in the field of biotechnology, as well as articles on topics ranging from gene therapy to hybridization array technologies. The site uses a cool popdown menu system that guides you deep into the world of biotech, where experimental drugs and vaccine approval are the stuff from which headlines are culled.

The site caters to all segments of the industry, from professionals to academic researchers to government regulators, even investors. There are a career center, profiles of companies involved in biotech research, lists of patient groups, educational programs, government organizations, and even a chat center. And for those who need to stock up on supplies for the lab, the Bio Online store claims to offer the widest selection of software for chemical and biological research on the Net.

Biospace offers many of the same features as Bio Online, but its emphasis is on the commercial and investment side of the biotech world. This is made abundantly clear at the top of the homepage, where you can check stock prices on your favorite biotech companies. The day that some biotech company clones a human, you're going to want to be watching the stocks on this site.

Evolution vs. Creationism

● http://physics.syr.edu/courses/modules/ORIGINS/origins.html

When we went out on a limb to say that evolution is a fact (it was a pretty short limb, we admit), we knew there were people who would disagree with us. That's fine; if there is anyplace where people are entitled to their opinions, it is the Net. This particular site, maintained by Syracuse University, takes great pains to present a variety of links from both the evolutionary and creationism camps, with links to the Institute for Creation Research and the Creation Research Society. More interesting are the links to discussion groups, which prove that even adults (alleged adults) can get hot and bothered by the same sort of dialogue that threw America into an uproar during the Scopes Monkey Trial.

This is all found under a great graphic of Charles Darwin sitting across from Michelangelo's painting *The Creation of Adam*. The site does contain a warning that some sites within the proevolution links might contain language offensive to some religious groups.

Functional Genomics

● http://www.sciencemag.org/feature/plus/sfg/

A hot topic for the new millennium is the human genome project. This website (Functional Genomics), sponsored by Science magazine, includes information about all aspects of genomics. The site is not necessarily a comprehensive resource; however, it is a good place to start looking for information about genomics. The site features headline news (with archives), lists, recent scientific papers, and information about upcoming scientific meetings. There are lots of links to other sites and scientific resources. Job listings for science careers, educational resources, and biotechnology stock prices and quotes are all included on the site.

The site has many features, but not all are free. Access to full-text articles requires a subscription to *Science* magazine and Science Online. Some other features are members-only and require a (free!) online subscription. Viewers have the option to search or browse topics and order articles. There's even a FAQ section and feedback forms. The site may not be comprehensive, but it is very thorough.

The Human Genome Project

● http://www.ornl.gov/TechResources/Human_Genome/

The Human Genome Project (HGP) is perhaps the largest scientific undertaking in history. Its mission? Simply, to identify all of the estimated 80,000–100,000 genes in the human DNA. Begun in 1990, and expected to be completed around 2003, the project is coordinated by the U.S. Department of Energy and the National Institutes of Health. In addition to its tagging of the tens of thousands of DNA genes, the project also aims to determine the sequences of the 3 billion chemical bases that make up human DNA, then store this information in databases, develop tools for data analysis, and address the ethical, legal, and social issues (ELSI) that may arise from the project. Not exactly your run-of-the-mill science project.

Each of these goals has its own section on the site. There is an extensive history of the project, as well as a DNA and genome primer. Of course, studying genetics carries the potential for raising controversial ethical issues (cloning, producing "tailor-made" babies, breeding for specific characteristics, etc.), and this aspect of the HGP is addressed in great detail, as the project claims to be the first large-scale undertaking to consider the ELSI aspects of its research. The site has audio files of interviews and radio shows about the project, as well as images of various chromosomes, molecules, and gene maps. There are areas for accessing free teaching materials, a glossary, and explanations of acronyms—in short, everything the layperson needs to understand what is being done here, making this a fantastic site for professionals and curiosity seekers alike.

Textbooks
MIT Biology Hypertextbook

● http://esg-www.mit.edu:8001/esgbio/

We believe that printed textbooks are soon to be a thing of the past, and there is proof in the Biology Hypertextbook. Developed specifically for an experimental study group at the Massachusetts Institute of Technology, this online version of the university's Introductory Biology course is available to anyone who stops by for a visit—and you don't even have to enroll at MIT. A world-class biology course from one of the world's premier institutions, all available for free—what a concept. Unlike traditional textbooks, this hypertext book has a searchable index and highlighted links to definitions and related sections, enabling you to, with the click of your mouse, jump quickly between, say, carbohydrates and recombinant DNA. The site is complete with photos and diagrams and, unlike "real" science textbooks, weighs and costs absolutely nothing.

Virology
All the Virology on the WWW

● http://www.tulane.edu/~dmsander/garryfavweb.html

Remember Ebola, a flesh-eating disease that broke out in various Third World countries several years ago? Well, Ebola is actually a virus, and viruses are microscopic organisms that treat humans as living playgrounds. In the process, viruses are responsible for a wide array of seemingly intractable health problems and diseases, from the flu to pneumonia to hepatitis to Ebola to AIDS; they are also the foundation for some of the nastiest biological weapons yet developed. In cases where human confronts virus, virus most often has the upper hand.

The study of viruses is called virology, and the site to learn all about virology on the World Wide Web is called, not surprisingly, All the Virology on the WWW. This site brings together a vast array of virus-related sites in one place, dividing them into easily searchable areas, including virology research and data, specific virus sites, AIDS/HIV sites, plant viruses, organizations, educational resources, and more. There is also a news section that pulls virology data from more than 200 sites including CNN, UPI, and Yahoo!.

It doesn't stop there. The site also has The Big Picture Book of Viruses with hundreds of micrographs of viruses and bacteria. The pictures may not look like much at first glance, but the names will ring a bell: bubonic plague, rabies, smallpox, syphilis, and so on. There is a bookshop on the site as well, and for those of you who need more in-depth background information, there are several online courses including an introduction to microbiology and infection and immunity.

[chemistry]

It's not everyday that the average person needs information on atmospheric chemistry, supramolecular chemistry, organometallic chemistry, or even heterocyclic chemistry. But for when you do—or for those professional chemists—these sites will lead to the best on the web for chemistry information. Start with the Information Retrieval in Chemistry WWW Server site (http://macedonia.chem.demokritos.gr/main.html), a colossal set of links, hosted by the Institute of Physical Chemistry, in Athens, Greece. It's divided into search areas for "extreme" and general-interest chemistry (from fun projects to education and books). Then click over to ChemWeb (http:// www.chemweb.com/), an online community and resource site for chemists and chemical industry professionals.

If all of this is Greek to you (forget that it's in English), maybe you need a basic course in chemistry. Luckily for you, there is a place online that teaches such a course, CHEMystery thinkquest.org/library/lib/site_sum_outside.html. A virtual chemistry textbook that features interactive learning segments, the site walks you through a typical high school chemistry course, from atoms and molecules to acids and bases, chemical reactions, thermodynamics, and even nuclear reactions. But make no mistake, this isn't your typical textbook stuff; here 3D images of molecular structures, and audio files help to explain concepts and content. You can walk through the "class" sequentially or jump to specific areas that you want to learn about. The next time someone asks you about delocalized molecular orbitals, you'll be prepared.

FYI, this is yet another brilliant site developed as part of ThinkQuest (an organization profiled in SCIENCE).

[dinosaurs]

Dinosauria On-Line

● http://www.dinosauria.com/

The *Gigantosaurus* of dinosaur websites, Dinosauria On-Line content is composed with a healthy mix of intelligence, humor, and opinion.

The Gallery section is a crowd pleaser, with excellent artist renderings, plus fossil photos taken on digs and at museums. The Journal and Dino-Dispatches sections record intelligent pieces on dinosaur paleontology accessible to experts and laypeople alike. The Omnipedia is a compilation of dino-specific materials from pronunciation guides and maps of ancient Earth to anatomical dictionaries and geological time periods. In the main section—this is serious stuff—before you leave, drop by the Dino Store and check out the Skullduggery; just don't tell the kids you went to Dinosauria On-Line and came home without the saber-toothed cat skull replica.

UC Museum of Paleontology

● http://www.ucmp.berkeley.edu/index.html

Volumes of historic and prehistoric knowledge at the Museum of Paleontology at the University of California in Berkeley are just a click away. Not only does this site have great text to accompany superb photos, but it includes profiles of important historical figures, research articles, and details of new paleontological discoveries as they occur. Attention has been paid throughout this site to capture the attention and imagination of children, but none of its content would be mistaken for kiddie fodder. It's a true-blue museum, only you don't have to wait your turn in line.

And in place of the usual, boring site map, the UC Berkeley folks have set up what they call a museum "subway"; view a map outlining routes to various destinations within the museum, and hop on the next train by clicking where you want to go.

[electronics]

Electronics Hobbyist

- http://www.eskimo.com/~billb/amateur/elehob.html

Need to know about maglev and LEDs? Don't have enough detailed information on Tesla coils and fluxgate magnetometers? If you answered yes, then the Electronics Hobbyist site should serve as the proper guide. This is a meticulously compiled page of hotlinks to the world of electronics. Everything here runs the length of a single page with nary a break—except for category headings, which include: Electronics Articles, Science Projects, Forums & Newsgroups, Webrings, Other Peoples' Electronics Hotlists, Various Other Hobbyist Sites, Electricity/Electronics Education, Miscellaneous Electronics Information, Circuits Archives, Magazines, Robotics, Electronics Suppliers/Stores, Embedded Processors, Weird Science, and Great Books.

YAHOO! ALSO LISTS: [electronics]

- **http://www.icon.co.za/~archimedes/**
  Archimedes: products for the electronic hobbyist or scientist
- **http://www.amazing1.com/**
  Information Unlimited: catalog for electronic hobbyists
- **http://www.meci.com/**
  Mendelson's Electronics Co., Inc.: surplus electronics and hobbyist type items
- **http://www.microfasteners.com**
  Microfasteners: online catalog for model builders
- **http://www.rpelec.com/**
  RP Electronics: sells a variety of electronic products for industry, education, manufacturing, and hobbyists

[energy]

Department of Energy (DOE)

● http://home.doe.gov/

This government site on "science, security, and energy" has information on energy-related science news, medical news, "greening the government," science education, and technological advances as accomplished by various DOE labs. The bulk of this site covers work done by various affiliates of the DOE in the area of research, which includes earthquake research, utility programs, energy conservation, and more. Of note here is the Science Education section, which contains an excellent set of links to science sites for kids.

[engineering]

Engineering encompasses so many different areas of specialization that the term becomes almost meaningless at the professional level. There are engineers of the electrical, civil, aeronautical, software, and mechanical types, not to mention those who drive trains. In an effort to provide some professional information about engineering in its broadest context, we've chosen these two European database sites. For specific areas of study, consult Yahoo! under Science > Engineering.

Engineering Electronic Library, Sweden (EELS)

● http://eels.lub.lu.se

Edinburgh Engineering Virtual Library (EEVL)

● http://eevl.icbl.hw.ac.uk/

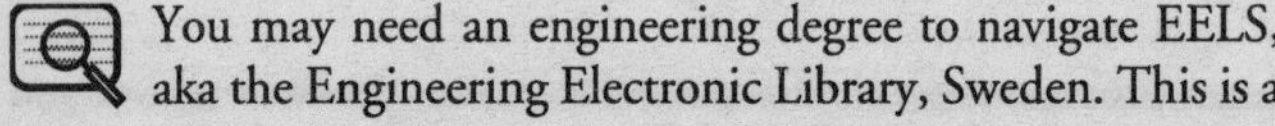

You may need an engineering degree to navigate EELS, aka the Engineering Electronic Library, Sweden. This is a

YAHOO! ALSO LISTS: [engineering]

- **http://www.ucd.ie/~food/hotlink.html**
  Agricultural and Food Engineering Around the World: extensive listing of WWW pages on agricultural and food engineering, most academic
- **http://www.er-online.co.uk/**
  Engineering Resources Online: quick guide and listings
- **http://www.englib.cornell.edu/ice/**
  ICE index to engineering resources from Cornell
- **http://www.technicaldoc.com**
  TechnicalDoc.com: Obtain product technical information, including drawings, specifications, MSDS, and cutsheets in Adobe pdf.
- **http://et.nmsu.edu/~etti**
  The Technology Interface: an online journal for the engineering technology profession serving education and industry

---

voluminous database that lists "all" engineering resources on the Internet. Though the site's graphics are limited to a little yellow map of Sweden, the search engine is as complex as they come, allowing users to search via URLs, site descriptions, site titles, or other components using linked fill-in-the-box descriptors. The site enables browsing by country or title, and includes hotlists of the most-cited individual engineering URLs and file directories. The professional will find a wealth of connections at EELS.

From Sweden, head south to Scotland, home of EEVL, a site that is truly a feat of Internet engineering. With its EEVL-eye logo leading each page, the Edinburgh Engineering Virtual Library has descriptions and links to more than 4,400 quality engineering sites on the Net. The library is the result of a four-year effort, designed to provide the education and research community with access to authoritative engineering information.

EEVL offers a complex variety of browsing and search options. In fact, its search engine is surely among the most far-reaching on the web; auto stemming, phrase searching, truncation wildcards, and resource filters make each search a logic problem in itself. EEVL allows U.K.-specific searches and links to more than 100 engineering e-journal websites and many engineering newsgroups.

The site includes a bibliography of guides to engineering information, listings of the most-visited sites each month, catalog additions and updates, and EEVL's All-Time Top 250 most-visited sites worldwide. Engineers who can't get enough can join EEVL's mailing list and contact the organization regarding its unusual-sounding EEVL Training and Awareness.

[environment]

Trying to present environmental issues to the public is always a double-edged sword. Environmentalists have often been labeled unfairly as extremists, concerned only with little-known species in hidden forests in countries with difficult-to-pronounce names. Either that, or they are derided as tree huggers.

As the sites in this section prove, neither of these preconceptions is accurate, especially in cyberspace. In fact, the web has become a startlingly accessible forum for exploring the issues of pollution control and environmental care, via level-headed reporting, brilliant design and presentation, and a sense of infectious urgency. The sites we review here run the gamut from those informing citizens about local recycling laws to others highlighting ecological hot spots around the globe to still others pointing out how both industry and Mother Earth are endangering the fragile environment we live in.

As a thematic group, these environmental sites represent some of the best that the web has to offer. Well-designed, thoughtful, and informative, they contain data that affects everyone; they are not for those people looking to simply indulge a hobby or find trivia. Instead, their compelling designs require you to sit and visit and do some thinking. As with the best of the Internet, they are worth visiting because you can learn from them, and find yourself amazed, and even overwhelmed, in the process.

Conservation International

● http://www.conservation.org/

When you think of ecologically endangered places—called biodiversity hot spots—usually such places as the Amazon River basin or sun-scorched regions of Africa come to mind. But guess what? California is a hot spot, too, and you can find out why here. Ecological disaster is a lot closer to home than you think, and the goal of Conservation International is to heighten your awareness of that. The organization has created a stellar site where visitors can learn about everything connected to conservation. It has information for all levels of interest in areas such as Scientific Activities, Conservation Resources, and In the Field.

The Global Biodiversity Hotspots list identifies ecosystems under the most imminent threat, as well as those wilderness areas that remain intact. This section features maps showing where the hotspots are; profiles the number of different species of plants, birds, mammals, reptiles and amphibians for the habitat; and calculates the size of the remaining habitat. Detailed program information for each habitat can be retrieved here as well. The Science section offers content on conservation biology and planning with analysis, along with information tools and links to training and support programs for institutions. In Resources you can read the latest conservation news; review publications and articles; learn about campaigns and workshops; and get detailed descriptions and purchasing information on documentaries for educators and conservationists, broadcast-quality wildlife nature stock footage, and workshops. A list of Internet resources on biodiversity and the environment is also included in this section.

All this scientific information is presented in an extraordinarily beautiful site designed with photos (including a gallery), illustrations, and an outstanding layout. It also serves as a reminder that conservation is not something that must take place in remote jungles half a world away; it might need to happen in your own backyard.

Earth's 911

● http://www.1800cleanup.org/

Cleaning up the planet begins with recycling. This site contains information that stresses the urgency of helping the Earth—hence the 911—and explores recycling on many levels, including local, national, global, personal, business, and even household hazardous waste. Each of the site categories is represented with a photographic image that, when selected, flashes information on the page regarding how to pursue and peruse that subject. Whether international or local problems, you'll find public service information and a virtual library of data. Enter your zip code and you'll be linked directly to your state's recycling information center, where you can find out how to dispose of your stuff (tires to toasters) in an environmentally responsible manner. Finally, a kid's section (Handy's Kids) incorporates colorful graphics and illustrations, contests, cartoons, games, and activities to drive the recycling message home.

Environmental Defense Fund (EDF)

● http://www.scorecard.org/

Air pollutants, water toxins, and pesticides on our food—enter this site at your own risk. You may want to leave the planet after you discover the many kinds of pollutants being emitted in your community. Simply type in your zip code and everything you wished you didn't know about local pollution will be presented to you, along with supporting facts and descriptions—in living color. Do you want to know how your county rates in the United States or how it rates relative to the rest of your state? Or how many people in your community face a cancer risk because of bad air? Ultimately, you probably *will* want to know who the polluters are and the kinds of pollution (toxic chemicals, animal waste) that pose the biggest threat to your area. You'll find it all here in depressingly data-driven detail.

In the center of the homepage is an environmental map,

and below it are several categories of environmental issues including hazardous air pollutants and animal waste from factory farms; roll your cursor over one of the issues and the map changes to reflect the data it has for that issue. Go farther into the site by clicking on a particular issue; for example, choosing hazardous air pollutants (HAPS) delivers the map with a corresponding legend and data on the cancer and noncancer risks posed by HAPS in your state. A scorecard combines Environmental Protection Agency (EPA) estimates and other data to come up with its findings. Other features include a pollution locator, pollution rankings, information about chemicals and their health effects, regulatory controls, FAQs, a glossary, and discussion forums.

But, hey, cheer up. At this site, you can personalize the Scorecard page so that it remembers your community and the information associated with it. If you spend enough time here, you'll want to use this feature because you'll get as mad as hell and want an easy way to e-mail polluters and government officials. Regardless of your interest in community involvement, you'll agree that the EDF has created an excellent model for building consumer support and advocacy.

Environmental Protection Agency

● http://www.epa.gov/

Think globally, act locally. That's the message of the EPA in its quest to protect the United States' natural resources. Everything you would expect to find from this organization is here on its excellent site: teaching concepts and aids; materials for concerned citizens, researchers and scientists, small businesses, and industry; publications; projects and programs; laws; and links to state, local, and tribal organizations, etc. You can also download software; access libraries, hot lines, and clearinghouses; find information on grants and funding; and check out links to other sites. You can also search for local information by entering your zip code in a search engine on the homepage.

New Ideas in Pollution Regulation

● http://www.worldbank.org/nipr/index.htm

Industrial pollution is the trade-off that many underdeveloped or developing countries have been willing to accept for economic growth. But pollution in one place, no matter how remote, can result in the toxic poisoning of the earth, air, and water on a global scale. Ugly and uneasy alliances form where locals want the dollars and companies need places willing to accept industrial hazards.

This site presents an incredibly gritty practical and economic look at pollution around the world, notably in developing countries. Run by the World Bank, it features recent research papers and information on different regions, operations, and projects pertaining to pollution control around the world. The News Headlines section features grim topics (such as "Valuing Mortality Reductions in India") and nearly two dozen categories offer data ranging from country reports to impact of markets. Further inside the site are briefings by topic and country, as well as a large resources section with pollution modeling and data, working papers, and EPAs of the world. Some of the presentations and papers are presented in pdf format requiring Adobe Acrobat, and occasional audio/videos require RealPlayer.

This review describes just a small part of the huge World Bank Group site, which contains a monstrous amount of economic-related research and analysis pertaining to various countries and global industries. The entire site is an amazing—and occasionally disturbing—store of research information.

PlanetDiary

● http://www.planetdiary.com/

PlanetDiary is a fascinating site that is also subversively educational and persuasive—and we mean that in an extremely positive way. According to Prentice-Hall, which maintains the site, "PlanetDiary records the events and phenomena that affect Earth and its residents. Each week, this site presents geological, astronomical, meteorological, biological, and environmental news from around the globe."

The homepage opens with a graphic of Earth, and six categories to choose from: Current Phenomena, Phenomena Backgrounders, Universal Measurements, Calendar, Archives, and Guide to PlanetDiary. Once a category has been selected, say Current Phenomena, a map of Earth appears with several icons marking locations around the world. Roll your mouse pointer over any icon and you'll get a description of what has taken place in that region, along with articles about the events. Fauna, floods, astronomy, earthquakes, radioactivity, severe storms, and volcanoes were all featured when we reviewed this site. Selecting an icon will take you to more information, including projects and activities (to help children cope with disasters), how to prepare for a disaster, and resources in your area. Finally there are links to other sites for more specific information.

The Universal Measurements section has cool tools for converting metric measurements and establishing timetables throughout the world, along with links to maps and general facts about Earth. One of the sections lets you check out *Na-*

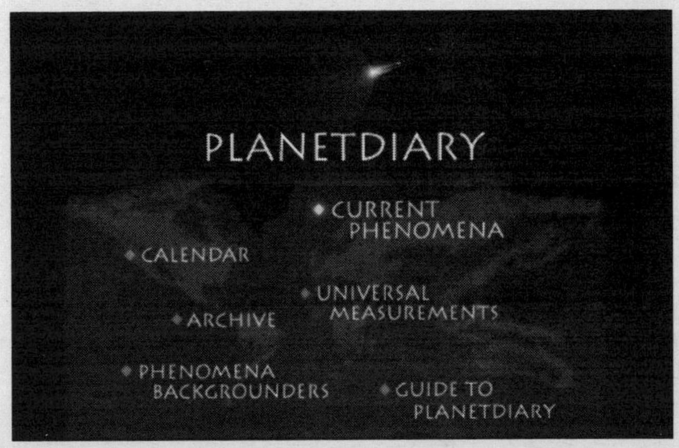

tional Geographic maps and also access city maps and information for any location in the world. You can also create a customized map of a specific region showing only the features you want. Or, using the TIGER mapping service link, you can type in your zip code and the U.S. Census Bureau will draw a map of your town, including bodies of water and roads. And while you're there, you can pick up population statistics about your city. The calendar is equally impressive, tracking major environmental events past and present, from volcanic eruptions of Earth-shattering size to city-shaking earthquakes.

You can easily spend hours at PlanetDiary studying the world; and the site is a surprisingly fun place to hang out with the kids on a rainy day, learning about the world through the myriad of activities of the planet itself.

[geology]

GeologyLink

● http://www.geologylink.com/

In contrast to the above site, GeologyLink provides multiple links and informational connections for those with only a novice's understanding of geology. The site serves as an introductory course in geology, which you might want to take in order to make sense of those pesky geological events like the earthquakes in Los Angeles or the volcanoes in Hawaii.

The Earth Today, the first in a series of topic headings found on the homepage, gives a comprehensive chronology of recent worldwide geologic events, with links to news stories and maps about each. In the News links you to recent general-interest stories about earth science, while the Hot Topic button provides a number of links related to a single subject, such as a recent symposium called "Life on Mars."

Inside Geology has links to lectures, subjects, news, and organizations worldwide, all grouped under the various chapter headings of a Houghton Mifflin geology textbook (the site's sponsor). The Virtual Classroom lets readers check out the lecture notes of educators at major universities, while Virtual Field Trips links them to geologic topics by geographic area, and the Glossary supplies definitions for terms such as "wave-cut bench," which may confuse any carpenters who stop by for a visit.

GeologyLink offers ample opportunity to purchase geology-related texts, and a click or two will instantly place you many layers into the Houghton Mifflin corporate crust.

GeologyNet

● http://www.geologynet.com/indexa.htm

[$] If you want to rock all night, here's the place to do it. GeologyNet describes itself as "your site for earth science software and information." "You" in this case refers to the geology professional, as this page is a combination link service, message board, and shopping mall for those who know the difference between schist and seismic schists. To put it bluntly, they know what they're digging for.

A huge clearinghouse of geological information, GeologyNet includes reams of relevant information and links for rock lovers. There is hot news ("Huge Oil Deposits Found under Caspian Sea" and "Big Losses in South African Diamond Mines!"), articles about microscopes of all shapes and sizes, gemstone identification, Windows and Mac screensavers, and much more. Products offered range from books and texts to mapping software to telescopes and microscopes to stickers that read *Geologists do it for ages* and *Geologists keep on rockin'*. The site is maintained in Australia, perhaps giving new meaning to the term Down Under.

[kids]

Research
National Science Foundation

● http://www.nsf.gov/

The National Science Foundation (NSF) is the country's preeminent independent, not-for-profit science organization. This government agency is responsible for promoting science and engineering through programs that invest more than $3 billion per year in almost 20,000 research and education projects. These programs cover areas as diverse as biology, computer technology, and polar sciences (the photos on its South Pole page make images of Hell look more inviting). The website also contains information on grants, contracts, legislative affairs, employment opportunities, the agency's administration, and the like.

ThinkQuest

● http://www.thinkquest.org/library/

The ThinkQuest Library is an incredible series of more than 1,000 websites developed by students participating in the ThinkQuest Internet-based education programs. These sites span a vast array of topics including Arts & Entertainment, Health & Safety, Science, Technology, and many others.

We've included several of the ThinkQuest (TQ) sites in this book, because we consider them to be generally extensive, far-reaching, and well-developed resources. For instance, the Science category is subdivided by discipline so that within, say, chemistry, more than 20 TQ sites have been developed, including ChemWeb (see our review under CHEMISTRY) to help students prepare for chemistry tests. This site, which serves as the main index and search engine for all the sites, also has information on the winners of ThinkQuest and ThinkQuest Jr. contests, plus connections to the IQ homepage, where you can learn

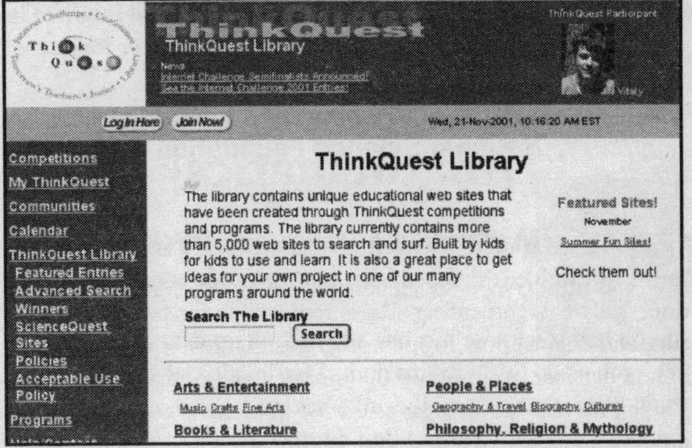

about the programs to which more than $2 million in scholarships and cash are awarded each year.

The Yuckiest Site on the Internet

● http://yucky.kids.discovery.com/

Children of the Internet age like to surf the web, but they still like grime and slime. The Yuckiest Site on the Internet caters to these rather conflicting tastes. The site, sponsored by Discovery Communications, Inc., makes science cool. Wendell, the worm reporter, guides kids through features of the site, including bug world (everything you always wanted to know about roaches . . . roaches?), yucky fun and games, and gross and cool body facts (burps and belches). Kids can interact with Wendell in the Ask Wendell section and learn more about Wendell and his friends in Worm World. There are a yucky poll and a What's Hot section to keep kids informed.

There are links to pages that let kids join adventure or science groups, quizzes, Discovery Kids anonymous message boards, Discovery Kids TV schedules, and the Discovery Kids game zone. Parents may be grossed out, but kids will love it. The website definitely lives up to its name as the best place for science (and yucky) entertainment.

[mathematics]

Martindale's Reference Desk

● http://www-sci.lib.uci.edu/ HSG/GradMath.html

If you had to choose just one site to look up data on mathematics, you'd do well to make it Martindale's Reference Desk. Strange as it may seem, this man has managed to create amazing indexes of fairly technical and advanced topics from across the web. The Virtual Mathematics Center is a catalog of Internet resources in a variety of disciplines, and the immense Math Center is filled with links grouped by area, the first of which connects to other Martindale's Reference pages, such as the Chemistry Center and the Physics Center (hey, even mathematicians have to look out for number one).

The math links are in groups including Journals & Preprints and Dictionaries & Encyclopedias. Courses, Tutorials & Databases leads to such links as a compendium of more than 9,000 online calculators or a page called Unsolved Mathematics Problems, maintained on the MathSoft corporate website. And what would a good listing of math courses and tutorials by subject be without a logical link? The one here leads to the Introduction of Logic for Liberal Arts & Business Majors, taught at Hofstra University.

MathLists

● http://www.math.psu.edu/MathLists/Contents.html

The really big problems in life still belong to the dedicated mathematicians. Who else would be concerned about giving the value of pi even more digits? Or try to come up with a number so big and final that you couldn't even add 1 to it? For those people, as well as the numerically curious, there is MathLists. This page, embedded in the website for the Penn State University Mathematics Department, is an excellent links resource for math websites around the world.

Using a self-described "primitive search engine" and a database, searches can be conducted in MathLists' main categories, which include General Web Servers, Related Topics (for example, physics department servers and math-education sites), Math Departments (at universities sorted by country and state), Societies and Associations, Institutes and Centers, Commercial Pages, Mathematics Journals, Mathematics Preprints, Subject Area Pages (from algebra to wavelets), Other Archived Materials (including links to Biographies of Women Mathematicians and the Young Mathematicians Network), and Mathematics Software. This site may not solve your math problems, but it just might get you closer to a solution.

MathSearch

● http://www.maths.usyd.edu.au:8000/MathSearch.html

Few of us ever do math in our heads anymore. With calculators being used as early as grade school, it's a wonder anyone can still recite basic multiplication tables, let alone do statistics and higher math.

Never fear: MathSearch is here. This site is a collection of more than 190,000 documents on English-language math and statistics from around the world. Maintained by the University of Sydney, New South Wales, School of Mathematics and Statistics, most of the links are associated with research-level and university mathematics material; it is serious students, researchers, and math professionals who will find the site useful on a regular basis.

In addition to its main search function, there is an index of the 60 most frequently linked pages—from the Geometry and Topology page to the Mathematical Association of America site.

[natural disasters]

NaturalHazards

● http://www.naturalhazards.org/

If you think that the world is a dangerous place, this site will assure you that you're right. NaturalHazard gives detailed descriptions of all disasters, including atmospheric and geologic, provides warnings and real time data, and points you toward products that help you weather the storm. The geologic area, for example, covers earthquakes and tsunamis, floods, slope failures, and volcanoes and details the location of the risk and the season of the risk and offers other Internet resources about the risk.

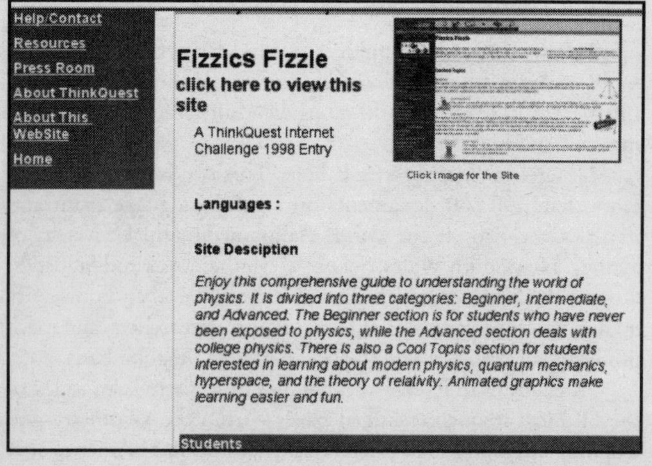

Help/Contact
Resources
Press Room
About ThinkQuest
About This WebSite
Home
Fizzics Fizzle
click here to view this site
A ThinkQuest Internet Challenge 1998 Entry
Click image for the Site
Languages :
Site Desciption
Enjoy this comprehensive guide to understanding the world of physics. It is divided into three categories: Beginner, Intermediate, and Advanced. The Beginner section is for students who have never been exposed to physics, while the Advanced section deals with college physics. There is also a Cool Topics section for students interested in learning about modern physics, quantum mechanics, hyperspace, and the theory of relativity. Animated graphics make learning easier and fun.
Students

[physics]

Fizzics Fizzle

● http://library.advanced.org/16600/

Don't know a quark from quantum mechanics? Not to worry. Log on to Fizzics Fizzle, a site whose quirky name belies its goal: to advance—or prompt—your physics knowledge. There are three levels of study to choose from here: The Beginner section is, obviously, for students who have never been exposed to the world of physics; Intermediate covers the physics curriculum generally taught in high schools; and the Advanced section covers the physics curriculum generally taught in introductory college physics classes. Click on a level and you're taken to the first page of the course, from which you progress page by page through an exploration of the often mind-boggling world of physics, in an easy and occasionally humorous format. Many of the concepts are illustrated with 3D images.

The site also features Cool Topics (interesting aspects of physics), Reference (formulas and values), Games & Fun Stuff, a forum for discussion, and links, and the customize option allows you to change the look of the site to fit your specifications (one of the few sites that offers this). If this was how they taught physics when we were in high school, we might have shown up for class more often.

PhysLINK

● http://www.physlink.com/

PhysLINK manages to balance professional-level data with content of interest to novices and amateurs. First-timers to the world of Newton and Einstein will find lots of areas to explore, while professionals will find value in the site's resources and links.

The site's Daily News is usually in essay form; other features are Science Software, Quotations, Ask Experts, Reference, Physics Fun, New Theories, History, Images, News, and numerous others. Some of these are especially noteworthy, such as the Physics and Science Reference section, for its links to other sites that provide data on physical constants and conversions and the table of nuclides. Ask Experts is a collection of questions and answers ("How many atoms thick is aluminum foil?" "Is it true that radio waves travel faster than X rays?").

PhysicsWeb

● http://www.physicsweb.org/

Designed for those bright enough to be conversant in physics, PhysicsWeb makes science infinitely cool. Along with the de rigueur news stories, there's a link to *Physics World Magazine*, an events page, and a listing titled Physics Jobs (posted on the site). A huge section called Best of PhysicsWeb, contains both a search engine and an index of topic areas.

[reference]

Infomine

● http://infomine.ucr.edu/

Been digging for serious science data and coming up empty? The mother lode awaits at Infomine. This is a wishing well full of "scholarly Internet resource collections" on physical science, engineering, computing, and math, and it's all searchable via a sophisticated, multilevel engine.

Infomine will be especially relevant to faculty, students, and research staff at the university level. It describes itself as "a comprehensive showcase, virtual library and reference tool containing highly useful Internet/Web resources including databases, electronic journals, electronic books, bulletin boards, listservs, online library card catalogs, articles and directories of researchers, among many other types of information." Phew! The table of contents lists all resources alphabetically. Be forewarned: Get extra batteries for your headlamp, because the list for the letter *A* alone contains several hundred links, ranging from Abbreviations to Aviation. Browsing by subject, keyword, and title also is available, and the search engine enables searches by keyword, subject, author, title, or any combination. Infomine is associated with the Libraries of the University of California, a sizable database of resources.

SciCentral

● http://www.scicentral.com/

Any site that offers its visitors a picture of a martini glass and pictures from the Hubble telescope on the same page knows how to mix business and pleasure. SciCentral does just that with lots of science links and plenty of scientific diversions for both the full-time scientist and the science enthusiast. The main section of SciCentral is categorized into Biological, Physical & Chemical, Health, Earth & Space, and Engineering Sciences areas. Other sections include Policy & Ethics, Research Highlights, and Science in the News. Within each of these sections are links to articles, companies, products, career resources, databases, institutions, funding resources, journals, discussion groups, and more.

Those not professionally engaged in scientific research will also find much of value here, including lesson plans for kids in K–12, After Hours Escapes (cool, more mainstream science-related sites, identified by the martini glass), discussions of artificial intelligence and replaceable body parts in Sciborg, a bulletin board, news and headlines, and scientific special reports from other media sources. This site succeeds in making science more interesting and, thanks to the After-Hours Escapes, a bit more intriguing as well.

[space]

National Aeronautics Space Administration (NASA)

● http://www.nasa.gov/

Space is the place at the NASA website, where you can learn everything there is to know—that isn't classified—about America's aeronautics and space research programs. We used to think it was cool when shots of space were televised from the lunar missions; here you can get those images and information whenever you're into outerspace.

NASA's homepage leads with a feature story and a jump to the Today@NASA page containing a daily online newsletter. From there you can go to one of NASA's Strategic Enterprises sections or to NASA for Kids, which features lots of projects and information, such as Build Your Own Martian Spacecraft and Amazing Space Activities. You can view a launch from one of three NASA facilities, get information on visiting NASA sites

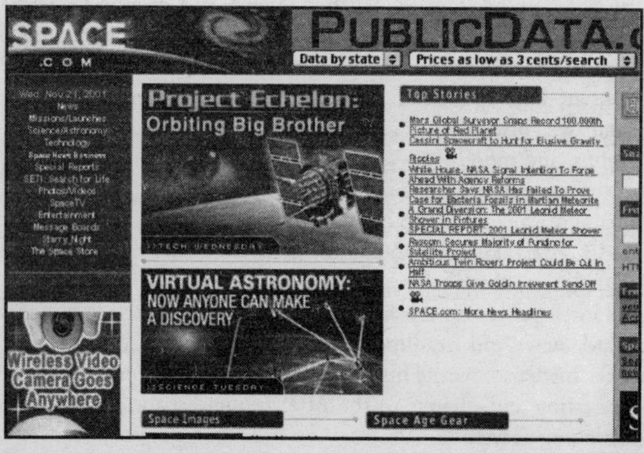

around the country, or learn about job, business, and research opportunities.

NASA has several cool websites, including the Mars Global Surveyor, Earth Observatory, and Women & NASA. Pictures of Space contains a vast archive of color photographs from NASA missions. Finally, there are more than 50 NASA Project homepages, among them, one for the Hubble Space Telescope, the Human Space Flight, the Mars Missions (which details four current missions to the Red Planet), and, for Doomsayers, an area on asteroid and comet impact hazards.

Space.com

● http://www.space.com/

Astronaut Gordon Cooper claims to have seen UFOs when he was on a training mission over Germany in the 1950s. A Swiss team of astronomers found a third extrasolar planet. A 300-pound meteorite crashed into the Moroccan town of Zag.

Is this another sci-fi site? Nope, this is Space.com, a serious science site that explores all aspects of space—breaking news, astronomy, exploratory missions, the strange space-related world of UFOs, and Area 51. Designed for space junkies, the site tracks missions, NASA budget fights, supernova discoveries, the plight of space contractors, even the stock prices of satellite manufacturers. Space.com also has a Space Imagined area that addresses space-based fiction, TV programming (with the inevitable *Star Trek* references), movies, and games. A chat room and message boards host a universe of spacey opinions. Short of spending time loosely tethered to a vehicle in orbit, Space.com may be the next best thing to being there.

[zoology]

Zoological Record

● http://www.biosis.org.uk/zrdocs/zoo/info/gp_index.htm

This small segment of the Zoological Record site is essentially an elephantine search engine that finds detailed data on animals. For instance, a search of "wolf" generated a list of links to 20 relevant sites, including Wolves of America and the North American Wolf Society. More than a cute, fuzzy animal site, it includes information for serious animal advocates and researchers, including updated Latin names, conference news, CD-ROMs, zoology links, and the like.

To search more broadly, go to the Zoological Record homepage, where you can pick your topic from the following selection: Protozoa, Invertebrates, Helminths, Arthropods, Insects, Chordates, and Vertebrates. From there, you can get even more detailed information about animal species.

SHOPPING

[auctions]

eBay

● http://www.ebay.com/

EBay needs no introduction. It is, simply, the Internet's most successful auction website, running more than 2 million auctions at any one moment (and claiming 1.5 billion hits a month).

To participate in any of its auctions, you must become a member (it's free); then you can bid on any auction in any category. The advantage is clearly on the buyer's side, as high-priced auctions are few and far between. And even if you don't "win" your object of desire this time around, eBay's volume almost ensures that a similar item will inevitably come up again—and soon.

On the selling side, using eBay is more involved. For starters, you need a website and a digital camera (so you can display pictures of sale items). Thereafter, organizing an auction of your items is a reasonably simple process, thanks to eBay's clear instructions and user support.

EBay functions under an honor system which means the buyers and sellers deal directly with each other. If problems do arise, eBay offers myriad solutions, including a $200 insurance policy on most items and escrow payments. A feedback system enables users to pay compliments or send warning alerts of a shady seller.

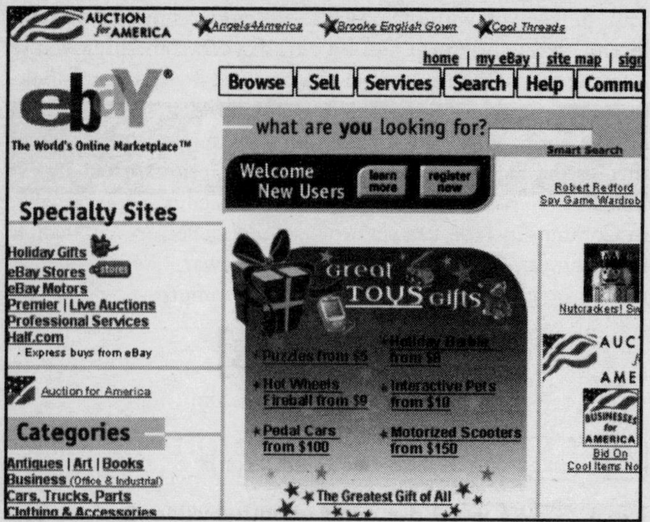

Overall, eBay is an enjoyable, upbeat online community—one that can become addictive. Not that we speak from experience or anything, but we do need to get back online now and check out our bid on that imported handmade sitar.

iCollector

● http://www2.icollector.com/

"Taking the antiquated out of antiques, iCollector has created, developed, and redefined the auction industry online." That's the claim this site makes, and it does a good job of living up to it. Running since 1994, iCollector is home to more than 200 auction houses, dealers, and galleries. It serves as a hub for these organizations, giving you easy and immediate access to hundreds of thousands of items for sale.

Once you become a member of iCollector, you can bid on a huge range of art and other collectibles, using valuable online tools to help you with the process. In Resources there is an item locator that will inform you by e-mail when something you're interested in comes up for sale. For instance, if you've been looking for that special '50s Eames chair for your den, My Agent will let you know when someone has put one up for auction. Then there is the Exhibitions section, which comprises virtual art exhibits where you can view the work of a specified artist. Finally, in Community, you can speak with other collectors about their finds and of course, "the big one that got away." Fortunately, at iCollector, there's always another auction tomorrow.

Sotheby's

● http://www.sothebys.com/

Going once . . . twice . . . SOLD! High-priced autioneering comes to the web courtesy of Sotheby's. One of the world's oldest and most venerable auction houses, Sotheby's has embraced the Internet with this useful and attractive site. Collectors of art and other collectibles can read a schedule of upcoming auctions at the firm in New York, London, and other locations and buy catalogs of the items to be auctioned. Site subject headings range from Ancient Works and Old Masters to Contemporary Collections, as well as more-focused categories such as British and Continental Ceramics and Glass, Works of Art, and Selected English and Continental Furniture. You can also read auction results from previous sales, when keeping track of, say, the current market value of a particular artist's work. "What's a Jasper Johns painting worth this week?" you may wonder. The answer: a lot.

Yahoo! Auctions

● http://auctions.yahoo.com/

If your local auctions aren't giving you the bidding buzz you've been looking for, then make the big leap and go international with Yahoo!'s auction site. Designed just like Yahoo!'s homepage, the site not only lets you select from a host of categories, but also allows you participate in auctions around the world. Can't find the object of your dreams in the U.S.? Try Denmark, France, Germany, Italy, Spain, Sweden, UK & Ireland, Australia & NZ, Hong Kong, Japan, Korea, Singapore, Brazil, Canada, or Mexico. Yahoo! has them all. Categories in each country include Antiques & Collectibles, Art & Entertainment, Business & Office, Clothing & Accessories, Computers, Electronics & Cameras, Home & Garden, Sports & Recreation, Toys & Games, Trading Cards, Travel & Transportation, and Other Goods & Services (such as health and beauty, real estate, weddings, etc.). While the range of offerings is huge, in some cases it helps to be fluent in the local language to narrow your search. It's all part of Yahoo's auction world, where you can view locally, and bid globally.

[beauty]

BeautyLink

● http://www.beautylink.com/

Not all of us can afford our own personal hairdresser or beautician to keep us looking our best or to give us makeup tips when we need them the most. But there are some beauty secrets everybody should be privy to: Dark circles under your eyes can be hidden with red lipstick; keeping your fingernail polish in the refrigerator makes it last longer; when applying liquid foundation to your face, let each paper-thin coat dry before adding more.

These and other beauty tips can be found at BeautyLink, a site that aims to give you the right information for the right look for you. Each section of the site—hair, beauty secrets, nails, even teen tips—is "hosted" by a cyberpersona with a beguiling name, including Blade Shearson on hair, Cyberteena on teens, and Pat Ansa on social issues. They offer insights to getting the most out of beauty products and more, importantly, how to use them. You can e-mail these specialists; others post their info and tips right online. For example, in the hair section, you can select the shape of your face from a group of icons, then read what experts have to say about the haircut that's right for you.

There is also a members' lounge for chatting about beauty concerns (registration is required), a gossip page (which makes you feel like you're sitting in the chair at the salon), and links to special offers and products.

Cosmetic Connection

● http://www.cosmeticconnection.com/

When you walk into a department store, the cosmetics counter is usually a bewildering maze of products and pitches. It's even worse when you go to individual beauty boutiques. What exactly is the difference between all these brands and products? What does the Body Shop offer that is different from Bobbi Brown? Or MAC and Mary Kay? How about Elizabeth Arden and Helena Rubinstein? Or Estee Lauder and Lancôme?

The Cosmetic Connection attempts to guide you through the makeup minefields by providing product reviews of dozens of name brands in a variety of categories, from skin care and makeup to anti-aging cream and lipstick. There is no makeup advertising on the site, so there appears to be no bias in the reviews; host Heather Kleinman and her "Cosmetic Connection Product Panel" give seemingly objective reviews and opinions on the products they scrutinize.

In addition to this core information is a link to a related site called Ask the Makeup Diva. Here you can get answers to e-mailed questions about makeup (such as, What's the difference between drugstore and department store cosmetics?). You can also have weekly updates of the Cosmetic Connection's weekly report e-mailed to you or connect to product manufacturers' websites.

SalonWeb

● http://www.salonweb.com/

Bad hair days are a fact of life. And unlike makeup, you can't fix a bad haircut with a washcloth and warm water. You can, however, try minimizing hair horrors with an online consultation from SalonWeb. There is a section that outlines the cuts, whether you have short or long hair. Of course, you still have to sit in a chair to get the deed done, so think of this as a first step toward mane management.

Spas
Club Spa

● http://www.clubspausa.com/

If your beauty regimen includes—or you want it to to include—visits to body and beauty spas, then this site will send you packing, literally, in the right direction. Spas, their resort counterparts, and even day spas (stripped-down beauty and massage sessions in your hometown) are listed at Club Spa's site, along with contact and accreditadion levels.

[books]

Buying
Amazon.com

● http://www.amazon.com/

$ For longtime Internet users, Amazon.com is like the microwave: It's hard to remember a time when it wasn't there, but it's not yet that old. The Amazon model has been replicated over and over on the web as a paragon of e-commerce, and for good reason. It makes buying stuff really really easy; plus it's a great starting place for research.

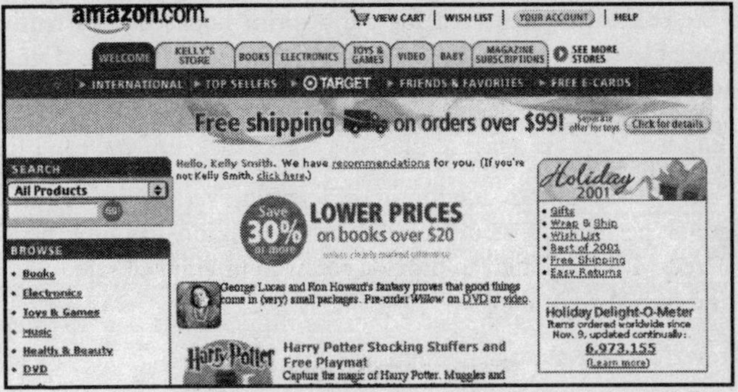

Although it started as a seller of books, Amazon now offers CDs, electronics, videos, and gifts and serves as an auction site. The Amazon methodology is so pervasive across the web now as to be almost self-explanatory: You pick a search category on the homepage (Books, Music, etc.), type in the name of what you're looking for, click the Go! button, and a list—sometimes a monstrous list—appears. If you choose to simply browse by topic areas or genres (mystery, romance, biographies), there are almost 40 contained in a pulldown menu.

Once you have your results list, you can jump directly to a particular book (or CD, etc.) and look over its capsule summary, which is usually accompanied by a review and reader comments, as well as the occasional author comment. A ranking calculator tells you how well the book is doing saleswise, relative to all the other titles Amazon carries—a feature that certainly has to be a humbling experience for most authors. When you've selected an item you want to buy, it gets added to your virtual shopping cart. You can opt to buy it right then and there (after giving your appropriate personal and credit card info), or you can save it and think about it for a while. If you leave the site and come back another time, your cart will still be waiting for you with your unpurchased items—something that never happens in a real store.

You can even search for out-of-print books not currently available on the site. Amazon will e-mail you directly if and when it finds the book you're looking for. With the addition of its auction component, items relating to the book you looked up will appear on the left side. As an example, if you looked up *Legends of Rock Guitar*, auction items featuring various guitars and guitar peripherals would be displayed. Amazon has now partnered with Bibliofind to provide access to millions of rare, used, and out-of-print books.

BarnesandNoble.com

● http://www.bn.com/

Focused largely on the sale of books, music, software, magazines, prints, posters, and related products, barnesandnoble.com has capitalized on the recognized brand value of its bricks-and-mortar stores to become the second-largest, and one of the fastest growing, online distributors of books.

Barnesandnoble.com profits from its focus on print products, which is far more targeted than Amazon's is today. Customers can choose from millions of new and out-of-print titles and read book descriptions, reviews, and excerpts. Among the features that make this site unique are the specialty stores, which include electronic books, academic and scholarly titles, and bargain books discounted up to 91 percent off the retail price. Other exceptional areas of the site are the Music Store and Online Courses, an exclusive list of approximately 50 courses per month.

[catalogs]

CatalogCity

● http://www.catalogcity.com/

The concept behind CatalogCity is almost too simple: Create a site that catalogues catalogs. Simple, yes, but clever as well. Here you'll find links to most of the big names (Lands' End, J. Crew) and hundreds of lesser-known catalog retailers arranged by category or in alphabetical order. A search engine acts as the primary guide through the site, but you may want to go with the index if you're not sure where that apostrophe in Lands' End actually goes.

In addition to linking you to catalog sites (complete with descriptions of the issuing companies), CatalogCity has sections offering gift certificates, gift ideas, catalog reviews, and, most important, sales and bargains. Inventory reductions, overstocks, clearance items, free gifts, and more are given ample space here, providing the online equivalent of a factory liquidation sale.

Cataloglink.com

● http://www.cataloglink.com/

Not getting enough mail-order catalogs? There are hundreds of catalogs out there, and they can be found at CatalogLink.com. Visitors can browse the catalog selection by category or use the search engine to find a catalog by name, category, or item. The site features a pick of the week and new catalogs.

This website is the perfect place when you are looking for a special gift. There are catalogs for things that we never thought existed. Items as varied as hand-painted Limoges porcelains, Smucker's jam, and Montecristo cigars can all be found in catalogs featured at this site. Have your credit card handy! Some catalogs are only available at cost, although many are free.

[consumer information]

It's hard to research something you're about to buy. Most of us don't store up several years' worth of consumer information magazines in anticipation of a purchase we might make down the road. It is precisely this kind of consolidated information at which the Internet excels in providing its users.

The Net enables you to cut through the consumer product clutter, giving you easily accessible research information anytime you want it. You don't have to store all those reviews; they're stored for you, at the sites listed below. A few of these names will be familiar to those of you who read consumer product magazines, and their sites serve as excellent resources now that they've headed to the web.

Consumer Product Safety Commission (CPSC)

● http://www.cpsc.gov/index.html

Want to hear about the latest product recalls? Know of a shoddy product that you want to report to the government? If so, this site is for you. The CPSC, an independent federal regulatory agency, helps keep American families safe by reducing the risk of injury or death from malfunctioning consumer products. When we visited, alerts from the CSPC included a sports water bottle whose cap can detach while drinking (a choking hazard), a snowmobile with faulty brakes, and a bicycle with handlebars that can suddenly fall off. Ouch.

You can also report unsafe products. Considering the thousands of new products that come out every year and the number of unexpected injuries that result from the bad few, this is a digital site worth bookmarking.

Consumer Reports Online

● http://www.consumerreports.org/

Just like its print parent, *Consumer Reports* magazine, this site is full of the organization's famous no-bull assessments of new technology and consumer products. There are free articles to read (such as "How to Spot a Problem Oriental Rug"), but to really get the most out of this site, you need to become a member or a subscriber to the magazine. Once you have your password in hand, you can read of the product reports. CR's most popular assessments are those covering new cars and trucks, many of which are included here. A powerful search engine will help you find a vehicle in the style and price range you want by producing a bevy of reports and reviews to read through to get the car of your dreams. The same is true for myriad other products—appliances, electronics, watches, and much more. Indeed, like the magazine, this site is a useful tool to help you avoid buying bad merchandise or getting ripped off by an unscrupulous retailer.

[fashion & clothing]

Fashion Net

● http://www.fashion.net/

Wish you could sit front and center at a fashion industry runway show? Need to know what was featured in the hottest collections for this season? Then pull up your chair and start eyeing the proceedings at Fashion Net. This site is a portal to the entire fashion industry, from its designers and manufacturers to its associations and schools. Sporting excellent video and slick graphics, as well as one of the coolest site maps around, Fashion Net's headings move like they're on a catwalk.

The site is divided into five primary segments: Fashion, Modeling, Beauty, Shopping, and Industry. Under Fashion is a section called Runway Shows, where you can view videos (using QuickTime) of the latest shows. Later, you can discuss who was wearing what in the Live Chat room. Links take you to fashion mags including *Elle, Vogue,* and some two dozen others, as well as to designer sites including Chanel, Dolce & Gabbana, Gucci, and Yves St. Laurent. The Modeling section also has another live chat, in addition to an advice component and links to major modeling agencies. In Industry, there are links to fashion schools, trade publications such as *Women's Wear Daily*, and a set of directories and services tailored to the fashion biz. Beauty and Shopping lead you to the products and their vendors.

[greeting cards]

Virtual Cards
All-4-Free Index

● http://rats2u.com/index.htm/

Need to cheer someone up with that perfect sentiment? Need to do it in the next few minutes? Sending a greeting from the Internet is almost instantaneous and you don't have to hunt around for a stamp.

Thousands of sites make it possible to send virtual greeting cards via e-mail. You simply select a card at one of those sites, insert the name of the recipient, add a greeting, and then submit it. The site notifies the recipient via e-mail that the card is waiting, and he or she logs in with a provided password to see the card.

All-4-Free is a guide to more than 2,000 free virtual greeting card sites containing some 50,000 card selections, arranged by indexes: Holiday and Festival, Special Occasions, Special Interest, and Special Feature. There are also links to sites offering cards relevant to impending dates and a section with more than 5,000 graphics sites for tracking down that special animated gif or screen background. Deciding between a card from Comedy Central's *South Park* or a True Friendship card from Victorian Sentiments may be a no-brainer, but at least you know where to find them.

[shopping for bargains]

One thing really rich and really frugal people have in common: They both like bargains. But the rich pay other people to find deals for them; you can use these websites to get the heads-up on really great deals.

Bottom Dollar

- http://www.bottomdollar.com/

Buyer's Index

- http://www.buyersindex.com/

Shopfind.com

- http://www.shopfind.com/

These three sites are essentially shopper search engines. They allow you to browse through general categories such as books, music, office products, electronics, movies, software, toys, and so on. Or, if you know exactly what you're looking for, you can type it into the search box and the engines will query various sites (including the big ones and some little-known discount warehouses), then show you a ranking of exactly how much each is charging for that product. This has turned up some remarkable—and money-saving—results. For example, we found differences of between $10 and $50 for a Sony 300 CD changer. By working with all three sites, you can scan literally hundreds of millions of products. So, from now on, there is no reason you shouldn't be able to track down the best price for anything. It might not make you feel rich, but it will make you feel smarter.

SOCIETY & CULTURE

[advice and help]

"I've been having an affair with my best friend's fiancee. They're getting married next week. Should I tell him?" All those people who write to newspaper advice columnists have problems. But by the time the advisors get back to these people—they have to sort through letters, write responses, and have them published—well, how much time has passed? Fortunately, e-mail and the Web have speeded up the process of getting advice. And these immensely popular columns translate well to the Net, both as spin-offs of their print form and as Internet-based advice sites.

Advice
General and Personal
Ann Landers

●

http://www.creators.com/lifestyle_show.cfm?columnsName=ala

Dear Abby

● http://www.uexpress.com/dearabby/viewda.cfm

Ann and Abby are twin sisters (born Ester and Pauline Friedman) who for years have been writing dueling advice columns. And now they both have websites that dispense the same content found in their daily—and hugely popular—newspaper columns. On the Web not much is different, except the visuals are much better, and there are archives. And of course, you're reading their columns on your computer, which adds a touch of postmodernism to their decidedly postwar approach to advice giving. You can also e-mail the ladies and buy their books while reading their words of wisdom.

Ask an Expert Page

- http://k12science.ati.stevens-tech.edu/askanexpert.html

When you're looking for help or advice, you invariably hear: "Ask a professional." At this site you can do just that. You can Ask a Valley Forge Expert, Ask a Water Testing Expert, or you can even Ask a Volcanologist: There are about a hundred different professionals in more than a dozen different categories, including science and technology, medicine and health, economy and marketing, literature and language arts, and personal and college advisors. These experts are located at sites ranging from newspaper columns to the Mayo Clinic; the actual Ask an Expert site is part of the New Jersey Networking Infrastructure in Education Project.

Young Adults
Help Me Harlan

- http://helpmeharlan.com/

Young Harlan Cohen is not your normal 30 year old. Offering advice for teens and 20-somethings, his Help Me Harlan column, which appears in over 50 newspapers, is a resource for level-headed feedback.

Given the occasionally puritanical replies and the opening image of Harlan's head, one gets the impression he's a clean-cut kid. He even edits out the dirty words. But if your 16-year-old were seeking help online, you might prefer he or she come here rather than, say, Savage Love.

Unlike most teen advice columns, Harlan's is not dominated by Q&As about sex, though he doesn't shirk the topic—he's fielded questions about everything from cheating lesbians to preteen promiscuity. But he also covers issues as diverse as parental relations, platform shoes, smoking, and hairy legs. And to encourage feedback, Harlan asks a Question of the Week (e.g.,"What's your worst roommate horror story?" and "Do you think we should bomb Iraq?"), printing all the responses he can. A well-researched Support Services page entitled "Go, Help Yourself" offers links to sites that address a wide spectrum of problems that plague the young, including eating disorders, drugs and alcohol, sexual abuse, and mental illness.

Savage Love

● http://www.thestranger.com/current/savage.com/

Welcome to Savage Love—and to serious advice on bedroom topics that would give Dear Abby and Ann Landers twin heart attacks. Dan Savage is known for offering sex advice that runs from the sardonic to the, well, savage. A bare-it-all columnist, Savage takes on any and all queries of the sexual sort, unabashedly addressing heterosexual horseplay, homosexual health, bondage benefits, and contraceptive concerns. And if you need more, you can e-mail the Savage One himself. His weekly advice is syndicated in various papers around the country, but the bonus at his website is that you can get the past month's columns in an archive and a direct link to his e-mail.

[apartments]

Rent.net

● http://www.rent.net/

Finding a decent, affordable apartment ranks right up there with having a root canal and doing your income taxes, especially if you live in a major metropolitan area.

Several sites on the Net offer assistance in finding apartments, including www.aptguides.com, and www.apartment search.com, and Rent.net ranks among the best with an excellent nationwide apartment guide along with a full complement of moving resources and online utilities.

Many options are available at Rent.net: apartments & rentals, temporary furnished suites (aka corporate housing), vacation rentals, and senior housing (retirement homes, assisted living, etc.). Additional resources include self-storage (thousands of facilities in North America), moving companies (products and services), and owner and manager listings. There are also links to entities you need to actually effect a physical move, some of which offer online discounts:Furniture Rental, Truck Rental, Yellow Pages, Movers/Shipping, Career Center, Insurance Center, City Guides/Local Info, Credit Center, and Auto Center.

To find an apartment, you have to drill down through a series of pages: state, city, and neighborhood. Only one city charges a fee to view its listings—New York City. Maps are available for viewing at the city level; and once you've narrowed your search, the site offers various pulldown menus that let you check out local resources and cost of living in that area. Depending on the market and the unit you're interested in, you can click on links to brokers, managers, owners, and so on, as well as photos and online tours. Finally, Rent.net's homepage features regularly updated articles about moving, with topics such as reviewing your credit report and planning tips. Now if there was only a site that made root canals this easy.

[astrology]

Astrocenter.com

● http://www.astrocenter.com/

How unique are you? How were the heavens aligned at your birth? Were the angels screaming or laughing? Astrocenter.com answers these burning questions and many more. Whether you are a skeptic or a die-hard astrology buff, you have to admit that the concept of an entire site devoted to these questions is intriguing. Maybe. But where else can you get a personalized and customized astrology reading, a personality assessment, and career information all in the same place? The site allows you to sign up for a daily email horoscope and to create a profile so you are greeted with a personalized horoscope page. You can even create horoscopes for your family.

Numerology and Chinese Astrology are offered in addition to traditional horoscopes. If you are a skeptic, the site is fun. If you are a believer, you will find lots of information that may help you navigate your life as easily as you'll navigate this site.

The Ultimate Original Science

- http://www.the-ultimate.com/space/astro.htm

With free time getting more tightly crunched by the daily grind, even taking a quick break to read your horoscope may seem like a luxury. Relax, the interactive mini-horoscopes are here. Bookmark this site for your daily loveline and find out if there is any hope in the cosmos.

At this site you will find some hard-core descriptions of certain astrological tenets (of an almost academic bent) coupled with somewhat kitschy graphics and an accessible approach. That said, there is a garland of Martian fire-flowers' worth of data, and some of the links are especially good relative to historical information and compatibility data.

[babies]

BabyCenter

● http:/www.Babycenter.com/

Need a baby name? Want to work for a company that is baby-friendly? There's a lot of things to learn about the world of babies, whether it's during preconception, pregnancy or actual parenting. A lot of that elusive parental knowledge can be found at BabyCenter.

By becoming a member of BabyCenter (it's free), you can create a personal page that tracks both your and your baby's development from pregnancy through toddler years, while providing you with helpful data every step of the way. From there you can visit any of the site's four categories—Preconception, Pregnancy, Baby, Toddler—each of which are filled with articles and advice from industry experts. A particularly brilliant area is the Tools & Calculators section, which has everything from an ovulation and ideal pre-baby weight calculator to a lullaby library and immunization scheduler.

A gateway section offers links to dozens of resources for health and safety, prenatal and postpartum care, child development, family, breastfeeding, special interest and fertility. Additionally, BabyCenter has a great online store for baby products (i.e., high chairs, strollers and car seats), toys, maternity and baby clothes, and a gift registry. There are images and detailed descriptions for everything it sells. If you've got a baby, or you've got one on the way, bookmark this site before all the screaming starts.

Baby Products.com

● http://www.baby-products.com/

Outfitting a baby or toddler is like getting an astronaut suited up for a moon mission—and nearly as complicated. At Baby Products.com you can view product information—from plane seats to double strollers and Chinese prefolded diapers—as presented by the manufacturers, then make head-to-head comparisons of these products (using a truly cool Shockwave control panel that calls up pictures and descriptions), create a budget for your baby and/or preschooler needs, and order the products. Sure beats having to wander down miles of aisles looking for this stuff—with the little tykes in tow.

Breastfeeding
La Leche League (LLL)

● http://www.lalecheleague.org

Breastfeeding is the way nature intended newborns to be nourished, but sometimes even nature needs help. New moms have difficulty getting their infants to breastfeed, and need coaching and a little assistance for things to flow smoothly. LaLeche League (LLL) is an excellent resource for mothers with nursing questions. Visitors can scan a collection of periodicals, find an LLL leader in their area, connect with a Web group of other mothers, find products, get information in different languages, and link to other websites.

The Newborn Page

● http://kidsource.com/kidsource/pages/Newborns.html

New parents crave information on their new occupations almost as much as they crave sleep. Once they realize that sleep is out of the question, they can come here for advice on infant health and education. The Newborn Page delivers sound and straightforward information for both new and seasoned parents. Articles and discussion forums address issues such as newborn safety, learning, health and medicine, preventative care and nutrition, and product recalls. There is also a hefty What's New section with links to news and articles of interest to parents, and a section of related websites with complete descriptions and a star rating system.

The Newborn Page is a subset of the Kidsource.com site, which provides information on children from one year old to the teens.

[charities]

National Charities Information Bureau

● http://www.give.org/

Thousands of charities around the world, from the Red Cross to Greenpeace, need money every day. Choosing between them—let alone finding them—is a difficult task for anyone wanting to donate money to a worthy cause. The Better Business Bureau has set up this site with the express purpose of helping people become informed givers. The site also details its "Standards in Philanthropy," which include criteria ranging from accountability to types of fund-raising efforts to annual reporting.

[conspiracy]

JKF Assassination Web Page

● http://ourworld.cs.com/mikegriffith./id3s.htm

There is enough data on the JFK Assassination on this site to keep historical revisionists and Oliver Stone busy for years. The main page is set up as an index that points to dozens of full articles within the site. Along the way, webmaster Mike Griffith presents incredible points of minutiae (a full page on the wounding of bystander James Tague), as well as categories of broader interest—such as how to buy the Zapruder film and links to other JFK sites around the Net. The site also keeps up with recent developments, theories, and people related to the conspiracy.

[crime and criminal justice]

Yahoo! has more than 100 categories of crime. This staggering number reflects the broad general—or perhaps morbid—interest in the topic. From serial killers to assassinations to the monitoring of city police forces to sensational trials, the awareness of all aspects of law enforcement and the criminal justice system has never been so prevalant in our society. The Web caters to that interest with thousands of sites, many related to specific crimes and advocacy groups. The sites listed here are the most interesting and intriguing Web approaches to the exploration of crime. They also tend to capture our attention with the same sense of voyeurism that true crime stories do, which makes them unusually entertaining despite our best efforts to remain detached and objective.

Anatomy of a Murder

● http://tqd.advanced.org/2760/homep.htm

Say you've been accused of a murder you didn't commit, and now you're getting ready to stand trial. The case against you is strong, and the only way to avoid a state-sponsored trip to meet Mr. Death may to be to plead to lesser charges. What do you do?

This is the premise of Anatomy of a Murder. Billed as a trip through the United States legal system, this site places the visitor in the role of a defendant in a murder case. Laid out as a story in twelve chapters, each chapter follows the chain of events involved in the discovery, investigation, arrest, and prosecution phases of a homicide. What makes this site so compelling is that each chapter offers a link to a Facts Behind the Story page that goes into incredible detail about what actually has taken place during the events described in the chapter. You'll learn the ranks that a police officer has to go through to become a detective, the types of fingerprinting powder used in homicides (four different kinds are described), the various forms and reports filed by the police, and definitions from the criminal code.

The site makes good use of photographs, and even offers "mood music" that serves as a soundtrack to each chapter. This site was created by students at Cranford High School in New Jersey as part of ThinkQuest (this group of websites is discussed under the ThinkQuest entry in the SCIENCE section).

APBOnline

● http://www.apbonline.com/

Think you can help the FBI track down serial killers? Want to have a go at figuring out what makes murderous lunatics tick? Then set your browser to APBOnline. In addition to putting you into the thick of investigations (we'll get to that in a minute), this site is like having a police scanner on your computer. Slick and engaging, APB-Online is described as "The source for police and crime news, information, and entertainment," and it walks the very fine line between informing and entertaining.

Of the site's nearly 20 different categories the most fascinating component is the Unsolved section. According to the editor of the site, Unsolved is "an interactive true-crime mystery—a new online journalism genre combining law enforcement source documents, enterprise reporting by APB's reporters and contributors, compelling narratives, interactive analytical tools, and the legendary profiling skills of ex-FBI Special Agent John Douglas." Indeed, Douglas, part of the FBI team that received national recognition for their psychological profiling of killers (and was glorified in the Thomas Harris books featuring Hannibal Lechter) gives this site his whole-hearted endorsement.

A huge amount of evidence is available on the site, including missing person reports, data on victims, timelines, and more. After reviewing this data, users can create their own profile of the possible killer (using pulldown menus), then compare them with

Douglas' assessment, and participate in discussion groups about the case. The first case posted was the Green River Murder case in Seattle, one of the longest running manhunts in the United States. An extremely interesting intellectual exercise, whether or not you're an armchair criminologist.

Bureau of Justice Statistics (BJS)

● http://www.ojp.usdoj.gov/bjs/welcome.htm

In 1996, the state and federal courts combined convicted a total of more than 1 million adults of felony crimes. With these kinds of numbers to deal with, the BJS is a statistician's dream site. A complete repository of information relating to U.S. crime—from statistics and analysis to trends and forecasting—the homepage lists more than 500 pages contained in the site, as well as intensive data sections. The Statistics About section includes Crimes and Victims, Criminal Offenders, the Justice System (Law Enforcement, Courts and Sentencing, Expenditure and Employment, etc.), Special Topics, and Crime & Justice Data from Other Sources. the Information to View contains Key Facts at a Glance, Data to Download, and Publications and Press Releases. A third section contains information about the BJS and its criminal record system.

The content is straightforward, covering topics such as homicide trends in the United States, victim characteristics (the elderly, teenagers, etc.), pretrial release and detention, and criminal case processing. The majority of the information is in text form, although dozens of color graphs present the data in easily digestible visual form. And a section of downloadable data is available to the user in spreadsheets; these files include crime, justice, and sociodemographic variables for use in analysis of crime. The BJS is yet another example of a well designed, extremely informative government-sponsored website—even if it is about the worst aspect of society.

Zeno's Forensic Page

● http://forensic.to/forensic.html

Forensics can be defined as the application of science to the law. It is used across the entire spectrum of the law, from examination of evidence found at crime scenes to the presentation of data during trials. Zeno's Forensic Page is an exhaustive index of several hundred forensic sites on the Internet, divided by categories, which include Forensic Science, Forensic Medicine, Forensic Psychiatry/Psychology, and Forensic Literature. Within these headings are sections on a vast number of topics, such as Arson, Handwriting, Hairs & Fibers, Toolmarks/Shoeprints/Tires/Locks, Toxicology, DNA/Serology, expert witnesses, associations, laboratories, and so on.

The site is maintained by Zeno Geradts, a forensic scientist at the Netherlands Forensic Science Laboratory (note the "to" in the URL).

[death and dying]

Coping & Planning
Death and Dying

● http://www.death-dying.com/

Discussions of death and dying are taboo in many daily social situations. As such, in our society it can be difficult to express grief. Death and Dying provides a simple online outlet for those facing perhaps life's greatest challenge. The site's mission is "to offer a safe haven to those who have lost a loved one to death, are anticipating the loss of a loved one, or who are facing their own death in the near future." To that end, D and D offers a number of ways to deal with those issues, from topic-specific chat rooms and message boards to newsletters and articles to discussions of legal issues. D and D, operated by a staff of professionals and volunteers, promises anonymity for the grieving. There's a Kids

Only section for young people dealing with grief, as well as a Fun Zone with an Escape Place that offers activities designed to take visitors' minds off of the stressful topic at hand. And, not surprisingly, one of D and D's most active areas is the Near-Death Experiences page.

DeathNet

● http://www.rights.org/deathnet/

Most societies are increasingly struggling with "dying with dignity" and "right to die" issues. This site looks at these issues head-on, without blinking. DeathNet brings together various sites that address the legal, moral, medical, historical, and cultural aspects of death. There are a dozen sections, including The Kevorkian File (favorable and opposing views), Art & Science of Suicide, the Living Will Center, Student Research Center, ERGO Center, Last Rights Information Center, Media Monitor, Tender Mercies, and a Garden of Remembrance. DeathNet will please some and upset others, but its honest look at our cultural attitudes towards dying—especially as it relates to terminal illness—should be required reading for anyone who feels strongly about the subject.

[genealogy]

Cyndi's List

● http://www.cyndislist.com/

Arcadian, Cajun & Creole, Prisoners & Outlaws, Nobility & Royalty: Those are just some of the categories you'll find at Cyndi's List, a massive index of Internet genealogy links (currently about 115,000 of them) maintained by Cyndi Howells, who has turned genealogy hunting on the Web into an art form. The information here includes many U.S. census records from the nineteenth and twentieth centuries, so be prepared to spend some serious time plumbing its depths. The links are broken down into categories that define the term melting pot: Handwriting, Methodist, Wills & Probate, Deeds, and Homesteads barely scratch the surface. With its broad scope, this site may lead you to find those missing branches in your family tree.

Family Search

● http://www.familysearch.com/

Need a copy of the 1851 British census? Got a feeling that there's blue blood running through your veins? Look no further, the answers are here for you. Compiled by the Church of Latter Day Saints (the Mormons), this premier genealogy site provides a starting point for tracing your family genealogy. Like any good genealogy site, there is a fast and powerful search engine that can give you quick feedback on relatives near and far. This writer plugged in his family name and was rewarded with two quick hits. Then again, the site posts a disclaimer noting that information sent in is not necessarily verified and should serve really as the beginning of a search, not the conclusion.

You can search through records of every type imaginable: census, death, court, military, religious, cultural, location, land and property, and many more. Family Search will link you to other Internet sites to expand your quest.

If you want to delve further into the site, you have to become a member. Thereafter, myriad options are available, such as the capability to collaborate with others to find family members, or to list your own genealogy website. There's even an online shop, where you can find genealogy software, including rare records. A fascinating site for both casual and serious genealogical enthusiasts.

Genealogy.com

● http://www.genealogy.com/

Genealogy.com explains "how easy and entertaining tracing your family history can be. Family history is a story of heroes and cowards! It includes adventure, drudgery, violence, tenderness, and thousands of yet-to-be-written stories about the unconquerable human spirit. These tales are not about fictitious characters, but about real people—your family."

Well, maybe this isn't your family exactly, but it still gives you basic tips for launching an ancestry search. You should be aware that a serious genealogical search isn't as easy as popping a name into a database. It's a fairly time-consuming task that can just begin on the Web, as Genealogy.com points out. But this site has many valuable and useful resources for that undertaking. For example, the basic search engine claims to have access to more than 325 million names from various sources. The SiteFinder is a comprehensive directory of genealogy sites on the Internet, featuring 71,829 categorized and cross-indexed links, with full descriptions. GenForum is a large message board system where you can post messages for others to read and reply, some of which, hopefully, may be relatives. If this isn't enough, there's a whole cache of helpful articles to help with matters like translating foreign documents, conducting online research, or icebreaking techniques for that overdue family reunion.

[girls]

Girl Zone

● http://www.girlzone.com/

What do girls want? That's been the subject of songs and story for centuries. This site seems to have answered the question for girls in cyberspace. Fun, loud, and chatty, this is just the kind of place you'd expect a websurfing teenage girl to hang out, especially if they want a lot of well-delivered, sound advice from writers who act as peers and speak from their own experiences.

There are a number of "rooms" to visit at Girl Zone, including Bodyopolis, Innercity, Around Town, and Downtown (note the city theme). Topics include articles on body, college, careers, opportunities, volunteering, film and music reviews, and Hollywood gossip. For example, in Around Town, an article titled "Girls Just Want to Have Funds?" offers sensible advice (like the kind parents constantly give in the wrong tone of voice) on managing money, impulse buying, and writing checks, all presented in teenspeak.

Other areas encourage communication and sharing of thoughts. Generally, the topics of the bulletin boards in the Girl Zone chat areas range from how to express your anger, to dreams, ideas, relationships, and body image.

There are some general rules for using the different chat areas, which, by the way, should be used by all kids on the Net; such as not giving out e-mail addresses, sticking to the topic, and skipping the bad language. Following in this theme is the Girl Zone Guide to the Internet, which offers practical and smart advice (again, from a peer's viewpoint). Teens can also sign up for free e-mail and shop for books and accessories. In short, Girl Zone encourages girls to make responsible choices and take charge of their lives—rrrright on!

YAHOO! ALSO LISTS: [girls]

- **http://www.agirlsworld.com/**
A Girl's World Online Clubhouse: explore the clubhouse, meet new friends, learn about grown-up women's exciting jobs, and share stories.
- **http://www.girlgeeks.com/**
Girl Geeks? The Female Side of Computing: explore the roles of women in computing in the past, present, and future. Includes video clips that need Quicktime or RealMedia.
- **http://www.health.org/gpower/index.htm**
Girl Power: diaries, games, puzzles, interviews with famous women. Girl Power is the power to be anything you want to be.
- **http://www.girlsplace.com**
Girl's Place: about social-minded, multi-cultural teen-age girls.
- **http://www.girlslife.com**
Girls' Life: this great site contains articles and features from the magazine as well as Web-only content, such as a help section, a place for you to be a critic, and much more.
- **http://www.gchannel.com**
girlzChannel: check out a channel just for girls. Get advice, play some Shockwave games, or just hang out.
- **http://www.gogirlmag.com/**
Go, Girl!: dedicated to getting girls and women of all ages and fitness levels involved in sports.
- **http://www.gURLwURLd.com/**
www.gurlwurld.com: website by, for, and about middle school girls. Read their thoughts about their all-girl history class, meet the TechGrrlz, and read quotations from famous women in history.

[gun safety]

The Gun Page

- http://www.prairienet.org/guns

We had a difficult time finding any site that really promoted gun safety. Given that guns are legal in the United States, and not likely to be outlawed anytime soon, we think there should be more Internet discussion on how to deal with the fact that people are going to own and use guns. Therefore, we're listing only one site in this section, namely The Gun Page. It is the only site on the Web right now that begins with a Safety First lesson and has links to other safety-related resources. If U.S. citizens are going to have guns and learn more about them, everyone interested in guns should start here.

[holidays & observances]

Holidays on the Net

● http://www.holidays.net/

From High Holy Days and Halloween to Mardi Gras and Mother's Day, it seems every day is a holiday somewhere. Holidays on the Net provides in-depth, interesting, and often amusing information about a wide range of national, religious, and nonsectarian occasions for frivolity.

The site has stupendous animated sections on holiday origins, plus celebration facts, party ideas, sound and song files,

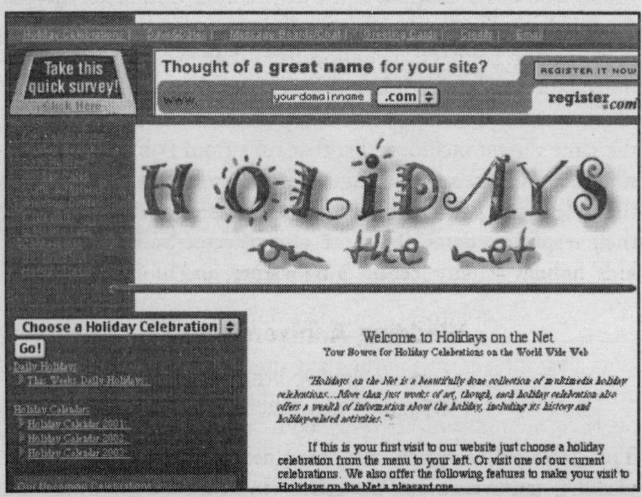

downloadable games, and crafts projects. Each holiday is presented as its own "site within a site," giving you a one-stop resource center for your holiday preparations. For instance, read about the Druids' influence on Halloween, then print out pictures for the kids to color; or send a virtual Halloween greeting card via e-mail, play some scary music on your computer, and get the complete text of "Eye of newt and toe of frog . . ."

The site's search engine will link you to websites related to specific holidays, or to calendars, horoscopes, message boards, virtual greeting cards, and selected books.

The Worldwide Holiday & Festival Site

- http://www.HolidayFestival.com/

Ever been in Paris on July 14th and felt like you were alone in the city, frustrated to find everything closed? Nothing ruins a trip abroad faster than learning your dream vacation has been put on hold by a holiday that you know nothing about.

The Worldwide Holiday & Festival Site can tell you in advance, who observes what, and when. Under Countries, there is an alphabetical list, and each entry links to individual locales and their specific holidays, including fixed-date events (such as national observances), and those whose dates change (religious holidays, seasonal festivals, etc.). The Religions category works in the same way: it includes a list that runs from Baha'i to Zoroastrianism. The site's search engine also identifies all the countries that celebrate a particular event, such as Easter or Ramadan, and their respective dates. This site also offers a business guide, a kids' holiday activity section, a bookstore, and more.

Wedding Anniversaries

- http://www.chipublib.org/008subject/005genref/giswedding.html

This single page displays a list of traditional and modern gifts for wedding anniversaries. Compiled by the librarians at the

Chicago Public Library, it covers every year from the first to the fiftieth, and every five years until 100.

In case you were wondering, the traditional gift for a one hundredth wedding anniversary is a 10-carat diamond. Start saving.

Party Planning
Birthday Party Ideas

● http://www.birthdaypartyideas.com/

The Birthday Party Ideas site is exactly what is says, a list of ideas for kid's birthday parties. There are a number of venues to choose from, including Aquarium, Ice Skating, Miniature Golf, Theme Restaurant, Tea, Racing, Animal Park, and more. There is a short discussion on ways to optimize the party, as well as invitation and game ideas. There are also links to products to enhance the experience; for example, paddleballs and a Beach Boys CD for a party at the beach (a large chunk of the site is dedicated to displaying these products).

You can get more ideas from a collection of reader-submitted ideas (rainforest parties, back to the '50s, etc.) link to party supply houses on the Net. So—dare we say it?—party on.

Party 411

● http://www.party411.com/

For something that's supposed to be fun, throwing a party can be a pretty damned stressful event. To keep you from losing your cool—or calling 911—dial into the Party 411 site instead. It can help you do everything right when giving a party for any of the following occasions: Anniversary, Baby Shower, Bar/Bat Mitzvah, Benefit, Birthday, Corporate Event, Graduation, Holidays, and Roasts & Toasts. Within these sections are articles and info under these headings: Party Themes, Party Games, and Planning Guides. There's also a forum where you can Ask the Experts (the Fashion Queen, the Party Doctor, the Party Girl, the Game Girl, and the Etiquette Queen). There you will find tips, facts, guidance—and reassurance—about all aspects of throwing a party, from choosing the right type of invitation to placing the fork on the correct side of the plate (always on the left, by the way).

The main page also features sections on Product News (the latest innovations in party paraphernalia), Party Themes, Specific Holidays and Special Events, Party Favors, Party Talk (a discussion forum), and links to "party pros" in different cities.

[kids]

There are tons of great kids sites on the web. Yahooligans (http://www.yahooligans.com/) remains one of the very best in this category in addition to the ones listed below.

Ask Jeeves for Kids

● http://www.ajkids.com/

Have your kids reached an age where you can't help them with their homework anymore? We suggest you go to Ask Jeeves for Kids (part of Ask.com). At this site, you ask any question—such as "How does a lightbulb work?" or "What is an elephant's trunk made out of?"—and the site returns several answers to your question and asks you to select the one that best meets your needs. You also have the option to narrow your request—an impressive feature. This site is a blast for kids of all ages, so pull up a chair—you may be here awhile.

Disney

● http://disney.go.com/

All together now: "Who's the keeper of the site that's made for you and me? M-I-C, K-E-Y, M-O-U-S-E." You guessed it—the mother of all mouse sites presents enticements and entertainment related to every aspect of the vast Disney empire. The homepage alone offers more than a dozen areas of interest, ranging from Movies, Music, and TV Shows to Games, Shopping, and Stories. Connections take you to the Disney Channel, Radio Disney, the many other Go Networks.

An Audio and Video button leads to a listing of Disney movies trailers for viewing, and audio samples of interviews from Radio Disney. Menus allows the user to jump easily between areas, one of which, Mouse House Jr., presents animated activities for the youngest members of your household.

For kids a bit older, fun family activities such as Ludwig Von Drake's Science & Magic Club can be found at J. Cricket U. And parents should visit the Vacations section, where they can read about trips to visit the Magic Kingdom (see our review under TRAVEL), plan an itinerary, and even make reservations.

Heck, while you're spending your hard-earned leisure-time dollars, besides visiting the Disney Store Online (where you can search for products by category, character or movie), why not head to Investor Relations and take part in the Walt Disney Company Investment Plan? You can try to make back some of that money you're spending on Pluto action figures.

Kids Domain

● http://www.kidsdomain.com/

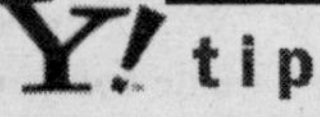

With online games, newsletters, contests, and more, Kids Domain is a great site for kids. But the name is misleading—the vast majority of Kids Domain is dedicated to information parents will find of interest, especially as it relates to computing. There's an archive of 600-plus software re-

Y! tip

When typing URLs, be sure to enter the correct suffix: .com, .net, .org., .edu, etc.

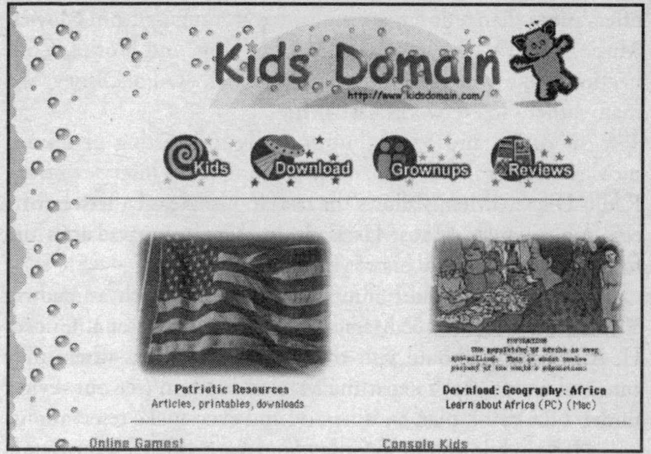

views and links to more than 1,500 downloadable programs and hundreds of other sites, all for kids and their families.

Four sections make up the site: Kids, Grownups, Reviews, and Downloads. For the most part, kids will prefer the Kids zone, playing games, downloading pages to color or demos to check out, or linking to an activity site. Parents will find the Kid Safety on the Web section in the Grownups Place area useful, as it provides information and links on many kinds of surfing protection. The homepage is regularly updated and lists new reviews, contests, and downloads, plus several featured games.

An area is devoted to helping kids learn to program computers that is full of tips on graphics and Web pages; it also has adult-oriented parenting and educational links. A type-in-the-box search engine is provided, and users can subscribe to the site's newsletter to get the latest information on Kids Domain updates. Probably you, more than your kids, will return to this site to take advantage of this impressive subject-categorized (math, language, etc.) catalog of shareware, freeware, and commercial software reviews and links.

[men]

Maxim

● http://www.maximmag.com/

If one corner of the Web can be considered a haven for a boys-only club, Maxim is it. Maxim's specialties are smarmy attitude and photos of fabulous "babes"—with their clothes on. That should be enough to get most guys into this site. From there they can read the articles. Maxim online provides a scaled-down version of the low-brow high-gloss men's magazine with all the departments, features, and columns found in the table-top model.

A section of the site is Girls of Maxim, which links you to a catalog of women who have been featured in *Maxim*. The homepage also contains a cheeky Joke of the Day, which is selected from reader submissions (a form is provided). The current and past issues of the magazine are available for browsing, as are 20 "classic articles" from the publication's relatively short past. Of course, contact info for both readers and potential advertisers is provided.

[mensa]

Mensa International

● http://www.mensa.org

If you can easily answer: "If it were two hours later, it would be half as long until midnight as it would be if it were an hour later, so what time is it now?" you can probably be a member of the Mensa society; if you're among the other 98 percent, you can only go visit the group's website. Whether member or outsider, the Mensa International site provides a clear understanding of what the group is all about and how to contact its members.

Are you the only SAT-topper who's into tap dancing? Is it okay that you never made it through health class? If you're a lonely Mensan and want to find out who else is out there, where they are, and what responsibilities come with being so gosh-darn smart, this site is the place for you. Come page through Mensa Information and Membership Benefits, or read the 3,700-word Mensa Constitution to find out about others who can match your Stanford-Binets. From this site you can also contact a Mensa pal in any one of 42 countries, subscribe to a newsgroup, or find a local meeting.

Most fun for all, though, is the Mensa Workout, where any user can take a 30-question, 30-minute test. (The test results for this visitor were headed with the caveat, "If you decide to take the Mensa test, you will not qualify for membership.") The real question begged by this site is whether you should try to join or just go pound your head against the wall. But you're smart enough to know that already.

[moving & relocating]

They say that moving is one of the five most stressful events in an individual's life. We're not exactly sure who "they" are, but we are inclined to agree. When you undertake to move, everybody has opinions, but it seems that no one has hard facts. With help from the sites listed below, you can make moving less of a chore and more of an adventure. Not that moving can ever be truly pleasant, but using these resources take some of the edge off.

HomeFair

● http://www.homefair.com/

You want to move; you just have to get out of the town you're in and find a nice place to live somewhere else—maybe anywhere else—in the United States or abroad. If you just knew where to start . . . HomeFair is a great place to begin to find out what it's going to take to live in major towns and cities around the globe. The site is essentially a set of tools—really calculators—that provide comparative living data such as cost-of-living differences between U.S. and international cities and a list of 10 cities that may be good choices for you based on lifestyle preferences, mortgage and moving rates, etc. The Mortgage section is surprisingly deep, containing dozens of calculators and articles to help you wade through this tortuous process.

There are sections on community and consumer info, as well as special offers from furniture rental and moving companies. Free crime reports and school reports are also available for those who aren't ready to be hounded by real estate agents. The simple design of this site does an impressive job of helping you navigate what can be a life-wrenching event.

Monster Moving

● http://www.monstermoving.com/

If the thought of leaving your moribund 1960 Thunderbird behind when you relocate to Zimbabwe is more than you can bear, than Monster Moving.com, a subdivision of Monster.com, can find you someone who will be more than happy to help you get it over there. You can use a variety of search mechanisms to find companies that can move everything from dogs to documents anywhere in the world. The results comprise a list of companies that meet your search criteria, with descriptions of their services, contact information, and hotlinks.

[mythology & folklore]

Bulfinch's Mythology

● http://www.bulfinch.org/

"Mythology is the handmaid of literature, and literature is one of the best allies of virtue and promoters of happiness. Without a

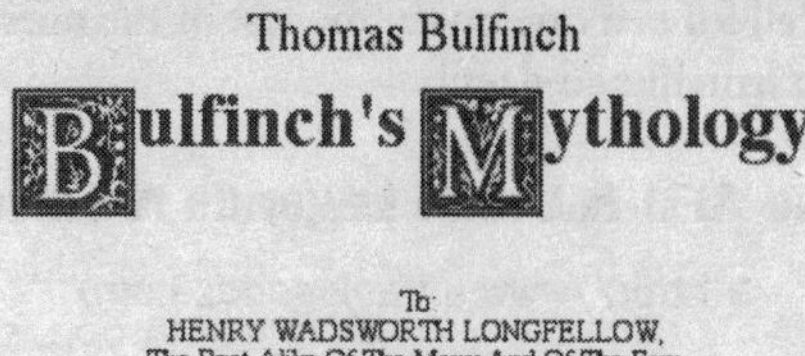

knowledge of mythology, much of literature cannot be understood and appreciated." So begins this amazingly detailed look at mythological tales of the Greeks, Romans, King Arthur, and Charlemagne, as originally compiled by American author Thomas Bulfinch (1796–1867). In addition to the text on the individual myths and characters, each story has numerous links that lead to footnotes or detailed maps that contain more levels of information about the ancient world's favorite gods and goddesses.

Thomas Bulfinch
Bulfinch's Mythology
To:
HENRY WADSWORTH LONGFELLOW,
The Poet Alike Of The Many And Of The Few,
This Attempt To Popularize
Mythology,
And Extend The Enjoyment Of Elegant Literature,
Is Respectfully Inscribed.
AUTHOR'S PREFACE
UPDATES
THOMAS BULFINCH
Volume I
THE AGE OF FABLE
OR STORIES OF GODS AND HEROES

The depth of information here is dazzling and complements Bulfinch's original work perfectly. With a scholarly eye to detail and friendly interface, this is definitely not a "hit or myth" site. In the story of "Meleager and Atalanta," for example, if you click on the kingdom of calyton where Meleager was prince, you are brought to a map page. This map contains locations specific to the story. Click on any of these areas and it will reveal another piece of the story's puzzle. If you then press on the Greek city of Agrinion, you go to a page about its Archaeological Museum with pictures of the museum's most important and relevant objects. This is all for just one myth; the rest of the tales are equally lavished with insight and detail.

The AFU & Urban Legends Archive

● http://www.urbanlegends.com/

Did you know that Walt Disney was frozen just before his death so that he would be resuscitated once a cure for cancer was found? Did you know that the Procter & Gamble symbol was created to reflect the company's pact with Satan? Did you know that you can see a cast member hanging himself from a tree in a scene from *The Wizard of Oz*?

Not.

These are all urban legends, those famous stories that "really happened to a friend of my brother's college roommate's dad" and other untraceable parties. This archive allows you to search for the most popular ones by category, which includes headings such as Animals, Celebrities, Collegiate, Death, Disney, Food, Medical, Movies, Products, Sex, Songs, TV, and others. Hey, and did you know that Ozzy Ozborne once bit the head off a bat? Uh, well, that one is actually true.

By the way, AFU stands for alt.folklore.urban, not All F***** Up. That's another urban legend. You can look up additional legends at the Urban Legends Reference Page (http:// www. snopes.com/)

Myth & Legend From Ancient Times To Space Age

● http://www.pibburns.com/myth.htm

From legendary creatures to UFOs, this site offers a broad array of links to sites that delve deep into the mysteries of myth and legend. Webmaster Philip Burns has compiled those esoteric sites into a set of topics that includes Crytozoology, Pirates, Legendary Creatures, Vampires, Werewolves, and more.

Legendary Creatures, for instance, leads to half a dozen sites about dragons, another half dozen on gargoyles, and more than twenty on mermaids. There are also great links to text from Grimm's Fairy Tales, as well as scholarly sites that explore the origins of specific myths.

[occult & paranormal]

The occult and paramornal are two areas of interest—or fear—that we don't usually talk about around the water cooler. There's something just too personal, or perhaps too weird, about these topics, depending on your point of view. In contrast, the Web is an ideal forum for indulging in a passion for, an avocation for, or even a disdain for, those mysterious realms that seem to be beyond understanding.

This category of the book is primarily the domain of the individual—the lone webmaster, as it were—largely because there are precious few organizations in this category with any staying power. So consider yourself forewarned: Good sites come and go, and you'll probably turn up more failed links in your search for the occult and paranormal than in any other area of interest.

That said, there are a few other things to keep in mind when visiting the realms of the occult and paranormal on the Web. Most important, realize that there are two types of people here: those who believe and those who don't. It is easy to detect who is who. Individual homepages usually have specific points of view, and address only one aspect of the genre (ghosts or vampires, for instance). Contrarians and skeptics tend to take on all the issues as a collective, lumping all categories together.

Our selected sites give you the healthiest dose of the category, pro and con. You can decide on the believing or not believing part yourself.

AvatarSearch

http://www.avatarsearch.com/

If you're looking for data on ghosts, witches, religions, werewolves, vampires, and even supplies, you can type in your needs here and be certain to get results. AvatarSearch bills itself as the "Search Engine of the Occult Internet" and has the results to back up its claim.

Like other engines this category-specific site has a complete search engine with pulldown menus for defining Boolean, partial-word, or case-sensitive searches. Results include all the pages found with the search term, a concise summary, and the category it falls under—such as vampirism, mysterious, strange phenomena, paganism and Wicca, and so on. The site also has cool links of the month, which have included Paganpath.com, Satanism.net, and Nocturnal Vision, the online Vampiric Community. Clearly, a wide variety of sites have been compiled under AvatarSearch's occult designation. A graphic calendar enables you to check out events around the Web by date, and provides you with a list—and links—to the sites sponsoring those events.

International Society for Cryptozoology

http://www.izoo.org/isc/

This is the official site of the International Society for Cryptozoology. Far from being a bunch of fanatics hoping to capture the Abominable Snowman, this scholarly group investigates a variety of creatures thought to be either mythical or extinct. The site discusses the discovery of past cryptids, such as the mountain gorilla, the okapi, and the Komodo dragon, and reviews some of the modern "monsters" being looked for, from oversized bipedal primates such as the Yeti and Sasquatch, to more the straightforward, including believed-to-be-extinct marsupials, birds, and carnivores. The site is punctuated with some truly excellent photographs and illustrations of these suspected cryptids.

Skeptic.com

● http://www.skeptic.com/

Ever wonder just what's up with those millennium cults or those alien abductions. Then spend a minute here getting a reality check. This is the homepage of Skeptic.com (publisher of *Skeptic* magazine), a group whose goal it is to present rational and intelligent debate on topics that are usually thought of as not being rooted in logic (alien abductions, conspiracies, etc.).

The Skeptic site is both informational and promotional (the society has members and publishes a magazine, as just noted). A News section takes various publicity seekers to task; also available are articles from back issues of the magazine, newsgroups, a hotline (for which you must enter your e-mail address), and links. The links alone are worth a visit; they point to hundreds of websites that promote skepticism or are guilty of promoting dunder-headed ideas (ranging from Holocaust-denial sites to automatically generated pro-Scientology sites, all of which are designed to swamp search engines).

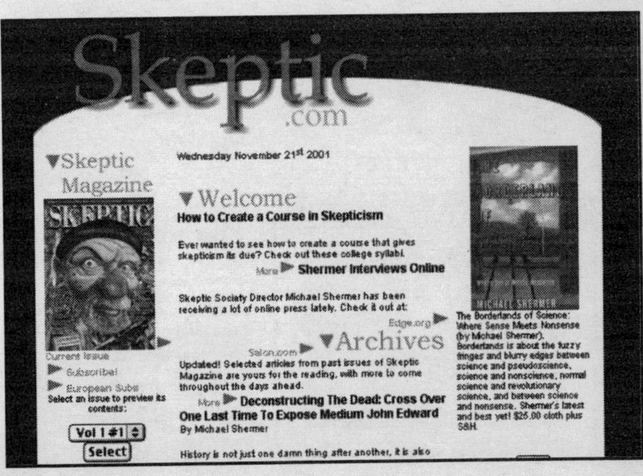

Strange Magazine

● http://www.strangemag.com/

This is a perfect example of what we call a "productivity reduction" site. If you start reading the front page of *Strange Magazine* online, you're bound to find something that catches your interest, and half an hour later, you'll realize you're still reading.

Strange Magazine reports on, well, strange things. It is not a promoter of fanaticism vis à vis unusual occurrences, but rather a reporter of weird stories, whether verified or not. An extensive set of articles describe the strange-but-explainable stories behind such paranormal icons as the Patterson Bigfoot film (where a reporter polls Hollywood makeup experts to explain who was behind the infamous home movie of Bigfoot).

The site is like a Chinese menu: Do you want to start with the article on "Accursed Sites of the World" or look at historical reports of red rain throughout history? Or do you want to read news about newly discovered lifeforms, then go on to the real-life kid who inspired *The Exorcist*? But the real question is, will you ever get back to work?

Vodun

● http://www.religioustolerance.org/voodoo.htm

Vodun is a religion practiced by nearly 60 million people, primarily in the Americas; Voodoo is an evil religion created by Hollywood. This is only one of the demystifying facts you'll find at the informative Vodun (aka Voodoo, Vodoun) page, which provides general background information on Voodoo, as well as more detailed discussions under the headings of Vodun Beliefs, Vodun Rituals, and Evil Sorcery (i.e., zombies). Additional resources are provided, with links and short descriptions of each, plus glossaries, a newsletter, and even a mail-order store specializing in supplies for certain types of Voodoo.

This site is part of the educational resources provided by the Ontario Consultants on Religious Tolerance. If your interest in cults and other religions extends beyond Voodoo, however, see our review under RELIGIOUS CULTS.

[parenting]

Childcare
ParenthoodWeb

● http://parenthoodweb.com/

Sleep: It's the one thing parents covet most for themselves (including this one) *and* their little middle-of-the-night marauders. ParenthoodWeb gets numerous points for dedicating a whole section of its site to this single issue. And that's just one of the dozens of excellent components of this gigantic site, which is several hundred pages deep. It seems to cover everything; there are reviews of the best minivans, support resources for gifted children, and discussions on such topics as "My husband doesn't do enough around the house" and letting kids sleep in your bed. ParenthoodWeb is filled with polls, surveys, and factoids (such as 56 percent of parents think their kids

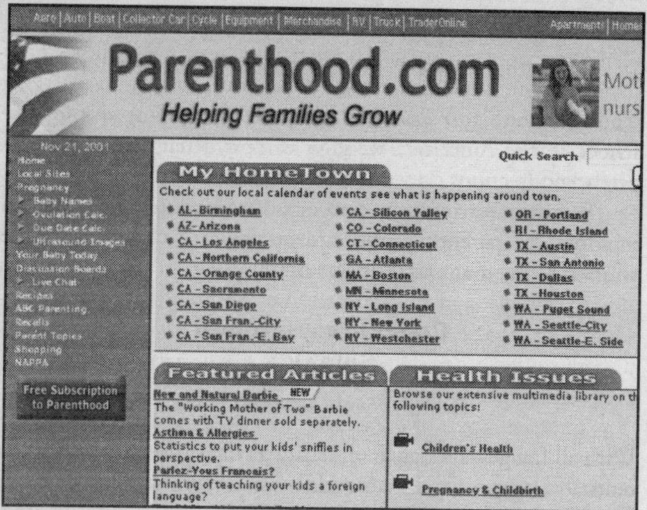

want more time together, but only 10 percent of kids feel that way). There are cribloads of tools, from pregnancy calculators and daycare searches to a baby store menu and recipe section, plus As the Pros sections and articles dealing with, for example, the "Terrible Twos" and separation anxiety. You might sleep better just knowing that this resource exists.

Parentsoup

● http://www.parentsoup.com/

Parentsoup.com is another excellent resource for parents, but it focuses a bit more on education and community issues than ParenthoodWeb. Visitors to this site can search Education Central by individual grades (from pre-K to senior in high school) or by subjects (such as home schooling, standardized testing, fun learning, and more). There are also "supplies": a college calculator, a kid's resume maker, and a school searcher. And there are chat sections for discussing topics ranging from private versus parochial school to raising gifted children.

On the community side, Parentsoup is divided into toddlers, preschoolers, grade schoolers, and teens. Within each of these communities are articles addressing concerns related to that age group (for example, the trials of moving during the school year or concerns over slow learners), chat rooms, and expert advice sections.

Parentsoup's resource category is impressive, with links to hundreds of parenting sites broken down by category. Give yourself a time-out and visit this site.

Computers/Internet
SafeKids

● http://www.safekids.com/

With all the good it has to offer, sadly, the Internet is also a potentially dangerous place for kids. To stay on top of potential problems while children cruise the Web, parents should stop by SafeKids, a site that offers tips, advice, and suggestions to help keep a drive down the information superhighway fun and interesting. It includes a Family Contract for Online Safety (which it recommends posting by the computer), rules for kids (such as not giving out personal information online), guidelines for parents (don't let kids meet in person with anonymous Net friends without your permission), and a discussion of privacy issues. There is also a downloadable PowerPoint presentation that serves as a safety slide show. Finally, there are links to resources such as "Safe Searching Site" and parental control software.

Fatherhood
Stay-at-Home-Dads

● http://www.slowlane.com/

If you're a dad who has left—or is contemplating leaving—the work-a-day world to spend more time with your children, pull off into Slowlane.com, one of the best-named sites on the Web. This online resource for stay-at-home dads (SAHDs, for short) is a great place to read about, link to, or talk about father-related issues. More importantly, Slowlane gives dads the opportunity to talk to other dads via numerous online chats, listservs, e-mail loops, and Web rings. SAHDs from Maine to California have set up their own chat groups to offer local and national support to home daddies.

The Written Word section contains book reviews, articles by and for dads, and links to newsletters and magazines, while the Working at Home section is for those who are, as one article puts it, "working two jobs for half the money." There's also information on the annual At-Home Dad Convention, where dads leave home to talk about staying at home, and several featured columns, such as the smartly titled "Stark Raving Dad." And Slowlane has a gift shop, so you can proudly boast of your SAHD-ness on a T-shirt or sweatshirt.

Fathering Magazine

● http://fathermag.com/

Fathers writing about fatherhood is the premise behind Fathering Magazine. This online monthly magazine contains original-content stories, news, articles, and reports by dads. Recent stories, in topic areas ranging from the serious to the humorous included "Child Custody Scandal" and "The Sleepover"; poetry is also part of each issue. Fathermag actively encourages fathers to write and submit articles for publication.

As in most magazines, this one has book reviews and regular commentary features. Several forums provide discussion groups on topics such as circumcision and children's health, and books about fathering are available in the online store (via Amazon.com), as are CDs, toys and books for kids. Finally, there are links to several children's clothing catalogs.

Foster Parenting
Foster Parents Care
(Child Advocates Resource Exchange)

● http://www.fostercare.org

This is a site for all those involved in the care of foster children, whether parents, guardians, social workers, or temporary caregivers. There are links to associations and foster care organizations, a database of recommended books, and lists of national to regional support groups. The Talkabout section enables both parents and kids to log in to different chat areas and forums to discuss adoption, education, and medical and legal help. Those that have been involved with foster care in the past will want to visit this comprehensive section that helps foster families reunite with each other.

Single Parents
Single Parents World

● http://www.parentsworld.com/

Probably there's no tougher job in the world than being a single parent. This site offers help to those beleaguered moms and dads on everything from leaving for work without a fuss to serious dating. Each section—Kids, Dating, Child Support, Survival, Ideas, etc.—is accompanied by an article addressing the main points of concern for single parents; in most cases, additional links offer more help with general parenting. A single parent's chat room is the place to go when you need to talk about carrying the weight of your family's world on your shoulders.

[people]

Biographies and Profiles
BioBytes

● http://www.biography.com/features/

John Gotti. Bill Gates. Charlie Chaplin. Princess Diana. These people loom large in our memories and daily lives. They might not all be ready for the full multi-volume biography treatment yet, but they are ready for BioBytes, a collection of one-to-two minute audio and video biographies on the Biography.com website.

This is the companion site to the Biography channel, hence a lot of the information is related to the show, including upcoming episodes and listings. There is also a section of excerpts from *Biography Magazine*, including feature articles and "where are they now" profiles. But it's the BioBytes that sets this site apart. Currently, there are a dozen of these clips (which require RealPlayer), packaged as brief looks at some of the big names of our time. Complete with narration and video, they are ideal for introducing viewers to the individuals in the series—and are good examples of what other sites that cover famous people ought to be doing.

Celebrities
CelebSites

● http://www.celebsites.com/

Marilyn Monroe has 41 of them. Marilyn Manson has 278. Websites, that is. CelebSites is where you go when you just can't bookmark enough Alanis Morrisette or George Clooney websites. Using the dedicated celebrity search engine, you can look for a particular celebrity by name, or you can look through celeb categories: actors, actresses, musicians, models, and athletes, plus genres such as movies or TV. There's a feature called Chat Watch that keeps you posted as to when celebs will be "appearing" online.

Historical Biographical Dictionary

● http://www.s9.com/biography/

Biographical Dictionary is a database composed of more than 27,000 topical biographies of famous people for your use in research, homework, or for trivial pursuits. To use it, type in a name, keyword, or date and—voila!—you get a short biography of that person. As a test, we inserted "Cromwell." Not only did we get a write-up on the noted seventeenth-century English politician, but we also got three other entries, including one for the little-known actor James Cromwell (*All in the Family*, *Babe, Star Trek: First Contact*). We then narrowed the search with the Puritan statesman's full name and got this entry: "Cromwell, Oliver (Old Noll), English general and politician; defeated Royalists at battle of Marston Moor 1644; 1st lord protector of England. Nice and concise. More familiar American historical figures are given a little more space: President Woodrow Wilson, for example, got 162 words of coverage. The

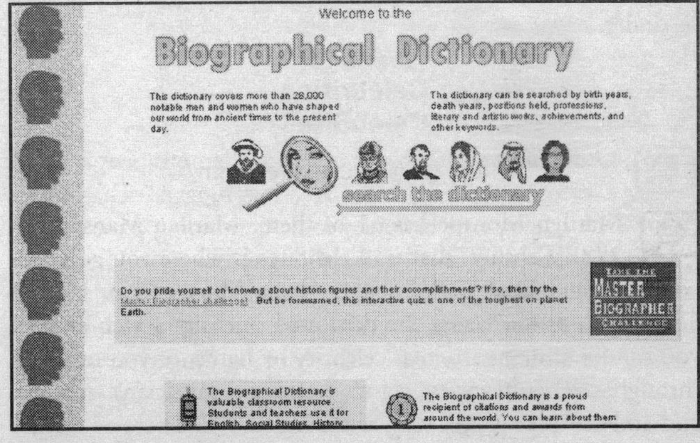

Biographical Dictionary is an ideal starting place to find the facts on the world's most famous—and infamous—folks.

Pictures
Classic Photos

● http://www.classicphotos.com/

[$] Is your den missing something? Perhaps it's a photo of Marlon Brando as Don Corleone? Maybe you need a picture of Grace Kelly in your kitchen . . . or bedroom. If so, visit this big online retailer of reproductions of famous photographs. A huge part of the classic photo collection consists of movie stars, sports legends, and musical acts, so whether you want a great snapshot of the Beatles, Babe Ruth, Bette Davis, or Jimi Hendrix, Classic Photos has an 8x10 or 11x14 image of it for sale.

You can also choose from still pix from movies, such as *Star Wars* and *Gone With the Wind*, among many others. Or, you can get old aerial photos of your neighborhood, vintage photographs of Midwestern cities, or special-interest images from these categories: motorcycles, breweries, police, gas stations, aviation, hunting, Native Americans, old cars and trucks, Coca-Cola, and more. Fans and photographers alike are sure to find something here to meet their glossiest needs.

Who 2?

● http://www.who2.com/

Only one website would categorize famous people under a category called Celebs Missing Fingers. That site is Who 2?, a database of famous people containing photos, bios, and links about your favorite celebrities and historical figures. In addition to straight facts, it classifies the rich and highly visible into strange, but amusing, categories such as Doctors Who Write, the aforementioned Celebs Missing Fingers, Disappearing Acts, Animated Babes, More Audacity Than Cranial Capacity, Presidential Sex Scandals, and These Actors Do Cartoon Voices. We couldn't resist the missing fingers category. There we found M*A*S*H's Gary "Radar" Burghoff, Boris Yeltsin, Telly Savalas, and the Grateful Dead's Jerry Garcia. Who knew?

By and large, this site is designed as a star-studded source. Plug in, say, Madonna and you'll get vital stats, links, a photo collection, and the following brief bio: "Birth Name: Madonna Louise Ciccone. Madonna released her first album in 1983. Once a streetwise bubble-gum-pop ragamuffin, she used a mixture of talent, cleavage, and relentless self-promotion to become one of the most famous recording artists of the 1980s. She has also acted in over a dozen movies. Madonna was married to actor Sean Penn from 1985–1989. Her daughter, Lourdes, was born on 14 October 1996. The father was Madonna's personal trainer, Carlos Leon." Anyone who needs more info should call the material girl herself. Now, "who 2" look up next?

Search WhoWhere?

● http://www.whowhere.lycos.com/

You might well ask: Is this a great people-finding tool . . . or evidence that Big Brother is running the show? The answer probably depends on what you want and why. With WhoWhere? you can plug in someone's name and find his or her address and phone number, and even call them via the Internet. Keep pressing and you'll find a map that shows his or her exact street and e-mail address. You're bound to need to find someone sometime somewhere—a long-lost college chum, relative, former colleague—so you'll want to bookmark this virtual Rolodex. This database is so comprehensive and useful that you might start thinking that WhoWhere? is watching.

Yahoo!'s People Search

● http://www.people.yahoo.com/

The world just got a lot smaller. The King Kong of people finders, this searchable database can help you find that long-lost relative in a jiffy. Plug in the appropriate names (surname required) and optional address info, and the search engine will return a list of candidates, including street addresses and phone numbers. You can further refine the search by adding e-mail addresses and public records.

We popped in names of old school chums and relatives, and were rewarded with lots of info in a hurry, all of it right on target. You could even use this site as an address book. Just bookmark it and refer to it whenever you need to look up a phone number or address in a hurry. Links enable you to phone them up via the Internet, too. You can also perform Yellow Page searches to find businesses in your hometown or across the country.

[pets]

It is often said that owners look like their pets. If this is true, we'd pay cash money to see the people behind the sites that populate (litter?) the Internet. There are thousands of pet sites on the Web (Yahoo! lists 73 categories—not sites, categories) ranging from the kitschy for kitties to the amazing for amphibians. Many of these are e-commerce locales that allow you to buy supplies for your pets; others are tributes to particular animals or breeds. You'd be amazed at how many sites there are for sugar gliders; we didn't even know what they were until we researched this section. Now we're thinking that maybe we should get one to go with the king cobra we can order online, or the equine washing system that we just bought.

On the Web, no animal is too big or too small to be included in the pet category (even spiders), so cuddle up to your favorite ani-

mal and spend some time at these pet-friendly sites where there are no leash laws and no one complains about the litter box.

Acme Pet

● http://acmepet.petsmart.com/

Think of Acme Pet as a virtual pet-lover's universe where pets rule and humans tend to their every need. Dogs, cats, birds, horses, fish, reptiles, and exotics all have their own areas of the yard (marked with their respective paw, claw, and fin prints). The yard comes complete with a library of articles, Clubs & Events and Chat & Forums sections, and a marketplace for buying an animal or its supplies. Feature stories, as well as anecdotes, are solicited from visitors and posted on the site. The community spirit is further enhanced with free e-mail and lots of opportunities to discuss pets to your heart's content. To round out the site, pet jokes and pet trivia (for example, the Southeast

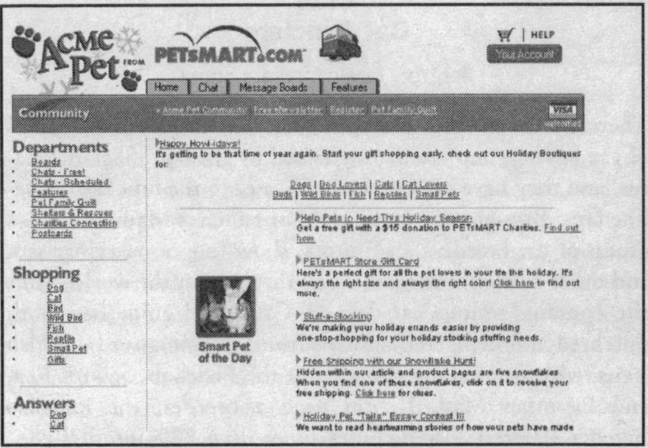

Asian Flying Squirrel can glide up to 350 feet) abound, making this an all-pet, all-the-time kind of place.

Birds
Birds n Ways

● http://www.birdsnways.com/

Any site that bills itself as the complete guide to exotic birds on the Net has to be doing more than winging it. Birds n Ways lives up to its claim, giving complete coverage on finches, budgies, conures, amazons, African greys, cockatoos, macaws, lovebirds, lories, parrots, cockatiels, parakeets, parrotlets, pionus, eclectus, senegals, and meyers. You'll find a collection of links to shopping, chit-chat, general information, legal matters, species data, veterinarians, clubs and associations, and everything else related to our fine-feathered friends.

Cats
Cat Fanciers

● http://www.fanciers.com/

There are cat people, and then there are *cat people.* Members of the latter group are distinguished by their professional status, and they have created a site to cater to the finickiest of feline fans. Brought to you by the Cat Fanciers Mailing List—a group of cat breeders, exhibitors, show judges, veterinarians, and other ailurophiles (cat lovers) throughout the world—this site contains serious cat data. A Cat Breed guide lists both purebred and pedigreed animals from Abyssinians to Turkish Vans, with stops along the way for the Pixiebob, Selkirk Rex, and Egyptian Mau. If you need a breeder, the Fanciers Breeder Referral List includes more than 800 Internet-connected breeders of pedigreed cats who are willing to act as referrals and to provide answers to questions about their breeds. Additional information is available on all things feline in Cat

Shows, Cat Clubs, Registries, Veterinary Medicine, Breed Rescue, Feline Welfare, and Shelter Information.

CyberCat

● http://www.cyberpet.com/cybercat

The *Mission Impossible* theme plays in the background of a cyberspace world of pet info. CyberCat's mission, should you decide to accept it, is to give you all the down-to-earth info you need on cats and their universe. No telling what happens if she fails.

As with CyberDog, this site is not for those only interested in the exclusivity of the professional cat societies. Here, various sections provide the landing pads for CyberCat's travels, and they mirror those of CyberDog: Breeders Showcase (info on various breeds), Pet Products (those available on the Internet), Services & Publications, Breed Info (detailed discussions of various breeds), Rescue & Breed Clubs (by region), PetChat (forums), WebBoard (postings), and other websites.

CyberDog

● http://www.cyberpet.com/cyberdog

CyberDog is the canine companion to CyberCat. Here, too, the *Mission Impossible* theme plays in the background at the CyberDog homepage, while you search for not-so-impossible-to-find information on all aspects of having a dog.

Eight sections lay the landing pads for CyberDog's travels. The Articles page contains myriad dog-lover-written pieces on subjects such as finding a pet, dog etiquette, and the always-important "Pets and Poop Patrol." Articles from the annual CyberPet writer's contest also are presented. Breeders features information and photos on one breeder for each American Kennel Club breed, and lists other breeders by geographical area. The Pet Supplies section groups Internet-available items under headings such as Books/Videos, Foods/Treats, and Health/ Grooming.

The PetChat and WebBoards areas are for registered users only; they are connected to the main CyberPet site, allowing entry into discussions on dogs, cats, horses, or other animals in an area called the Zoo. Rescue and Clubs provides links and/or e-mail addresses for related organizations around the country, while Other Web Sites allows searches by topic to find links of interest.

Perhaps the most thorough and useful section of CyberDog is Breeds Info, where detailed discussions on each dog breed can be found, along with search tools for breed by size, suitability for children, and overall intelligence.

Exotic
Exotic Pets on the Internet

● http://www.pet-net.net/exotic.htm

Amphibians, Chincillas, Ferrets, Gerbils, Guinea Pigs, Hamsters, Hedgehogs, Hermit Crabs, Insects & Spiders, Llamas & Alpacas, Mice & Rats, Prairie Dogs, Primates, Pot-bellied Pigs, Rabbits, Raccoons, Reptiles (with the categories General, Lizards, Snakes), Short-tailed Oppossums, Skunks, Snails, Sugar Gliders (an Australian marsupial—no, we'd never heard of them either). Need we say more? Each one of these section headings has its own set of links, from professional to personal, on the Exotic Pets page.

Fish
Fish Link Central

● http://www.fishlinkcentral.com/

Web surfers are always warned to beware of fishy sites, but Fish Link Central (FLC) is one we recommend. This vast compendium of info for the home-fish enthusiast, FLC has just about everything you need to know, whether you're a beginning hobbyist or an expert. As further proof of its reputation, more than 2 million people have visited the site in three years.

Among its many departments are Fish Photos (with 500-plus photos of freshwater fish), the Internet Resources, Fish Software, Agencies, Breeders and more, Fish Article Database, and the all-important FAQ/Helpsite, which is staffed by a group of volunteers who will answer any scaly questions you might have. This fun site also includes a number of fish games, including Fishrace. Fish fans with a sense of humor? Yes, indeed. They certainly hooked us.

Reptiles
Kingsnake

● http://www.kingsnake.com/

Not many people keep pets that could kill them, but those who do never underestimate the dangerous allure of a 15-foot boa constrictor. Of course, being well-informed minimizes the fatality potential, so reptile lovers should bookmark this site. Kingsnake.com is the

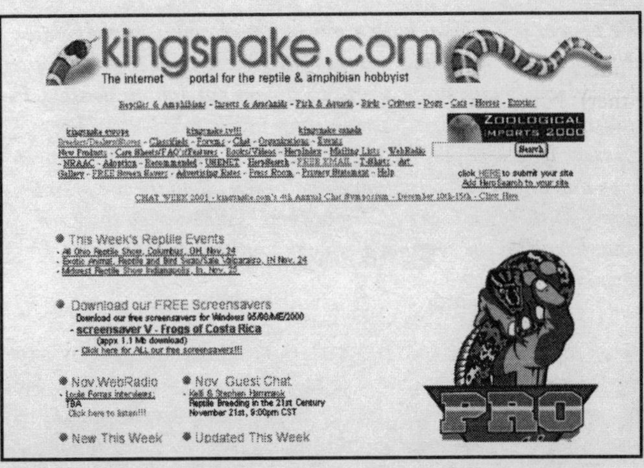

category, er, killer site for fans of reptiles, and it contains a truly eclectic bunch of links. Go from Jurgen's Garter Snake World to the German Society for Herpetology, and from there you can explore "the world of the bush viper" and exotic locales such as DragonFarms, where you can actually purchase the potently poisonous black mamba or spitting cobra.

The site features sections on breeders, retailers, chat area (with the appropriately titled Snake Room, Lizard Room, Amphibian Room, and Turtle/Tortoise Room), forums, herpindex and herpauctions, as well as events, online magazines, feature articles, the National Reptile & Amphibian Advisory Council, and reference guides. A twice monthly radio show originating from the website, which covers such herp issues as cornsnakes or Honduran milk snake morphs, sets this site apart from nearly every other pet site on the Net. Of course, you'll want to keep these pets apart from every other pet anyway, otherwise they might just eat them.

[religion]

We present this section with a minimum of commentary, because religion is a personal and serious issue. We've tried to include sites devoted to as many of the world's primary religions as possible, including some major sects. Sects within major religions will get coverage wherever possible, but not every sect has a huge site or a huge amount of followers (some don't even allow the use of computers, so there's a Catch-22 right there). We've tried to be reasonable within the confines of a book with no, er, religious agenda.

Anglicanism
The Anglican Domain

● http://www.anglican.org/

We like the way the Anglican Domain introduces its purpose on the Web: This site serves a dual purpose: to educate people about the church and to provide a means for communication between members and member churches. Sections include About Our Church, Official Web Pages (which are produced by national churches, provinces, dioceses, and parishes), Church Words, and Make Your Web Site.

Baptists
Baptists International Network

● http://www.baptists.org/

There are almost as many different Baptists groups in the United States as there are Baptist churches, and Baptists International Network will lead you to all of them. From A–Z, The site links you to different churches. You have several options to choose from: City & State, pastor's name, church name, zip code or even telephone number.

Buddhism
Buddhist Information Network

● http://www.buddhanet.net/

This is one of the most spectacular sites on the Web—in any category. Not only is the information about Buddhism thorough and intuitively arranged, but the site boasts incredible images and brilliant design. The best place to start is the Contents Page, which provides a lengthy and alluring guide to every facet of BuddhaNet. Over a hundred links are summarized here; highlights from them are complete texts, discourses, biographies, regional traditions, and teachings for children. Each section and its

respective pages are just as intricate, with mind-boggling attention paid to detail and content depth. There are also directories, a BuddhaZine, pages on meditation, studies, death and dying, and much more.

Catholicism
Catholic Information Center

● http://catholic.net/

From the Pope to places of worship, the Catholic Information Center is a comprehensive resource for Catholics about Catholicism. Catholics can get information Papal Encyclicals, teachings, documents, Magisterium, the Papacy of Pope John Paul II, and see the Holy See mission to the UN, or access Catholic directories and periodicals, liturgy, devotions, vocations, movie reviews, dioceses around the world, the Catholic Encyclopedia Project, daily readings, and a news ticker provided by *Catholic World News*. The site also features a Church Locator that, amazingly, lists of all the Mass times for all the churches in the United States.

The Church of Jesus Christ of Latter-Day Saints (Mormons)

● http://www.lds.org/

Probably no other religious organization has embraced technology to the degree that the Mormons have. They have invoked the power of the Web to create online genealogy sites and libraries and to fund some of the earliest machine translation systems. Thus, it comes as no surprise that their site is among the most advanced on the Web.

The site is, however, divided simply, into: Languages, Basic Beliefs, Family History, Family Resources, and Media Resources. Clicking on Languages informs you that content is available in 41 different languages (including Tonga), perhaps more than on any other site on the Web. The beliefs of the Mormon religion are compiled in sections titled Articles of Faith, the Book of Mormon, a Family Guidebook, and Testimony of Prophet Joseph Smith.

For non–Latter Day Saints members, the genealogy section will be of primary interest. We provided a complete review of it in this guide under GENEALOGY. The primary component of the section is the FamilySearch Internet Genealogy Service (FIGS), launched as part of the Mormon mission to trace family lineages around the world.

Hinduism
The Hindu Universe

● http://www.hindunet.org

The Hindu Universe is really the Web universe for the Hindu religion. The site is primarily a directory, in the style of Yahoo!, arranged in 14 headings: Arts, Customs, Worship, Internet Books & Resources, Dharma & Philosophy, History, Temples & Organizations, Interfaith Relations, God Sages & Gurus, Sciences, Scriptures, and Social & Contemporary Issues. As with all good directories, visitors can dig down further into their areas of interest (under Worship, for example, are links to Bhajans, Puja, Shlokas, Festivals . . .).

The Hindu Universe also features a calendar, a list of upcoming events, a glossary, Seva programs, digital postcards, chat rooms, news, books, and an interactive section. A particularly strong element of the site is a cool Java applet that creates a window on your browser to serve as a remote control for guiding you around the site.

Islam
IslamiCity in Cyberspace

● http://www.islam.org/

Followers of this ancient religion have staked out a decidedly high tech piece of the Internet, utilizing the full multimedia capabilities of the Web to connect to the Islamic community. IslamiCity is the digital gateway to Islam around the world. The site, reportedly more than 6,000 pages deep, is full of photographs, links, quotations, archived audio and video, as well as teachings, scripture, and news. IslamiCity provides two search engines for its viewers: one for doing a site search and one for doing Qur'an searches.

The site is divided into these areas: Bazar & Shopping, Community & Social, Education, Business, News, Mosque & Religious, Multimedia, Travel, and World ePort Center. A link to Live TV from Saudi One Channel and Dubai Channel enables viewers to watch the broadcast of prayers; there are also links to online radio (archived clips of recitations, lessons, and commentary) and CyberTV (webcasts on 10 different channels).

Note: the URLs islam.org, islamic.org, and islamicity.org all lead to this site.

Judaism

Maven

● http://www.maven.co.il

Like having a Jewish grandmother always around to dispense advice, Maven is a haven for information about Judaism on the Web. This site links to more than 9,000 (yes, that's nine with three zeroes) extremely well-categorized sites. These cover a wide variety of conventional topics, from communities, entertainment, and food—all selected based on their relevance to Judaism—to the Holocaust and anti-Semitism, Israel, and Judaica gifts. Maven also offers information tailored for specific Jewish sects; for instance, visitors can browse through the Communities & Synagogues listing by designating Conservative, Orthodox, Orthodox Union, Reconstructionist, and Reform.

Lutheranism

● http://www.lutherans.net/

Modern day followers of Martin Luther will find a complete guide to all aspects of their religion at this site, from history to online hymns. It is an exceptionally well-designed site—by any standards—with three dozen categories ranging from Advocacy and Campus Ministries to History, Music Resources, and Theology. There is an index of congregation websites, Bible study tools, random Bible verses, and even a Christian jukebox that plays MIDI file hymns online while you're surfing. The site also has links to related sites around the world (e.g., the History section contains links to German research sites). Lutherans.net was created by John Link of the Trinity Lutheran Church in New York as part of his research in expanding his church's youth ministry. The site is part of the Luther Ring ("the easy way to surf Lutheran sites on the Web!").

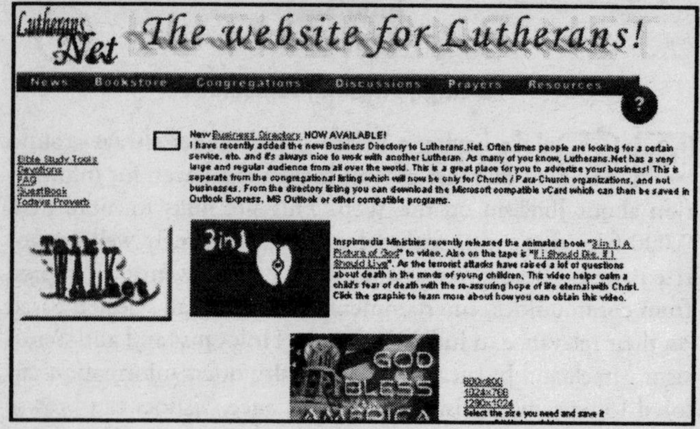

Methodist
Methodist Archives

● http://rylibweb.man.ac.uk/data1/dg/methodist/methlink.html

The Methodist Archives and Research Centre is a collection of documents and materials important to the Methodist religion and its history. The site is maintained at the John Rylands University Library of Manchester, England, which gives it an academic orientation. There are links to more than 100 resources pertaining to Methodist doctrine, history, and research. These are divided into 12 sections, among which are The Methodist Church in Britain and Ireland, and Heritage Sites in the United States; Early Methodist Manuscripts and Printed Collections; and United States Conference Archives. Visitors can scan this information as it pertains to specific countries, collections, news, and world events.

New Age
Spirit Web

● http://www.spiritweb.org

Spirit Web is a repository of many New Age teachings, pursuits, and interests from yoga to UFOs, among them a Focus of Spirit section, an event calendar, and news. Main topics include Channelings, Lightwork, Meditations, UFO Sightings, Yoga Paths, and Theosophy. Each section takes you to what is essentially a new homepage within Spirit Web. Each main category has subtopics; reincarnation, for example, has headings for Reincarnation and the Self, Karma: Meaning & Definition, Transpersonal Hypnotherapy, and Personal Reincarnation Examples. They link to full articles. And by becoming a member (free), you can take online classes, receive mailed updates, and have access to chat rooms.

A unique feature of Spirit Web is its substantial TV and audio/video archives, culled from a variety of sources, including conferences, interviews, and webcasts. They cover a breadth of topics from joy and higher consciousness to encounters and women in religion. In short, through Spirit Web, you can channel your spirit via every digital medium the Web has to offer.

Taoism
Taoism Information Page

● http://www.clas.ufl.edu/users/gthursby/taoism/

Many Westerners have probably heard of the I Ching or of the practice of feng shui, and many in corporate management circles have heard of the classic text known as "The Art of War." Few, however, are likely aware of the Taoist origins of these things. For enlightenment, go to the Taoism Information Page, a site that is part of the World Wide Web Virtual Library (see under LIBRARIES). With an impressive scope, this site serves as a virtual teacher in the ways of the Tao. It is an index that serves as a launch point to scholarly, philosophical, and exploratory study of the Tao. Specific areas include Introductions to Taoism or Daoism, Chinese Language & Culture, Chuang-tzu or Zhuangzi, I Ching, The Sun-tzu Art of War, Alchemy and Feng Shui, Taoism and Modernity, and a handful of others. Deep within this virtual library are complete translations of Taoist texts, links to practical information on feng shui and I Ching, and reference sources for sites and ventures related to Taoism.

Virtual Religion Index

● http://www.rci.rutgers.edu/~religion/vri/index.html

You can explore the world's religions without going to theology school by spending some time with the sacred texts at this Rutgers online classroom. A truly remarkable site, the Virtual Religion Index serves as the best place to begin any singular or comparative study of religion—yours or anyone else's. Maintained by the Religion Department at Rutgers University, the site is a collection of links to resources for most of the world's religions. The categories include: American Religions, Ancient Near Eastern Studies, Anthropology & Sociology, Biblical Studies, Buddhist Studies, Christian Tradition, Comparative Religion, Confessional Agencies (such as Protestant religions), East Asian Studies, Ethics & Moral Values, Greco-Roman Studies, Hindu Studies, Islam, Jewish Studies, Philosophy & Theology, and Psychology of Religion. Each of these has a set of annotated links that will guide you sure-footedly along your path to spiritual enlightenment and theological wisdom.

[seniors]

Housing
National Council on the Aging (NCOA)

● http://www.ncoa.org

NCOA is the organization that started the Meals on Wheels programs for the homebound elderly and created Foster Grandparents for active older Americans. Attending to the broad concerns of America's aging population, this site has data on everything from jobs for seniors to legislation, advocacy, and social security.

ThirdAge

● http://thirdage.com/

Mature web crawlers need fun on the internet too. Thirdage.com is a website geared towards a more experienced audience: first-wave baby boomers, now in their mid-40s through 50s. Consumer product companies fund this free site that has features on health and beauty, love and family, horoscopes, money, and travel. There is an area for chats and discussions, games and jokes, and quizzes. The personals section let's you meet other people with similar interests. There's a recipe finder and electronic postcards. There's even a poll and a newsletter.

Want to spice up your love life? Try a romantic dinner recipe. See if the time is right with a romantic horoscope. Explore the twelve ways to find a new love. Want to learn something new? Try the free online courses. This site has so many features that we can't list them all. Thirdage.com proves that baby-boomers are still 'booming' and reminds us that people of all ages can find their niche on the 'net.

Travel
Elderhostel

● http://www.elderhostel.org

Elderhostel, a program that has been around for nearly 30 years, gives people over 55 the opportunity to travel to more than 80 countries, and participate in programs at universities, national parks, museums, conference centers, and other learning sites. Head to Ireland to learn about art and theater, do some jungle studies in Brazil, or learn about ancient civilizations in Turkey; these are but a few of the hundreds of trips offered by Elderhostel. You can review the travel packages, check out the requirements, and book the trip all on this site. The only thing Eldershostel's Web page doesn't do for its clients is pack their bags for them.

[UFOs & alien abductions]

It is wonderfully ironic that the Internet was a creation of the government and the military-industrial complex, the same alliance that purportedly keeps the real information about UFOs under wraps and shrouded in mystery. But if the Internet had not been born, the UFO and alien abduction interest groups would have had to invent it. There is no better medium for disseminating the photos, rumor, classified information, innuendo, and technical analysis that is core to the UFO world. Newsletters are too slow and not graphically intensive. Radio is okay, but not much fun to look at. TV is always a source of questionable reliability. At the end of the day, the Internet fills the bill nicely.

International Center for Abduction Research

● http://www.ufoabduction.com/

If you want to know about human egg and sperm harvesting by aliens and interplanetary neurological procedures—and, hey, who doesn't?—you can get more than you ever dreamed right here. This site is so well organized, and treats its subject matter so seriously we weren't sure whether to put it in the business section or under religion. Maintained by author Dr. David Jacobs, who claims to have investigated some 750 cases of UFO abduction, the International Center for Abduction Research site points users to FAQs, Straight Talk, an Abductees Speak section, Hypnosis, a list of Jacobs' books and upcoming presentations, and a Questionnaire. Straight Talk is the main area, where topics addressed include: How many people are abductees? Who is abducted? hybrid babies, and mindscan. The individual sections are oddly academic discourses on the matter at hand.

UFO Seek

● http://www.ufoseek.org/

This searchable directory and news source is an extra-terrestrial researcher's fondest dream. Its huge scope contains links to all things in the world of UFOs as well as daily news on UFO-related stories from around the globe. Here's a brief selection of the subjects you'll find covered: sightings, alien abduction, crop circles, Roswell, Area 51, Presidential comments about Groom Lake, cattle mutilation, life on Mars, conspiracies, a huge A-to-Z directory of related websites, online video segments, and more. And this is just the beginning. If you can't find it here, maybe the truth *isn't* out there after all.

Area 51
Area 51 Resources

● http://www.nauticom.net/users/ata/resources.html

Not counting JFK's assassination, probably no other subject on the face of planet Earth serves as fodder for so much conjecture and conspiracy speculation as that small strip of land outside of Las Vegas, Nevada, known as Area 51. This is especially true on the Web.

At the Area 51 Resources page, you can begin your investigation into the world of experimental aircraft, pirated alien

YAHOO! ALSO LISTS: [weddings]

- **http://www.blissbridal.com/**
  Blissbridal.com
- **http://www.castle.net/~energize/CMRP/index.html**
  Ceremony Music Resource Page: contains links music selection lists, CD resources, sound files, and information.
- **http://www.geocities.com/~toddandrobyn/destwed.html**
  Destination Wedding Ring: for sites that feature weddings you have to travel to.
- **http://www.wam.umd.edu/~sek/readwed/readwed.html**
  Personal Wedding Pages on the Net
- **http://www.ultimatewedding.com/**
  Ultimate Internet Wedding Guide: posts engagement announcements, provides wedding information, and offers a listing of links to professionals.
- **http://www.waycoolweddings.com/**
  Way Cool Weddings: weekly links to the best wedding sites on the Web.
- **http://www.weddingcircle.com/**
  Wedding Circle
- **http://wedding.gogrrl.com/**
  Wedding goGrrl: guide to listings including apparel companies, planners, articles on cultural traditions, and honeymoon information.
- **http://www.weddingchannel.com/**
  WeddingChannel
- **http://weddings-online.com/**
  Weddings Online: contains links to information, resources, and professionals.

spaceships, and an expanse of desert so secret that even the U.S. government won't acknowledge its existence. The page is divided into four categories: All-Terrain Links, Internet Links, Print Resources, and Area 51 Merchandise. These contain everything from chat rooms, interviews, and photo galleries to lengthy essays, magazines, and arcade games. Links are to: Area 51 Photos, Aircraft Tested at Area 51, Sources of Area 51 News, Area 51 Spoof, Area 51 Contractors (including Lockheed Martin and Johnson Controls), and Preconfigured Searches for Area 51 information (on Yahoo!, Alta Vista, Excite, and others).

[weddings]

The Knot

● http://www.theknot.com/

"The #1 Wedding Resource and Gift Registry" makes the big-day planning fun and easy. The site is loaded with ideas and advice for the happy couple, their wedding party, their parents, and distant relatives. Planning is an in-depth section, as are those offering tips on beauty, etiquette, and managing a budget. Love & Life sets you up for a lifetime of blenders and bread-makers, and exhaustive advice is available on buying a home and money matters. Completely clueless grooms-to-be can get engagement education by reading articles on 50 Ways to Pop the Question, Popping the Question By Birth Signs, and Astrologically Correct Proposals. Women still waiting will want to check out Getting Him to Ask. Face it guys, there's nowhere to hide.

Via the Local Services directory, you and your betrothed can find bridal shows, learn the local license laws, and locate hundreds of jewelers, photographers, and florists in or near your hometown.

And just when you think the whole thing is too overwhelming and less fun than a mother-in-law on a honeymoon, you can read the Weekly Features for such entertaining pieces as The Worst Wedding Song Poll and a registry list for characters on the

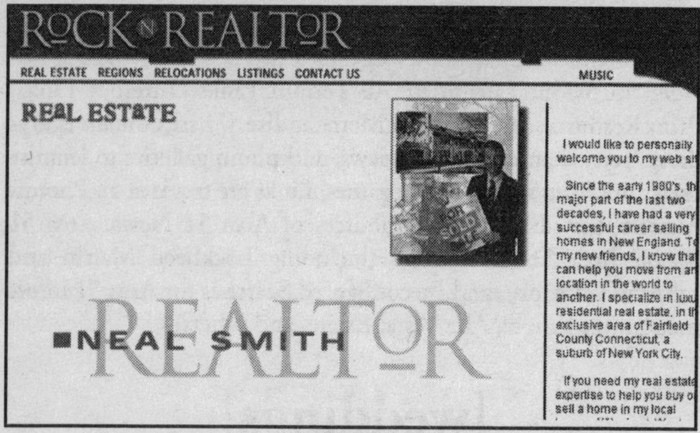

TV sitcom *Friends*. If you dig deeply enough, there's probably even a sock-warmer resource in here to help take the chill off those cold feet.

[weird and bizarre]

One person's weird is another person's wonderful. The Web has more weird stuff on it than any combination of circus sideshows or houses of horror, and more unusual stuff than a garage sale at Pee Wee's playhouse. You can find your own weird stuff by searching Yahoo! under weird, or perform a search for your particular kind of weirdness (hey, each to his or her own). The weird sites here don't fit into any other category (although we've scattered plenty of weird sites throughout this book). If you need to get weirder, be our guest. There's room for everyone and everything on the Web.

Rock 'n' Realtor

● http://www.nealsmith.com/

A rock 'n' roll drummer from one of the world's most famous bands sets up shop as a high-end realtor. Sound like the premise for a sitcom or the continuing exploits of the most at-risk member of Spinal Tap? It is the real life of Neal Smith, a refugee from the original Alice Cooper group, the glam-rock band that helped make wearing dresses a guy thing. This site is amazing (and we mean that in a good way) because it demonstrates how the Web can be used to capture any premise, real or imagined, then provide a home for it.

In a seeming disconnect, on one part of the site, Smith presents the expensive houses he's offering for sale in the upscale Connecticut and New York bedroom communities just outside of Manhattan. Then with a click of a drumstick, er, mouse, he takes you to scenes from his life as Cooper's drummer, when he provided the rhythm on anthems such as "School's Out" and "No More Mister Nice Guy," (not to mention the memorable drum intro to "Billion Dollar Babies"). Sound bizarre? It's not; it just shows how incredibly diverse the Web can be.

Webb Page Confidential

● http://www.phoenixnewtimes.com/extra/dewey/index.html

Dewey Webb—his real name—has been writing about oddities for the *Phoenix New Times* for decades. He brings his curious affection for the strangeness of daily life—and for the odd curios, collectibles, and characters that our society produces—to his own Webb site. Features include cult-movie reviews (for example, *X, Y, and Zee* starring Elizabeth Taylor, and the Siamese-twin thriller *Chained for Life*), Objects of the Week (Larvet's Original Worm Snacks and a "Say No To Drugs" ballpoint pen syringe), his own version of the Death Pool, and personal photos with second-tier celebrities (such as Barry Williams from *The*

Brady Bunch). The site has extensive archives and is updated every Wednesday, which isn't frequently enough.

The Weird Places

● http://www.deiman.nl/weird/

From the Adult Children of Alien to Scary Squirrel World and 50 Years of Band-Aid, this is a list of links to several hundred of the weirdest sites on the Web. That really says it all. This is the only entry in this book that we cannot even begin to describe, because you have to see the sites to believe them. All we can say is that it's hard to believe that thinking beings actually spent time creating some of these places.

[women]

Femina

● http://femina.cybergrrl.com/

Femina Web Search is different from many other women's sites in that it provides a gigantic directory of links to the best women's sites on the Web and categorizes them in the process. More specifically, they are sites "for, by, and about women." Using a Yahoo! style directory, you can search either by keyword or by topic areas that include Arts & Humanities, Business and Finance, Education, Girls, Media and Publications, Computers and Science, Regional, and Health and Wellness. We challenged a few female friends to come up with something that wasn't listed at this site and they couldn't do it.

Femina Calendar highlights events of interest to women and girls; Femina Mail sends you updates on the site (registration is required); Best Sites for Women lists, well, best sites for women; and FeminaNet lets you connect to other women online to discuss topics from academic research to work-related. Go girl. Or in this case, cybergrrl.

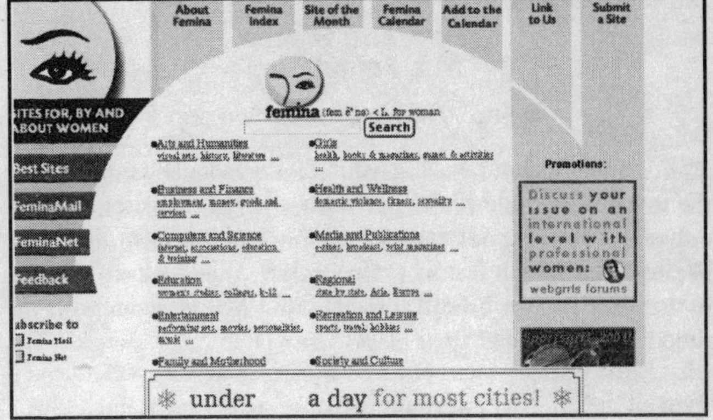

iVillage

● http://www.ivillage.com/

Imagine being able to get your trusted friend's advice whenever you need it. This image can come true at iVillage, a women's online community.

The site provides women with tons of tools to manage daily life. You can, for example, track your pregnancy or create a custom timeline to help you plan all the details of relocating. Search several subsites such as Fitness & Beauty, Food, Career, and many others. Additional areas include Working from Home and the Women's Auto Center. Wondering about how to avoid osteoporosis? Go to the AllHealth area. Want to know how to react when your 11-year-old admits to smoking? Find out from the experts of ParentSoup (see our review under PARENTING). Worried about money? Use MoneyLife's Interactive Toolkit to check on your financial health or to plan your retirement.

In most areas iVillage has set up bulletin boards and scheduled chats where you can share your thoughts and experiences.

You can also post your questions to peers and experts. iVillage changes the featured articles in each section daily, so it's always worth coming back.

Ms. Foundation

● http://www.ms.foundation.org/

Ever thought about having your teenage daughter peek over your shoulder while you're nervously trying to impress her with what you're doing? Or maybe you're an ambitious young female trying to figure out just what the heck is going on every day behind those mysterious office walls? Since Ms. Foundation is the organization that invented "Take Our Daughters to Work" Day, that is the primary focus of its no-nonsense website, where you'll find all the information about this once-a-year event, including a checklist for girls to help them prepare for this day, a guide for parents, and information for teachers, community organizers, businesses, and sponsors. If you plan to participate in this important day and need supporting material, there's a whole catalog of promotional items you can order.

Also at the site are the foundation's other programs to empower girls and women; health issues and economic security are also briefly described. If you're a young woman, don't miss the extensive resource list in the Girls Area, with lists of books, magazines, articles, and links to related sites.

National Organization for Women (NOW)

● http://www.now.org/

   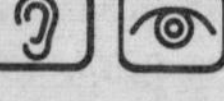

NOW "is dedicated to making legal, political, social and economic change in our society in order to achieve our goal, which is to eliminate sexism and end all oppression." This site gives women (and interested men) immediate access to information about the organization and its issues. It also serves as an excellent starting point for women's advocacy. Don't come here for idle chatter; this is a place to get fired up about key issues. Find out what's happening, and what's not; watch video clips and hear speeches from the 1996 Fight the Right March in San Francisco.

The sites focal point is a photo of the famed 1996 march; it is surrounded by category links and a search engine link. Users can click on the photo to get a historical overview of the march, which includes video and audio presentations. From there, the site's content covers everything you should expect from a women's advocacy site—abortion rights, economic equity, affirmative actions, women in the military, violence against women, and legislation. There is also NOW chapter information, general information and history, news, membership data, feminist merchandise, and Internet resources.

[world cultures]

Country Studies—Library of Congress

● http://lcweb2.loc.gov/frd/cs/cshome.html

How much do you know about other countries and their cultures? Let's pick Mongolia, for instance. You probably didn't know that its worst water pollution was caused by the waste from a wool-scouring factory; that a quarter of its population has families of seven or more members; that its society is based on pastoral nomadism; and that its higher education system takes its cues from Russia. All this and more is courtesy of The Library of Congress Country Studies section.

This leviathan site presents the history, culture, growth, population, linguistic characteristics, family units, religion, social mobility, geography, and evolution of more than 100 countries—and that's just a sampling of the main topic areas, all of which are arranged alphabetically in a table of contents, for easy access. A visit to this mega site is free and unlimited, so there is no reason not to learn more about the world outside your own.

Another site of interest is the World Cultures section of Geography World, a colossal collection of annotated links, that leads to some great and often-overlooked sites on the Web. They include sites for aboriginal studies, cultural gestures, languages, holidays, recipes from around the world, and many, many more. This site is a subset of the magnificent Geography World site, which contains more than two dozen other categories relating to geography and culture. Brad Bowerman, who teaches high school geography in Pennsylvania, is the webmaster of this outstanding site, which rivals any other topic-specific index on the Web.

[young adults]

Advice
Adolescence Directory On-Line (ADOL)

● http://www.education.indiana.edu/cas/adol/adol.html

You are not alone. Your problem, no matter how strange or horrible, has confronted someone else. The Adolescence Directory On-Line site features links that address nearly every conceivable tough issue a teen might encounter during his or her adolescent years. These include Conflict & Violence (resources about violence prevention and peer mediation), Mental Health Issues (depression, eating disorders, development, etc.), Counselor Resources (info on professional organizations and links), Teens Only (homework help, sports info, games, zines, etc.), and Health & Health Risk Issues (alcohol and other drugs, sexuality, AIDS, acne, obesity, and more). Once you get into this site, you'll find hundreds of links that provide both informative and professional data on each of these teen concerns. Most important, the site shows that these concerns are shared by nearly every teen on the planet.

Teen Advice Online

● http://www.teenadviceonline.com/

We recall that one of the worst things about being a teen was not knowing who to go to when you had a serious question about dating and sex, or whether or not your haircut really made you look like a geek. Mom and Dad usually weren't the right choice (since they *made* you get that geeky haircut), and your friends were often at the root of some of the problems you were seeking to solve. Today, thanks to the Internet, teens have a variety of places to find help (check out our ADVICE section), and one specifically geared to teen issues called, not coincidentally, Teen Advice Online.

Site counselors write articles and answer e-mailed questions. The main topic areas include Dating, Innocence Lost, A Day in the Life, and Get Help. Sample articles include "Don't Love Me Anymore," "Dating Who You Want to Date—Not Who Your Friends Want," "The Big, Bad Breakup," and "The Fine Art of Flirting." A search engine lets you look for info on relationships, sex, school, substance abuse, parents, and personal appearance (perfect when your haircut does make you look like a geek).

College

CollegeXpress

● http://www.collegexpress.com/

Mapping Your Future

● http://mapping-your-future.org/

There are plenty of sites that can help you pick out colleges and universities, and we've profiled a few under EDUCATION. CollegeXpress serves more as a guidance counselor to answer your questions about dorm life, college sports, financial aid, drinking, roommates, and living away from home. All of these are found in different departments of the "college," which include its Sports Source, Student Center, Admissions Office, and other virtual buildings. As soon as you enroll on the site, you have free run of the campus, so try out college online before you try out college in real time.

When you're ready to enter "real" college, click over to Mapping Your Future (http://mapping-your-future.org), a site that provides counseling for those who have figured out what they want to be when they grow up.

Dating
CTEEN

● http://welcome.to/cteen

Did *Phantom Menace* do justice to the other three Star Wars movies? Are emergency contraceptives safe? When is the right time to start having sex? Who is responsible for a person's eating disorder? Questions like these may seem totally unrelated, but to the average teenager, they may all be part of the same conversation.

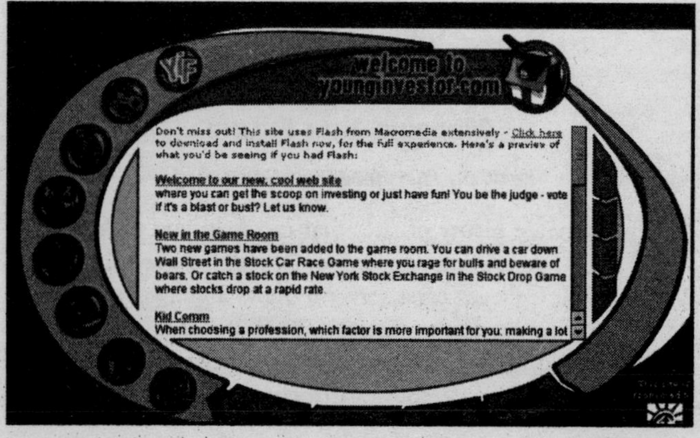

CTEEN tackles the eclectic issues of the typical teen day in an online zine that resembles a scaled-down version of *USA Today,* although the sections read more like the *New York Times*: Technology, Lifestyle, Careers, Chat, and Search. Readers can submit a question to CTEEN, join real-time chats, or browse through the site's numerous and diverse articles.

Money
Young Investors

● http://www.younginvestor.com/

The Young Investor site is for the Alex P. Keaton in all of us, with games and projects that will appeal to mini-moguls—and perhaps their not-so savvy parents.

Enter a world of games involving stocks and bonds—which sounds vaguely like the real world of investing. Would be Warren Buffetts can play the Stock Market Game, a simulation that teaches kids about finances and investing. Next up is Money-Tration, a memory game that can be downloaded or played online, a Young Investor Trivia Game, and a Currency Crossword, along with several others. For serious adolescent investors, there is the Young Investor Fund, an actual fund maintained by Stein Roe Mutual Funds, which outlines the process of investing to youngsters who want to start socking it away today.

Two other features are: the Measure Up Survey that rates a visitor's knowledge of finances against other young investors, and a College Calculator that—presumably—lets kids know that at some point all this money becomes very real.

News
ChannelOne

● http://www.channelone.com/

Most real news is written for adults (we're not talking about the watered-down cheesy stuff on celebrities, record releases, and movie openings). ChannelOne is different; it takes teen interests and channels them into several different areas News (which recently included how to help ongoing relief efforts in earthquake zones), Music (learn how to do something cool like play the guitar), Games & Contests (daily challenges and the chance to win prizes), and Homework (homework help, deadlines calendar, and volunteering). Within each of these are articles and areas dealing with social issues such as illiteracy and animal rights. It's not Ted Koppel and *Nightline*, and that's the point: it addresses global issues in a way that will interest kids.

SPECIAL THANKS

Dozens of people helped make this book the tremendous reference you now hold in your hands. First off, thanks to everyone at BPVP: Byron Preiss, who made this book happen; Dinah Dunn, who ran interference and performed editorial feats above and beyond the call of duty; Megan Scanlon; and especially Howard Zimmerman, who provided a voice of sanity in an otherwise insane race against the clock. Then there are a host of people who have promoted and provoked my interest in various subjects over the years, giving me enough confidence—and ammunition—to tackle the monstrous diversity of topics in this book. Their answers to my questions have helped me learn more than any school could have ever taught me: Thomas Werge, John Kunkel, Michael S. Johnson, Bill Brahos, Randy Parker, and Al Mowrer. I should also note that this book was written and edited in different cities all around the country, and I am grateful for the sanctuary provided by the Hamilton Building in New York, the Tucker Greco family, and the Philip Chapnick family.

On the corporate side, this book owes a debt of gratitude to the work and vision at HarperCollins of Cathy Hemming, Matthew Benjamin, and especially Megan Newman; Jennifer Price at Yahoo!; and John Leonhardt at Panic Entertainment Group. For editorial production and design a heartfelt thank-you to copyeditor Janice Borzendowski, proofreader Kathy Huck, and designers Tom Draper and Erin Bosworth.

This book would not have the diversity it does without the contributions of the writers who hacked their way through the web with virtual machetes, trying to provide a clear view of the Internet terrain. I could not have done this without them and their collective sense of determination, humor, and good will. This book is as much the work of Buzz Morison, Silke Fett, Trini Newquist, and fellow comrades-in-arms Rich Maloof and Pete Prown as it is mine.

I'd also like to thank my parents, brothers and sisters, and their families, all of whom are a constant source of inspiration and comic relief. And immense gratitude goes to my immediate family—Trini, Madeline, and Katherine—without whom I'd still be wondering which way was up, or if the Internet ever ended.

Finally, this book is dedicated to Katherine.

HP Newquist

CONTRIBUTORS

Silke Fett, who contributed to the business, pregnancy, outdoor activities, and women's issues sections of this book, is currently the web manager for Carnegie Hall in New York City.

Rich Maloof is an independent editor and author based in New York City. His contributions here include sites on music, dating, law, wrestling, hobbies, and sports.

Buzz Morison is a Minneapolis-based freelance writer and editor for publications such as *Rolling Stone, City Pages*, and *Request*. His contributions here include sites on geology, geography, science, music, health, finance, theater, sports, parenting, teaching, and engineering.

HP Newquist is the author of nearly a dozen books, including *The Brain Makers* and *Virtual Reality*, and numerous articles on a broad spectrum of topics. He wrote entries for every section of this book and edited the book as a whole.

Trini Newquist is the author of *The Phoenix Baby Resource Guide*, a reference work for new parents. Her contributions here include sites on food & beverages, health, finance, hobbies, houses & homes, and parenting.

Pete Prown is the editor of the garden magazine *Green Scene*, for the Pennsylvania Horticultural Society, and the founding editor of *Guitar Shop* magazine. His contributions here include sites on art, auctions, gardening, cooking, finance, history, music, and houses & homes.